UNTOUCHED

First published in the United States of America in 2009 by

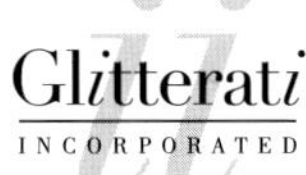

Glitterati
INCORPORATED

Glitterati Incorporated
225 Central Park West, Suite 305
New York, New York 10024
www.GlitteratiIncorporated.com
Telephone: 212 362 9119
glitteratimedia@gmail.com for inquiries

First edition, 2009

Design: Sarah Morgan Karp/smk-design.com

Library of Congress Cataloging-in-Publication data is available from the publisher.

Hardcover edition ISBN 13: 978-0-9822669-0-8

Printed and bound in China by Hong Kong Graphics & Printing Ltd.
10 9 8 7 6 5 4 3 2 1

UNTOUCHED

Johnny Rozsa

COMMENTS BY Susan Sarandon

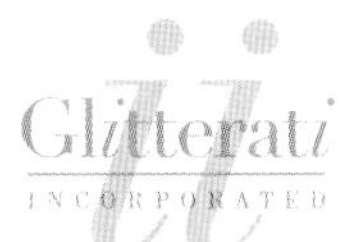

Glitterati
INCORPORATED

Contents

Images L to R: Jackson Five; Sister Sledge; Robert Mitchum

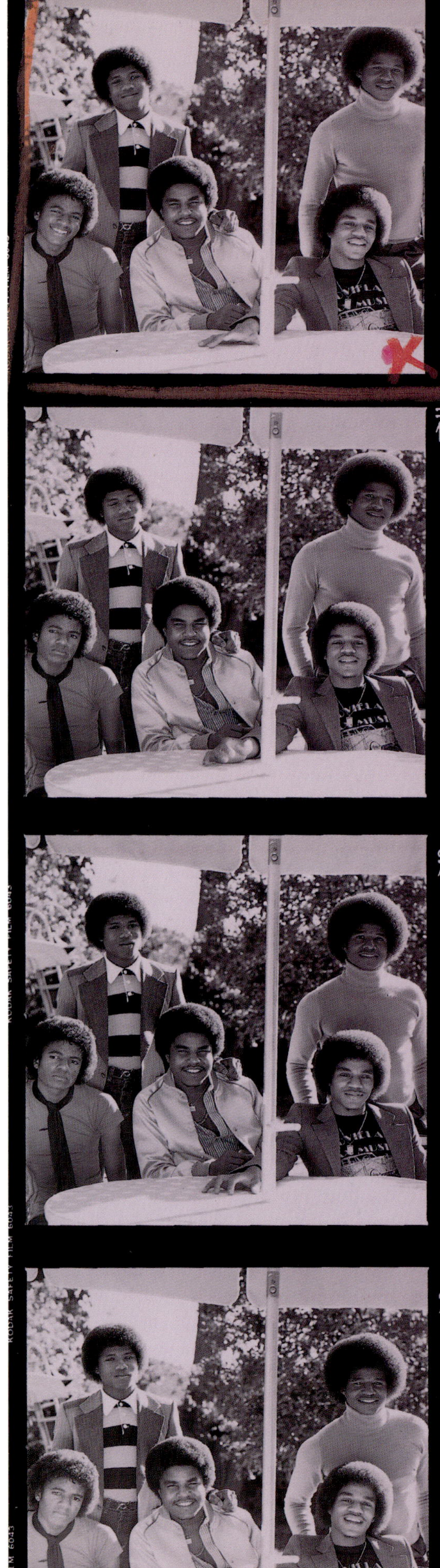

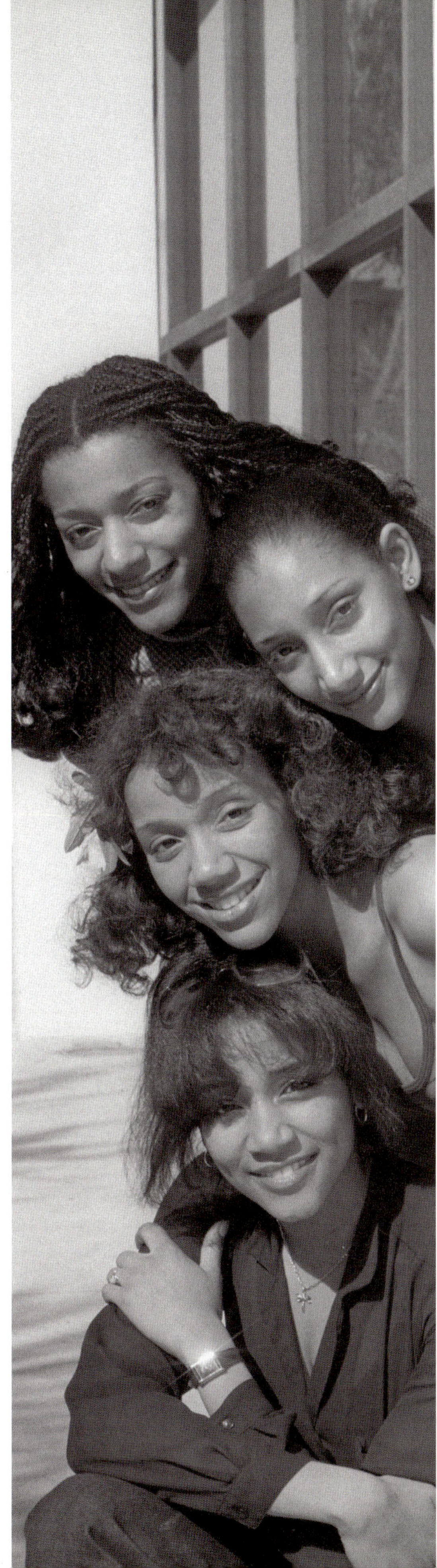

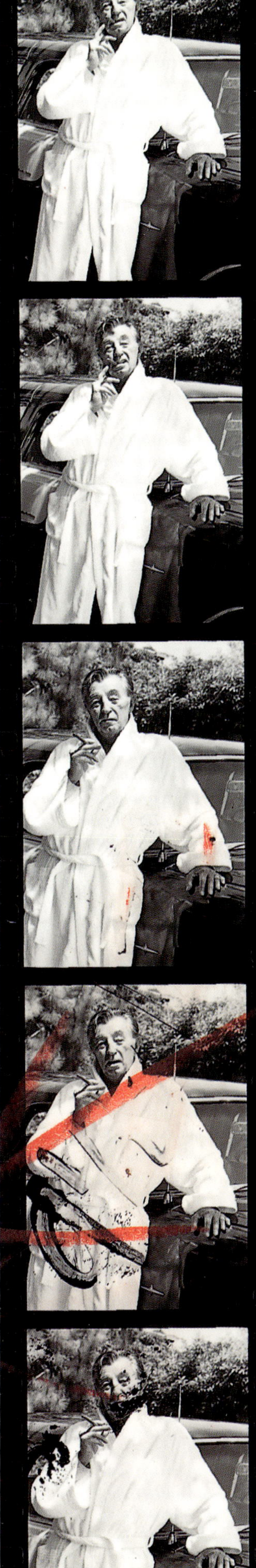

Contents

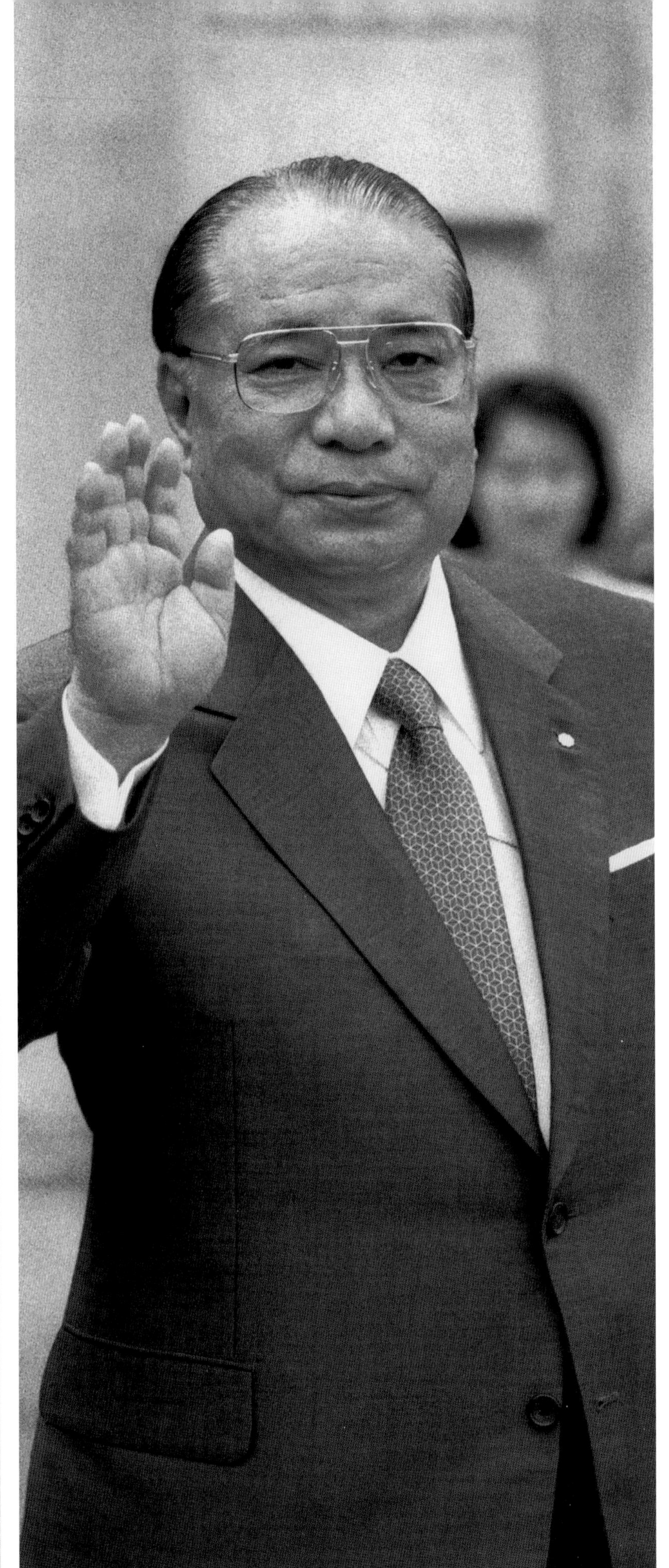

Dedication To Daisaku Ikeda, President of the Soka Gakkai International, my mentor in life.

The book is also dedicated to my mother Lisa, to my sisters Julia and to Eve, whose idea it was to get it together, and to Veere Grenney, who is the epitome of friendship, integrity and style.

Images R to L: Daisaku Ikeda; Molly Ringwald

Comments

Just being around Johnny was an event. Things happened: lots of laughter and spontaneous seizing of the moment. But then those were the days; before I had children and before AIDS made the world so much more monotone.

We met socially with Ian McKellen, Philip Sayer, Marilyn, Rupert Everett and the like! The shoots came later and were seamless transitions from personal to professional. They were fun, they were spontaneous, and eventually they were with children present.

I've never really liked to do this part of the job, but Johnny made it pretty painless. He was prepared—armed with a concept, but still fun and fast. For me that was important.

Looking at the photos now, I remember thinking then that I look pretty hilarious—still do. It's nice to see them. I remember my daughter being at the later shoot and playing in my sweater. . . and now she's a movie actor. Johnny should shoot her— for the next book.

Susan Sarandon
New York

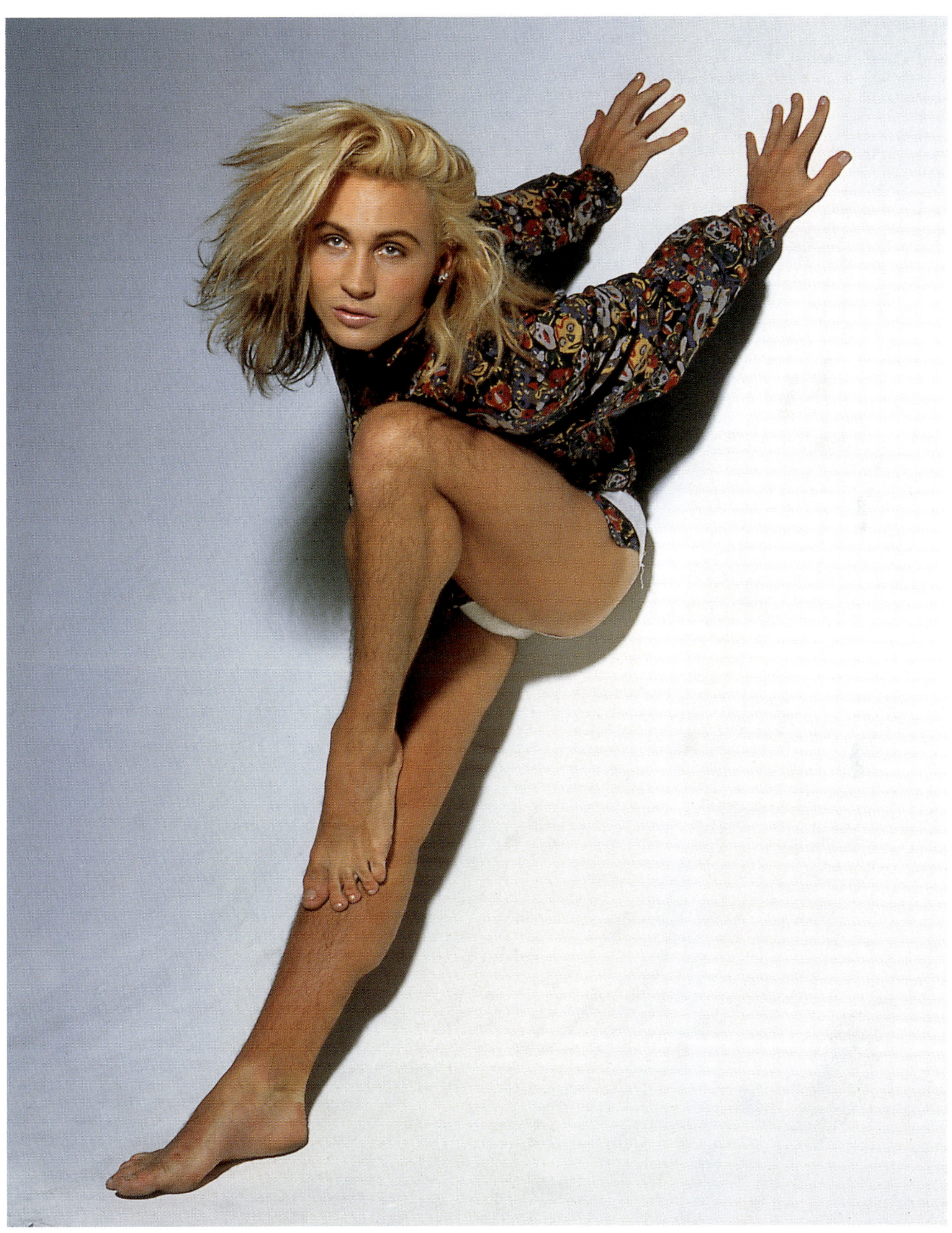

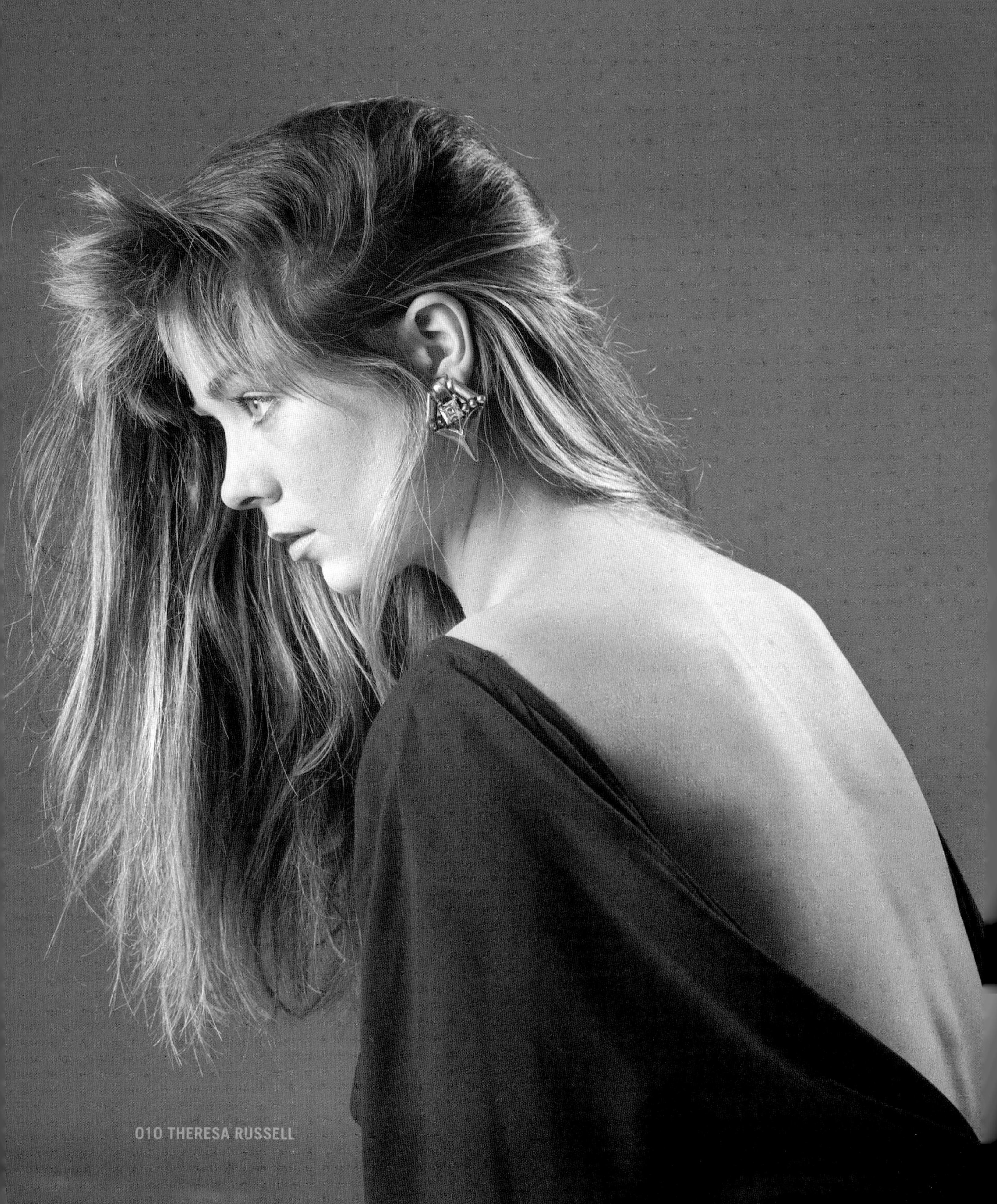

010 THERESA RUSSELL

Introduction

This is a collection of my portraits of iconic actors, musicians, and personalities, all taken before the days of Photoshop, digital cameras, and publicists. Few of these images have been published before; all of these photographs are untouched and were shot in London, Los Angeles, or New York.

While in Los Angeles to do a photo session in one of the penthouse suites at the Chateau Marmont, I shared the elevator with an elderly chic lady who had a magnificent emerald ring on her age-spotted hand. Grabbing it, I asked to admire her ring. Horrified, she glared at me while I checked out all its facets. I looked up at her face and suddenly realized that I was clutching the hand of French cinema star Jeanne Moreau. The planes of her lined face were bewitching, even in the light of that elevator. It was untouched—except for a flash of coral lipstick—and beautiful.

A photograph is like a blink. It lasts for a fraction of a second and yet a portrait can capture a whole story. Light can be harsh and bright, or it can be soft to create a mood.

Photography is instantaneous, but there is a progression of a photographer's style, of the way one sees and learns throughout one's life. These days it is so easy to erase a wrinkle or bag or to bleach an image. What has happened to the way we look at images? Everything is plasticized. Skin does not have to have pores and breathe. Erasing a "flaw" is a snap! A 34A-sized chest can immediately become a 34B with two clicks of a mouse. All this has its place. I am not against retouching when it improves an image, but our generation now depends on it and on the knife, and this dependence makes everything that we view too sanitized, too homogenized. Here, between the pages of this book, is a collection of images of celebrities that I have been lucky enough to photograph, often times just one-on-one, before the digital age.

I was born and grew up in Nairobi. It is a stunning and remote place—full of light, exotic animals and wild people. Every day was a day of exploration, visual treats, and beauty. Living in Kenya made me curious.

Then, in the early sixties, I was enrolled in Repton, an all-boys' school, which to me was the complete opposite of everything I had known until then. My school uniform was a gray herringbone suit. There were dull, short, wintry days in Derbyshire, and yet, even back then, I heard the sounds of change, of Dylan and The Beatles. I had a great art teacher who helped me "see" and who taught me to develop my sense of color, texture, light, and shape.

Change was everywhere. I pored over fashion magazines with David Bailey's clean images of Jean Shrimpton, marveled at the quirky beauty of models Jill Kennington, Donyale Luna, and Patti Boyd. I was influenced by the works of Irving Penn and Richard Avedon, with their clean backgrounds, and even by George Hurrell's fabulously lit portraits of movie stars from the studio era of Hollywood.

One summer, I interned at British *Vogue*'s art department with Barney Wan and watched as he laid out stories by photographers Norman Parkinson and Helmut Newton. I learned that the way a photograph was cropped made it better. I loved the techniques of black-and-white printing in the dark room, even the smell of the chemicals and the slithery feel of the negatives.

After college, I ran a vintage clothes shop in Covent Garden, stocked with racks of furs and chiffon dresses, everything from the glamorous beaded boleros of the 1920s to 1940s' floral day dresses. I spent my days washing and ironing while meeting fashion editors, models, actors and photographers who came in to borrow clothes for their shoots. They were creative and doing what I soon realized I wanted to do, rather than sitting in a store full of schmatte.

I was social, too. I was invited to all the "in" parties. I met everyone who was anyone and, maybe because I was a bit exotic, people loved having me around, and I became part of the London scene. I frequented Vivienne Westwood's shop on the King's Road. I knew Galliano after he left St. Martin's. I was friends with theatre actors like Ian McKellen, Philip Sayer, and Ian Charleson. I was curious about people and what made them function. I went to concerts because I adore music. I've been around Bob Marley, Nina Simone, The Jacksons, Ella Fitzgerald, Frank Zappa, and Madonna. I watched Dusty Springfield record at the old Philips Studios in Marble Arch. I hung out at BBC House while singer Julie Felix recorded the first ever color variety show for BBC 2.

Soon, I bought my first Hasselblad and started shooting my friends and getting little jobs in magazines. I never enjoyed taking snaps of people at parties. Being a paparazzo was not my thing. I rather preferred having people pose for me, with controlled light, in a studio environment. I loved the process of watching my friend Stevie Hughes bring out the best in a person's face with his magical make-up, and seeing how Ray Allington could transform windblown hair into stunning shapes and textures. Blitz, the club, started and I met Boy George and Marilyn. In a SoHo bar one night, I spotted Leigh Bowery and Trojan and felt that they would be terrific subjects to photograph.

Then, publicists did not control shoots and art directors tended not to boss me around.

But often times, a public relations person or an editor would call me to see if I could photograph Dolly Parton or Christian Slater or shoot stills on a video (for Whitney Houston) or on a movie set (for Ellen Barkin). I was commissioned to work for some of the best magazines and my reputation as a photographer has grown. For all those who sat in front of me and my camera, I offer my sincere thanks.

Johnny Rozsa

New York, New York

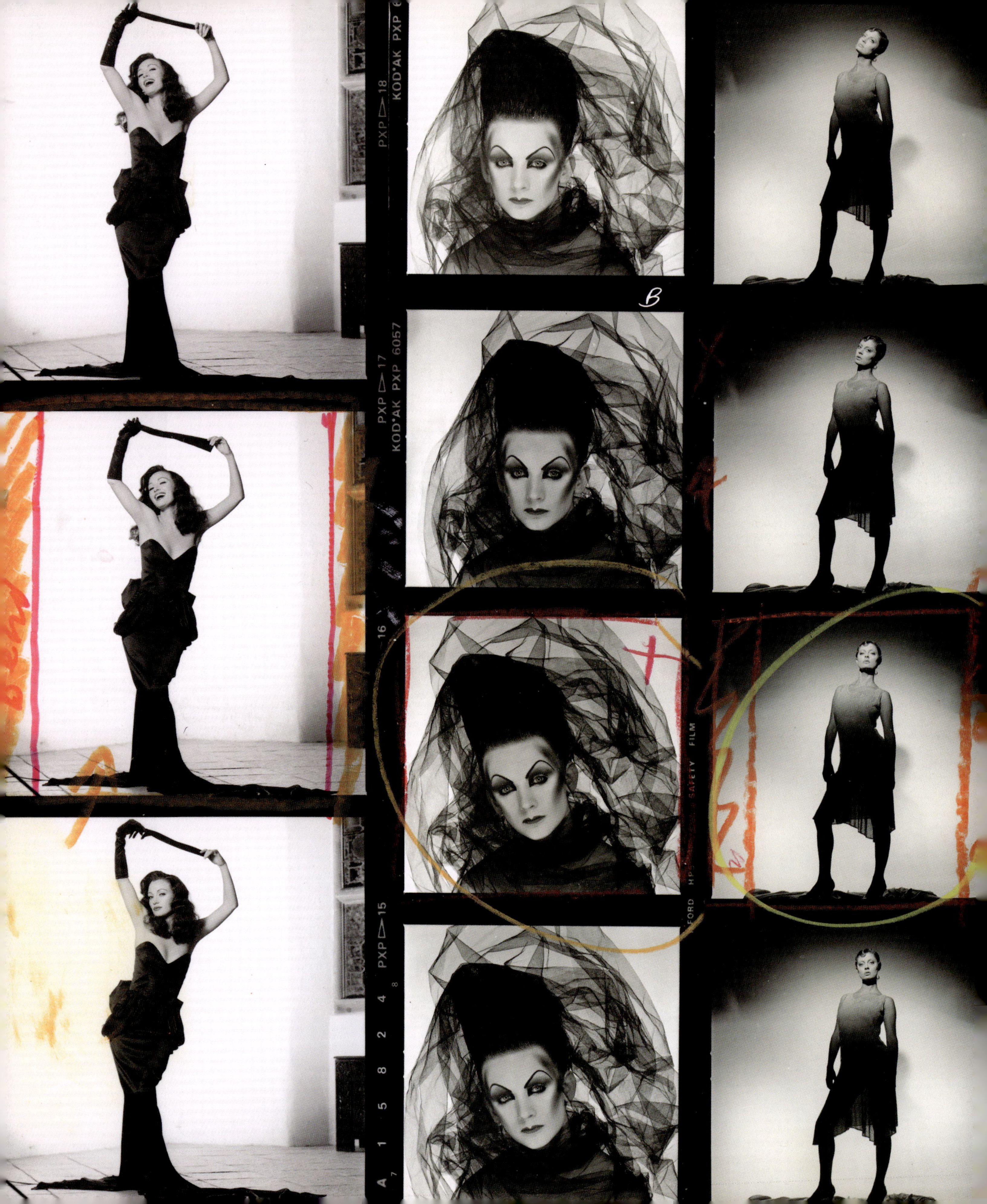

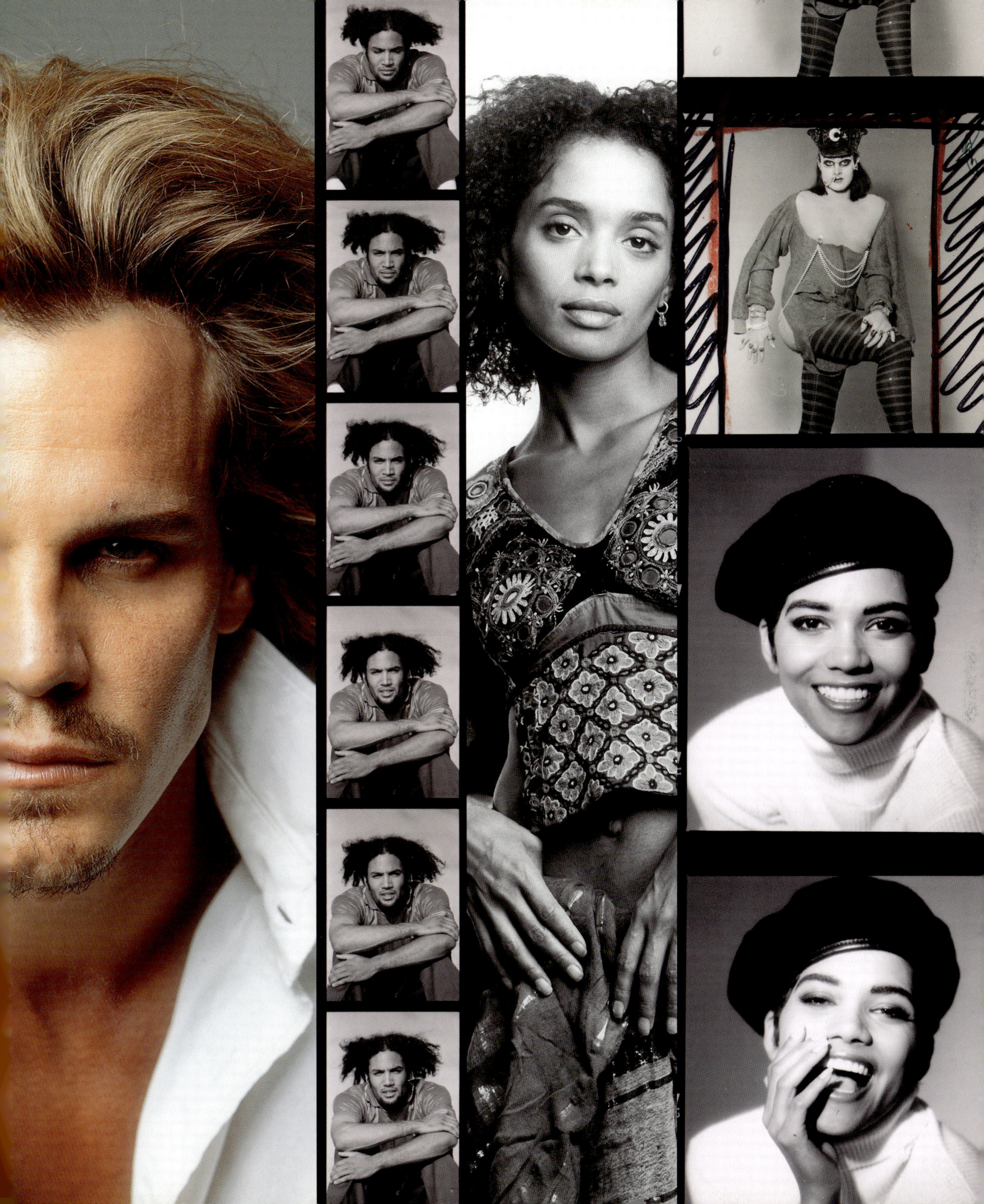

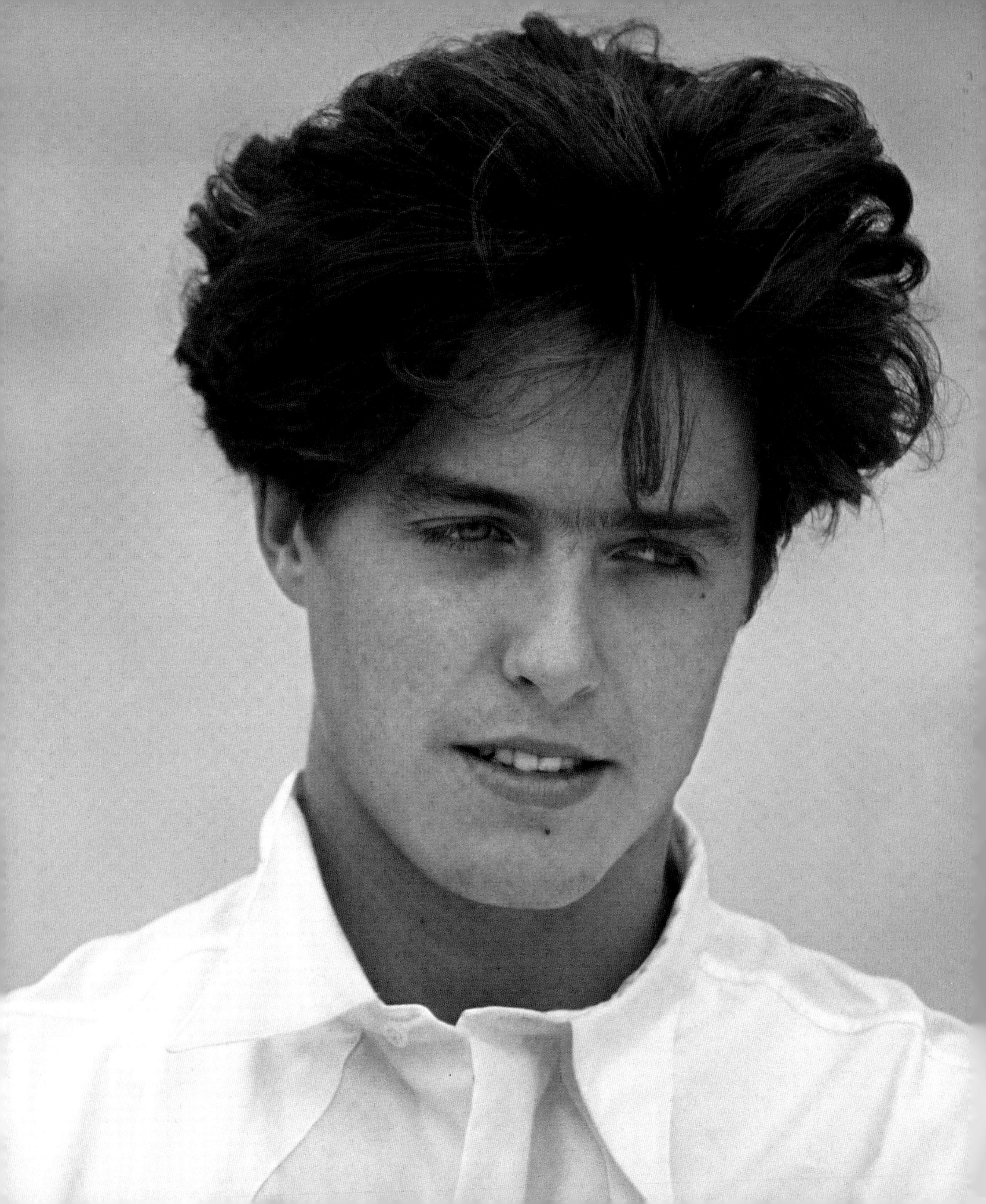

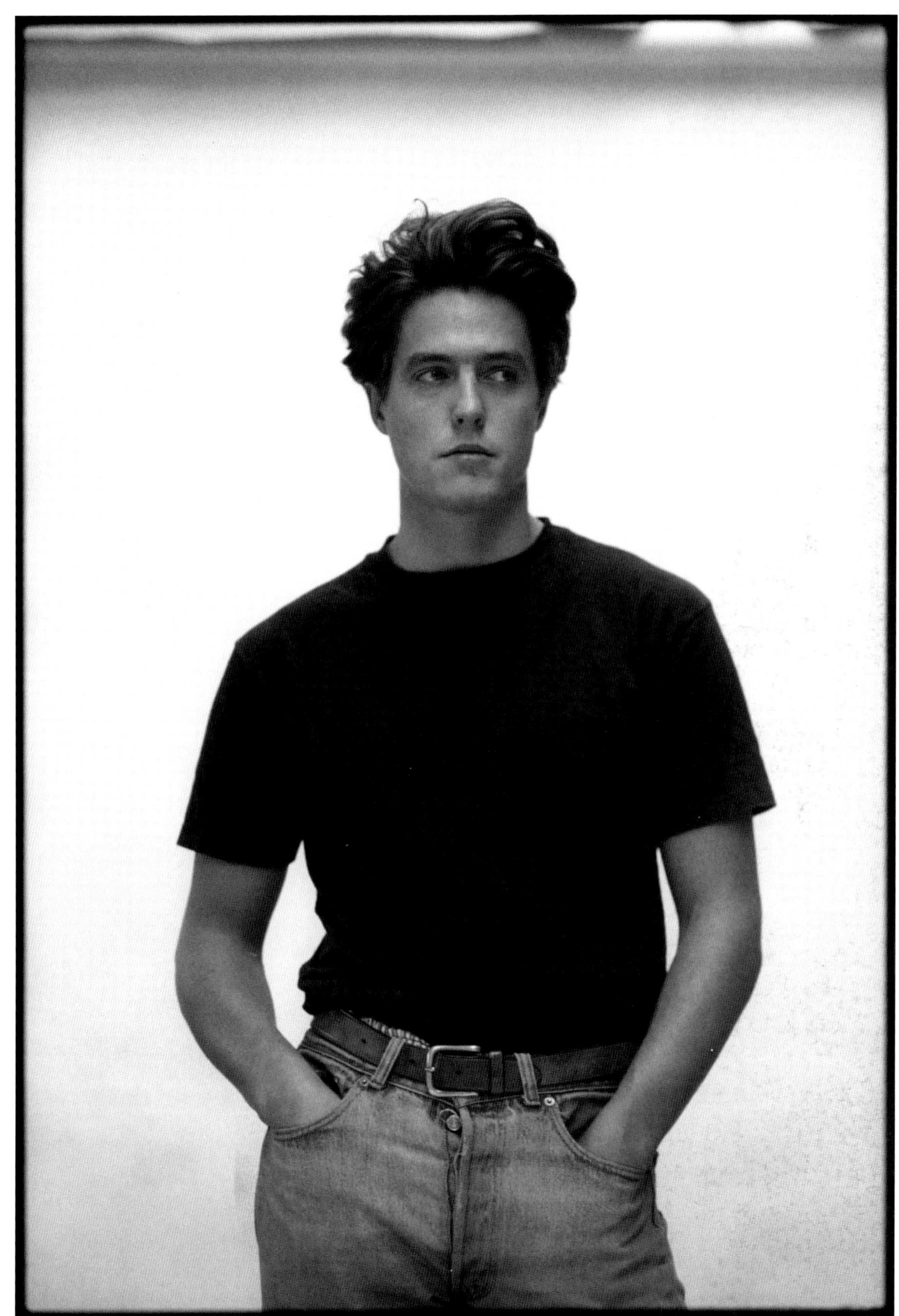

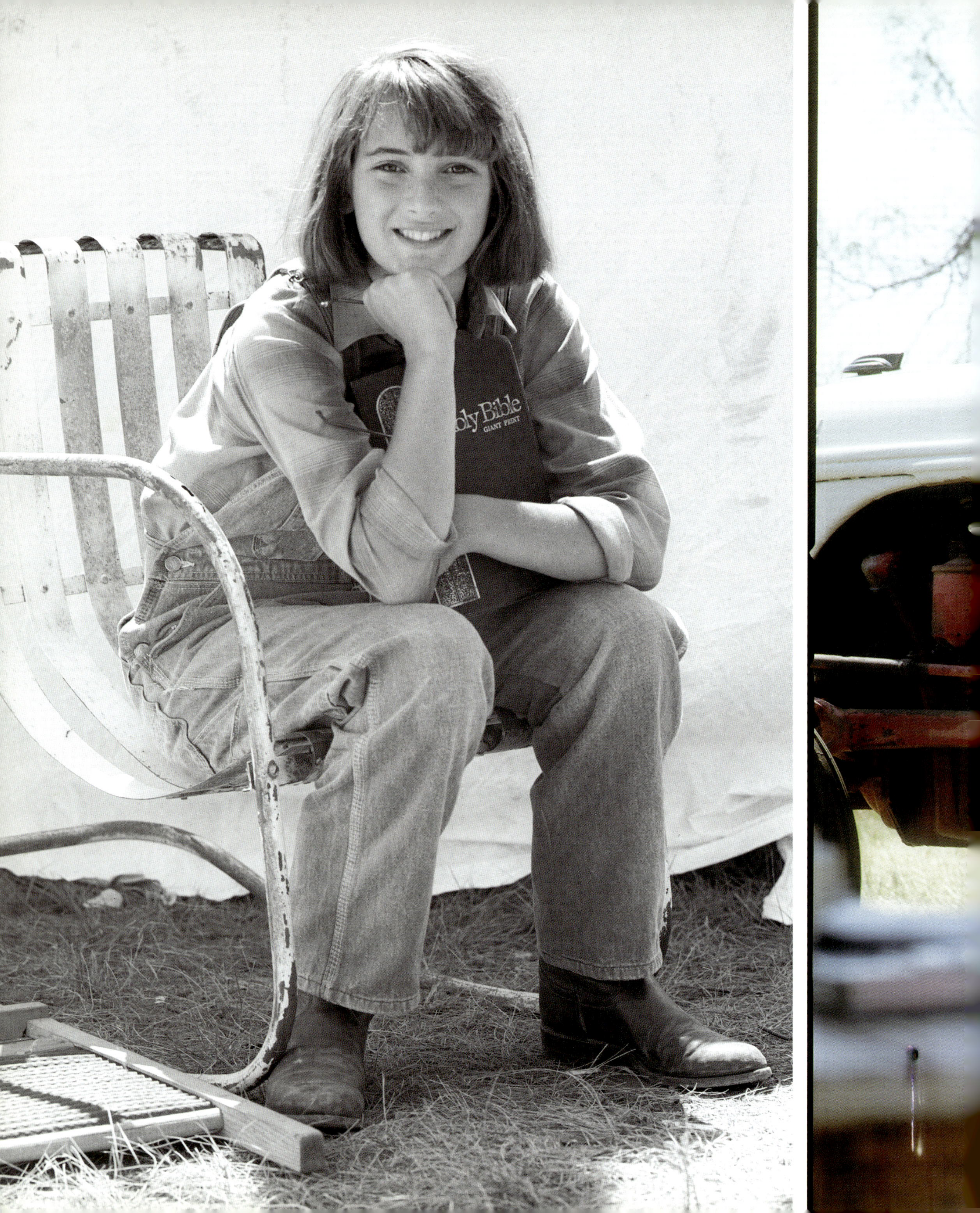

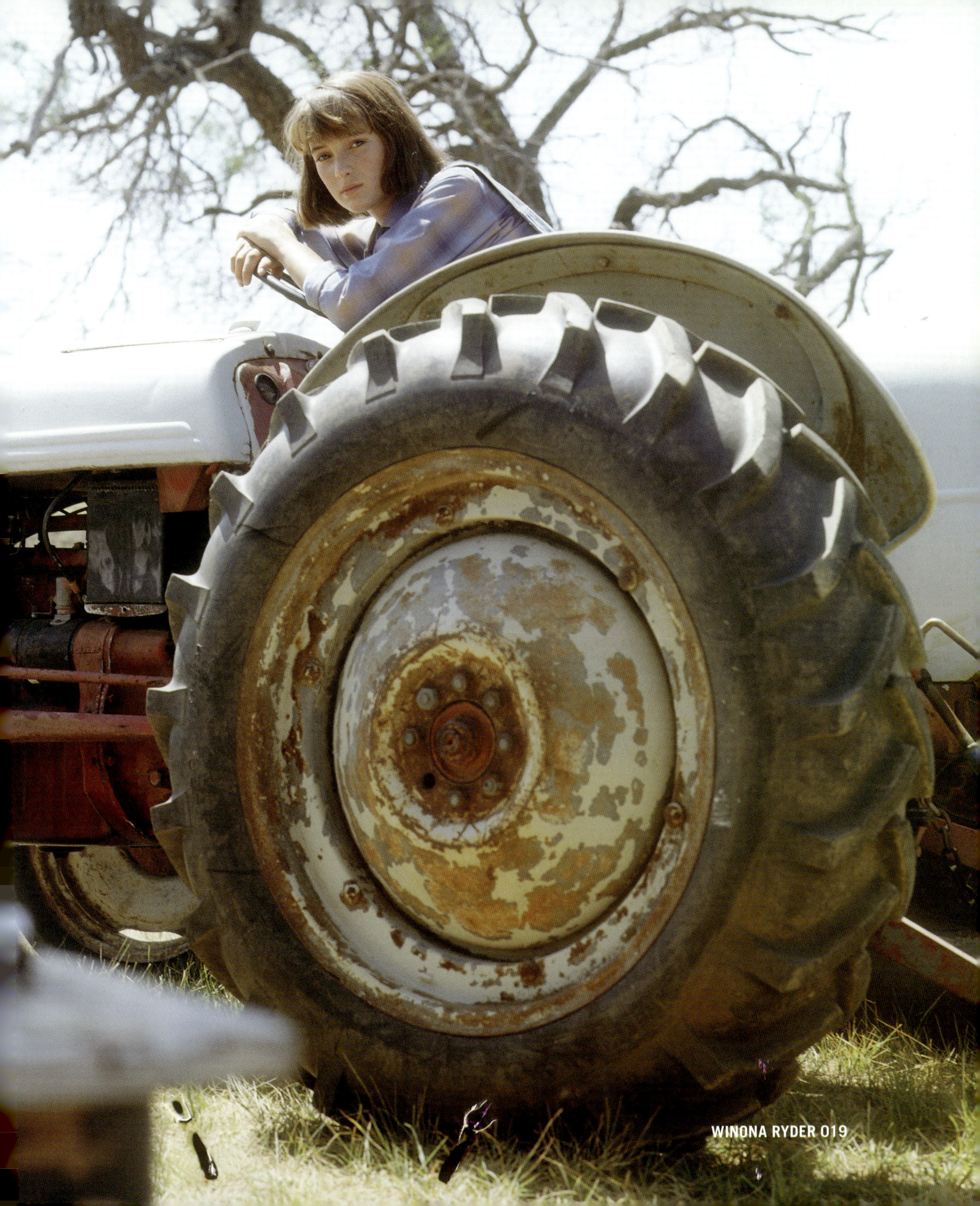
WINONA RYDER 019

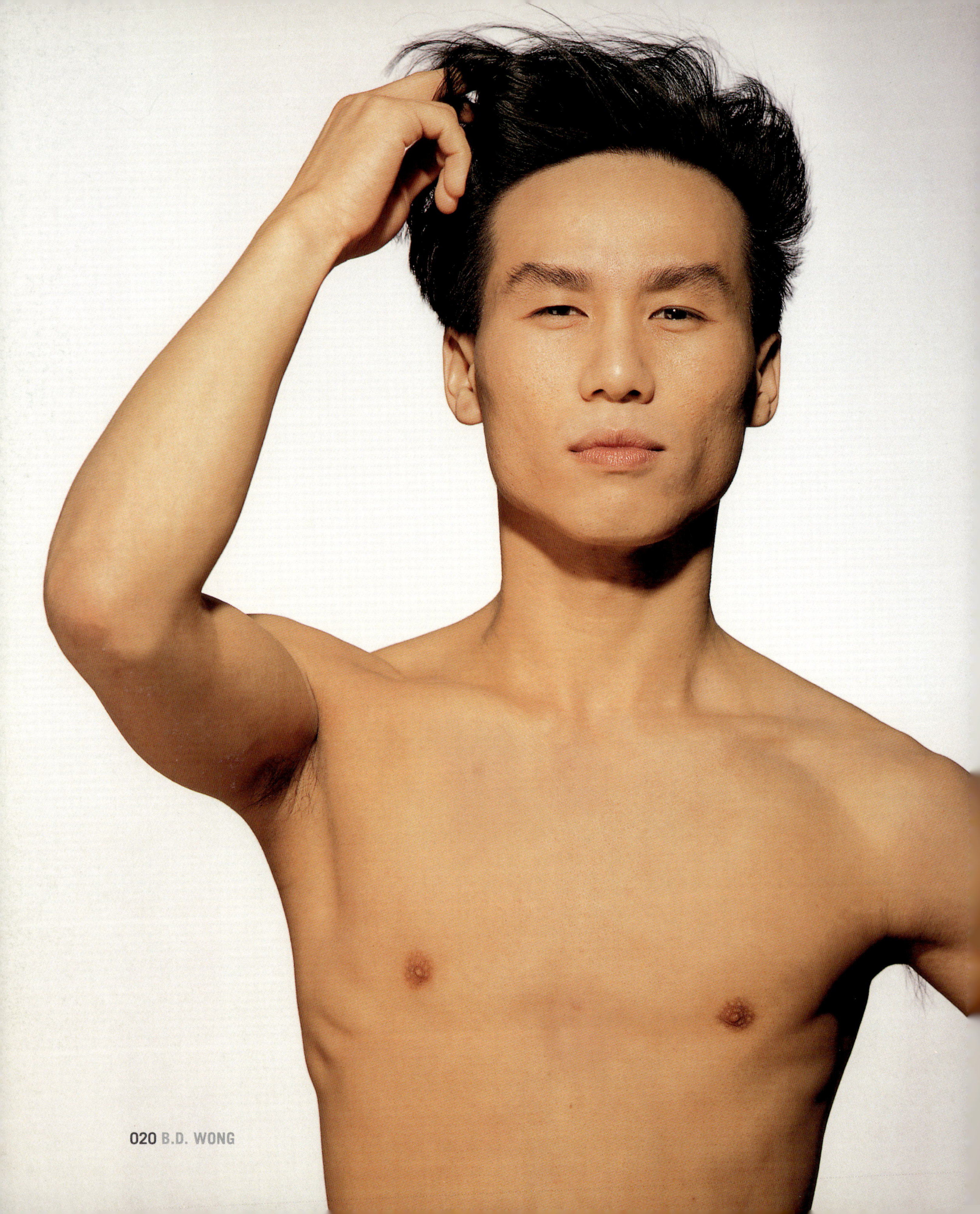

020 B.D. WONG

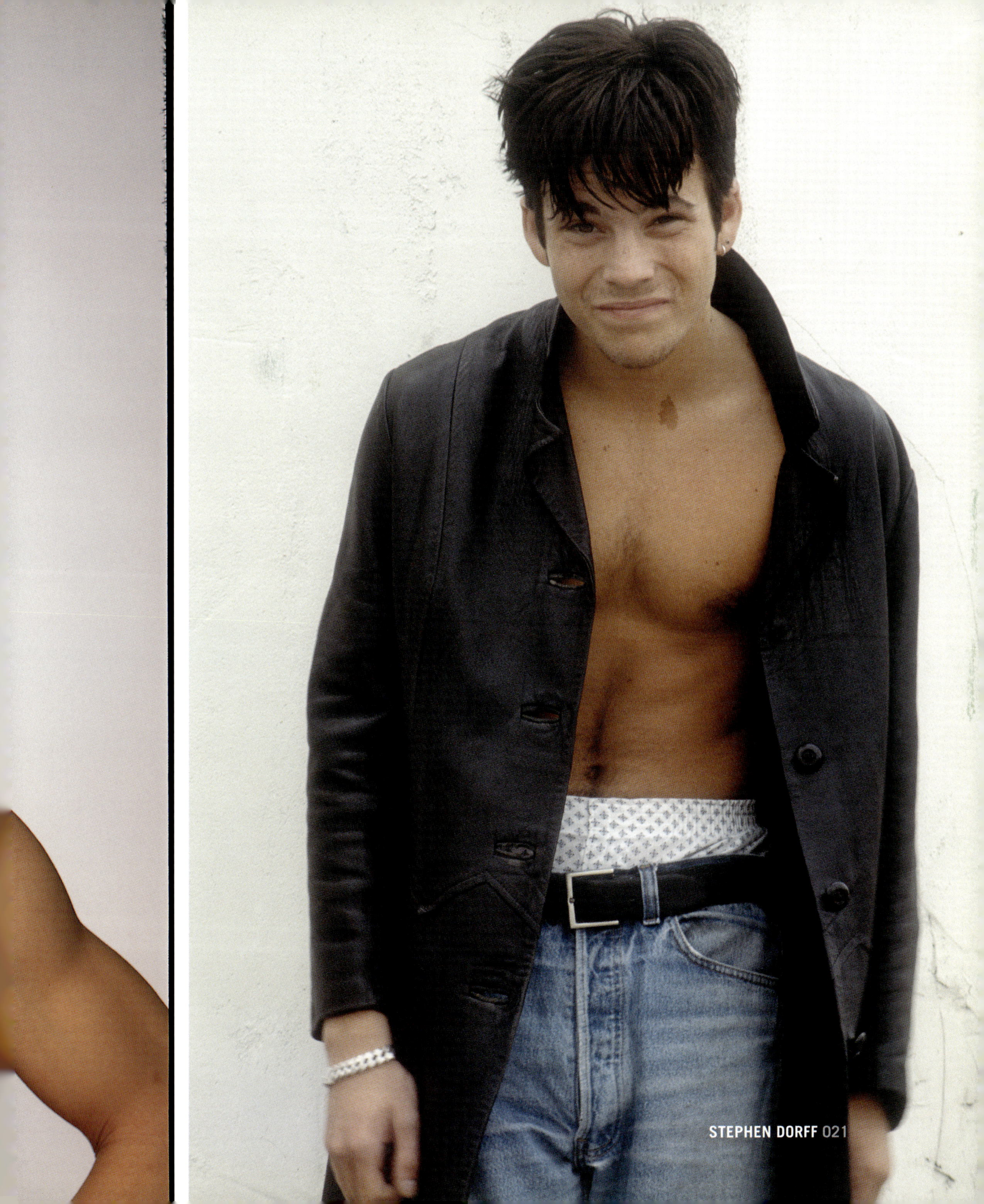
STEPHEN DORFF 021

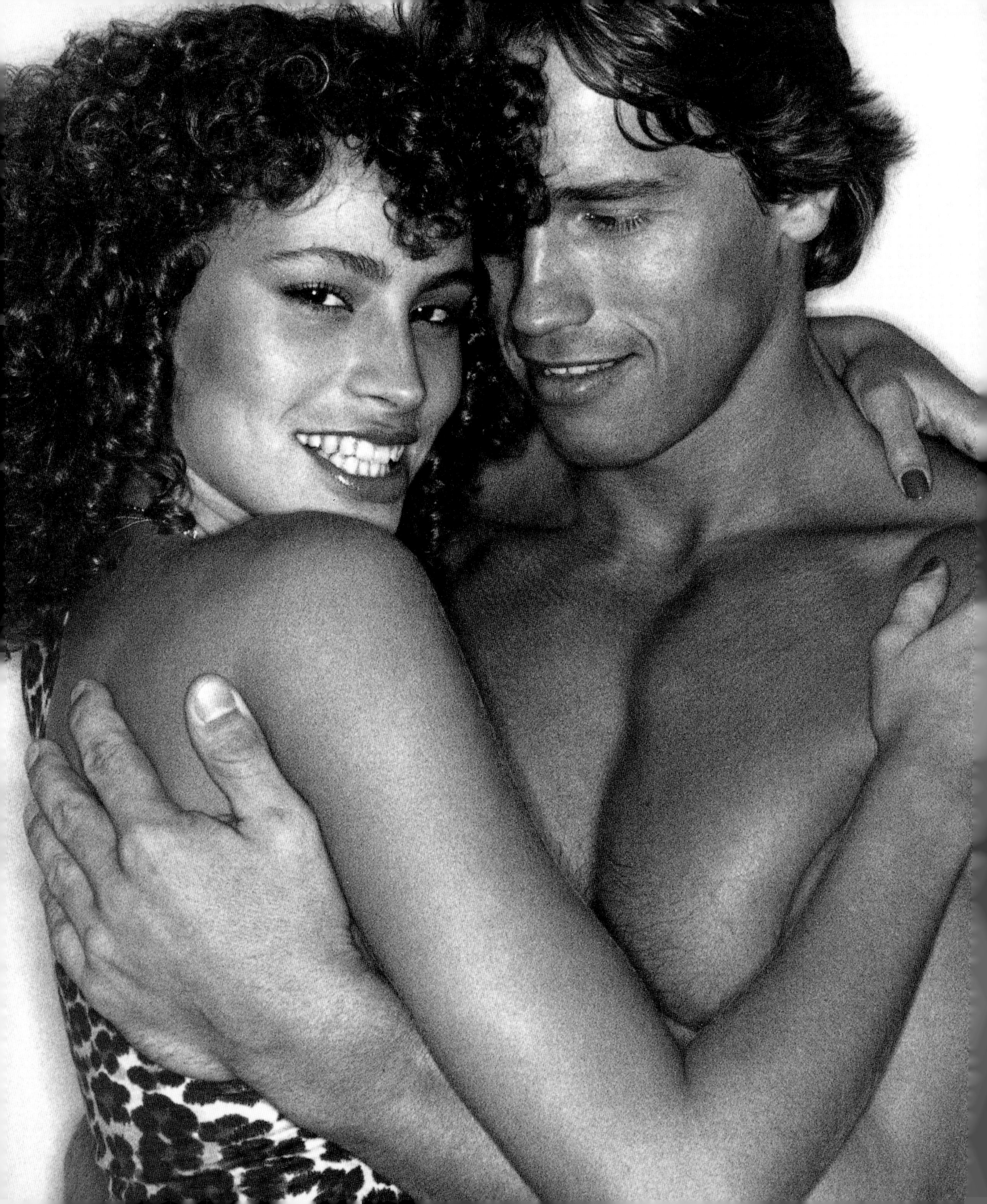

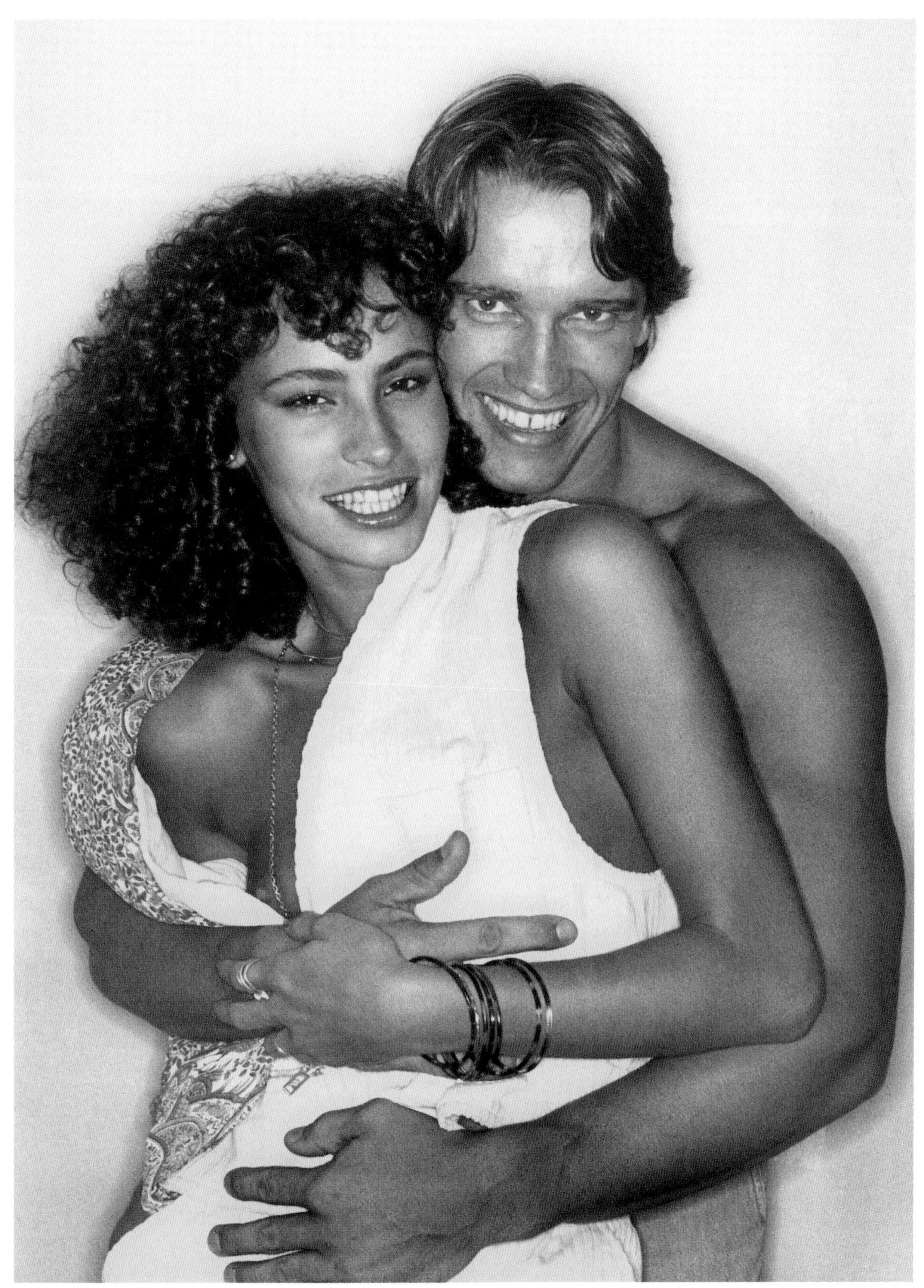

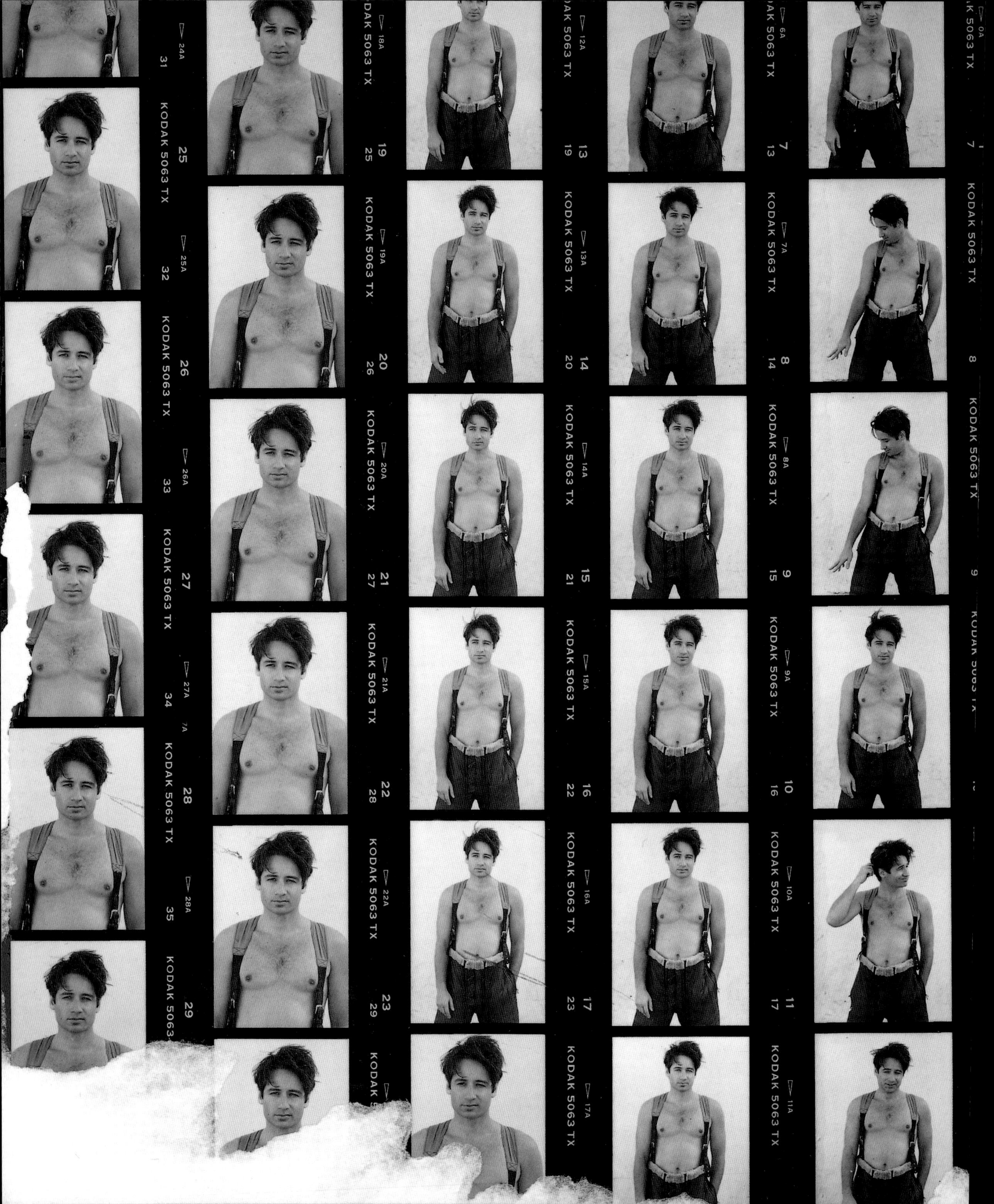

KODAK 5063 TX

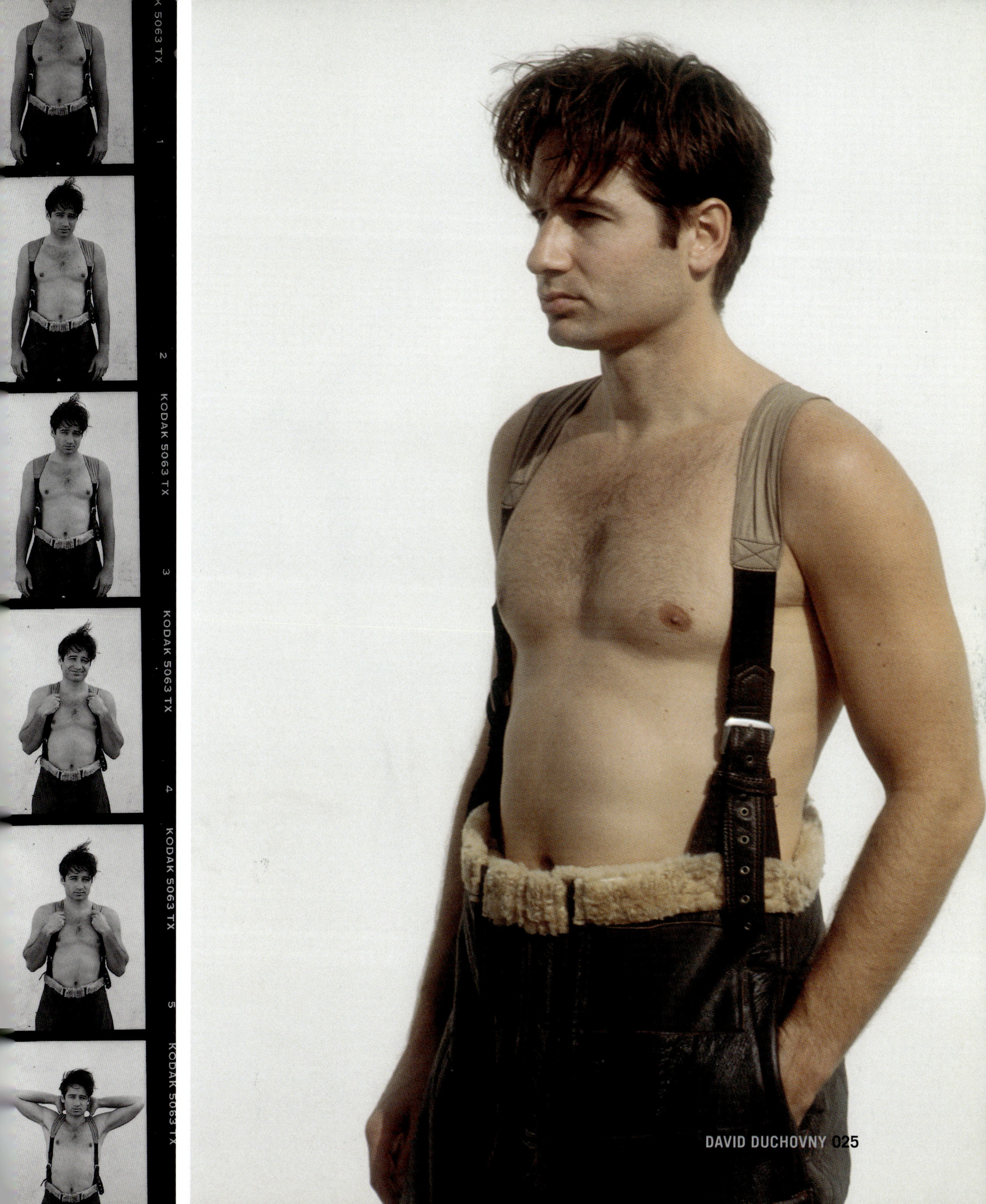

DAVID DUCHOVNY 025

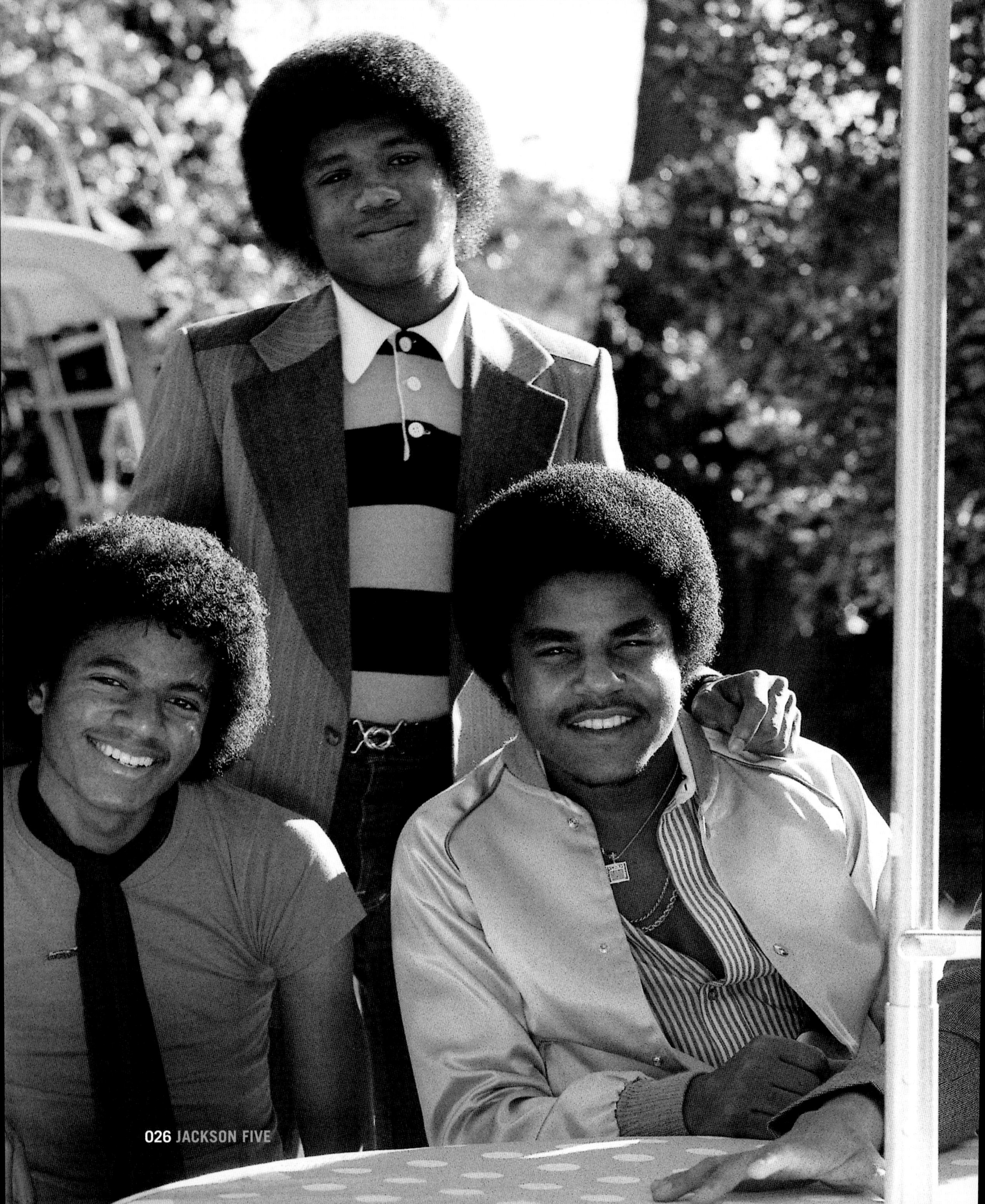

I was commissioned to photograph the Jackson Five for *Ritz* in the early seventies when they were at the height of their fame. I asked my friend, Marsha Hunt, to do the written interview and we were extremely excited to meet the whole family at their compound in Encino, California to see what they were like and how they lived. When I photographed them they all had these huge afros, so I decided to backlight them so their 'fros would give them an angelic glow. They were very pliable—they did whatever I asked. When Marsha and I left in the car, on the Ventura freeway, we were both gobsmacked at how difficult she had found it to talk to Michael. She thought he was an idiot savant because he was so mesmerizing on stage, while every time we spoke to him during the shoot one of his brothers would have to answer for him. He was about fifteen. I photographed the Jacksons outside because we were never invited inside the house.

I was commissioned to photograph the Jackson Five for Ritz in the early seventies when they were at the height of their fame. I asked my friend, Marsha Hunt, to do the written interview and we were extremely excited to meet the whole family at their compound in Encino, California to see what they were like and how they lived. When I photographed them they all had these huge afros, so I decided to backlight them so their 'fros would give them an angelic glow. They were very pliable—they did whatever I asked. When Marsha and I left in the car, on the Ventura freeway, we were both gobsmacked at how difficult she had found it to talk to Michael. She thought he was an idiot savant because he was so mesmerizing on stage, while every time we spoke to him during the shoot one of his brothers would have to answer for him. He was about fifteen. I photographed the Jacksons outside because we were never invited inside the house.

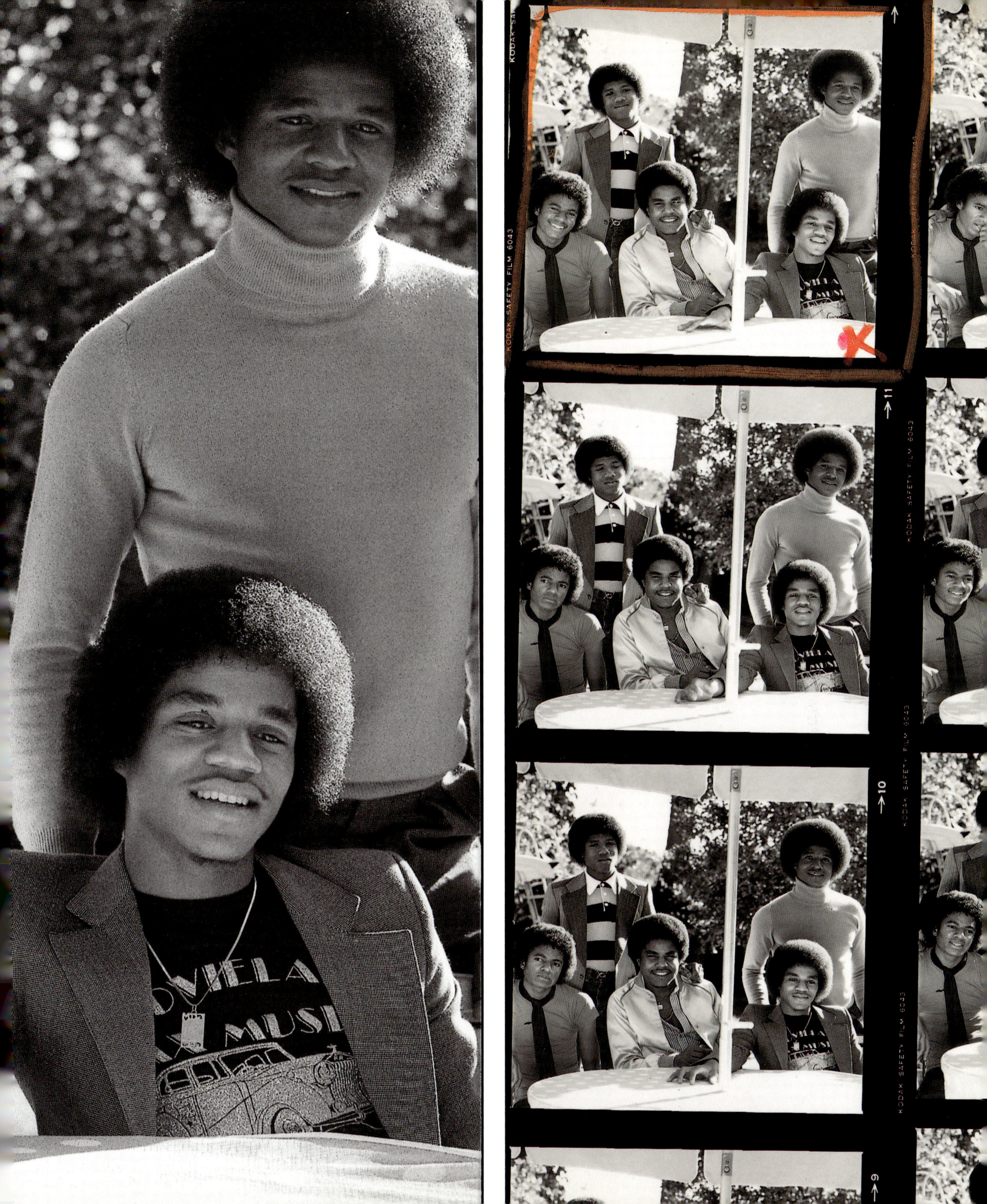

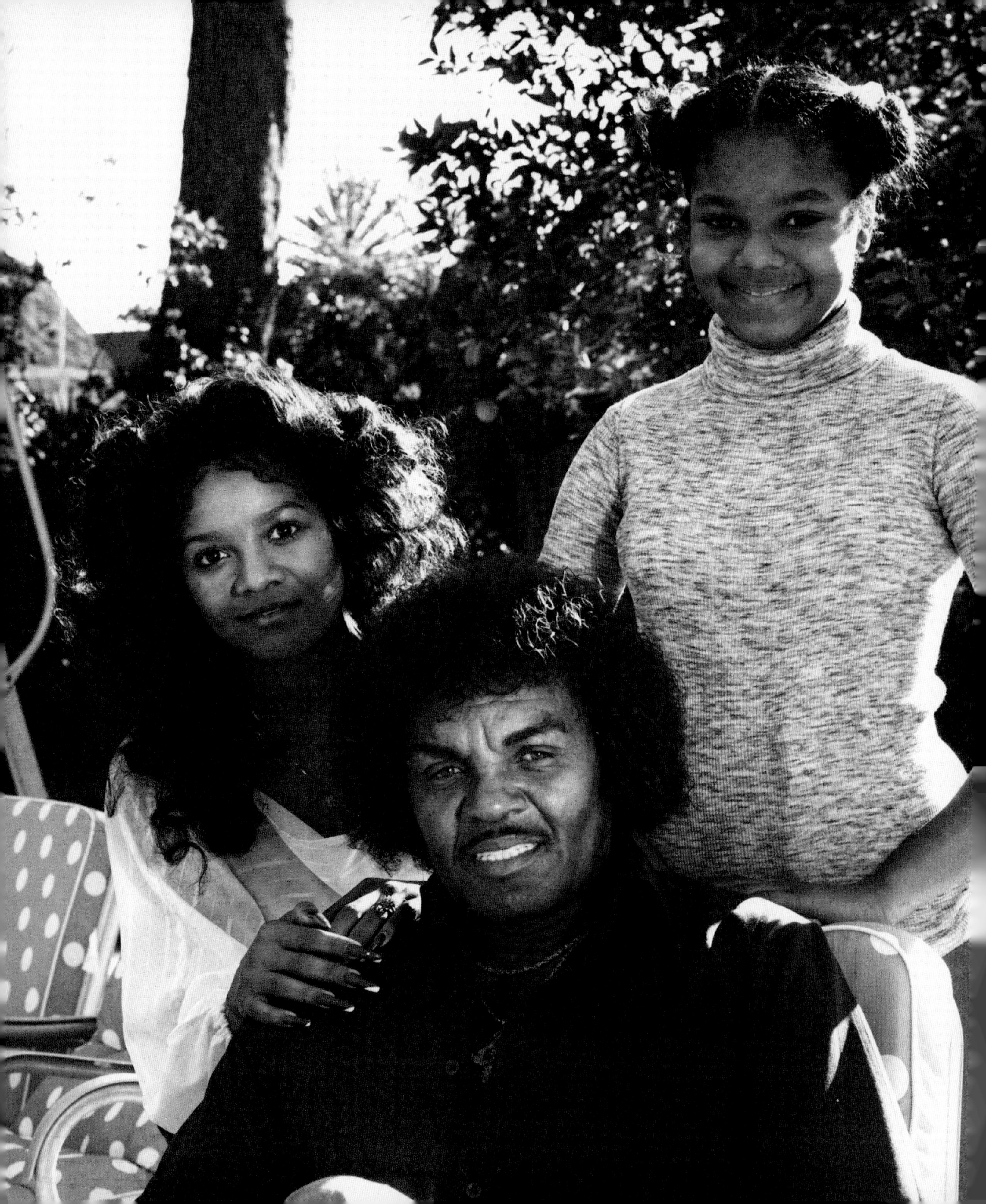

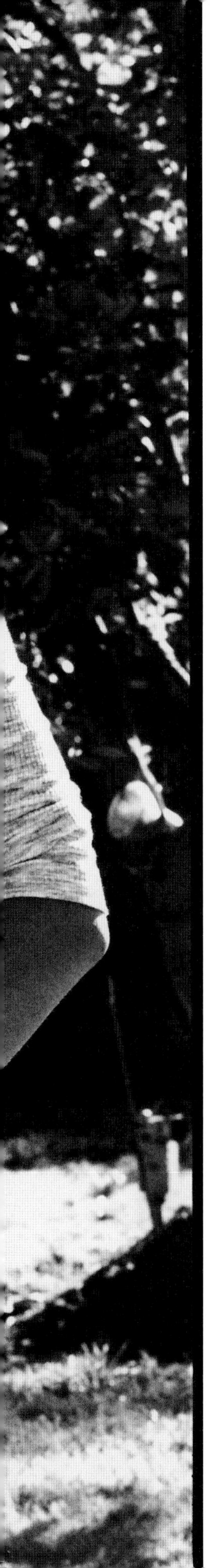

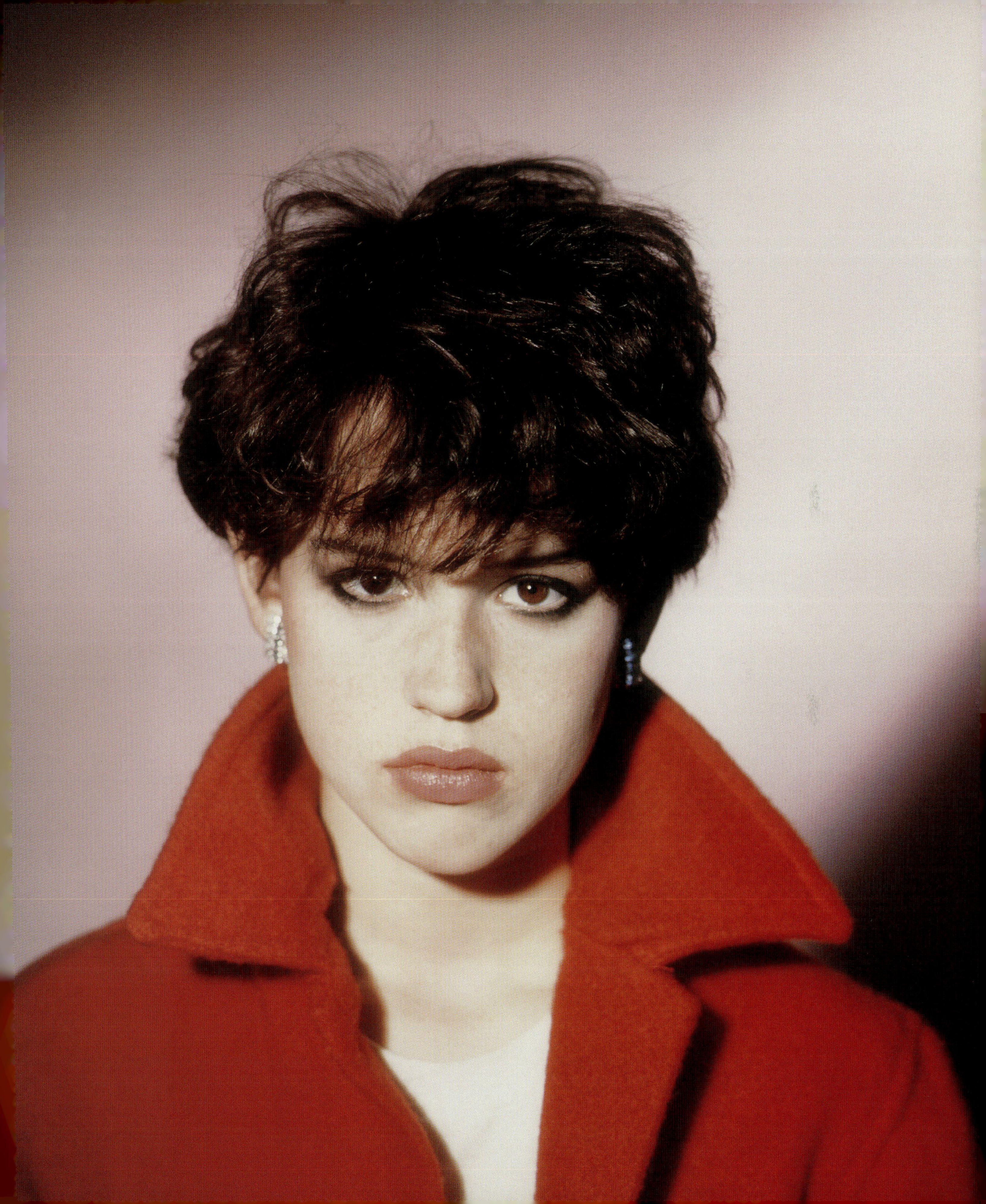

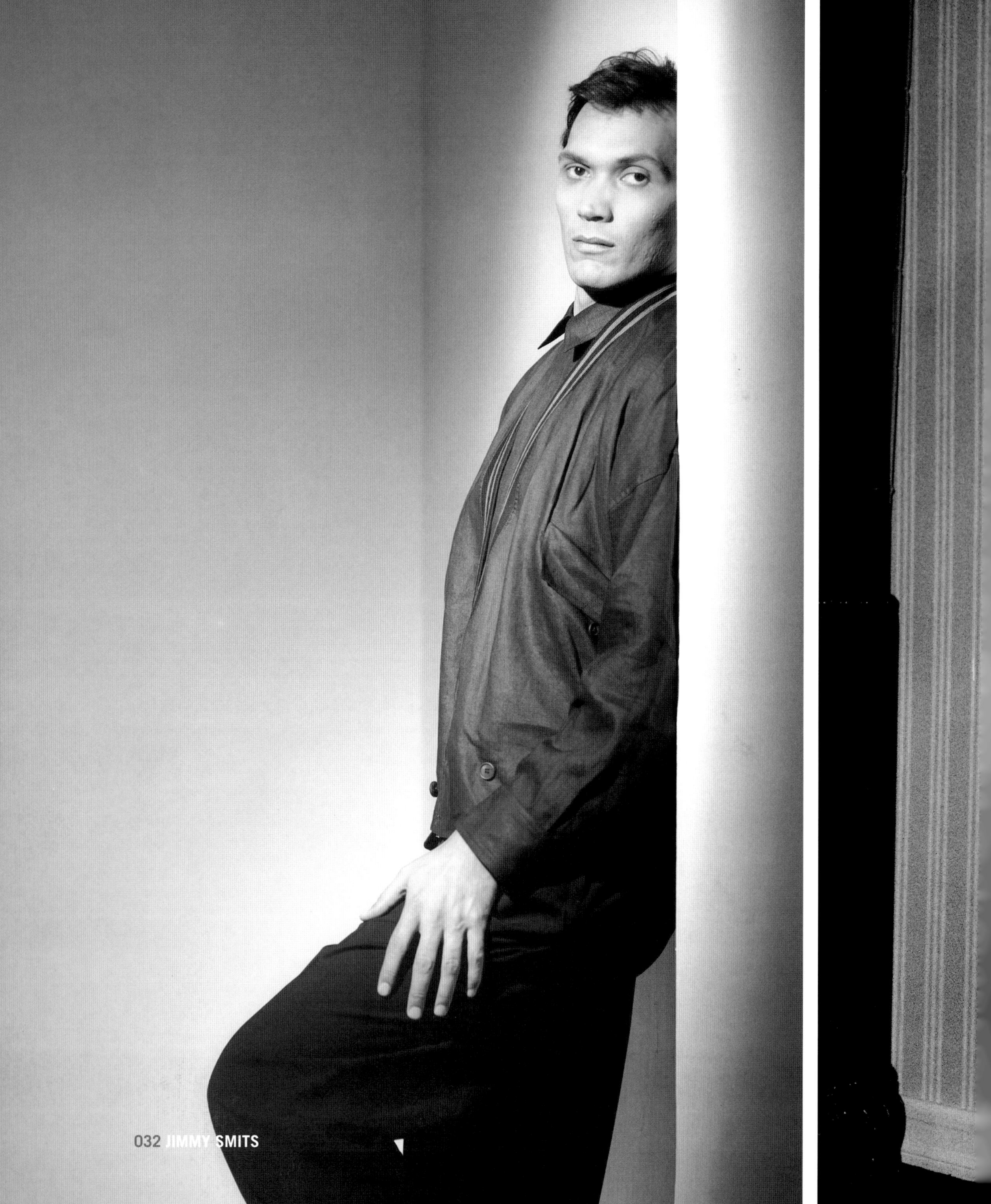

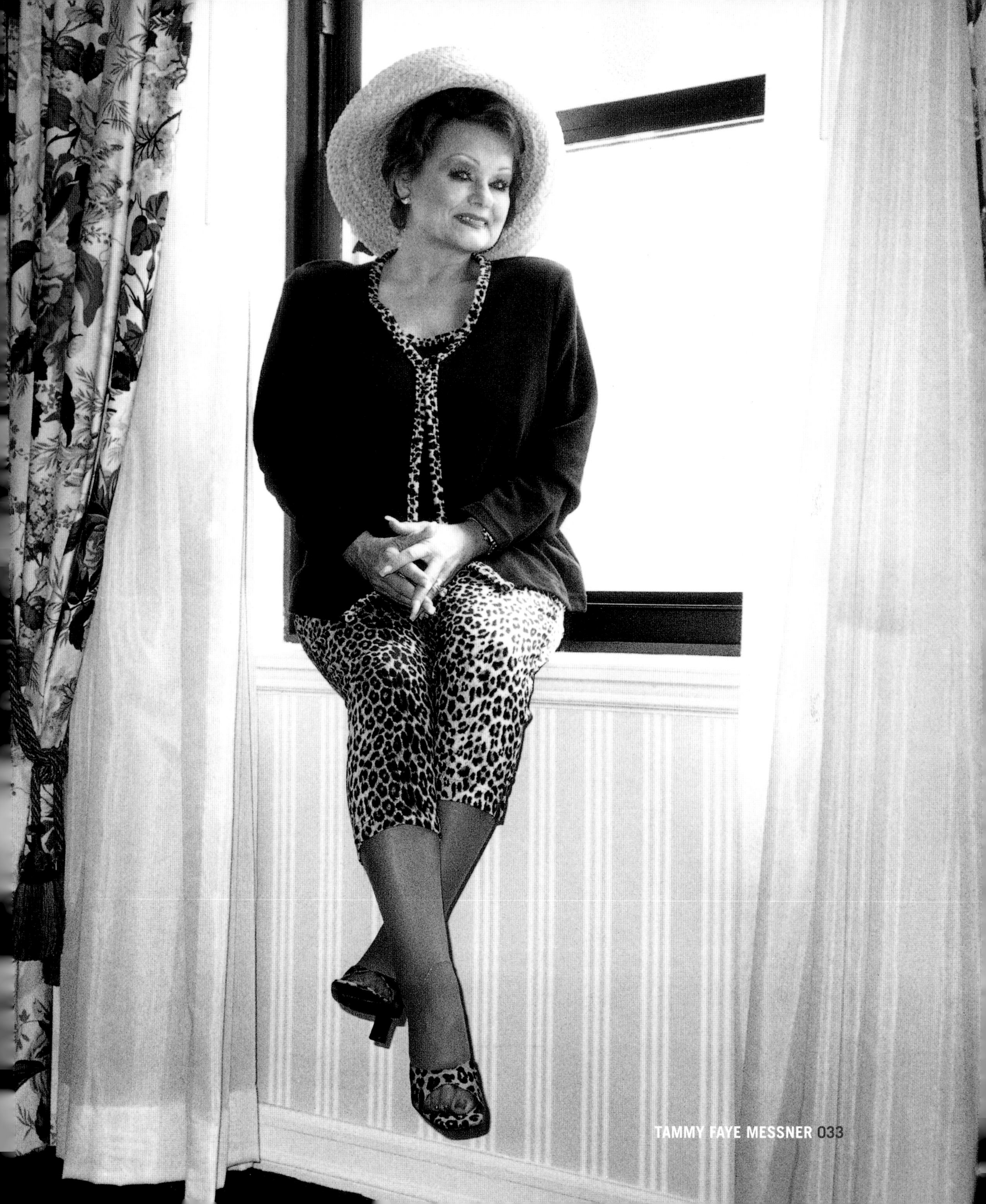

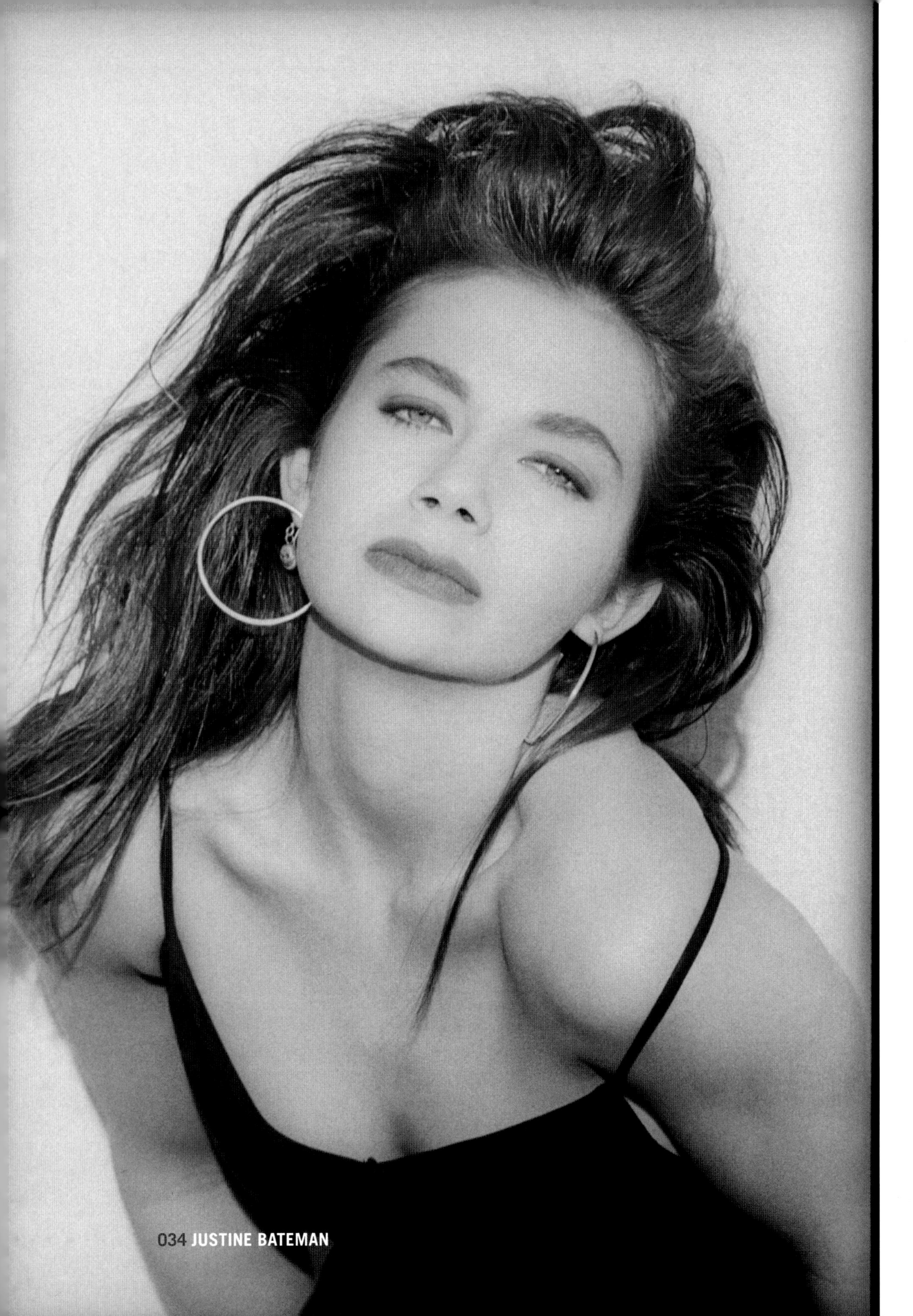

034 **JUSTINE BATEMAN**

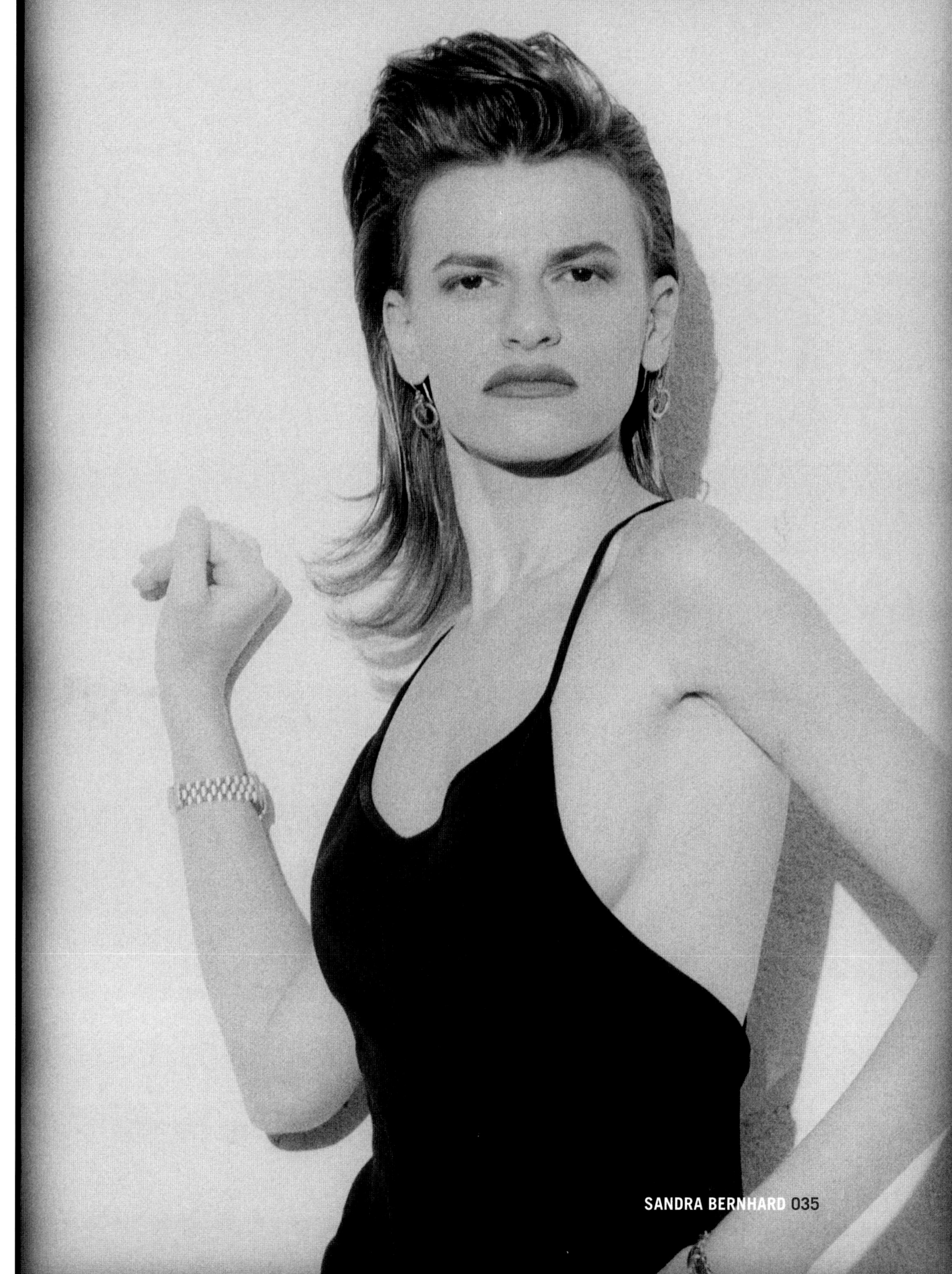

SANDRA BERNHARD 035

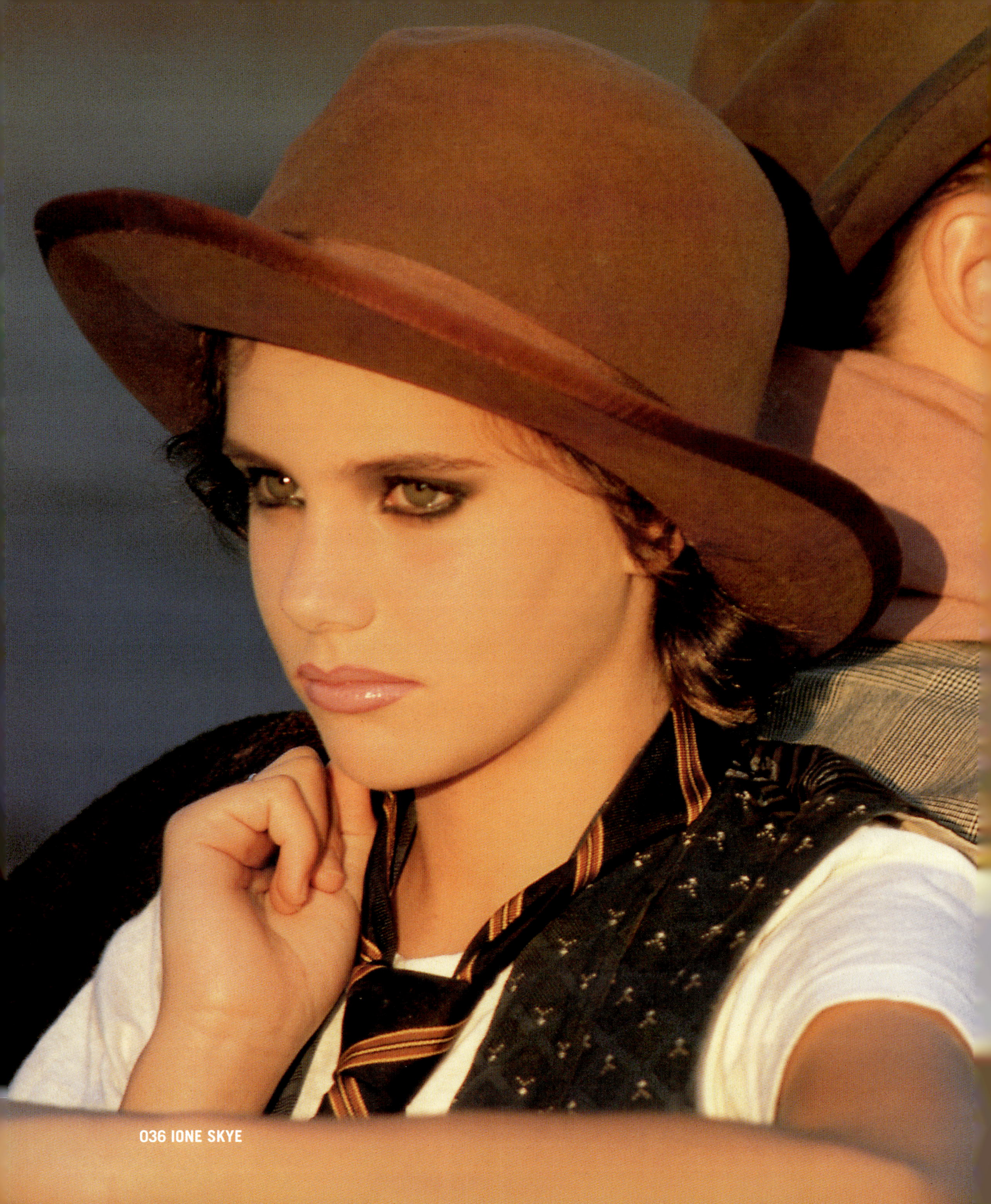
036 IONE SKYE

After
The
Lost
Boys
. . . and
still
riding
high.

After The Lost Boys ... and still riding high.

Enid, Ione's mother, is a saint. I met her in the early eighties when I first got my Green Card. She had a gorgeous husband and two young kids, Donovan and Ione, and, with the little money she had at the time, made her house a cozy hub for friends with dinners every night. Ione, a pre-teen, was a stunner and I fell in love with her like a daughter. One evening, Paul Starr (my friend and a make-up visionary) and I were feeling bored and creative, so we grabbed some flesh fishnets and a boa and headed down to Hollywood Boulevard to snap Ione looking like a Vegas showgirl. Half an hour later, Ione was scrubbing off her mascara and soon we were at the table, *en famille*, eating some delicious pasta and salad! Two years later, she starred in her first film, *The River's Edge*.

Enid, Ione's mother, is a saint. I met her in the early eighties when I first got my Green Card. She had a gorgeous husband and two young kids, Donovan and Ione, and, with the little money she had at the time, made her house a cozy hub for friends with dinners every night. Ione, a pre-teen, was a stunner and I fell in love with her like a daughter. One evening, Paul Starr (my friend and a make-up visionary) and I were feeling bored and cre- ative, so we grabbed some flesh fishnets and a boa and headed down to Hollywood Boule- vard to snap Ione looking like a Vegas show- girl. Half an hour later, Ione was scrubbing off her mascara and soon we were at the table, en famille, eating some delicious pasta and salad! Two years later, she starred in her first film, The River's Edge.

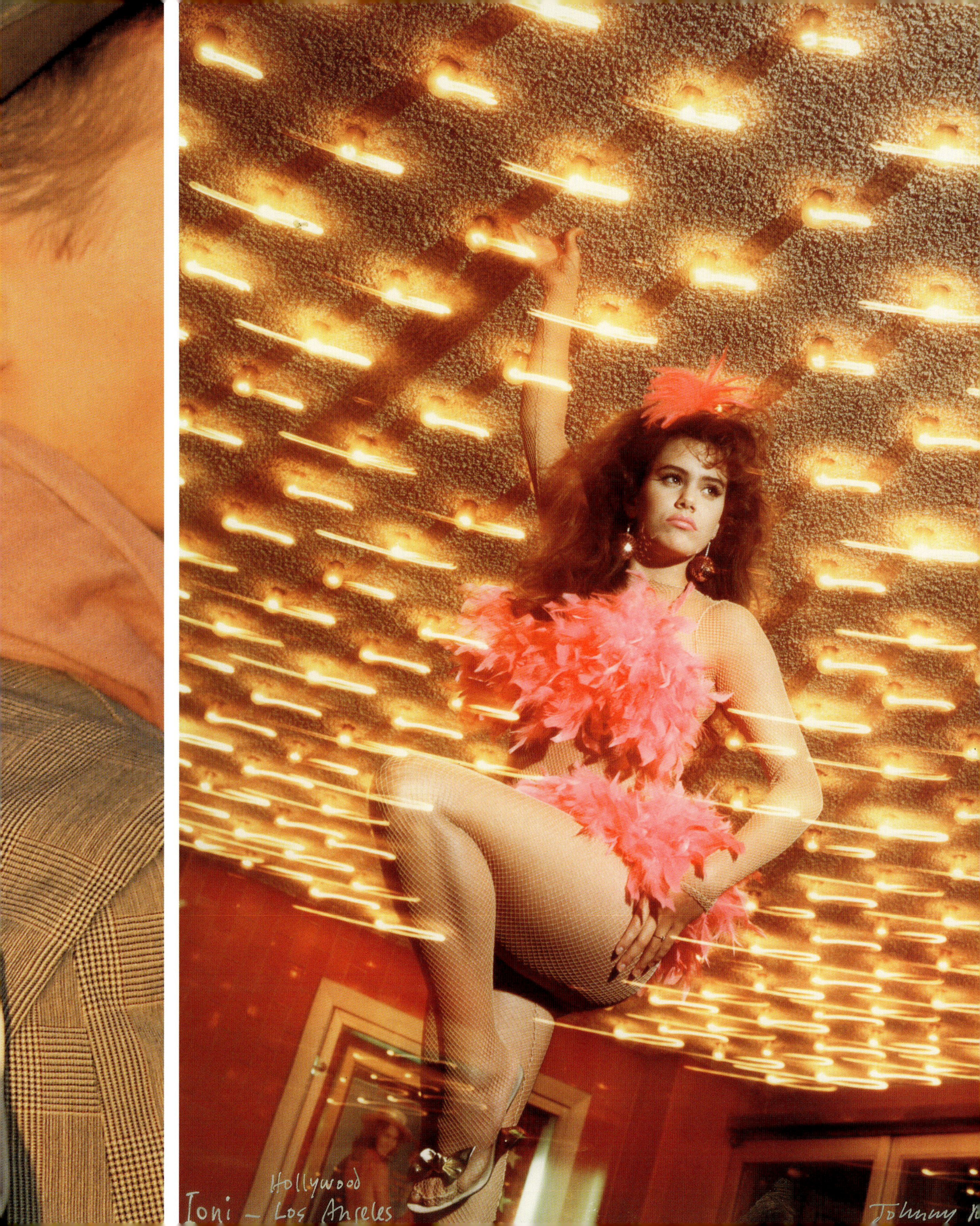
Hollywood
Ioni - Los Angeles
Johnny

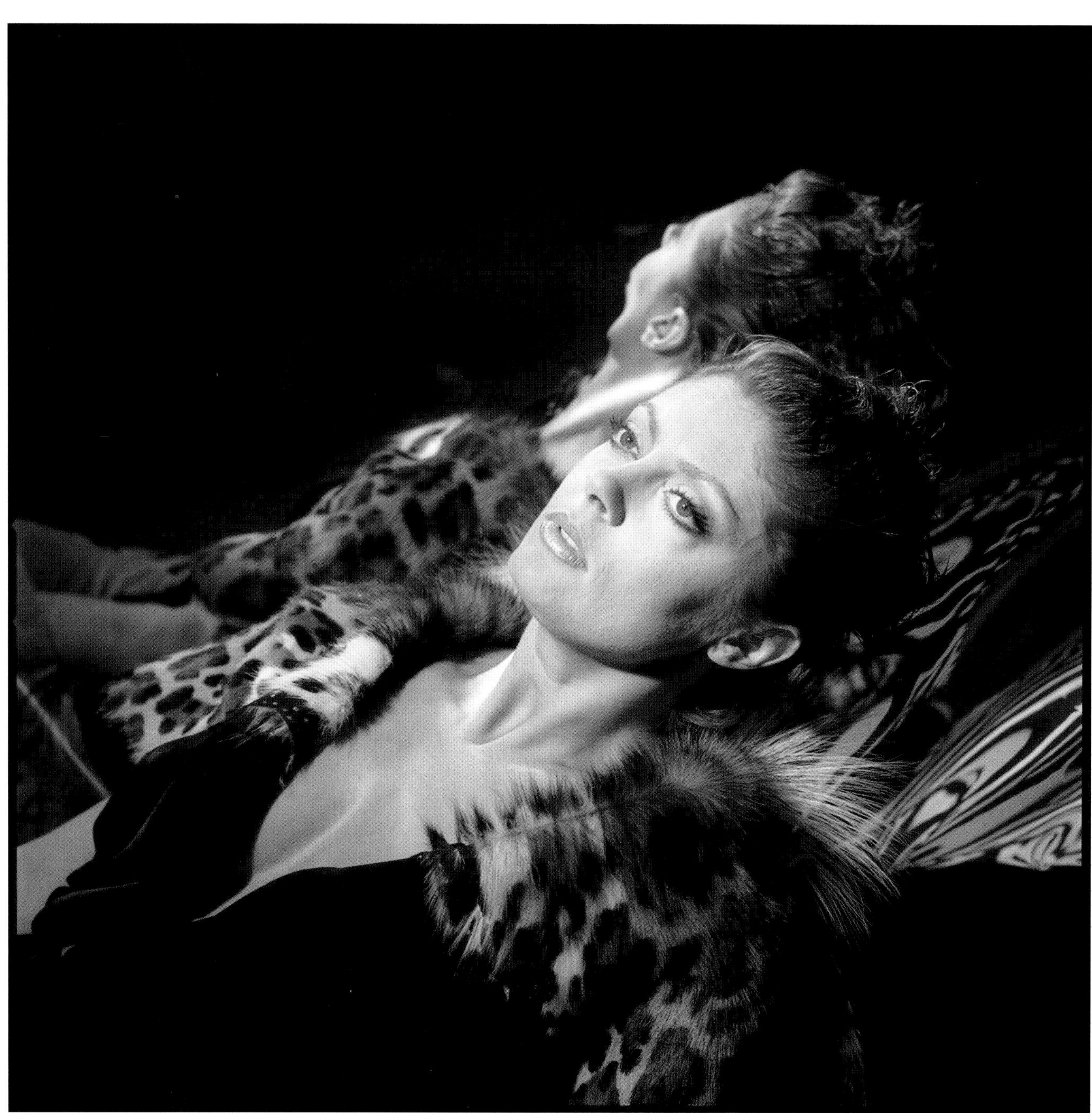

038 SUSAN SARANDON

I spent two days on the set where she wore the famous gold bra and hot pants. I built my own little stills studio and watched and waited and waited! What I realized about Mariah Carey is that she has the wittiest sense of humor and can get down with the best of the best of those with a quick mind.

I spent two days
on the set where
she wore the famous
gold bra and hot
pants. I built my own
little stills studio and
watched and waited
and waited! What I
realized about Mariah
Carey is that she has
the wittiest sense of
humor and can get
down with the best of
the best of those with
a quick mind.

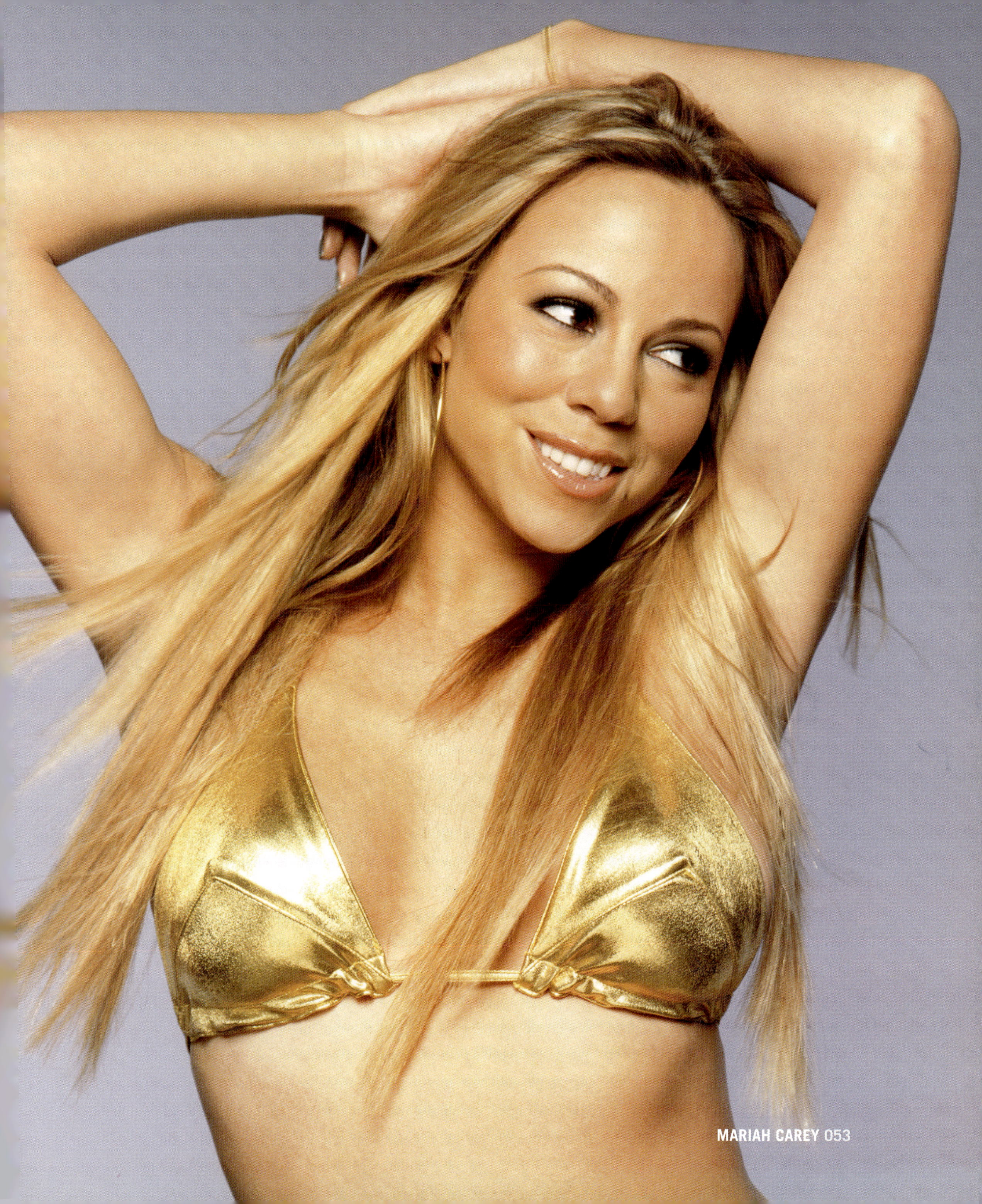

MARIAH CAREY 053

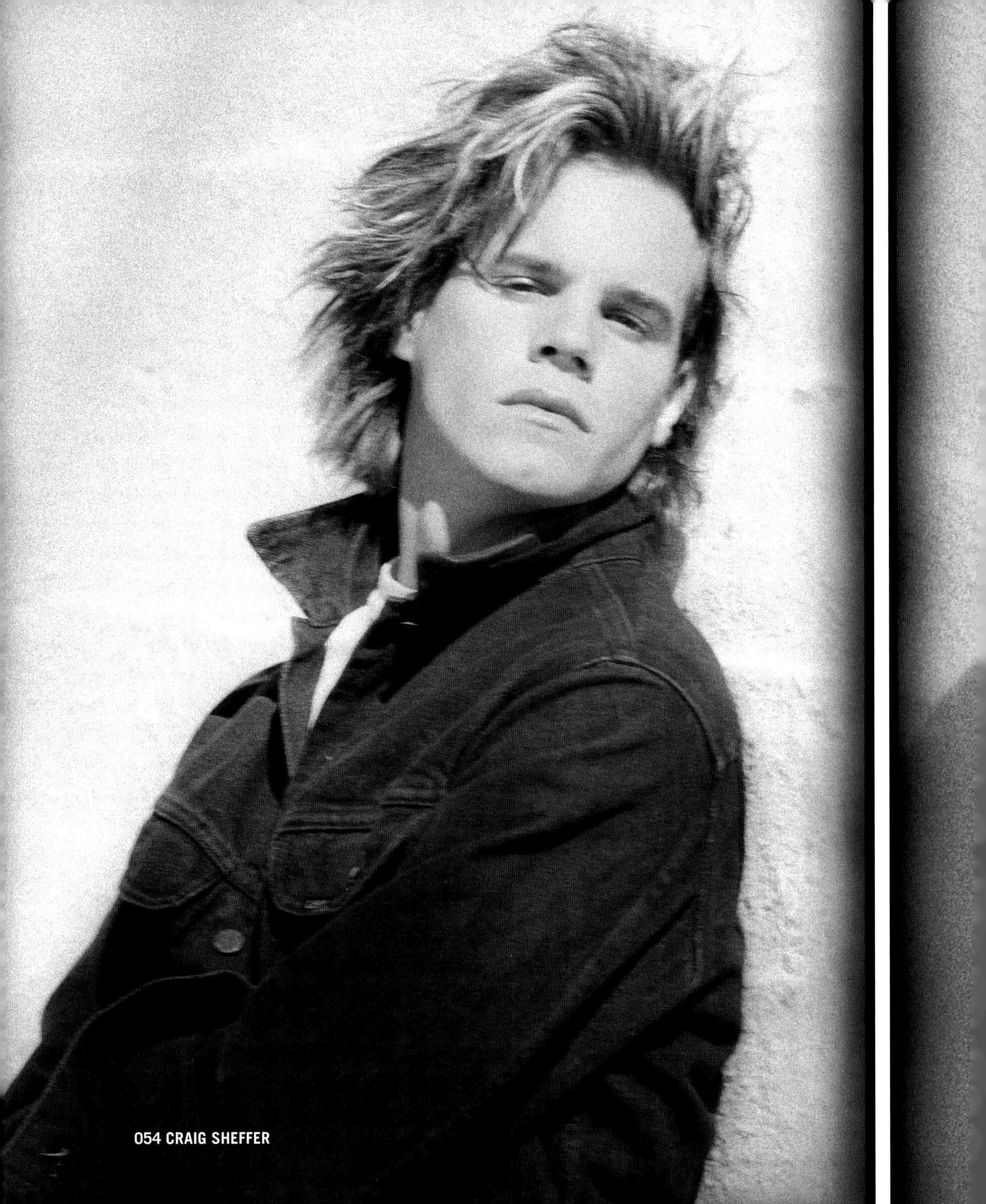

054 CRAIG SHEFFER

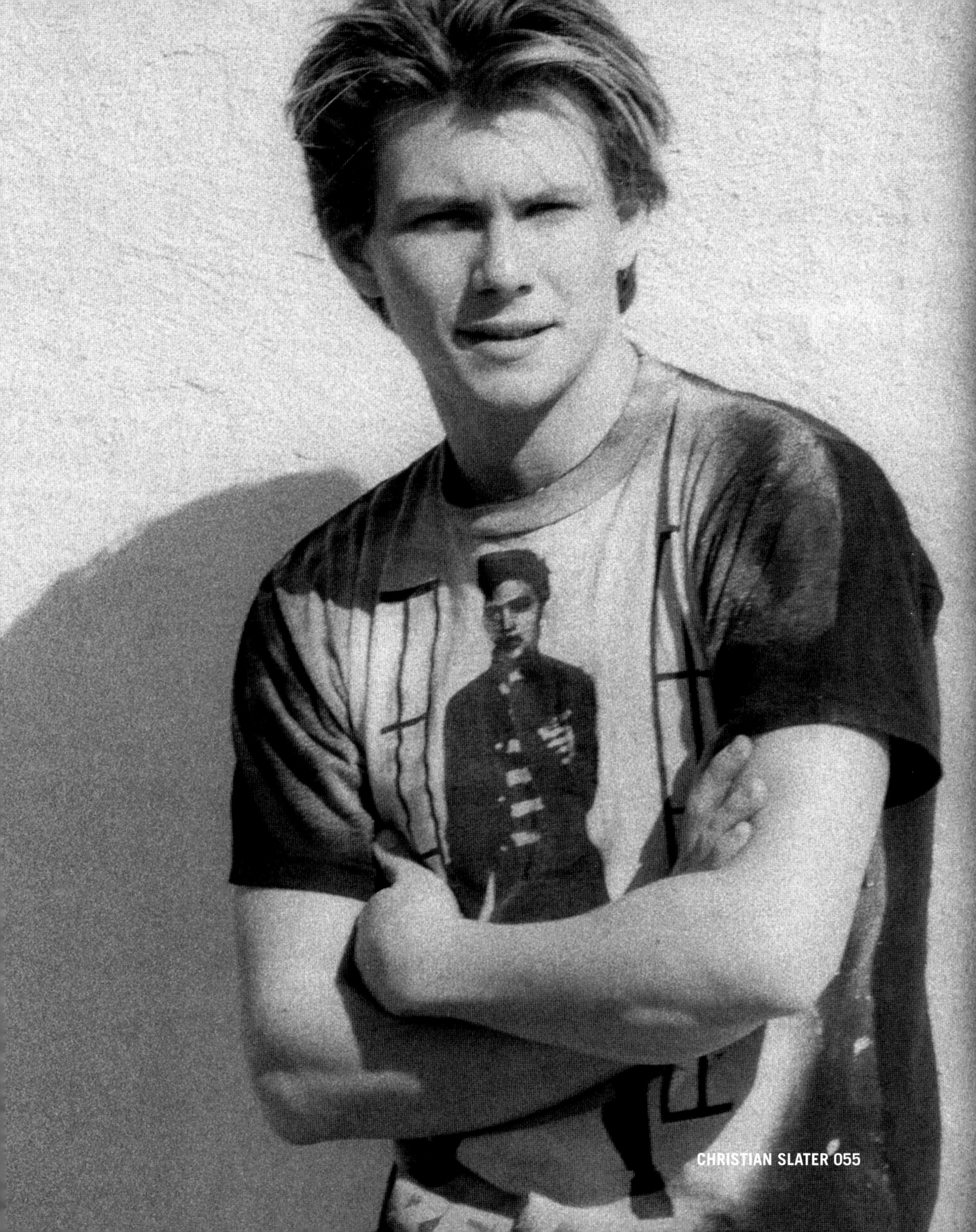
CHRISTIAN SLATER 055

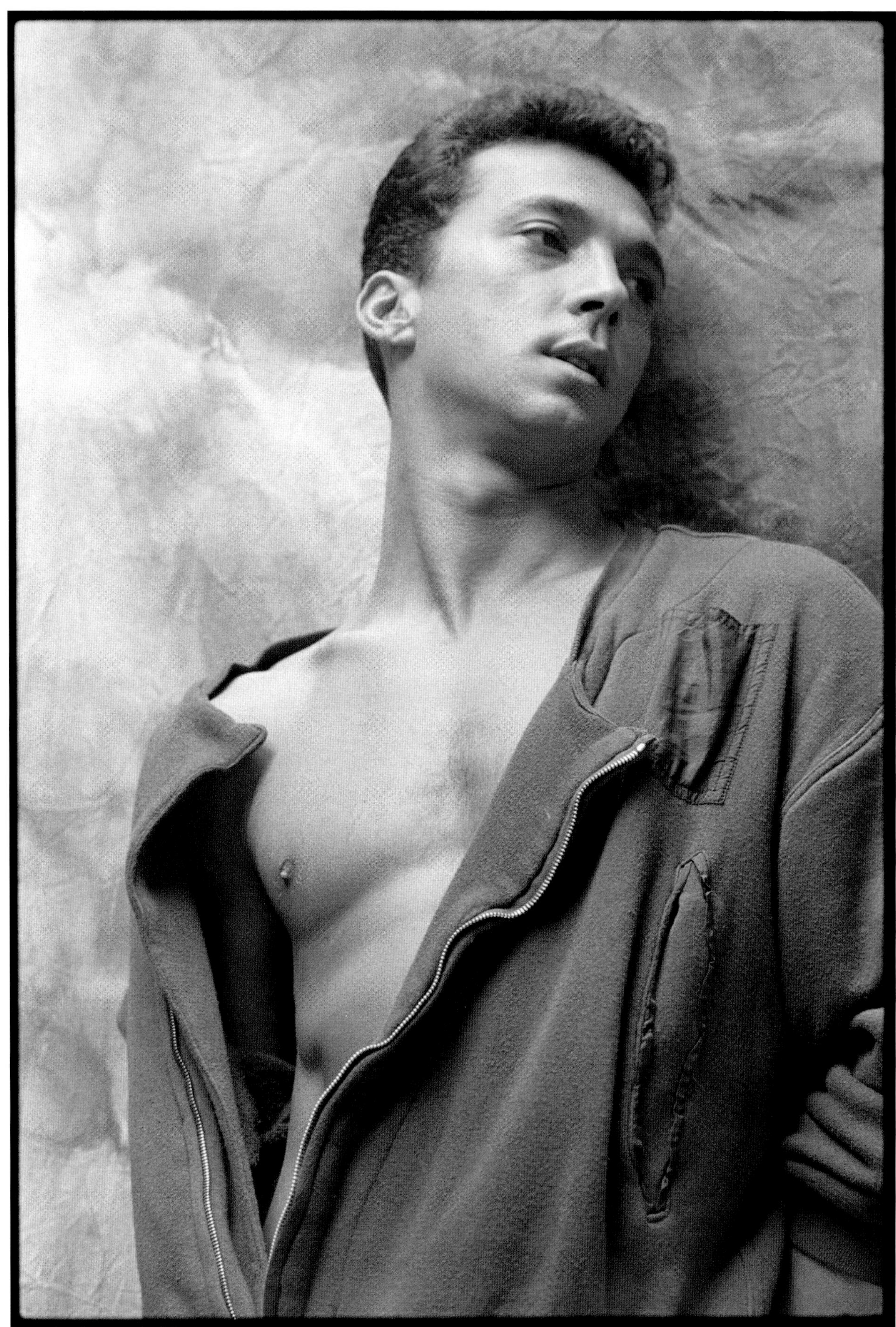

 BRUNO TONIONI

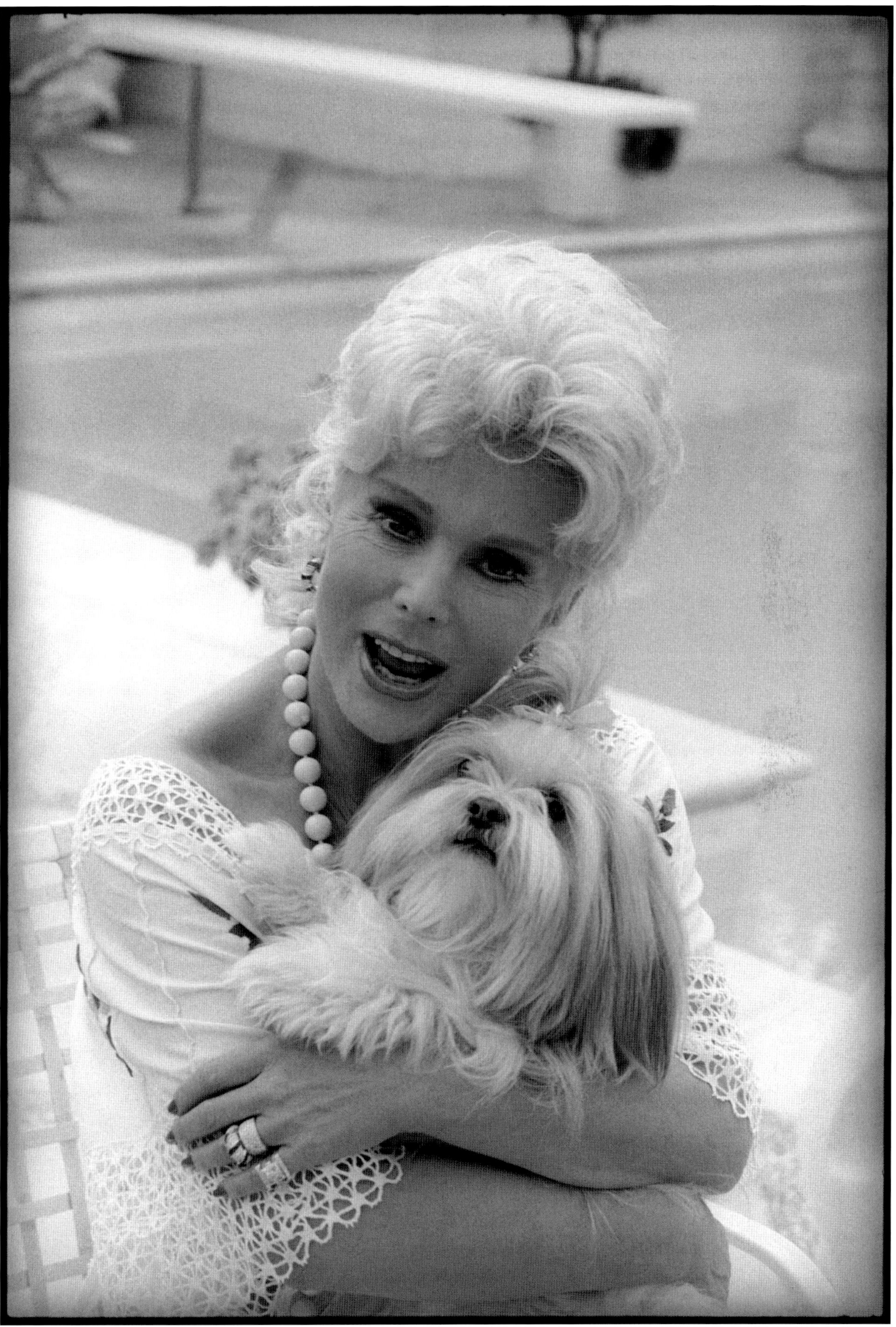

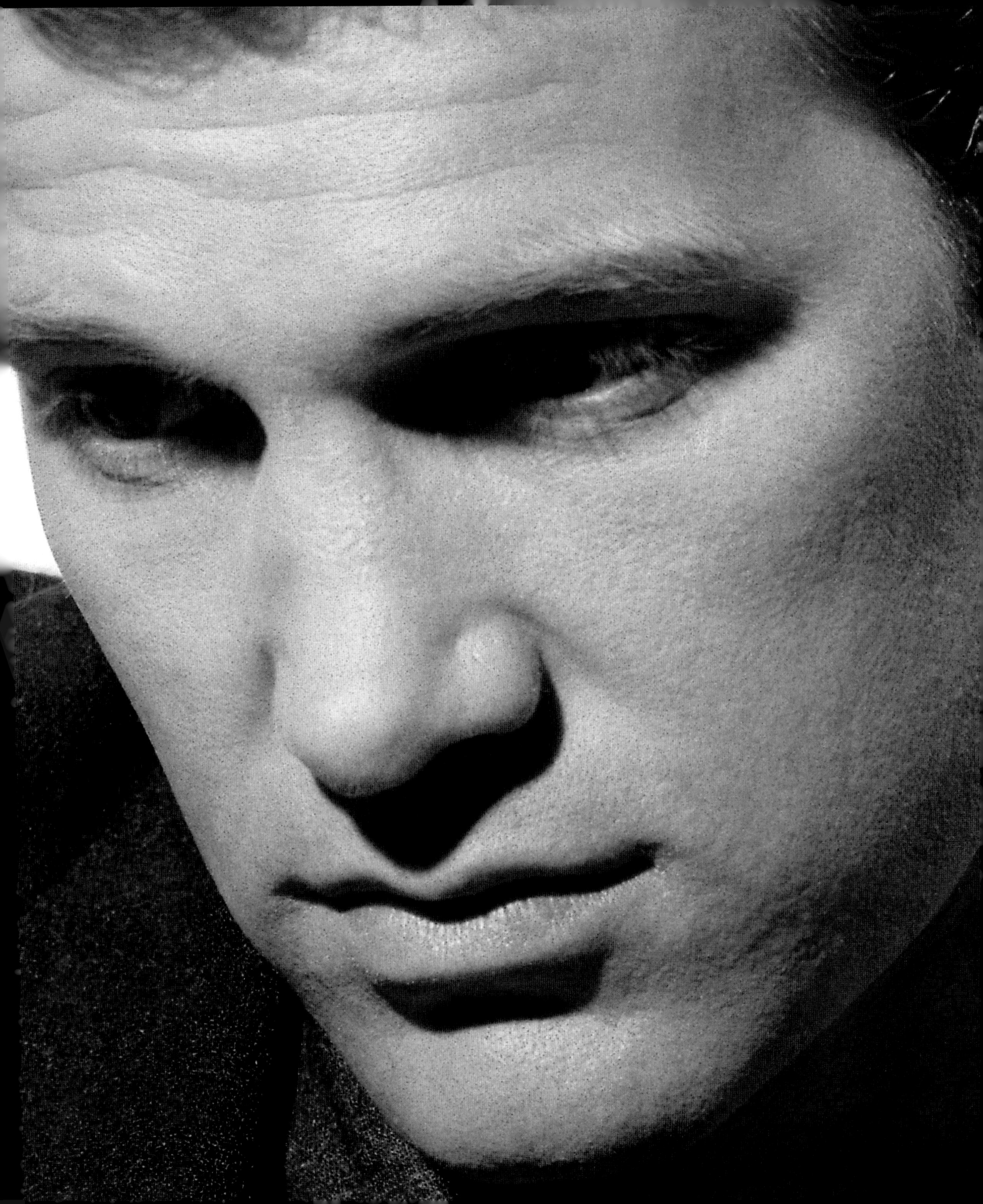

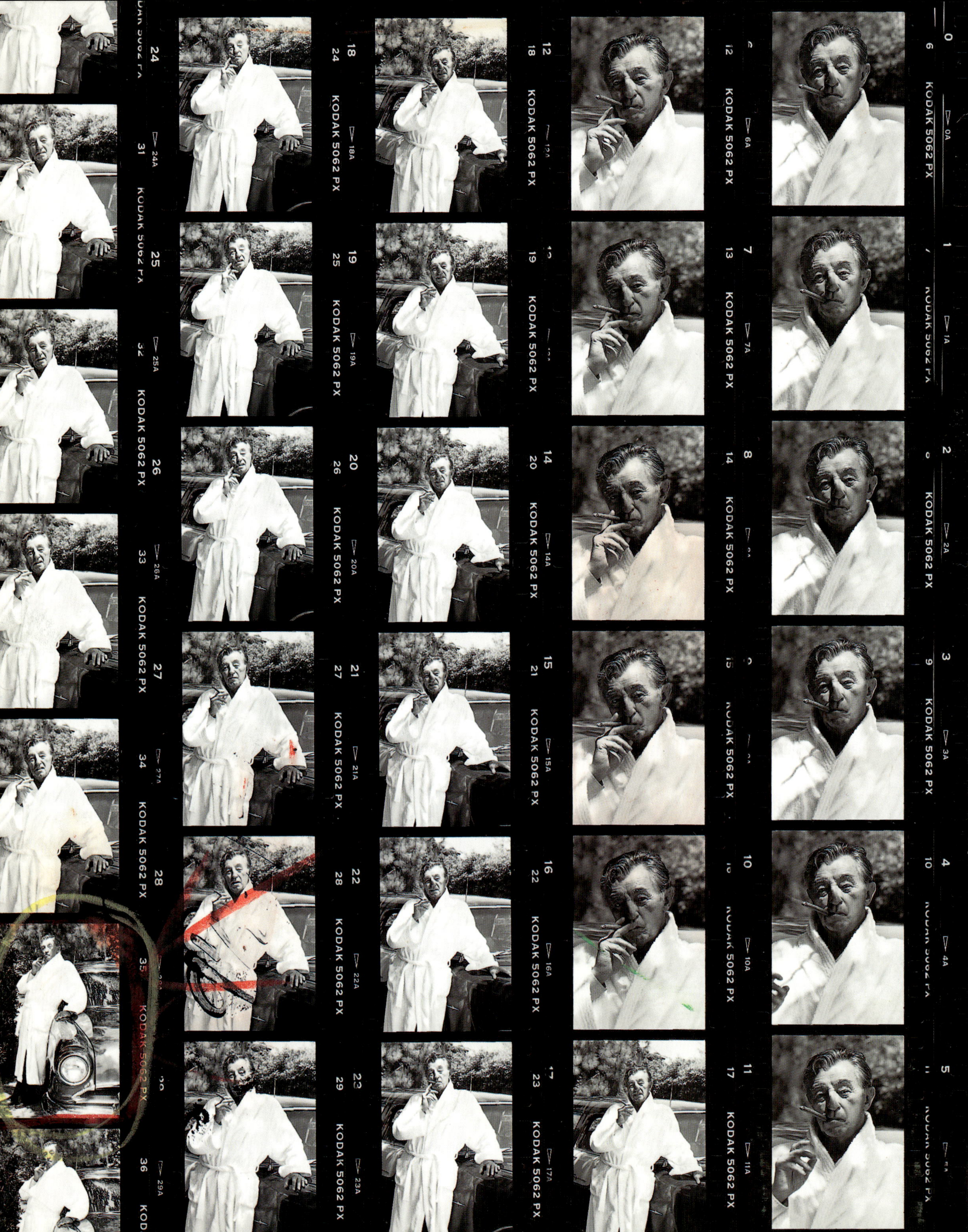

He is a true Hollywood legend and a bona fide star! I was super excited to photograph Robert Mitchum at the El Encanto Hotel in Santa Barbara. Our appointment was at midday, but by two o'clock he still had not appeared. I had one of my assistants scour around the location to look for him and he found Robert propped up at the bar with four empty martini glasses in front of him. It was a boiling hot day. I could not imagine how this eighty-year-old man was able to stagger from the bar to my four outdoor locations over the next two hours, endlessly spouting hysterical stories about the old days. The photograph I love most is this one, where I threw a toweling robe on him, stuck a cigar in his mouth and propped him up against a 1950s' "Woody" station wagon, meant to evoke the time at the peak of his huge film-star career. The sun was at a forty-five degree angle making him look craggy and fascinating. I'll never forget watching him drive off behind the wheel of his own car, totally inebriated, while I thought to myself, "if he makes it home alive, it'll be a miracle!" He did, but this was one of his last photo shoots ever.

He is a true Hollywood legend and a bona fide star! I was super excited to photograph Robert Mitchum at the El Encanto Hotel in Santa Barbara. Our appointment was at midday, but by two o'clock he still had not appeared. I had one of my assistants scour around the location to look for him and he found Robert propped up at the bar with four empty martini glasses in front of him. It was a boiling hot day. I could not imagine how this eighty-year-old man was able to stagger from the bar to my four outdoor locations over the next two hours, endlessly spouting hysterical stories about the old days. The photograph I love most is this one, where I threw a toweling robe on him, stuck a cigar in his mouth and propped him up against a 1950s "Woody" station wagon, meant to evoke the time at the peak of his huge film-star career. The sun was at a forty-five degree angle making him look craggy and fascinating. I'll never forget watching him drive off behind the wheel of his own car, totally inebriated, while I thought to myself, "if he makes it home alive, it'll be a miracle! He did, but this was one of his last photo shoots ever."

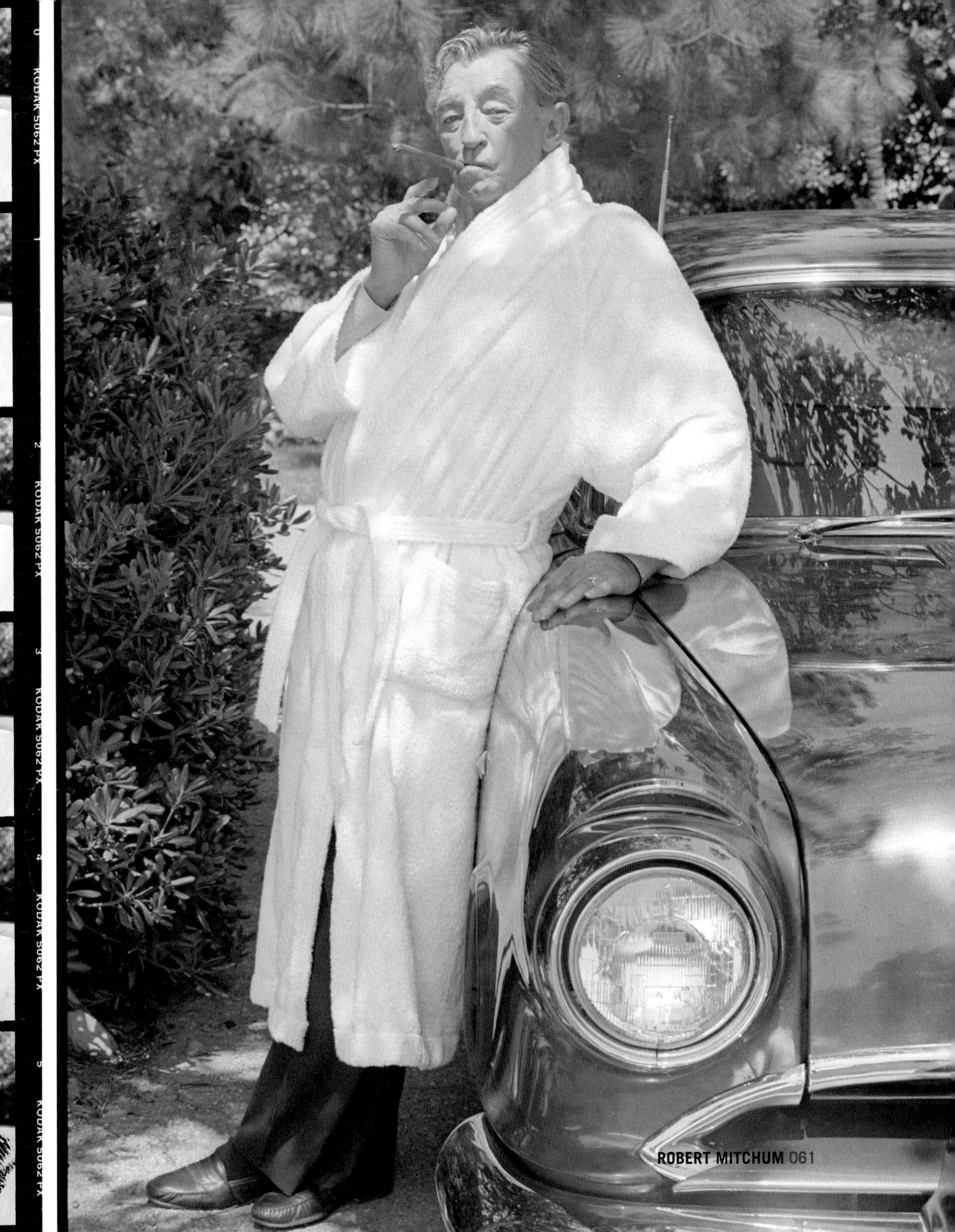
ROBERT MITCHUM 061

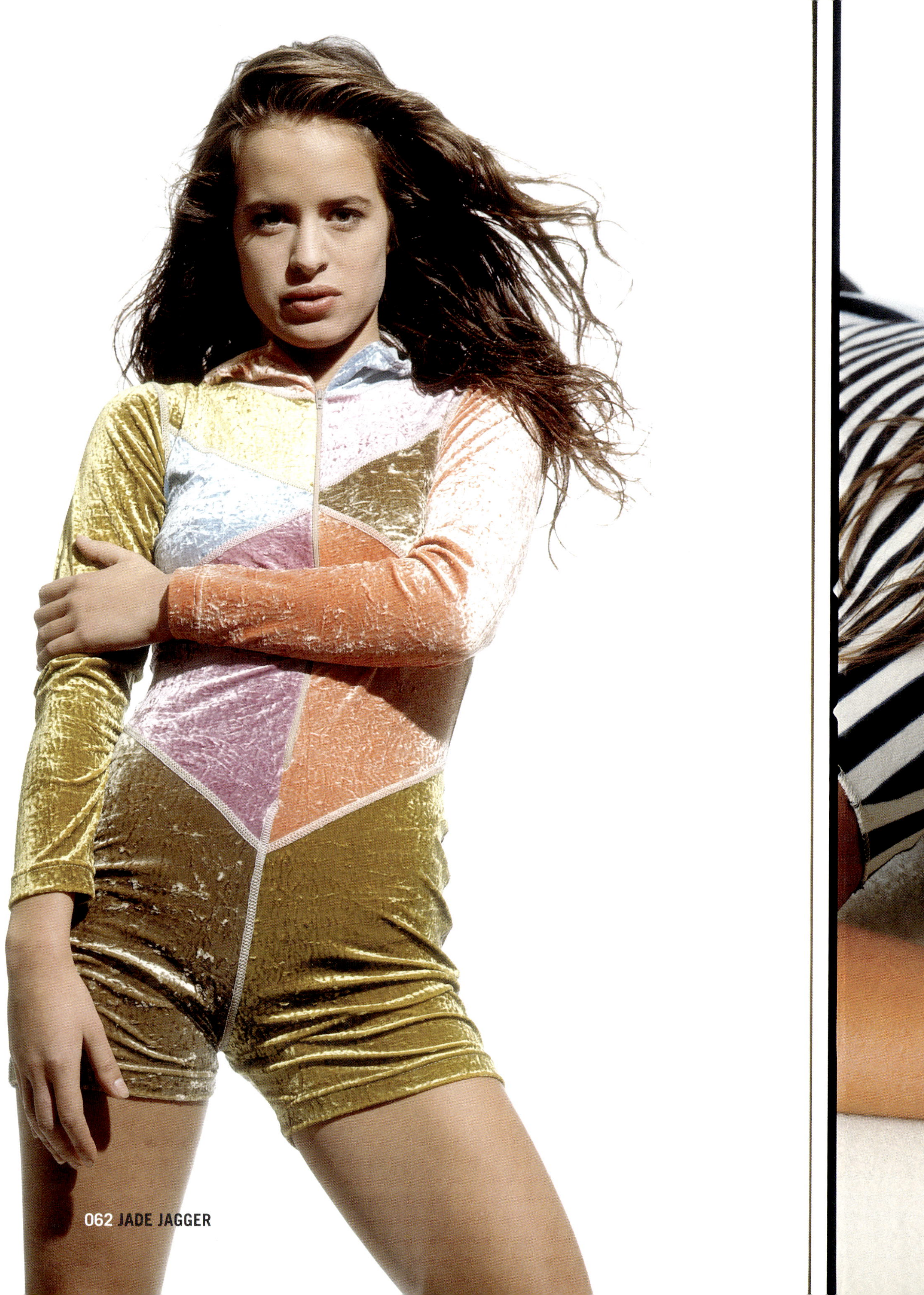
062 JADE JAGGER

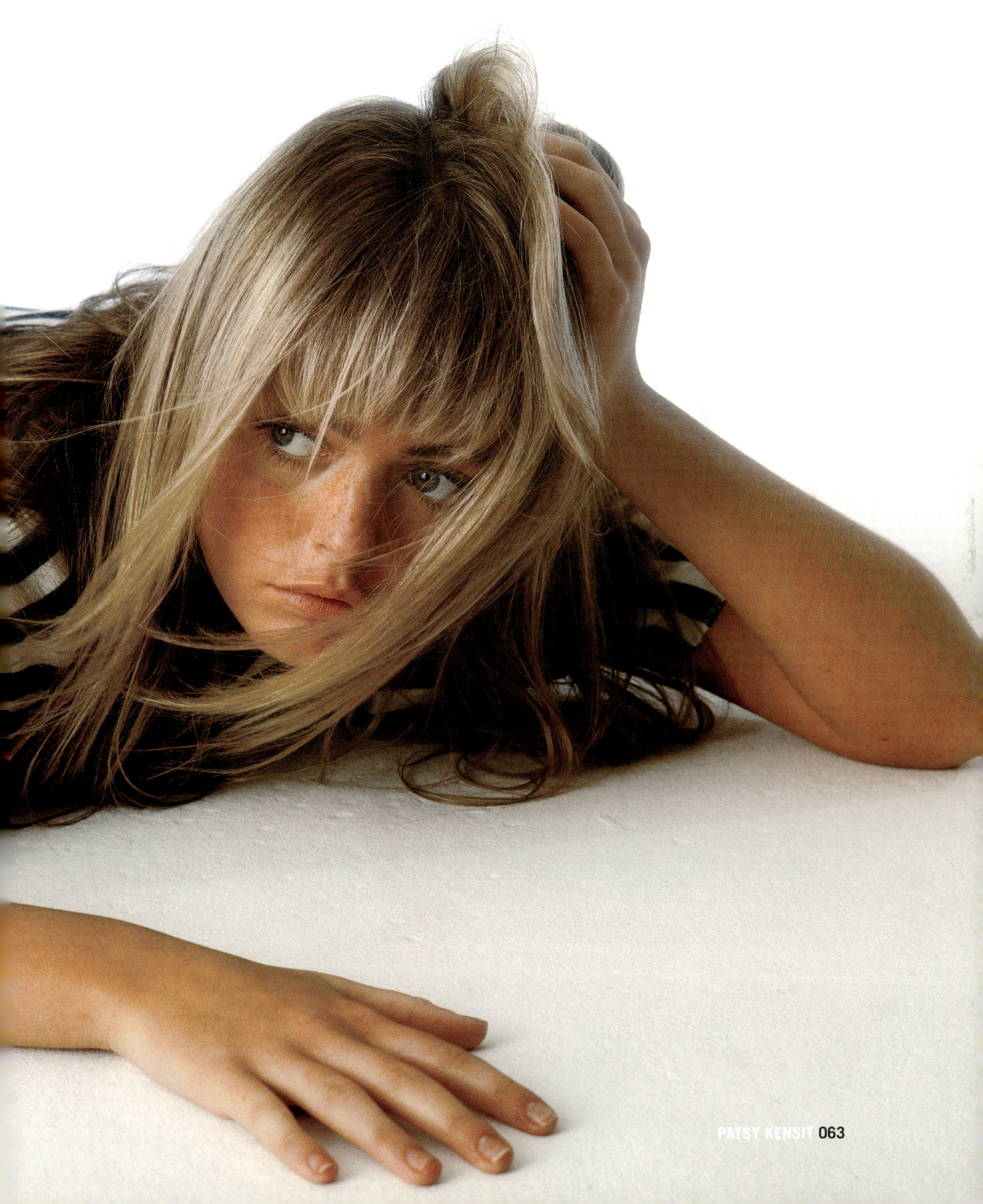

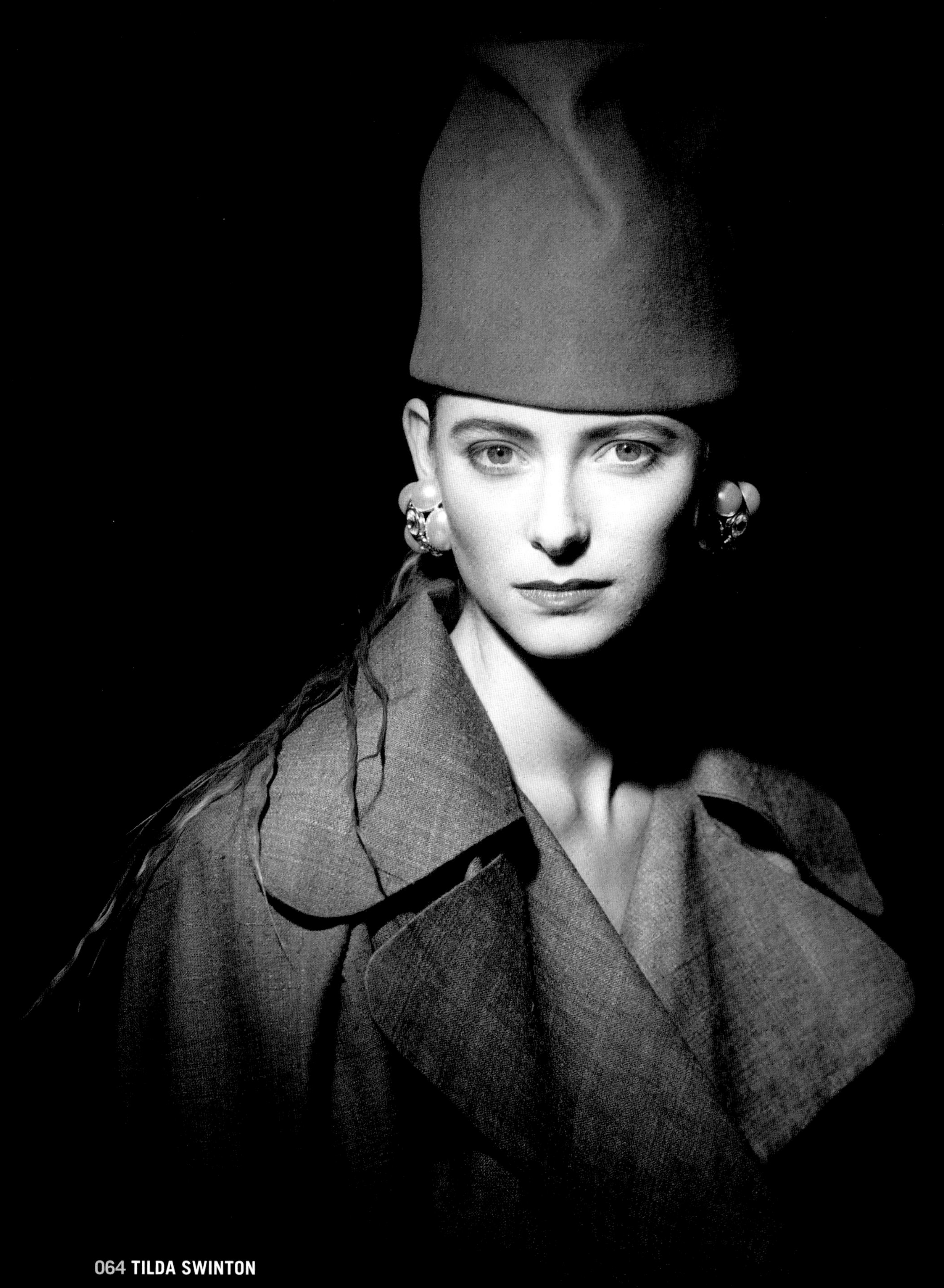

064 TILDA SWINTON

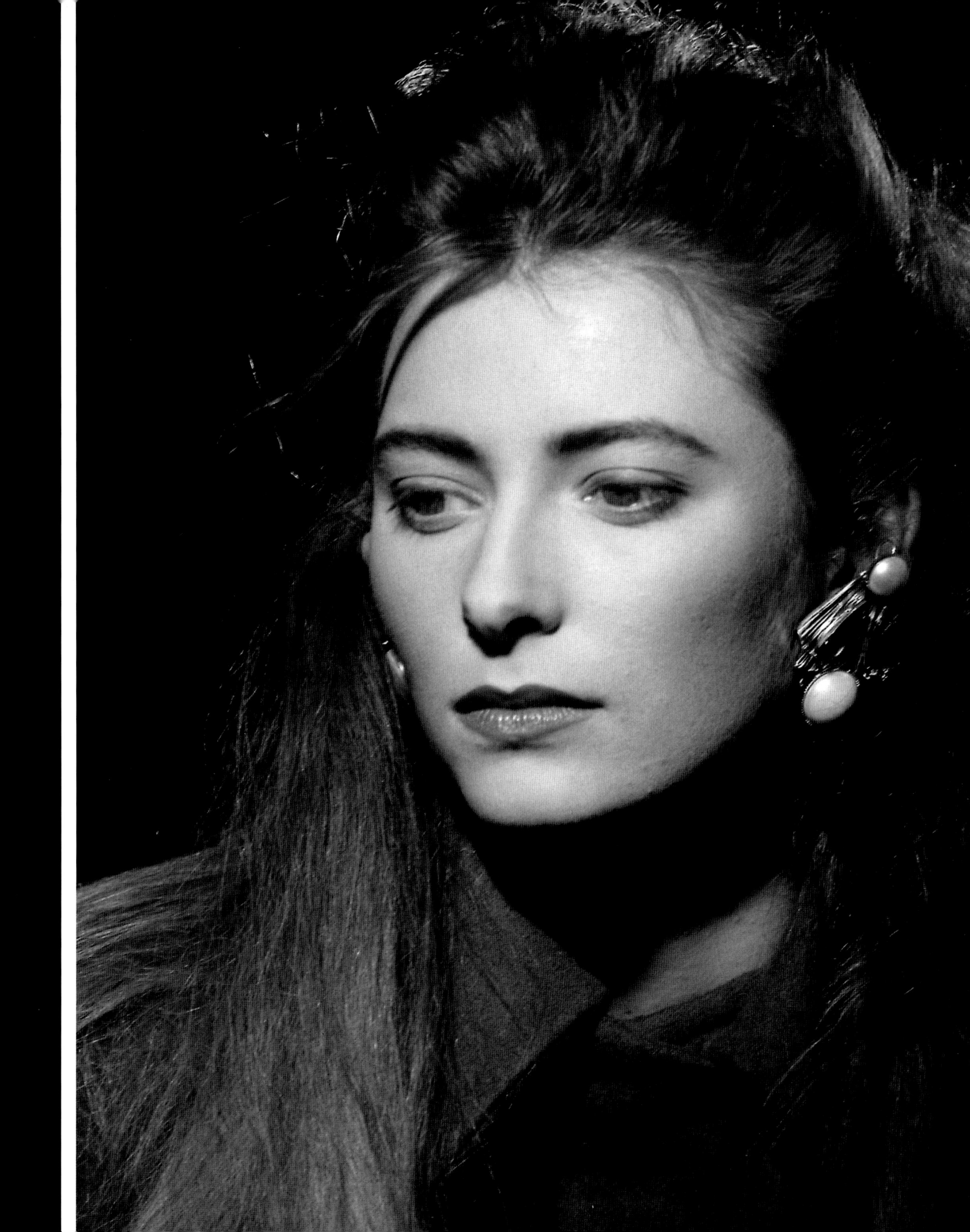

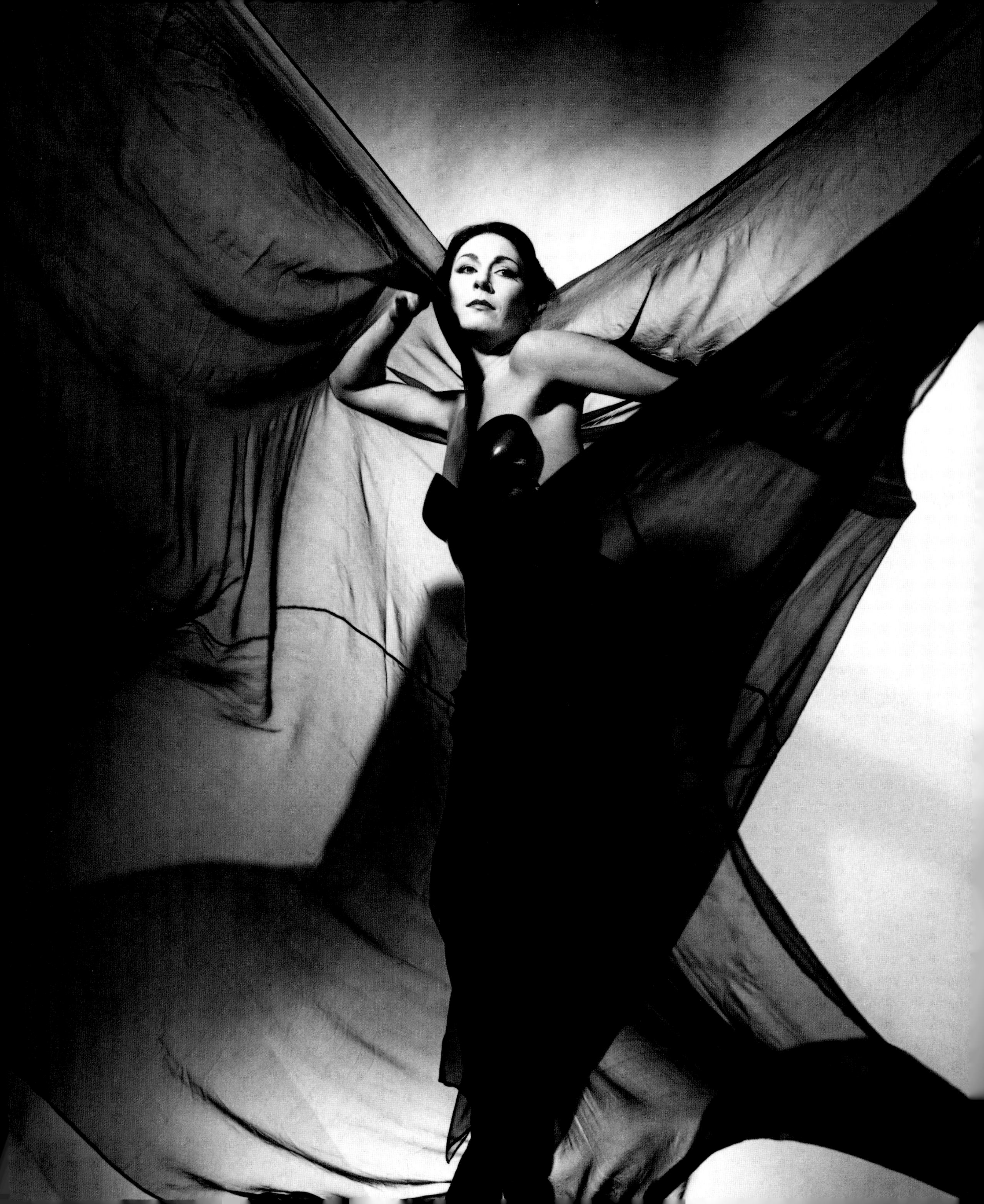

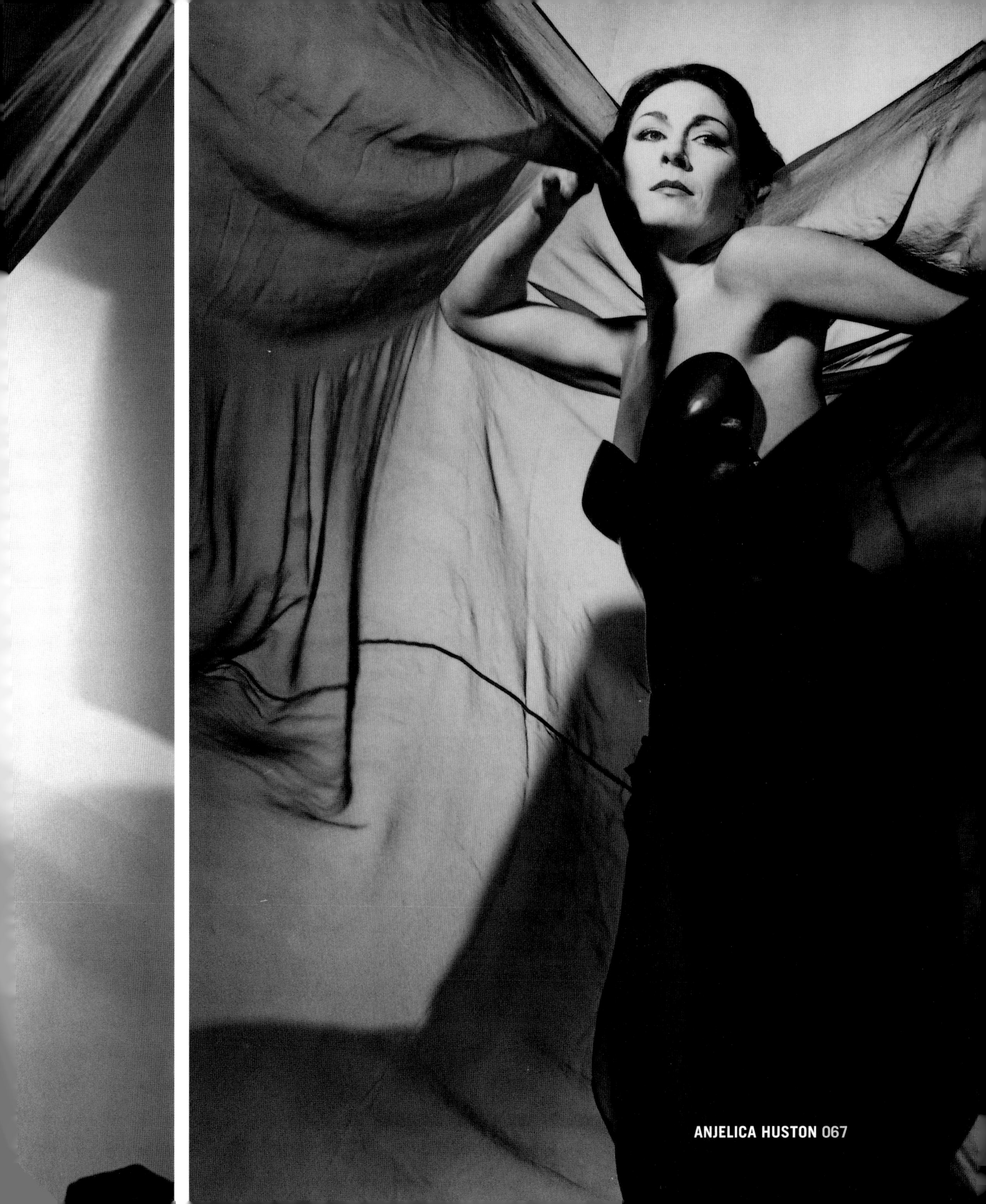
ANJELICA HUSTON 067

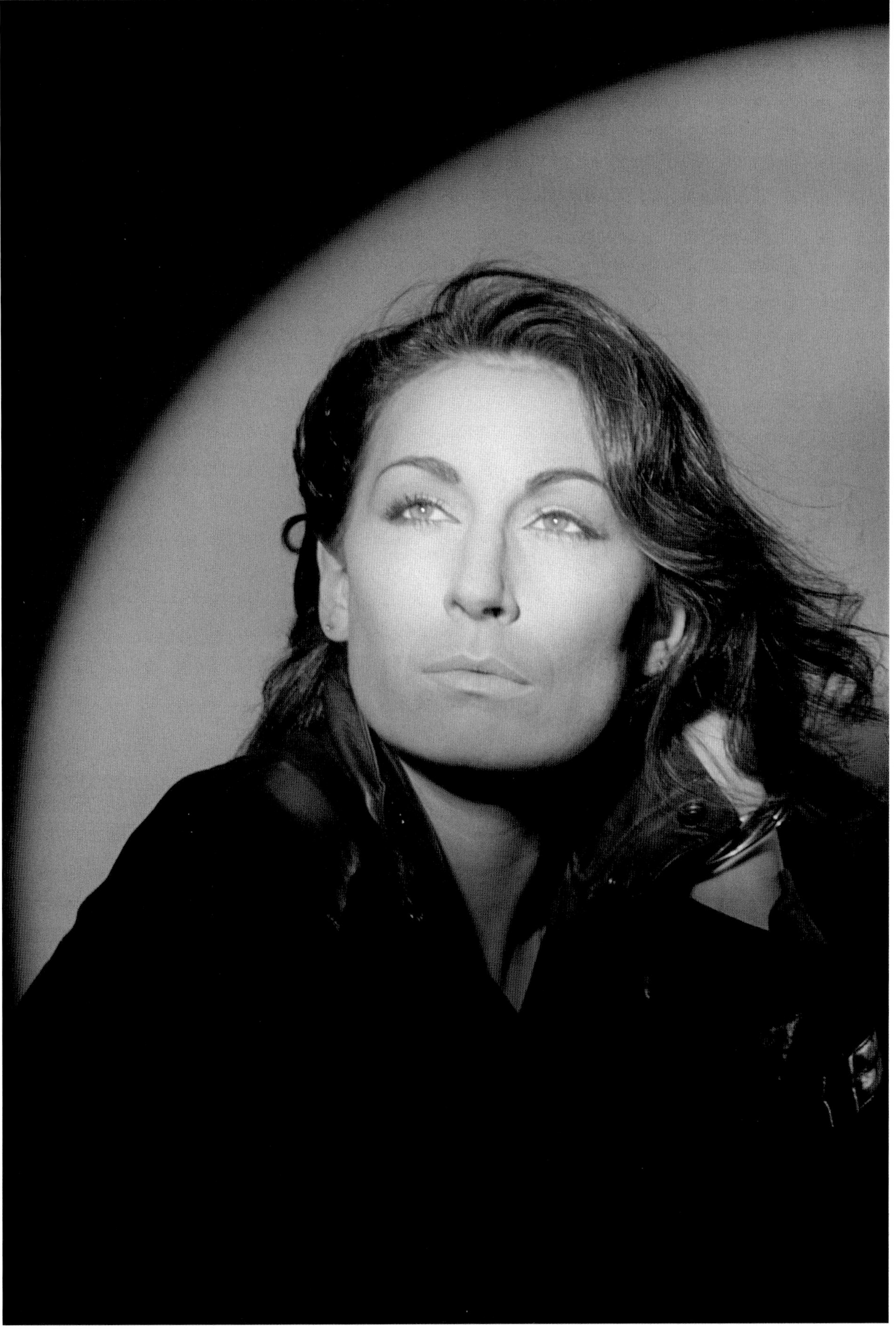

I sought her out. I had seen her in *Jungle Fever* and on television in *Queen* and thought she would be fun to photograph. She arrived at my Melrose Avenue studio alone and we started off lightly. Then we added more eye make up and a red lip, and walked round the corner where she posed against the fence. Towards the end of our session, Halle (who is now known best for playing Dorothy Dandridge and for being an Oscar winner) spun around and whooshed up her ballet skirt. What a blast! What fun!

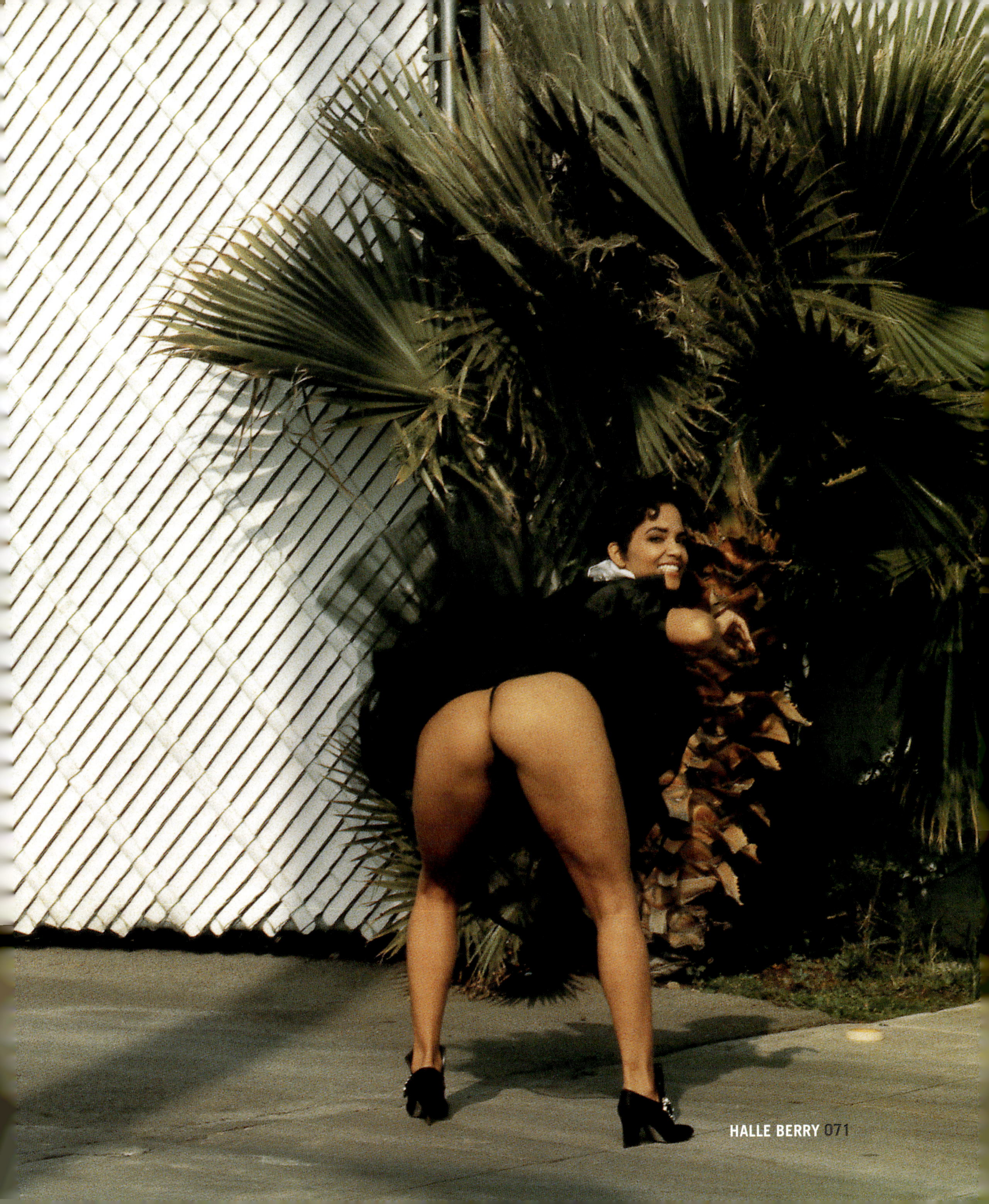
HALLE BERRY 071

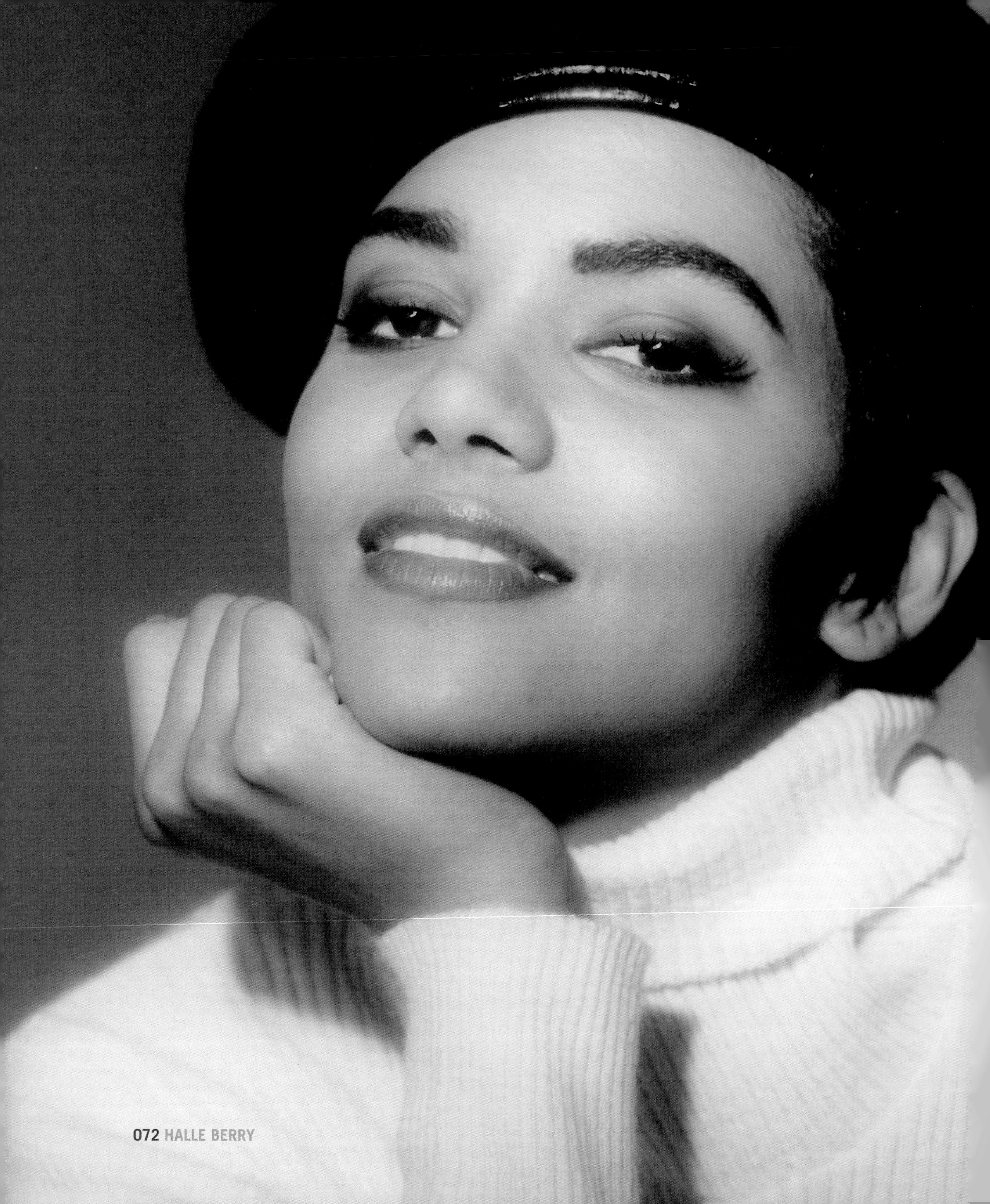

072 HALLE BERRY

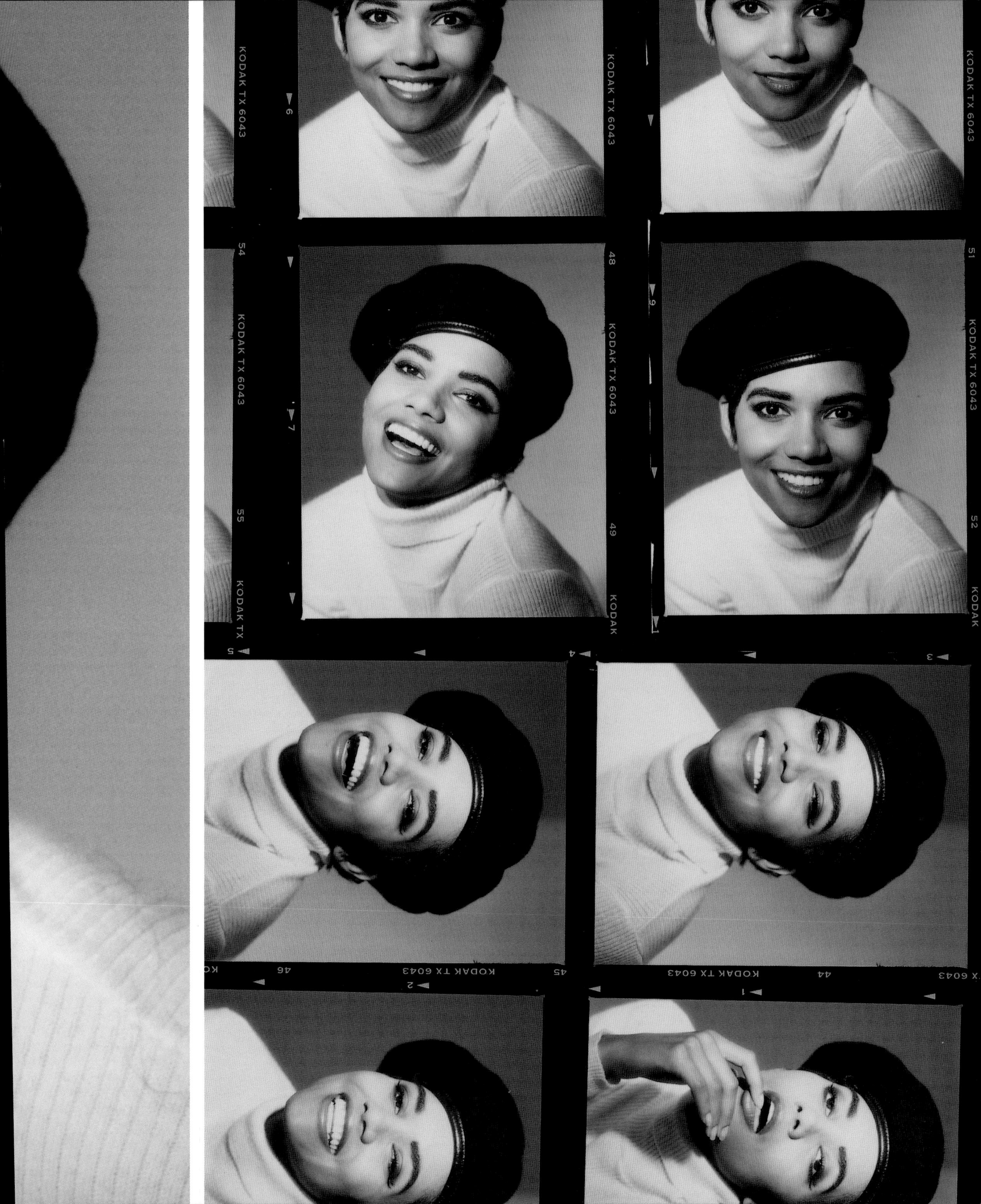

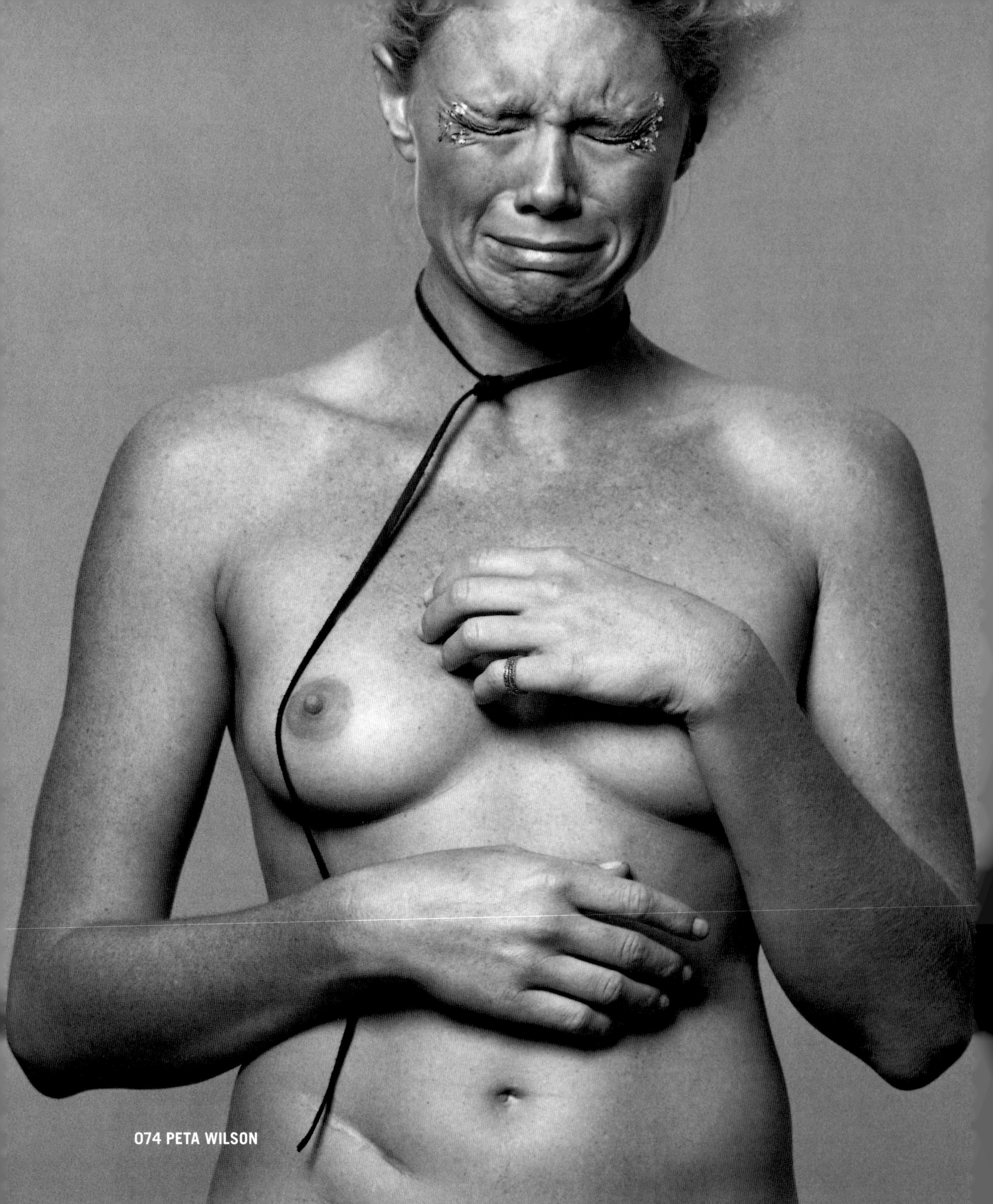

074 PETA WILSON

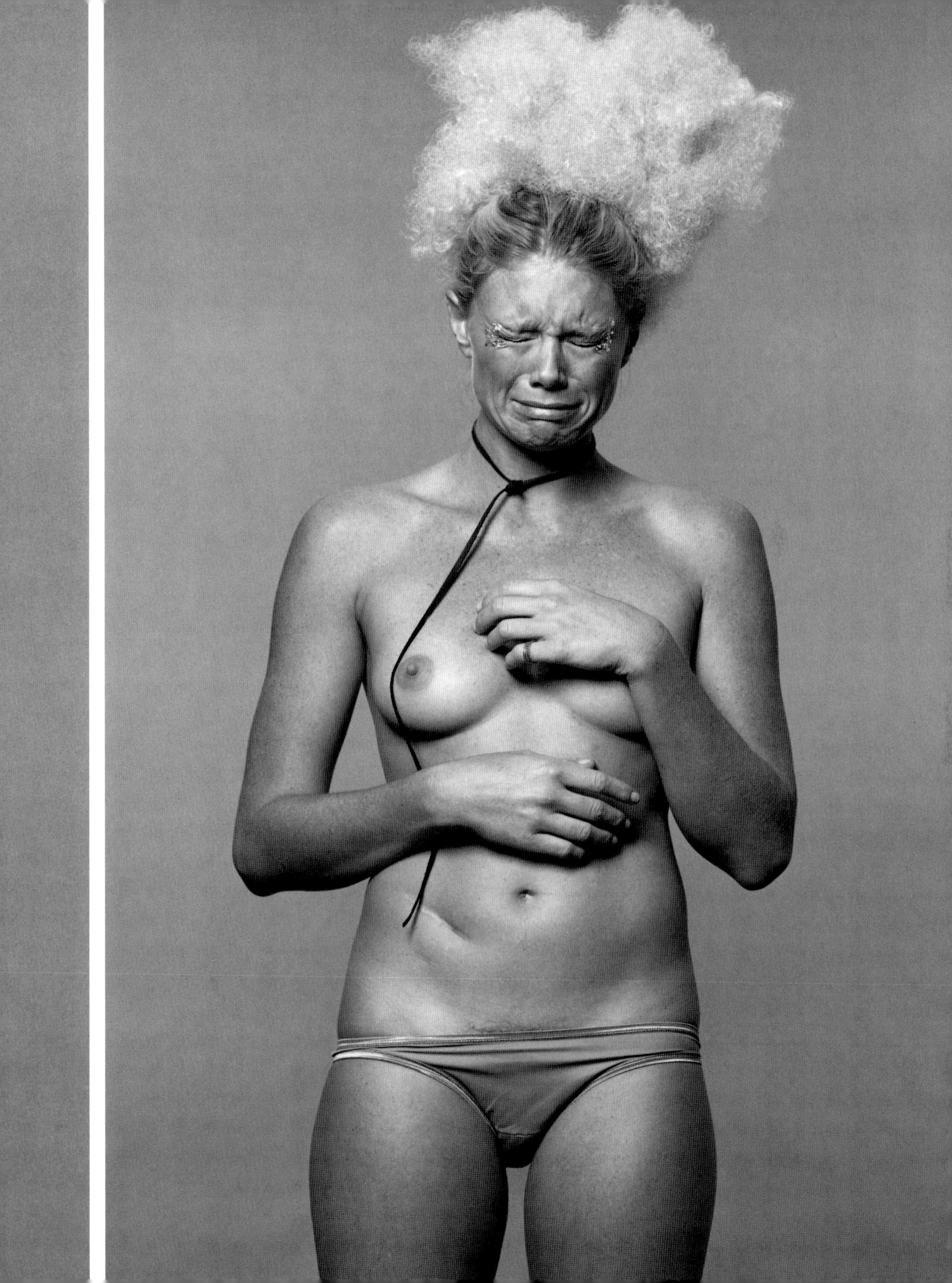

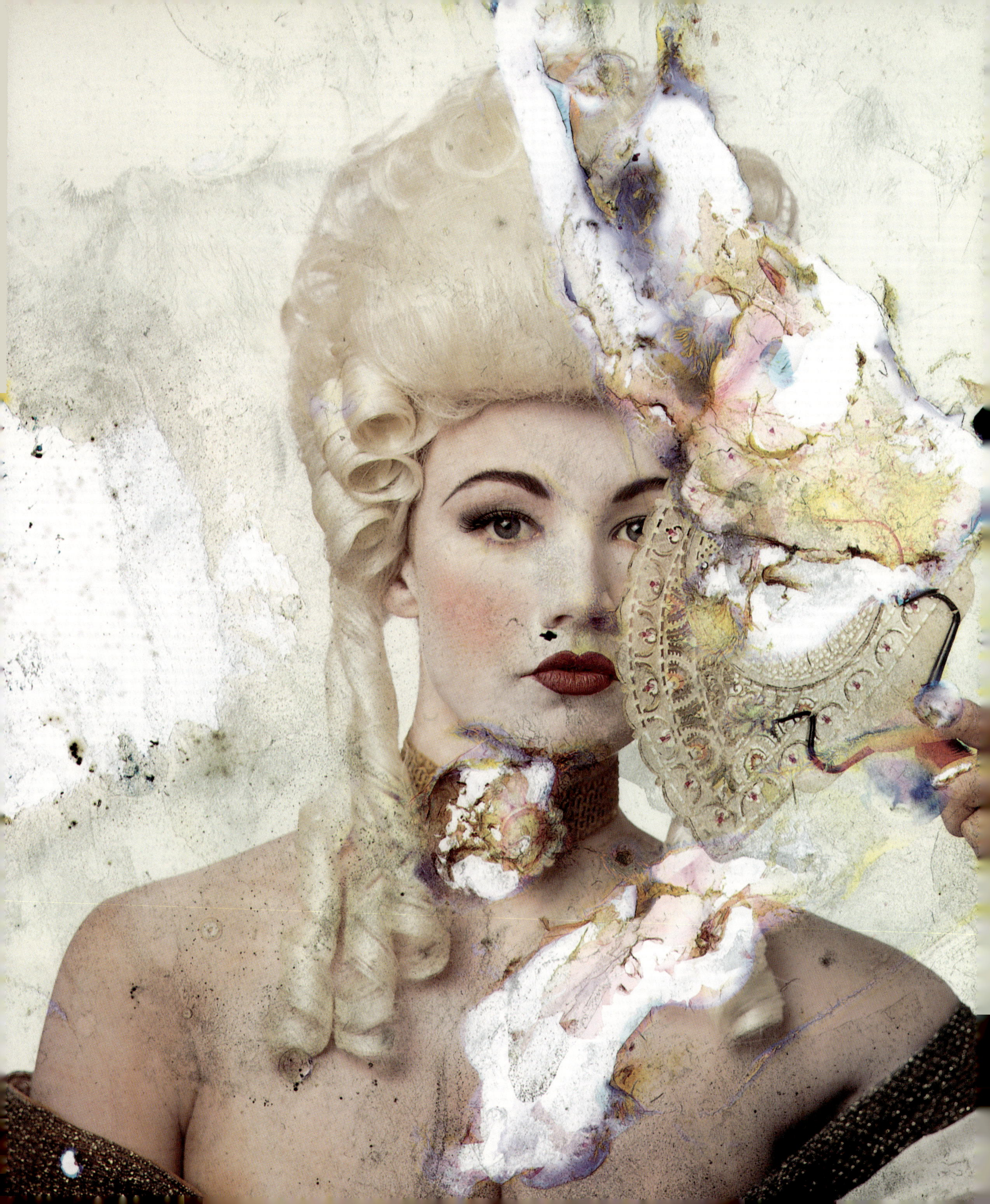

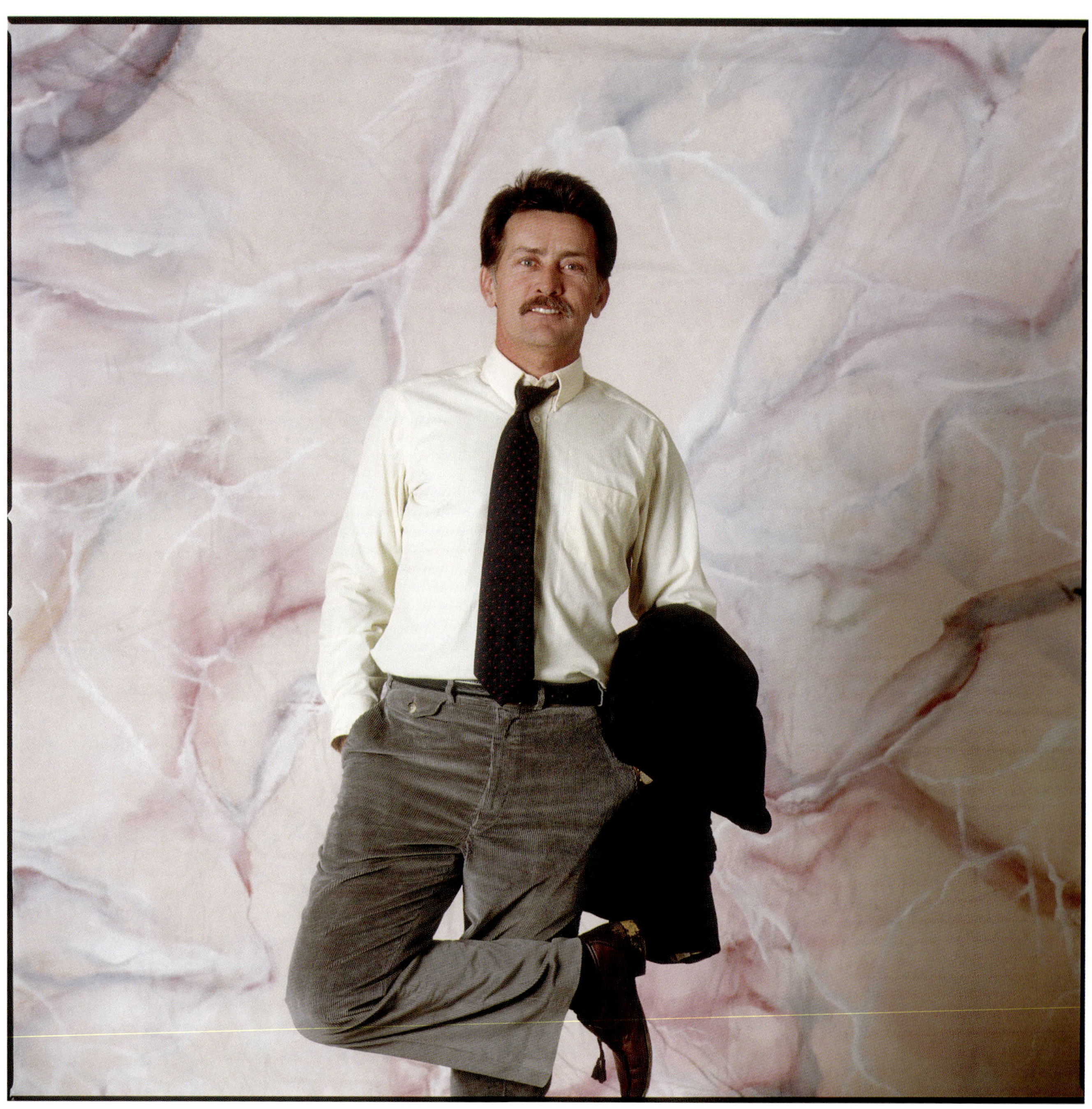

078 MARTIN SHEEN

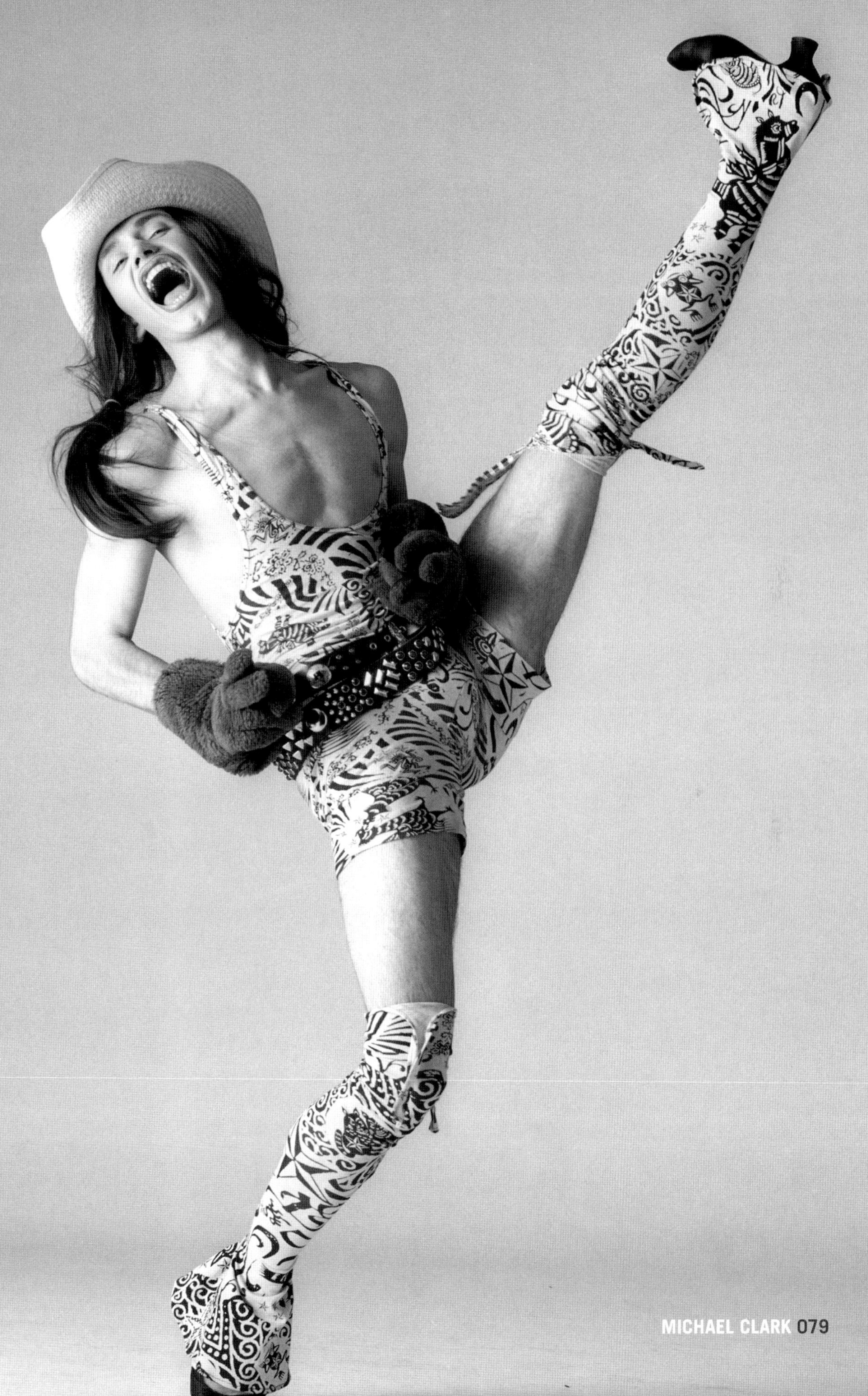

MICHAEL CLARK 079

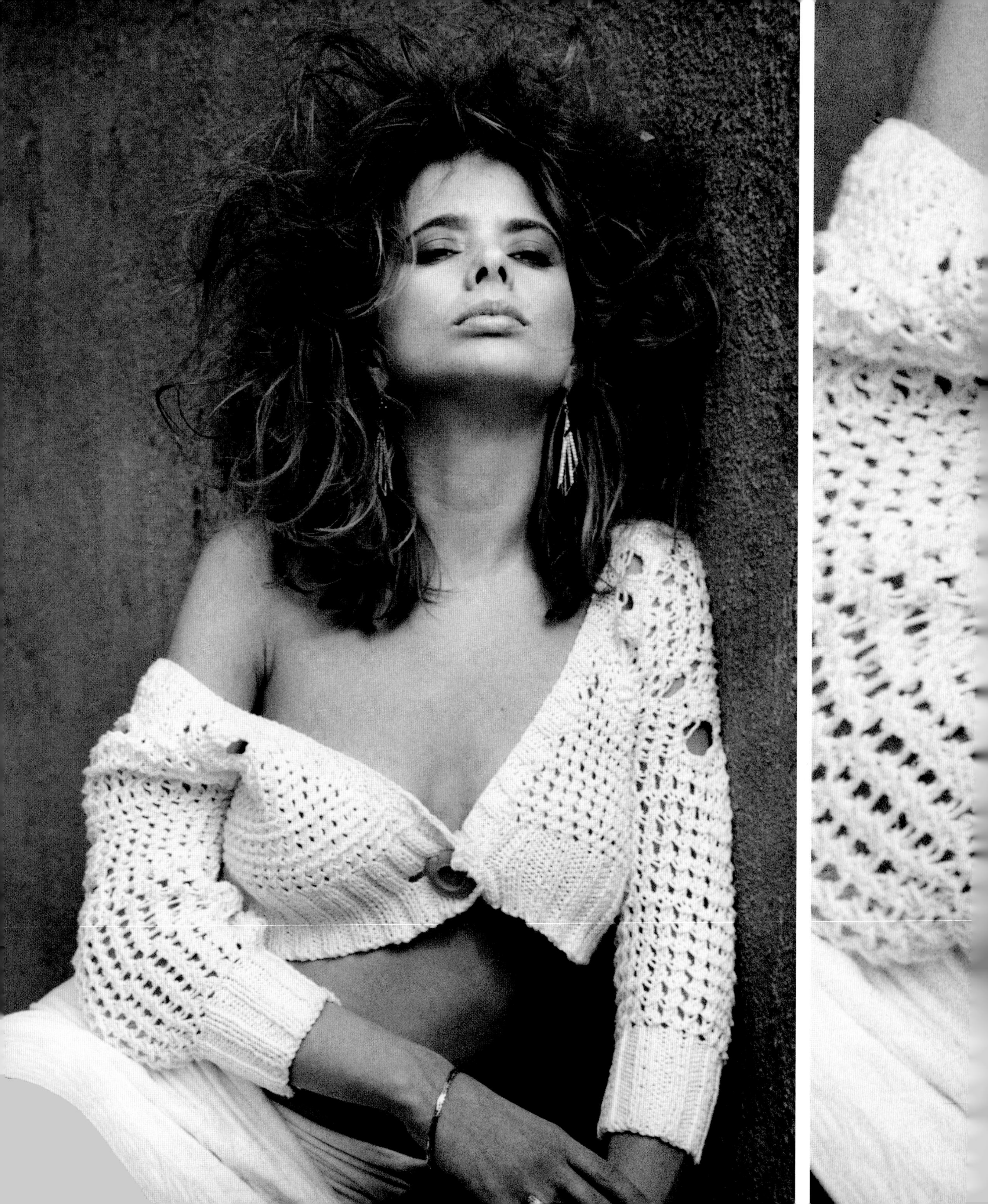

Will she ever speak
to me again after
backcombing her
hair and spraying it
and re-backcombing
it? The "Body Map"
clothes were teeny
tiny and I thought
she needed some
more volume up top.

Will she ever speak
to me again after
backcombing her
hair and spraying it
and re-backcombing
it? The "Body Map"
clothes were teeny
tiny and I thought
she needed some
more volume up top.

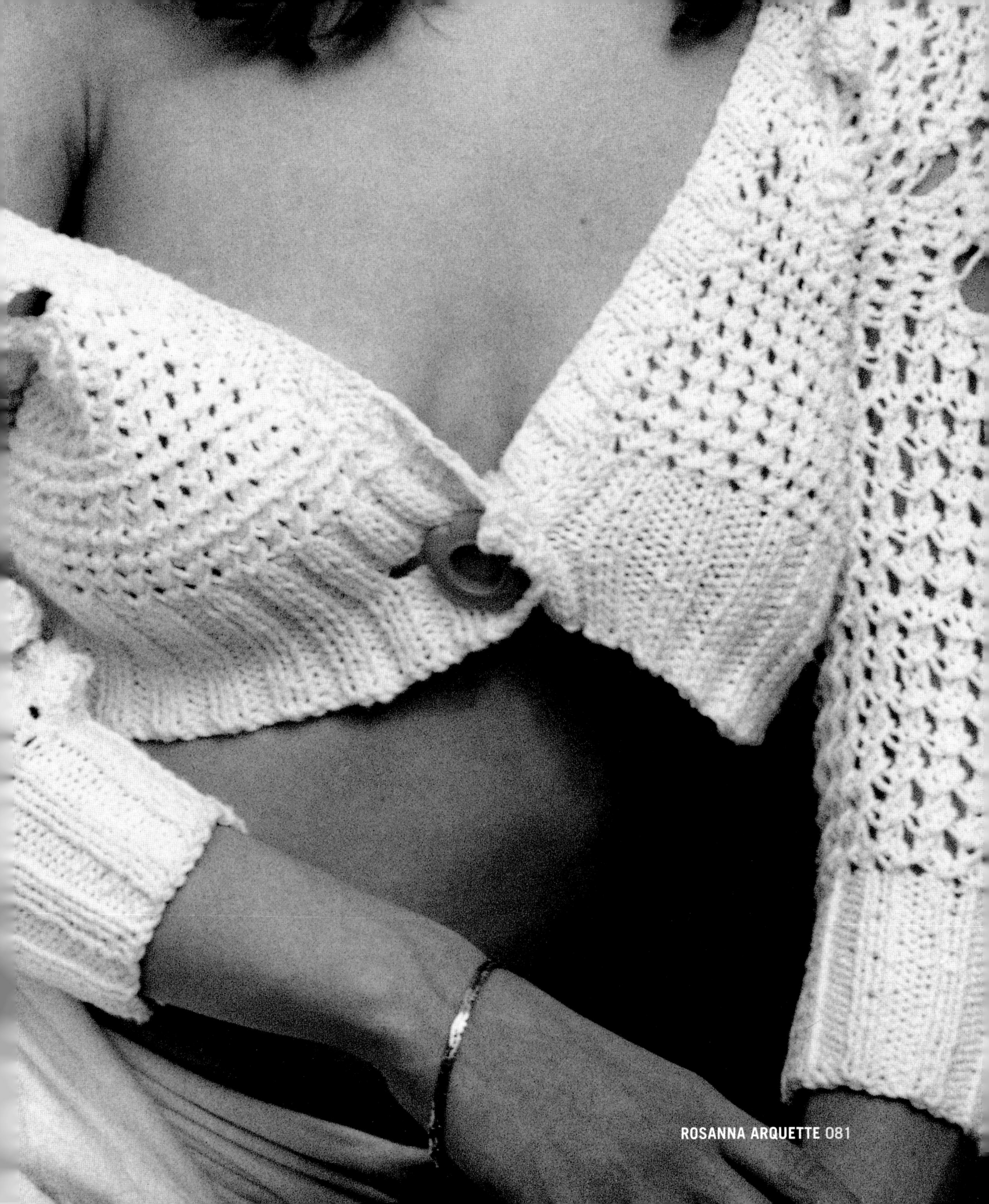
ROSANNA ARQUETTE 081

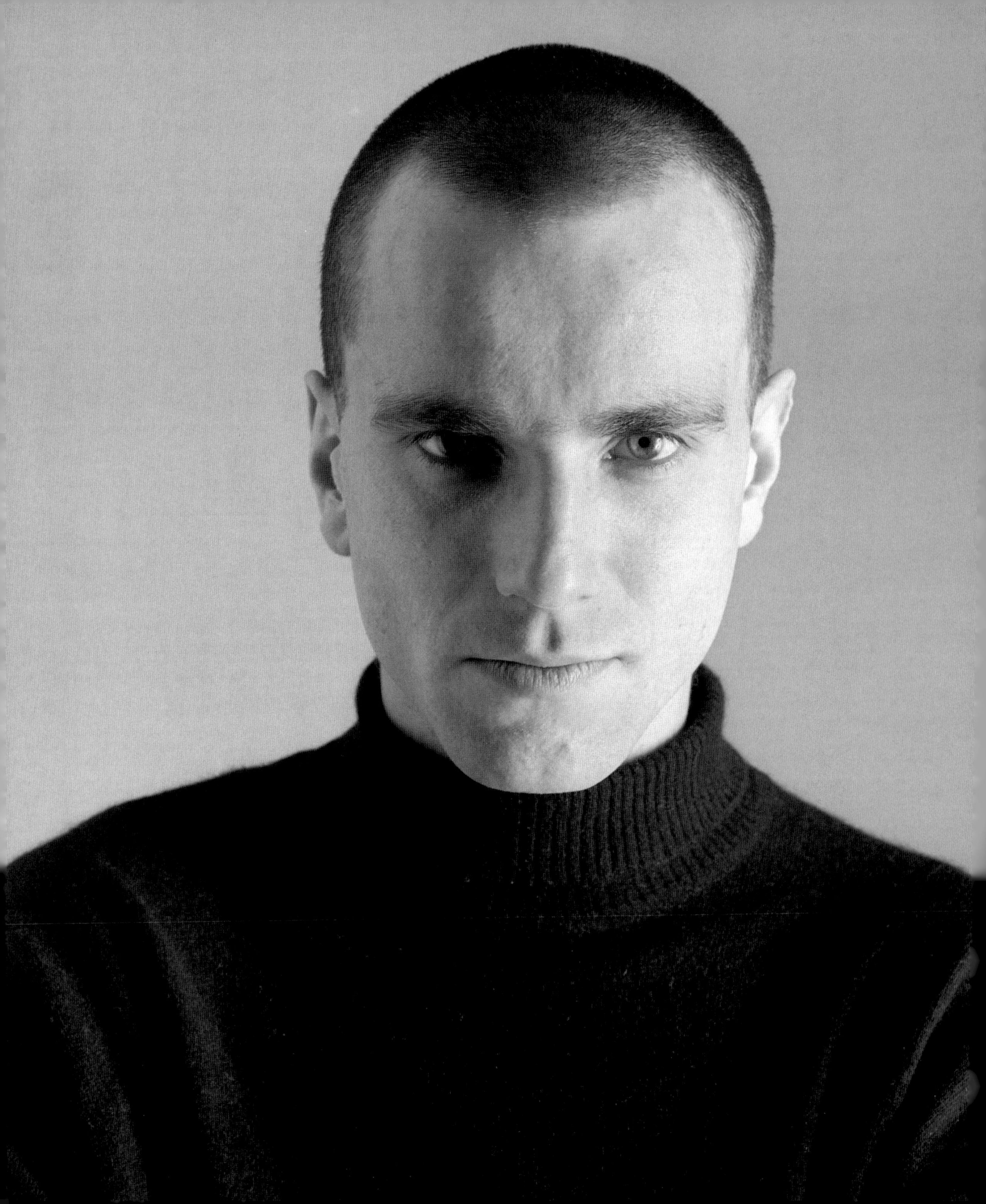

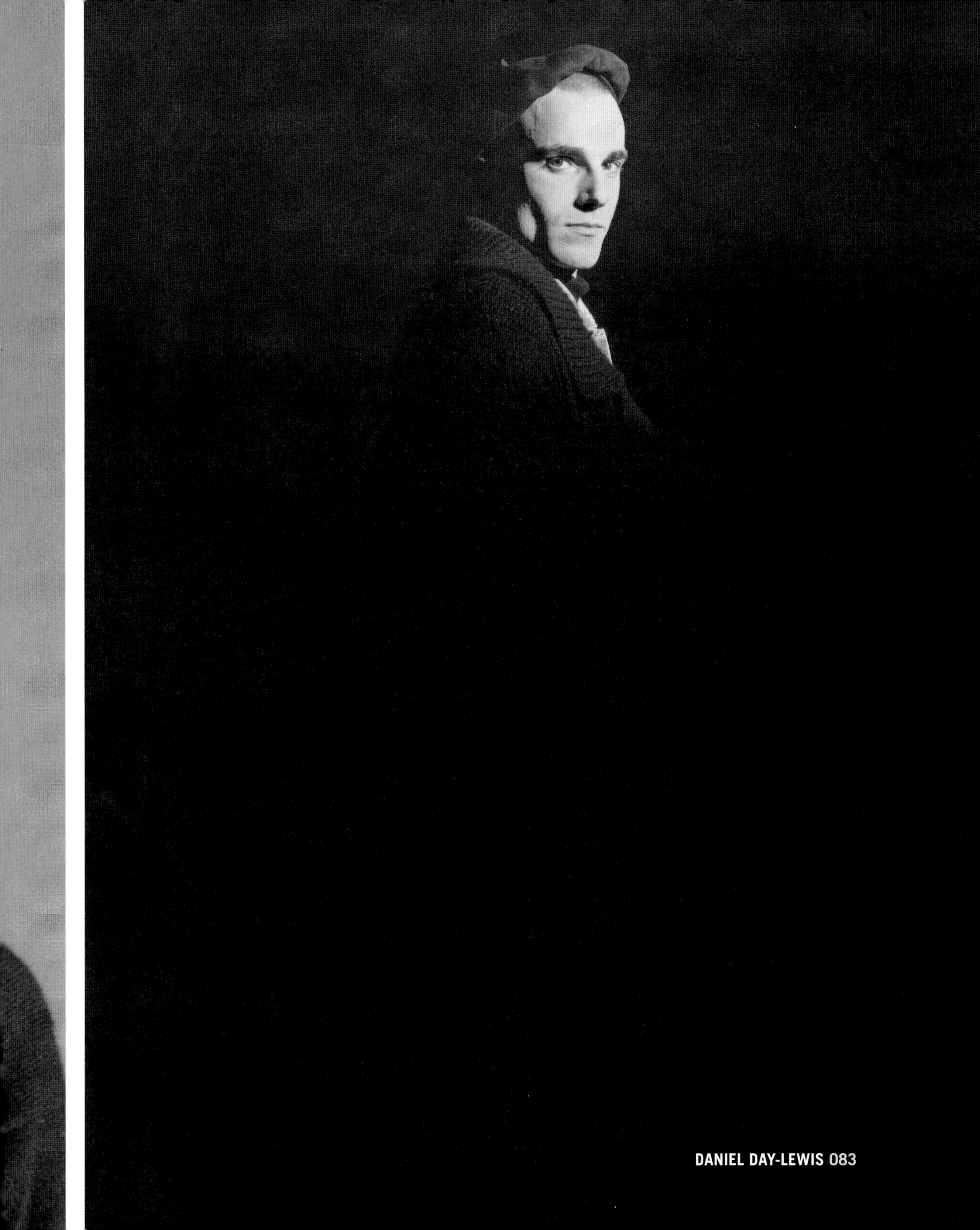
DANIEL DAY-LEWIS 083

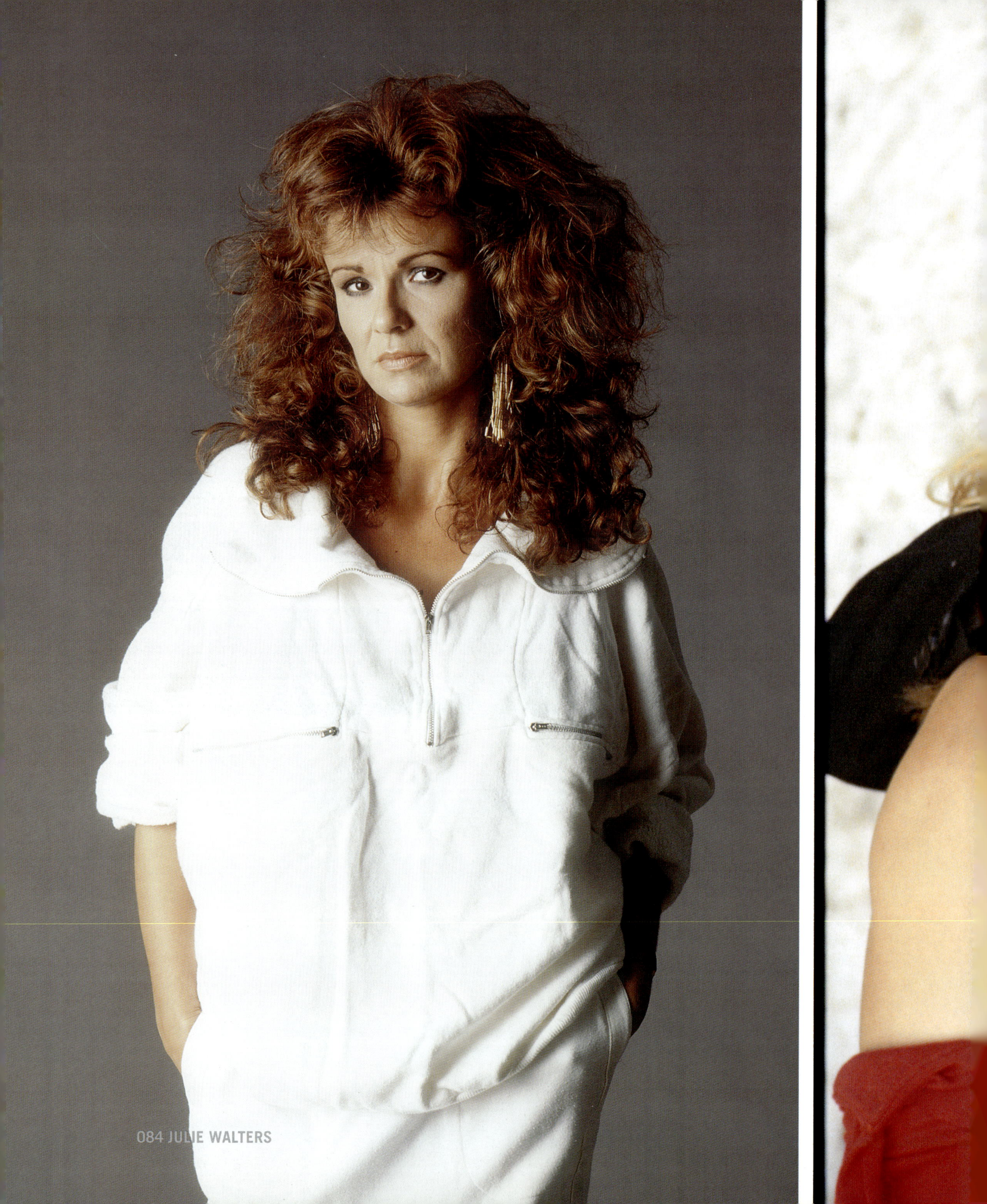

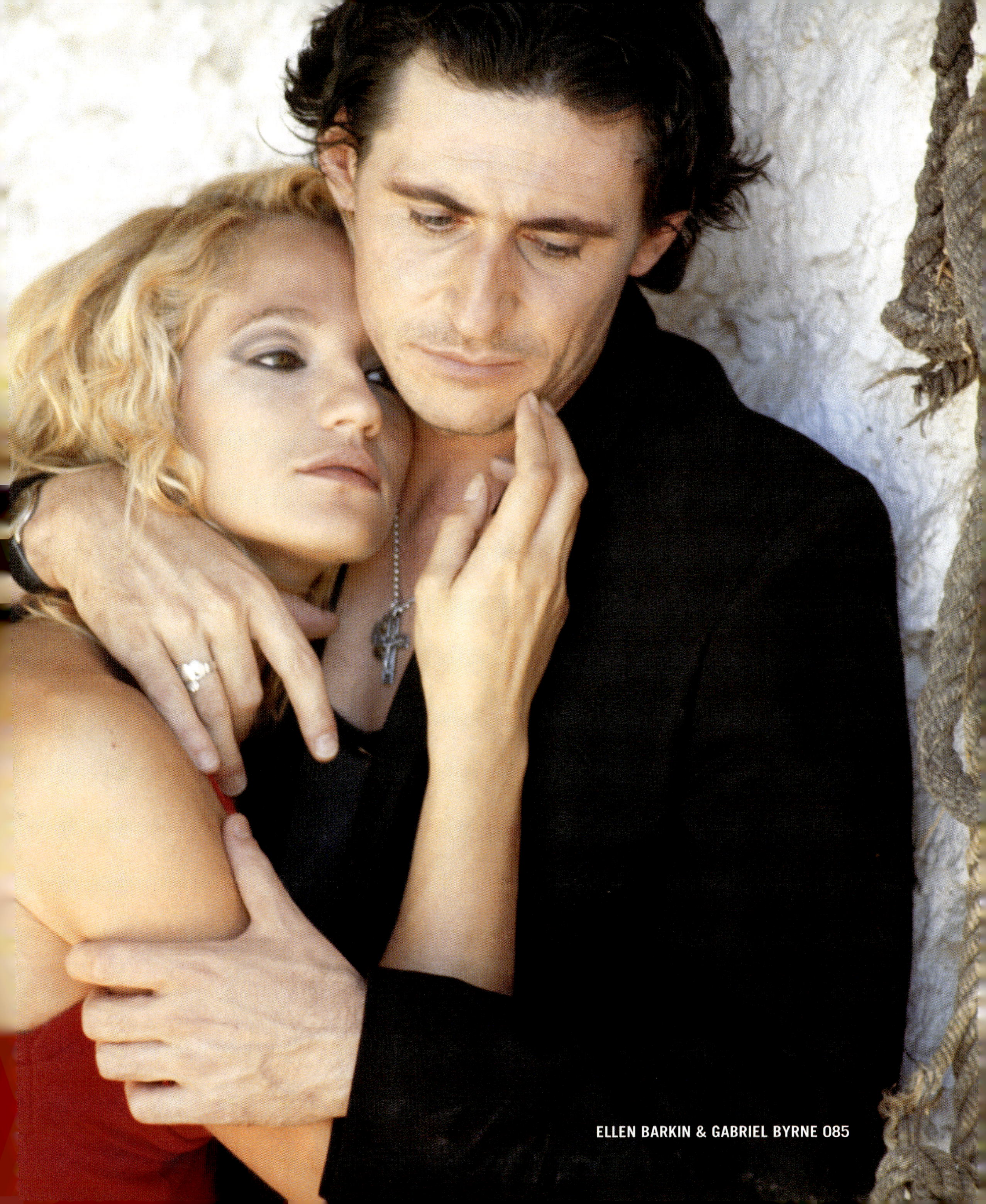

ELLEN BARKIN & GABRIEL BYRNE 085

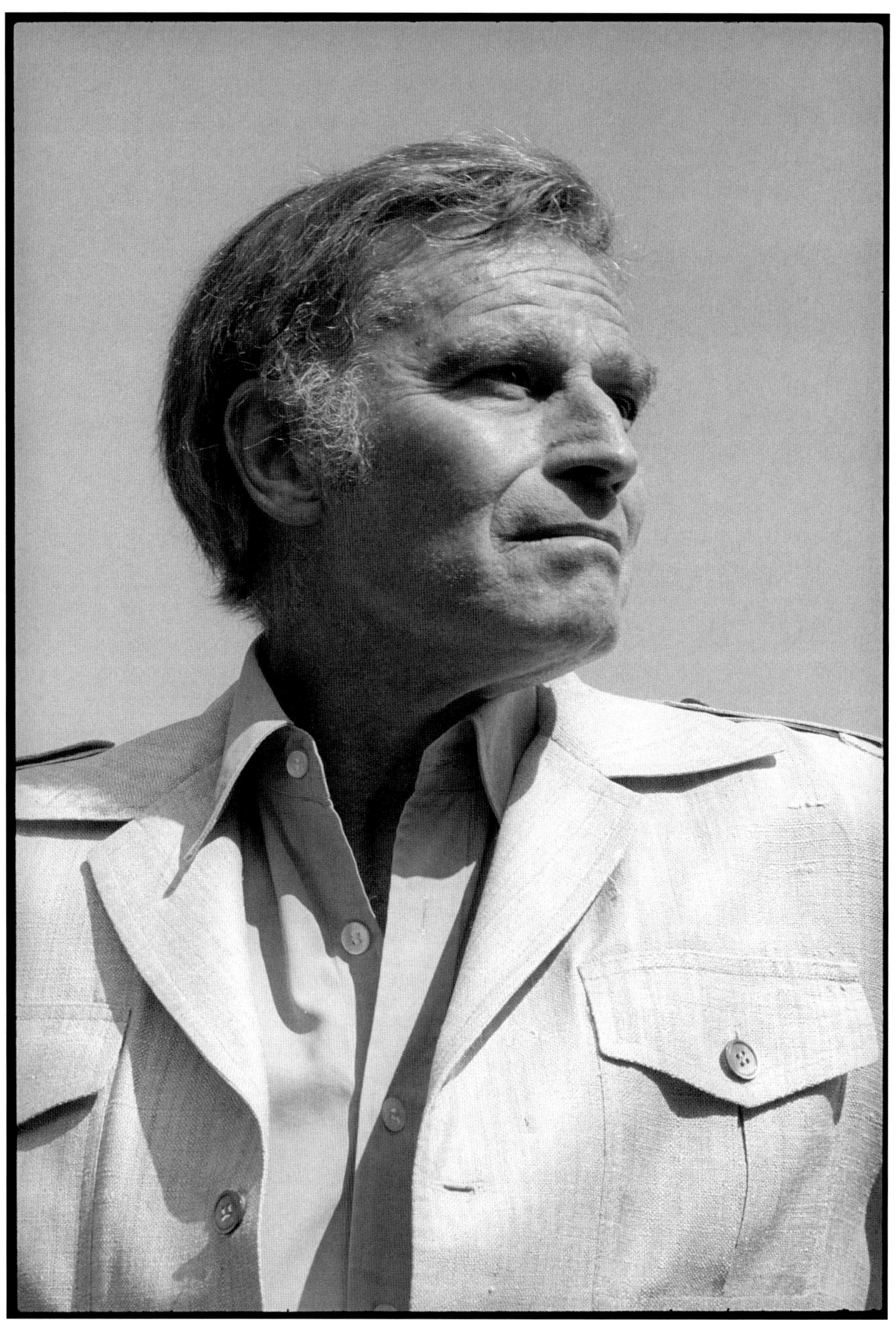

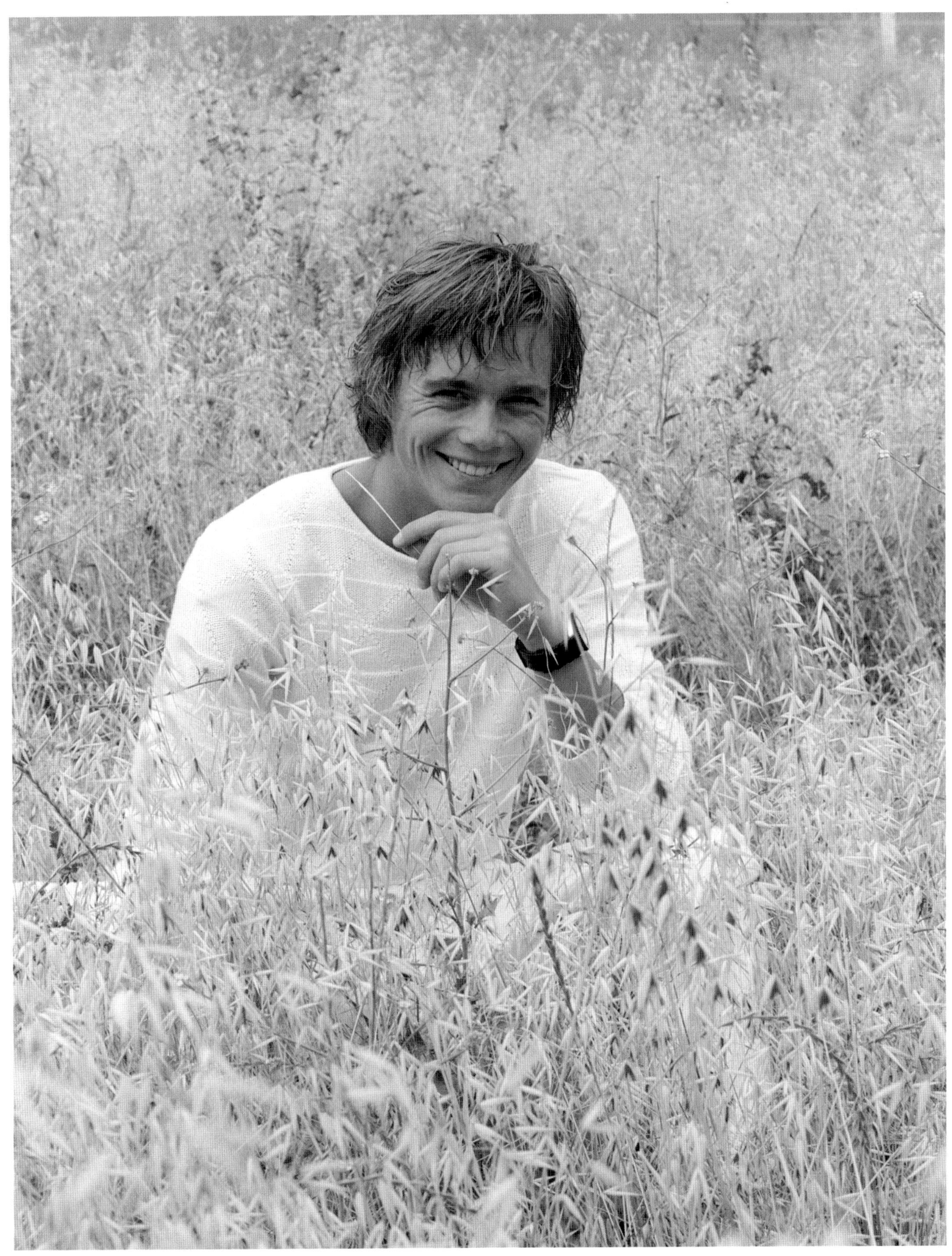

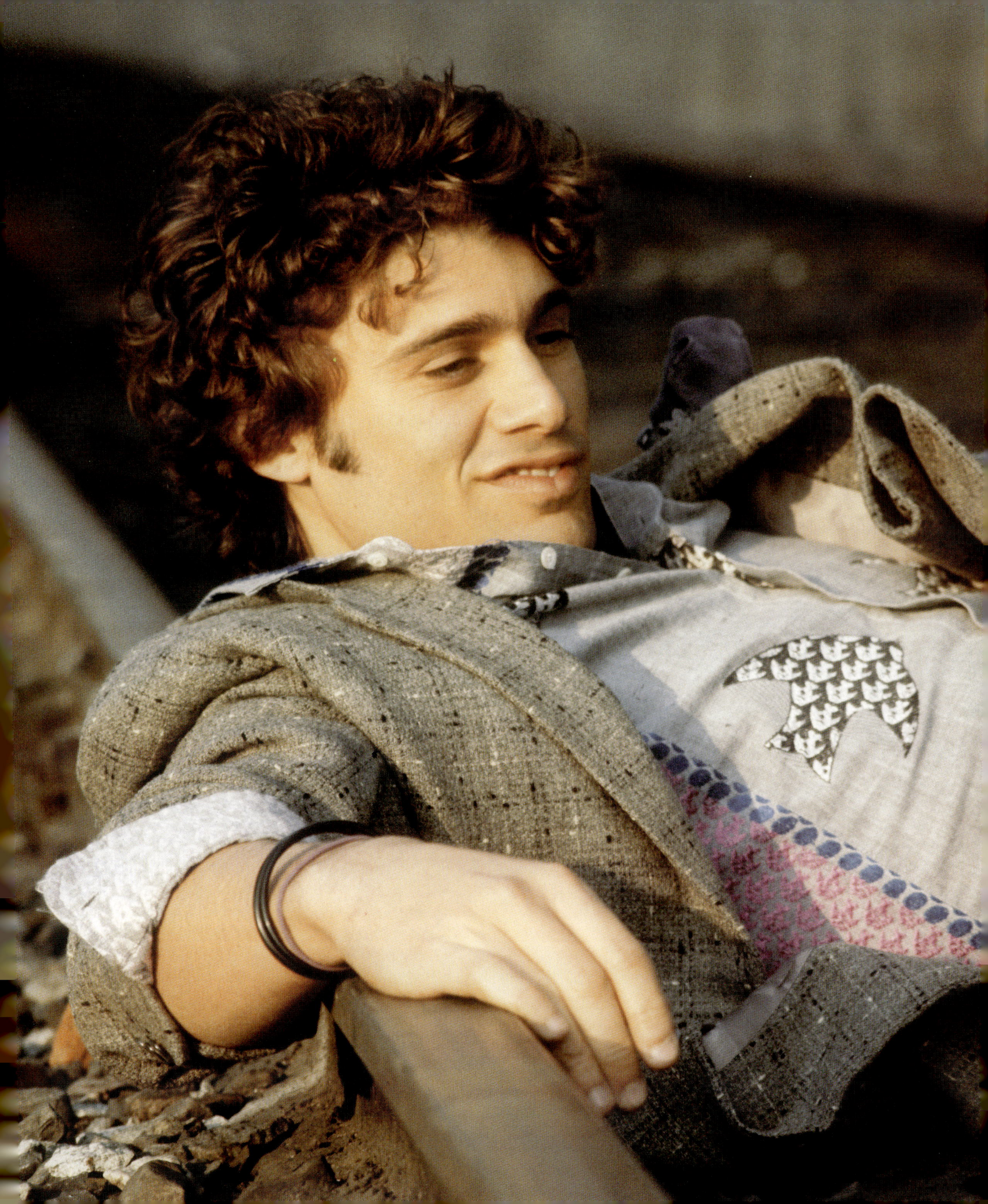

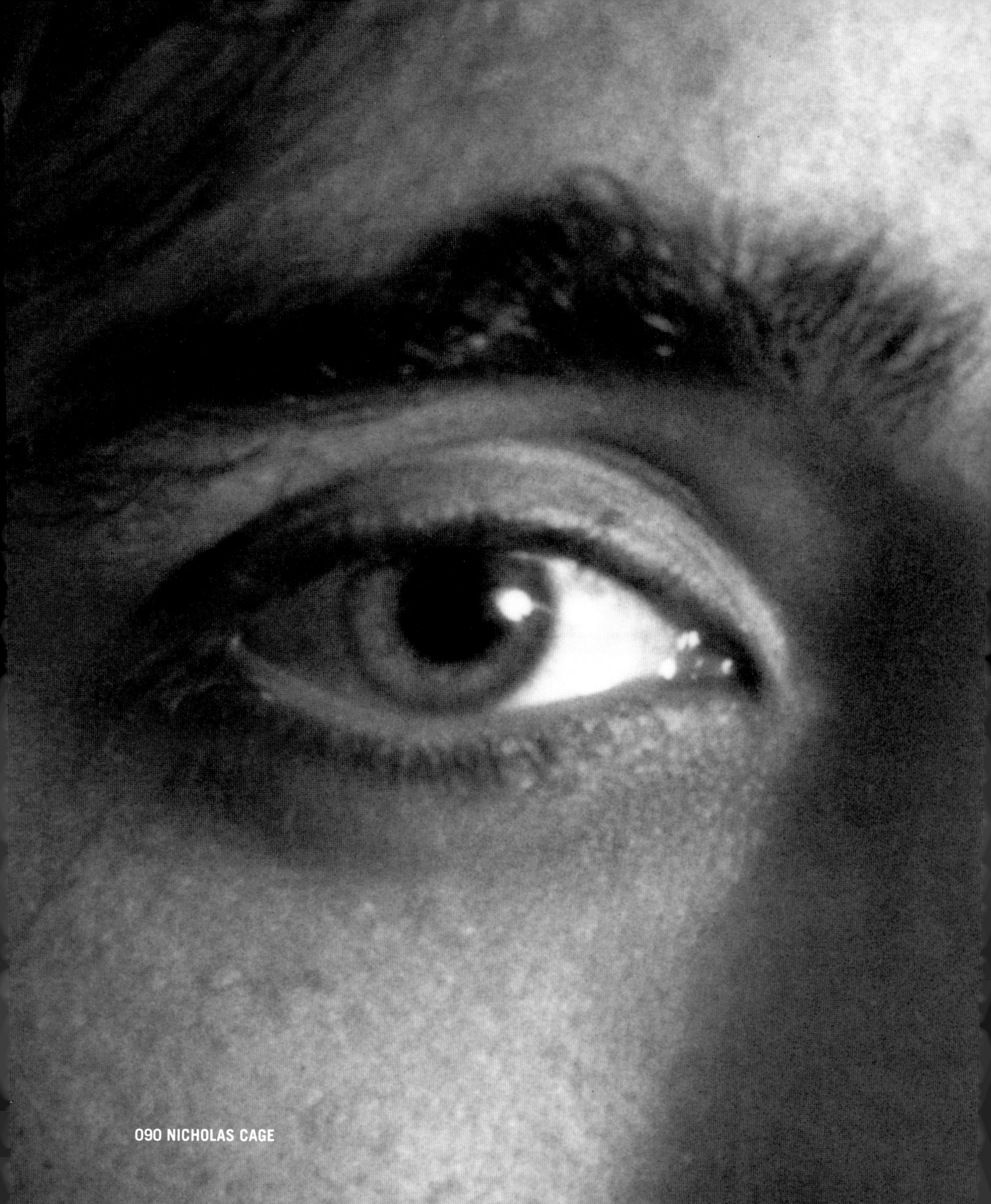

090 NICHOLAS CAGE

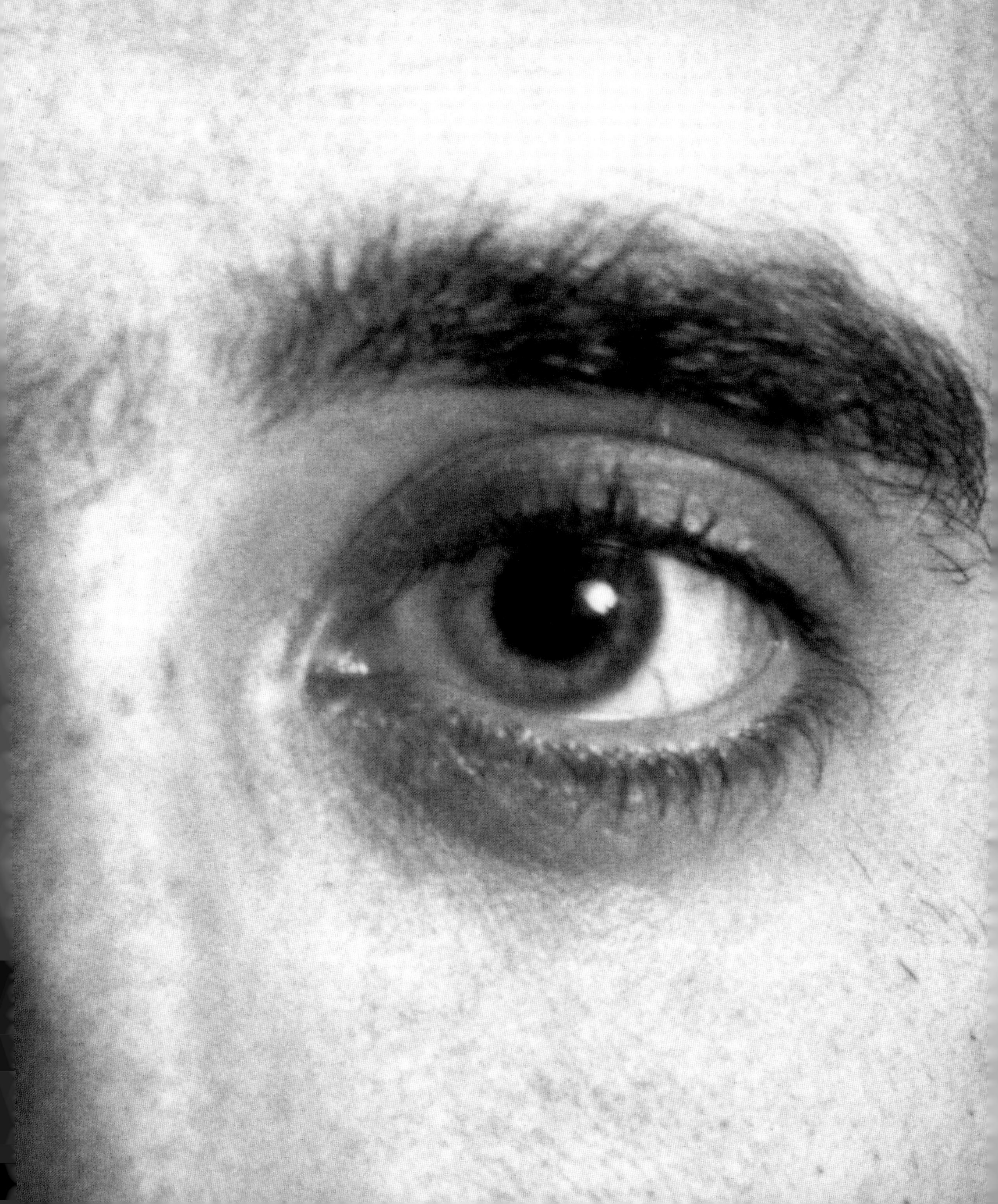

I photographed Carmen Electra in Hawaii for her first calendar. When we first met, at Jerry's Deli in the Valley, I wanted to get an idea of what direction, what theme, what clothing to go for. Carmen reminded me of Raquel Welch. She had brown hair, tanned skin, leathery bikinis—a *One Million Years BC* feel— and Carmen agreed.

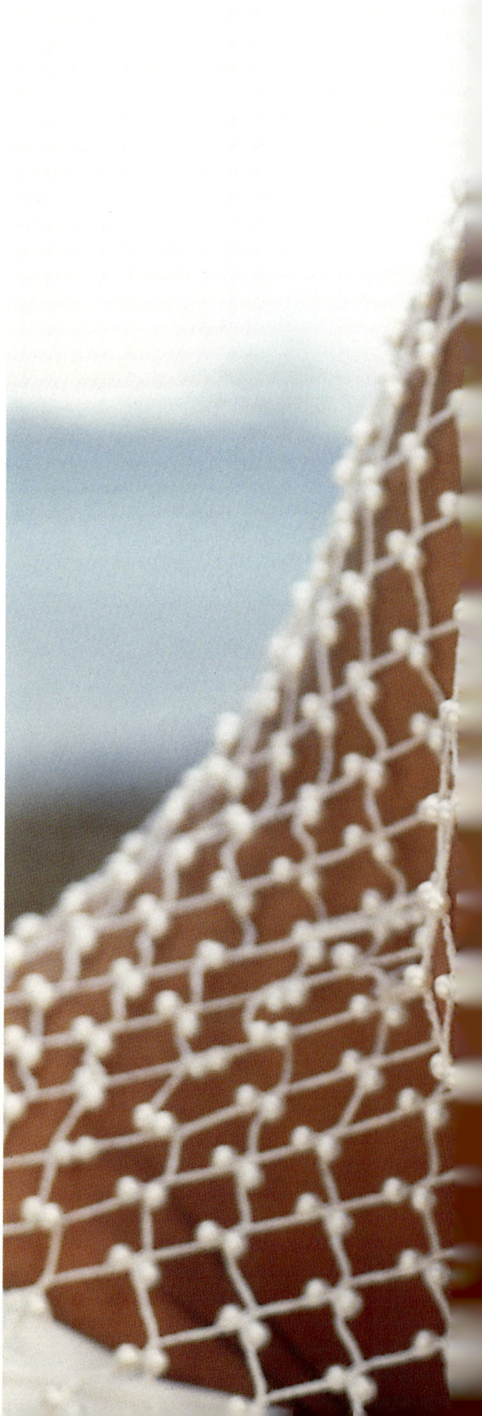

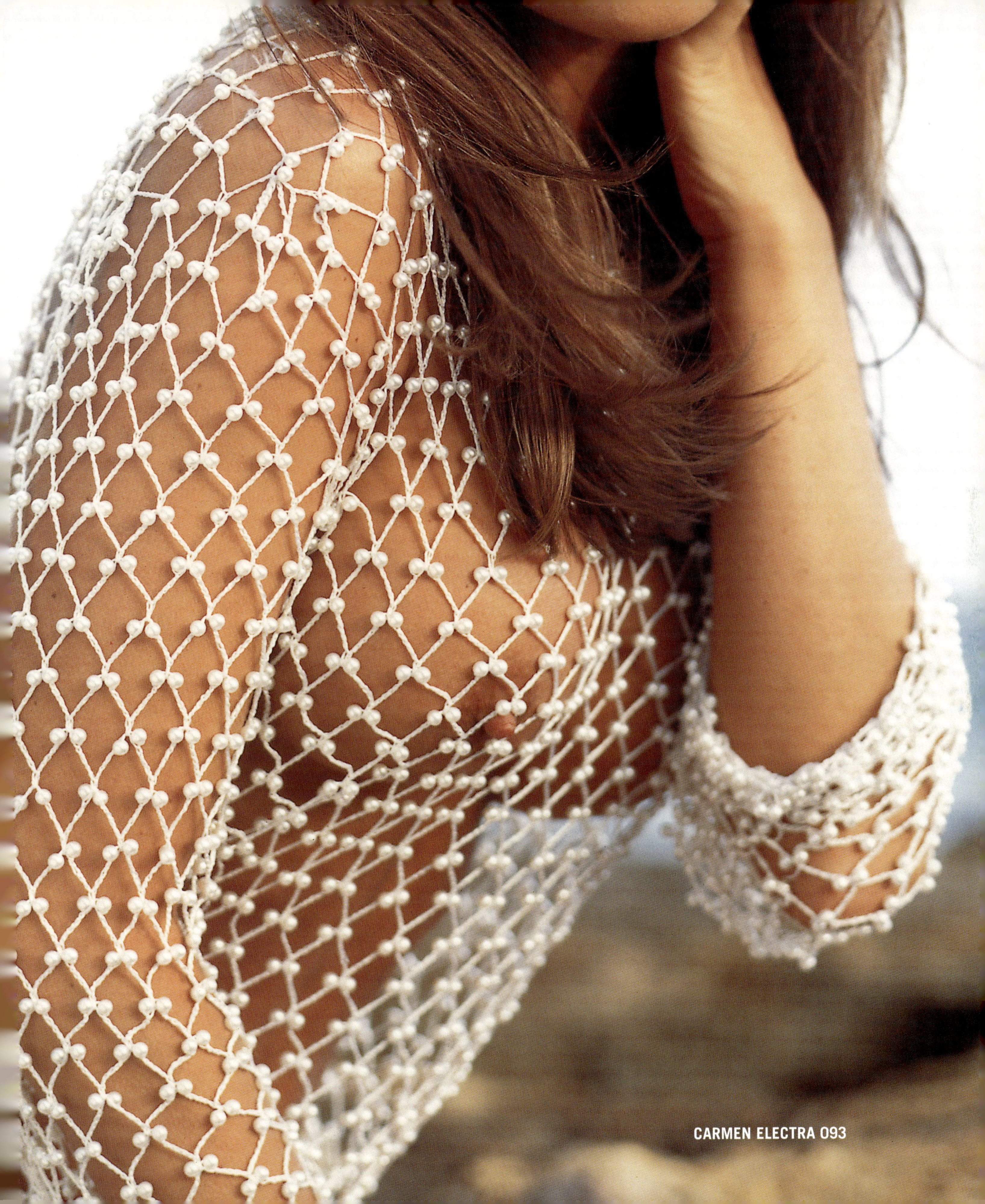
CARMEN ELECTRA 093

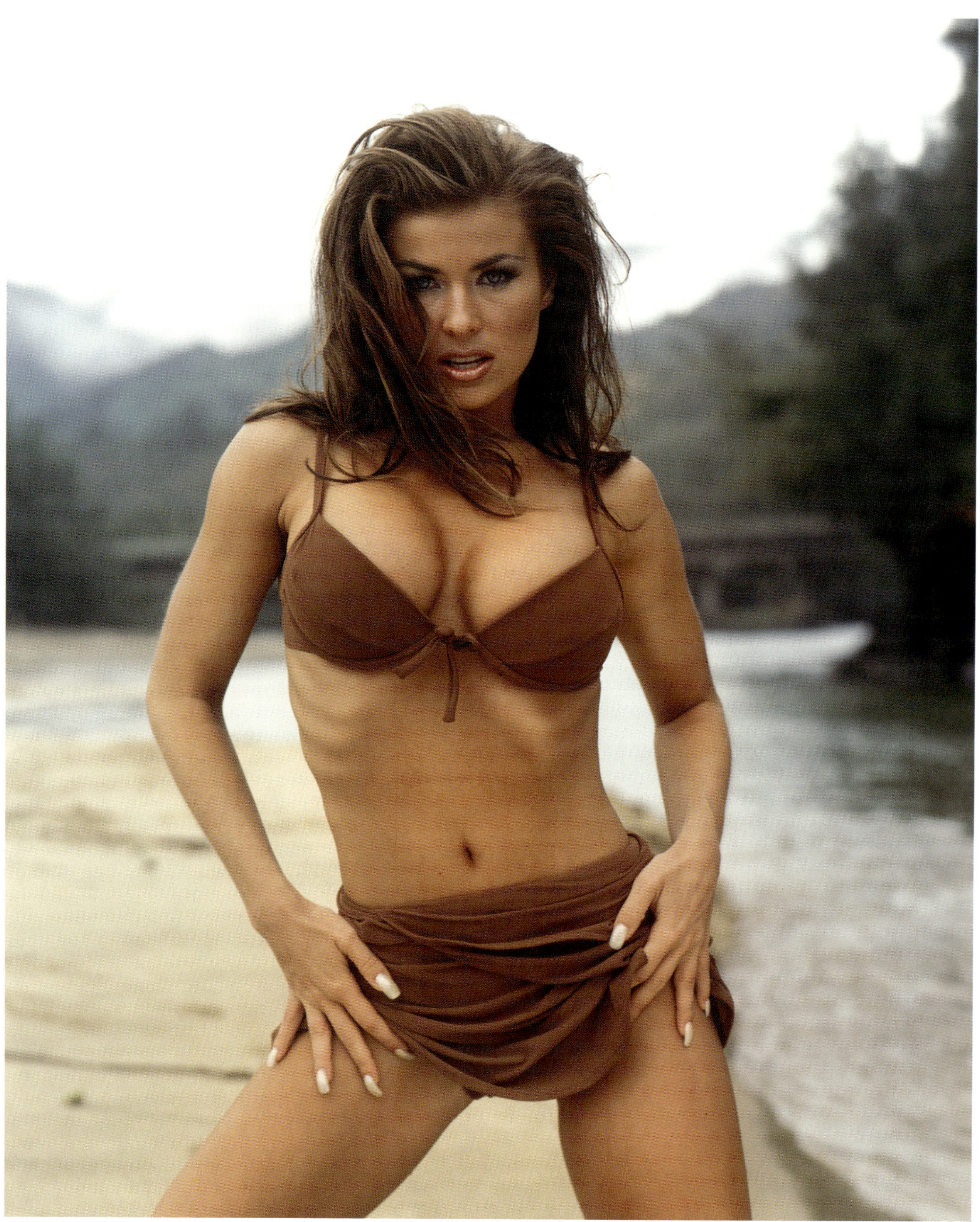

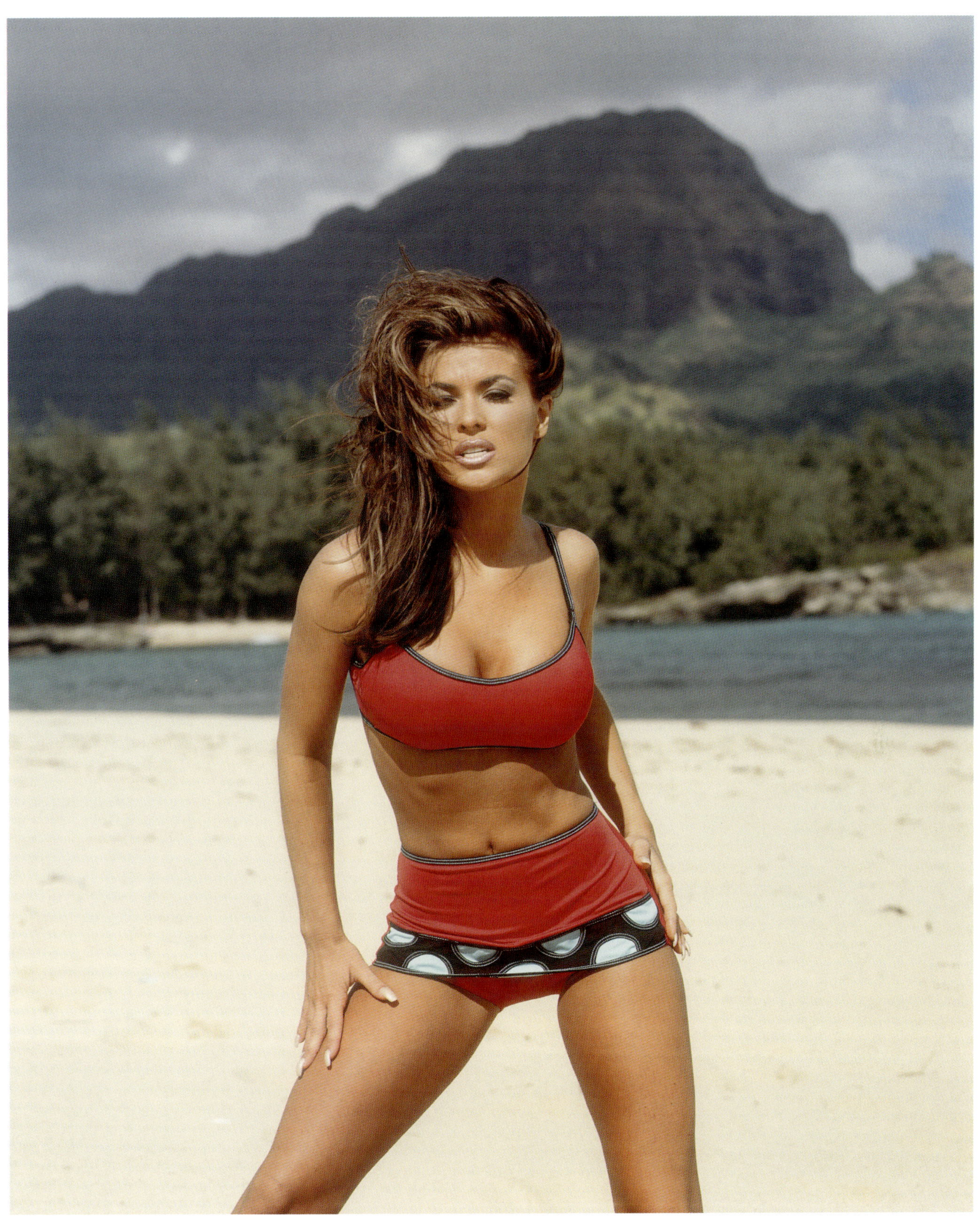

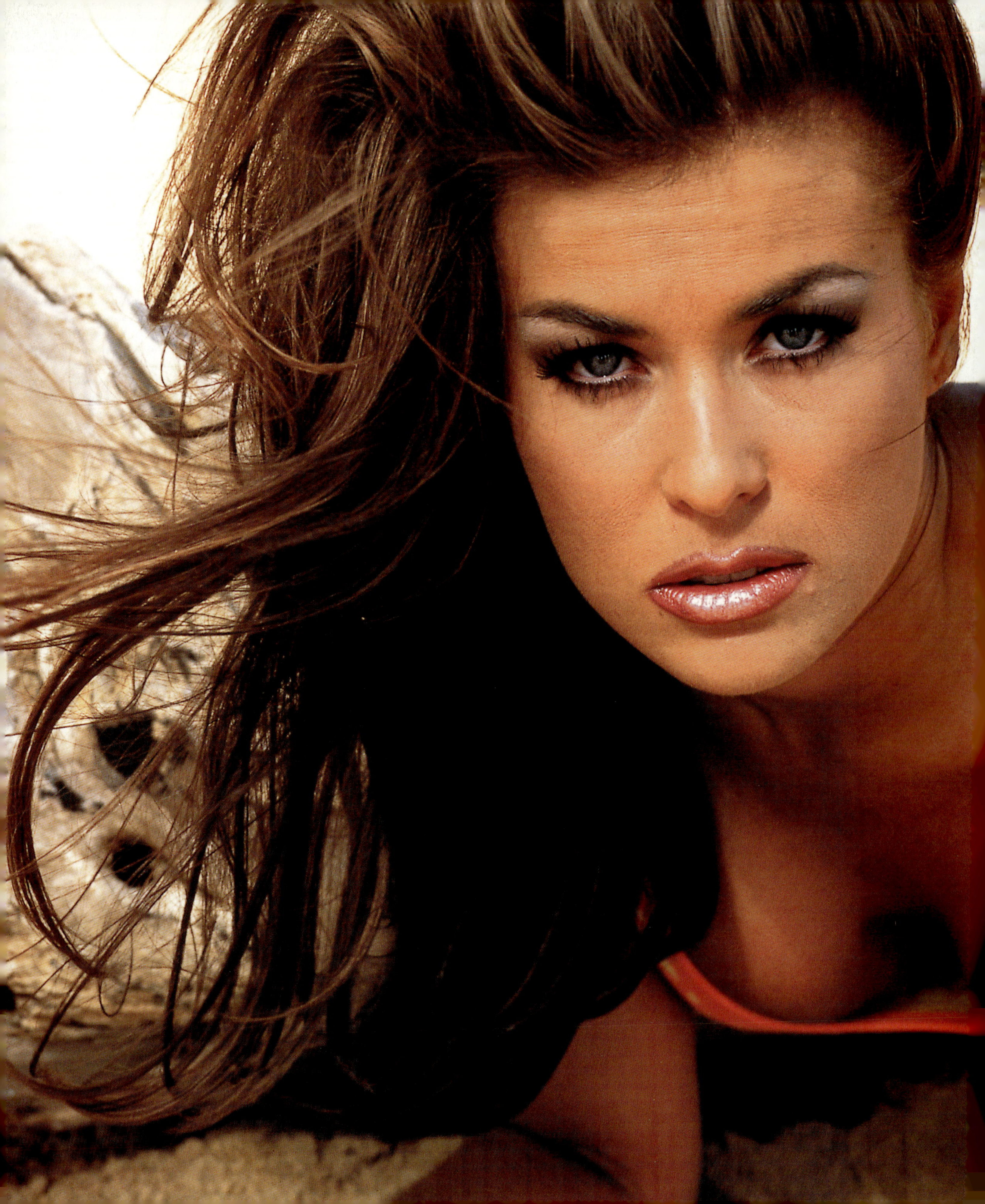

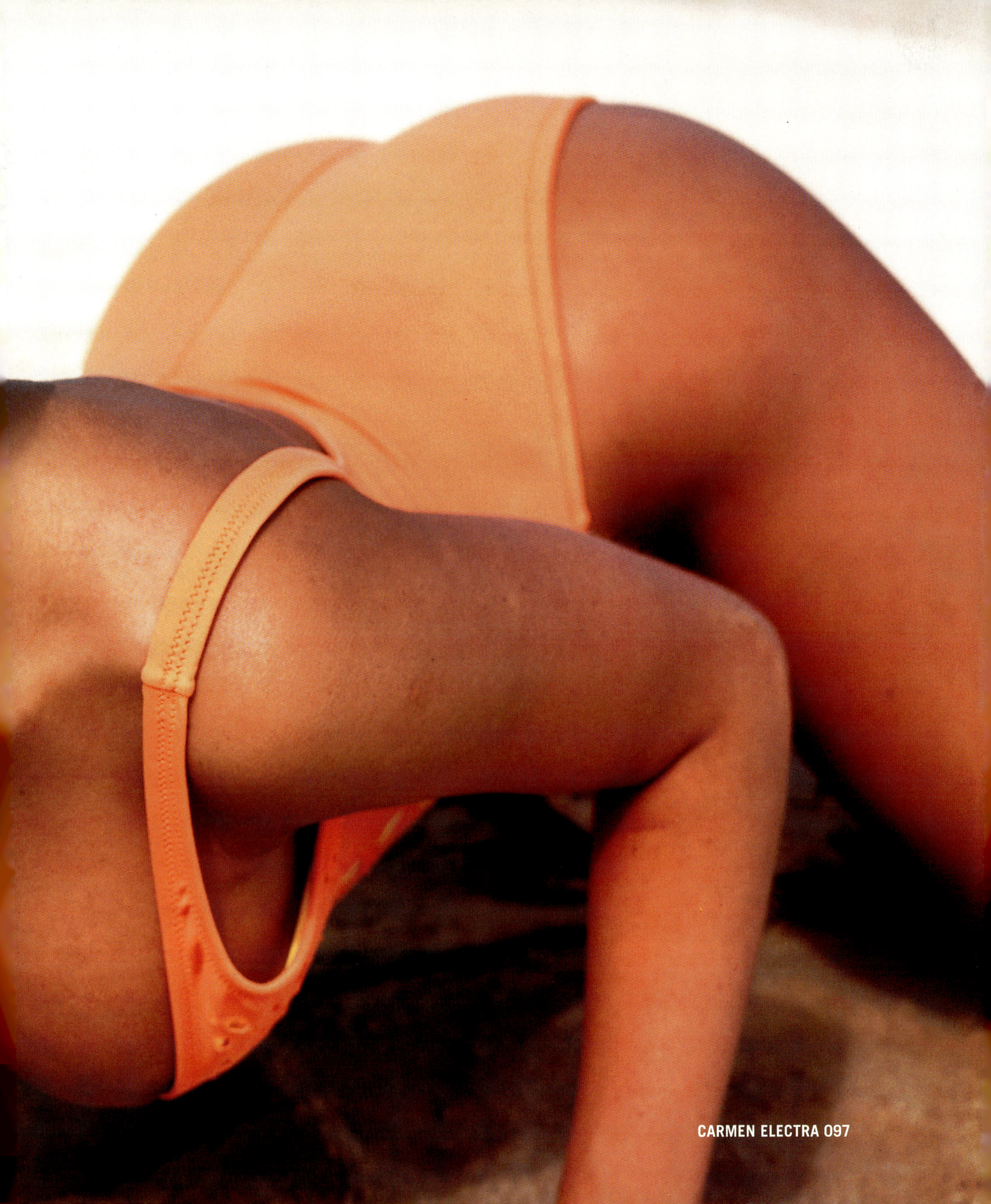
CARMEN ELECTRA 097

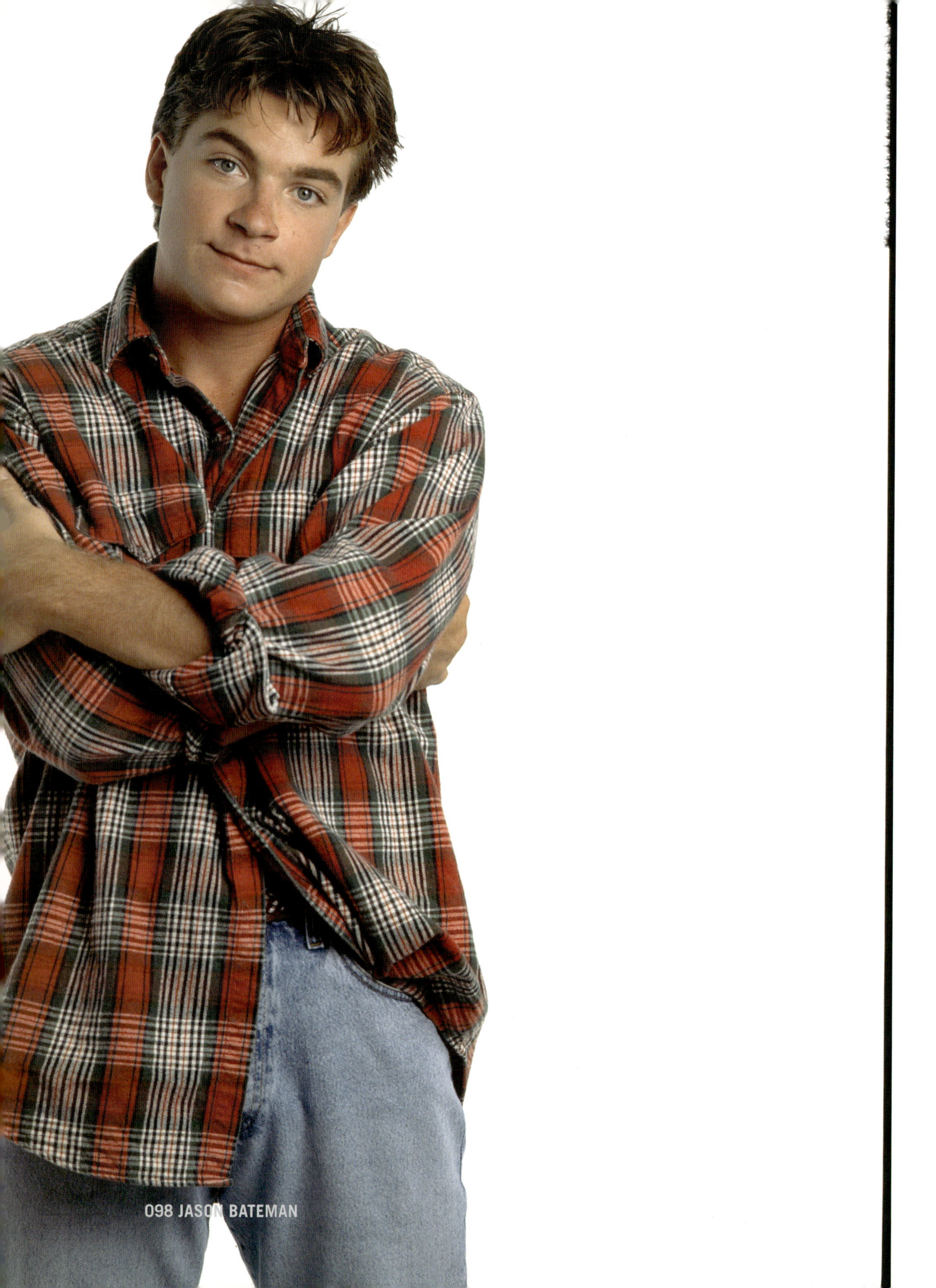

098 JASON BATEMAN

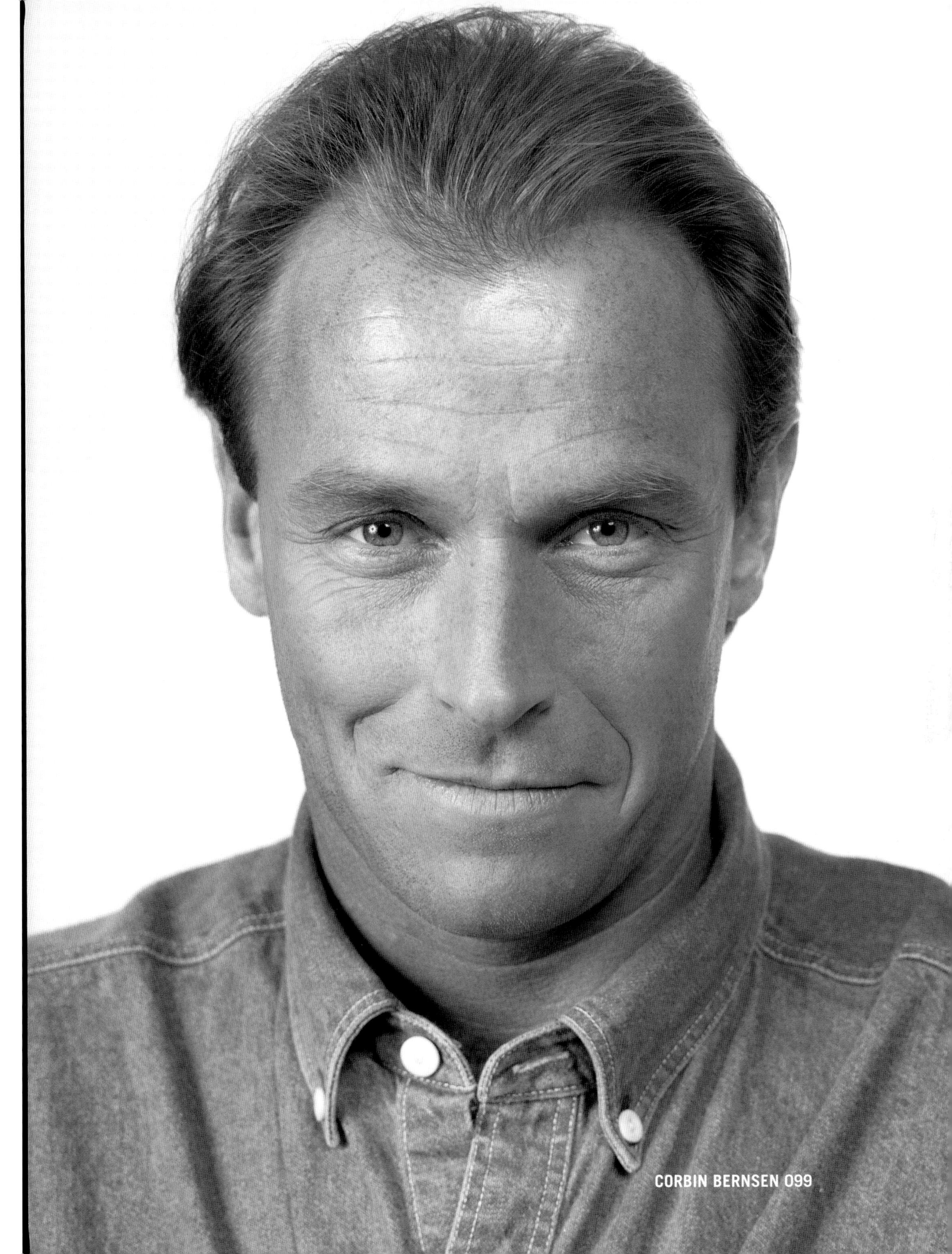

CORBIN BERNSEN 099

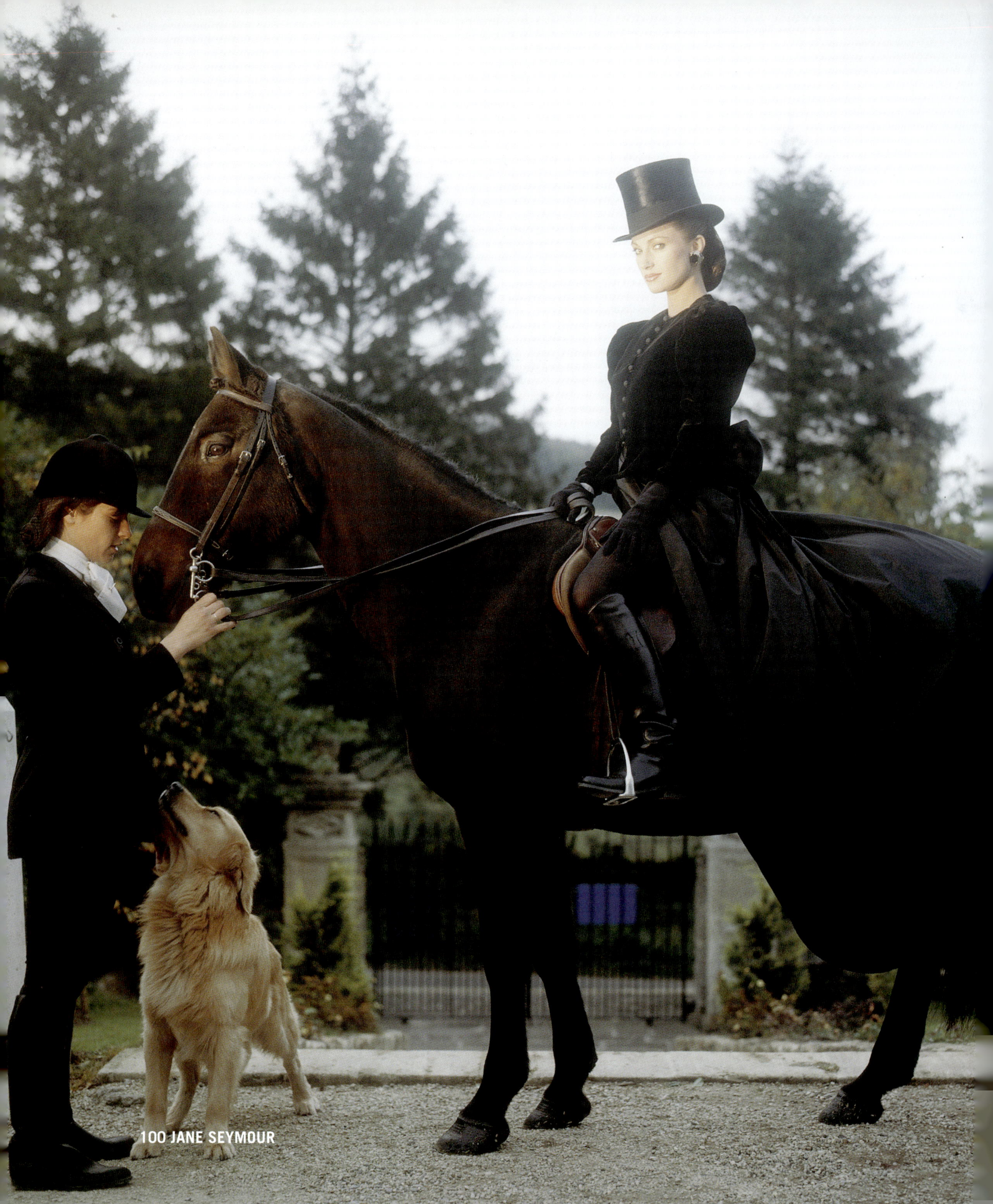

100 JANE SEYMOUR

I photographed her in her Wiltshire country estate to illustrate her book on *Romantic Living*. We did several different looks—Rita Hayworth as Gilda, Marie Antoinette and a wisteria nymph. This English horse-woman soon after transformed herself into a homestead doctor on *Dr Quinn, Medicine Woman*.

I photographed her in her Wiltshire country estate to illustrate her book on Romantic Living. We did several different looks—Rita Hayworth as Gilda, Marie Antoinette and a wisteria nymph. This English horsewoman soon after transformed herself into a homestead doctor on Dr Quinn, Medicine Woman.

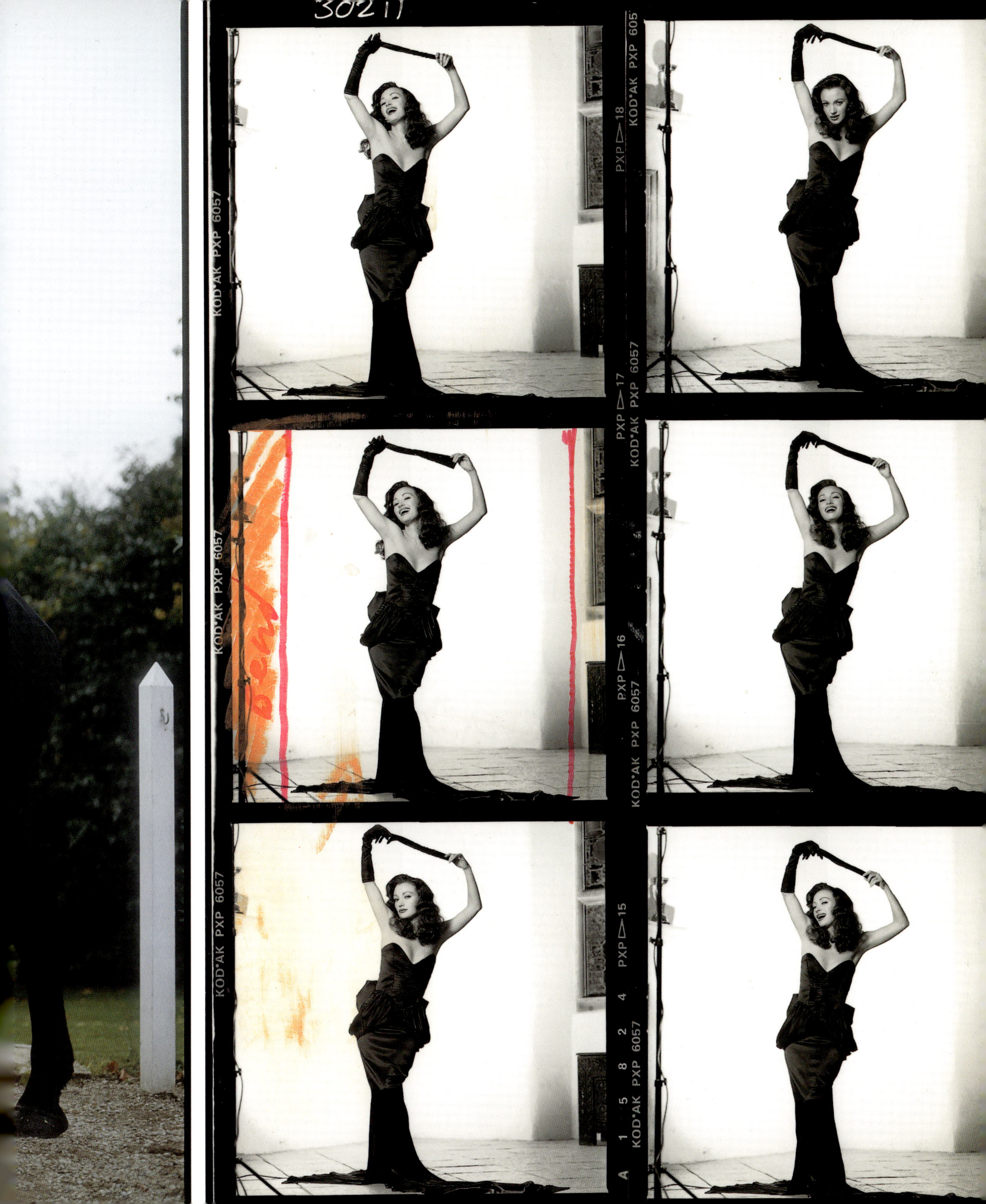

30211

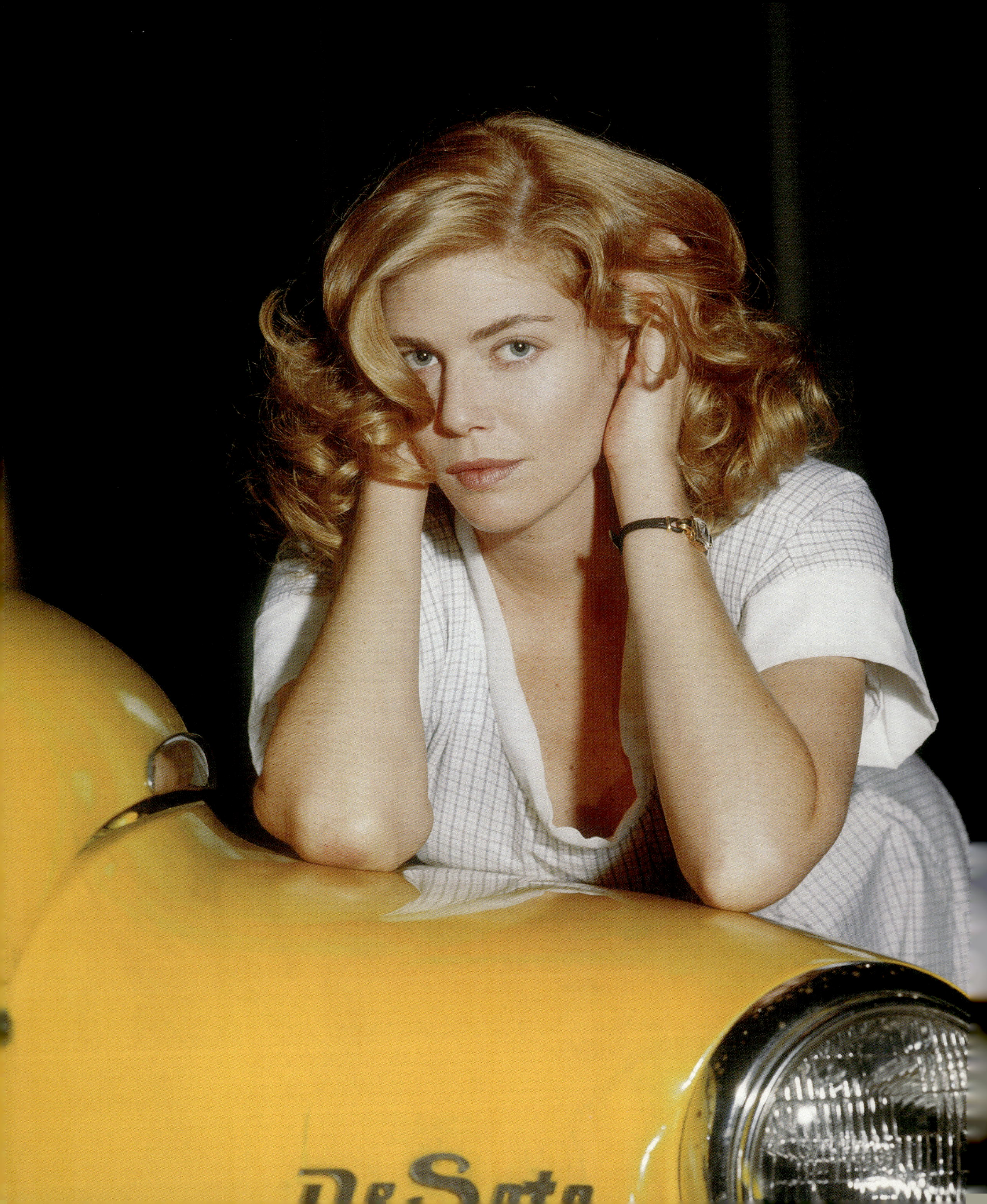

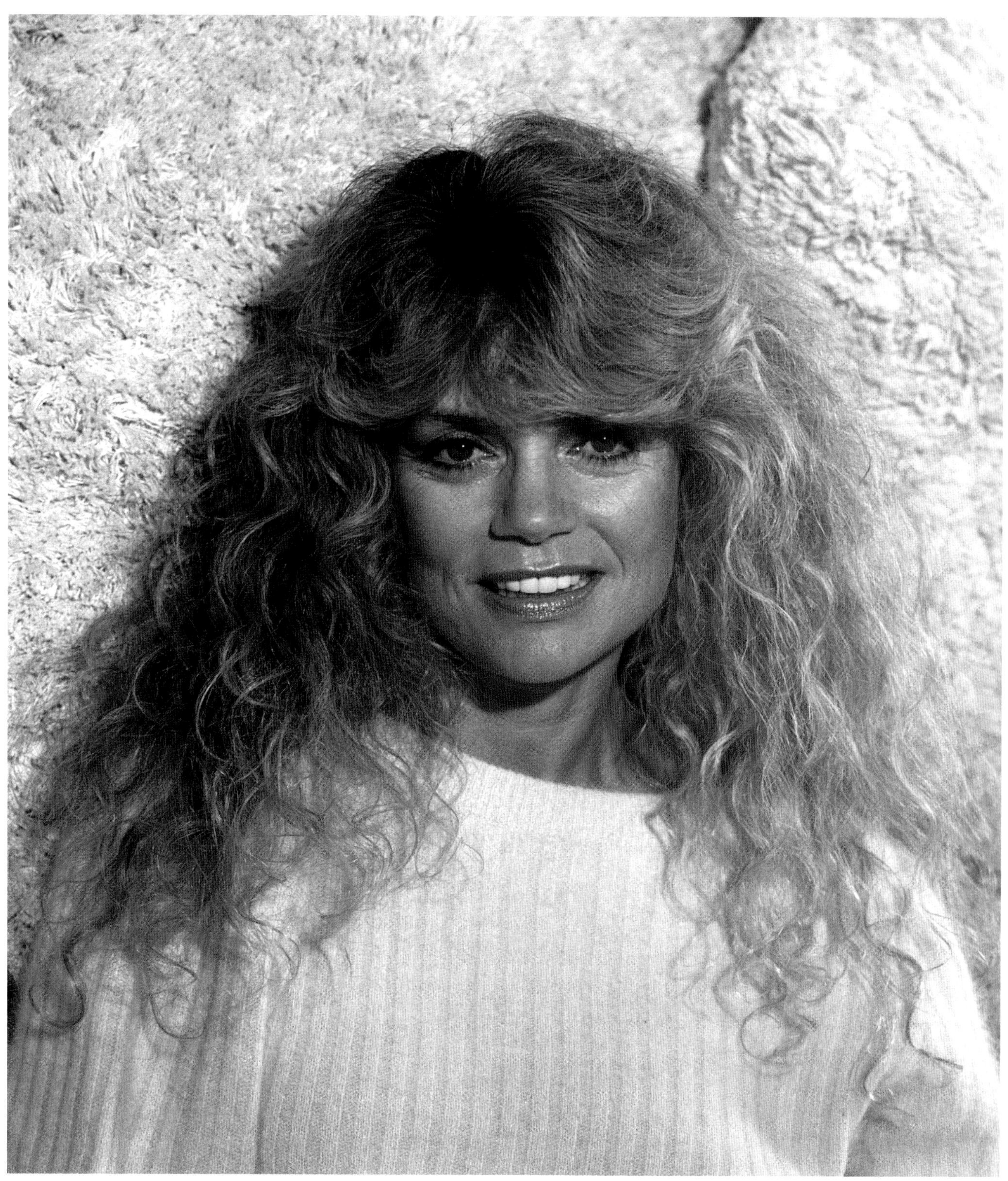

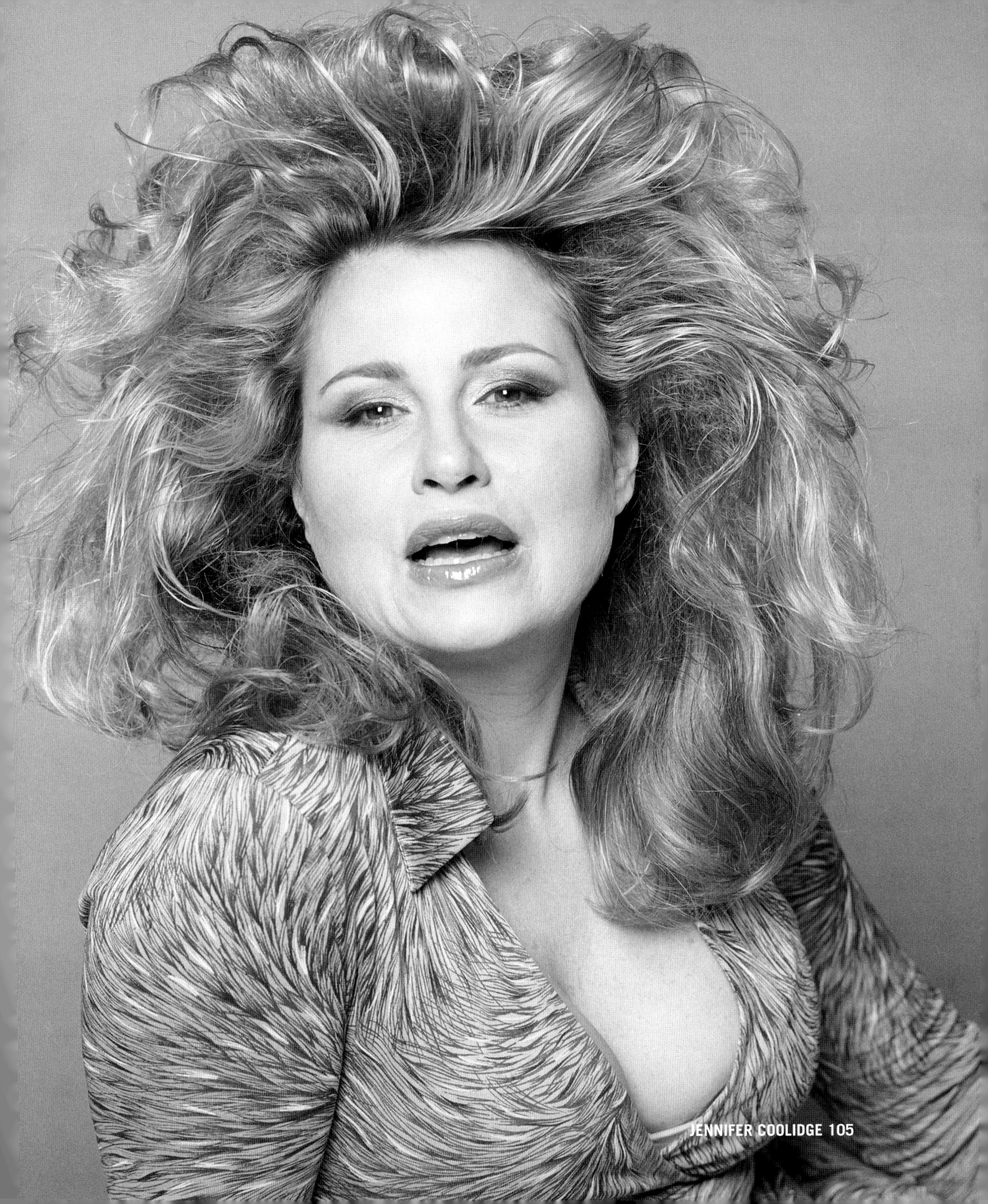

JENNIFER COOLIDGE 105

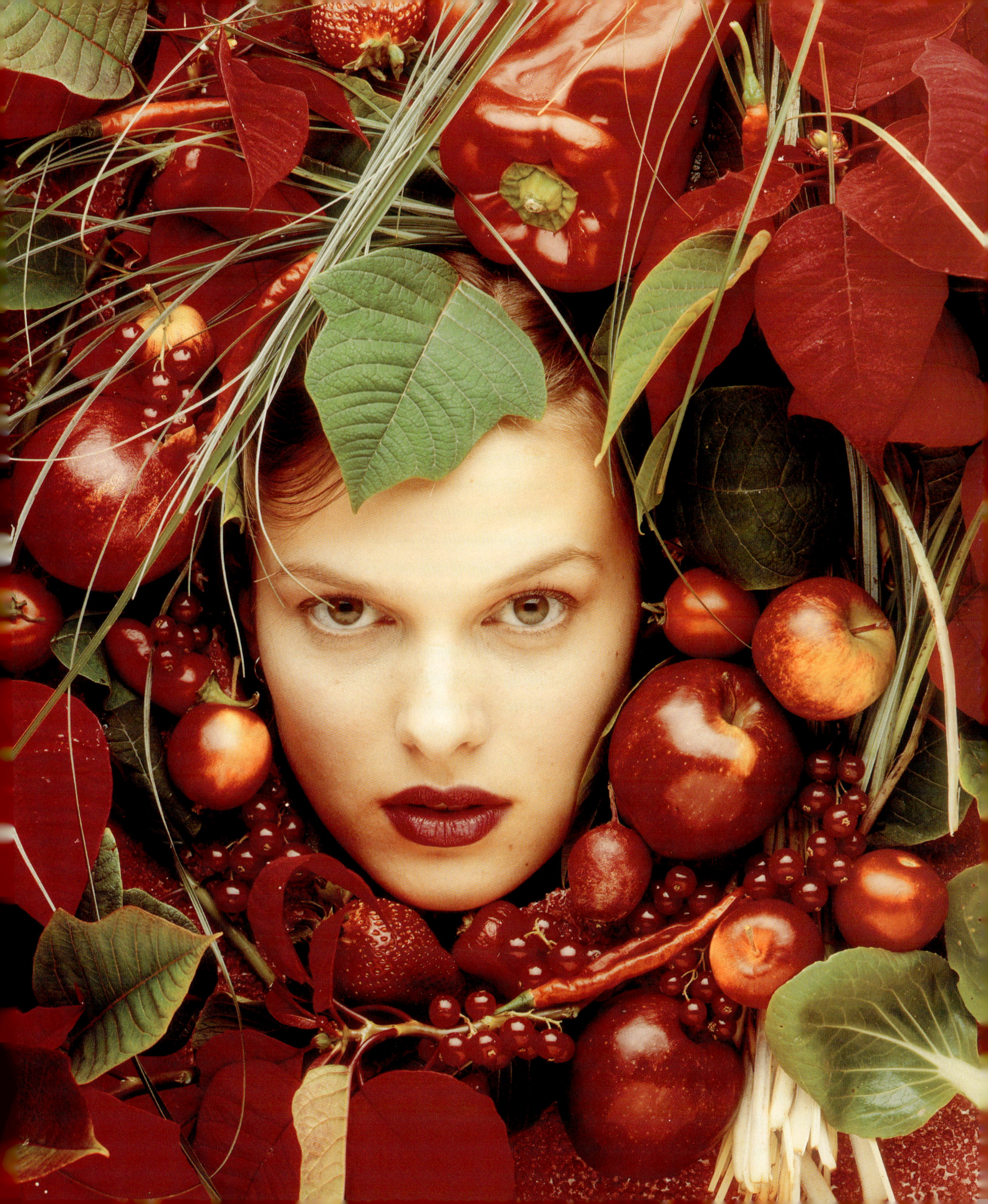

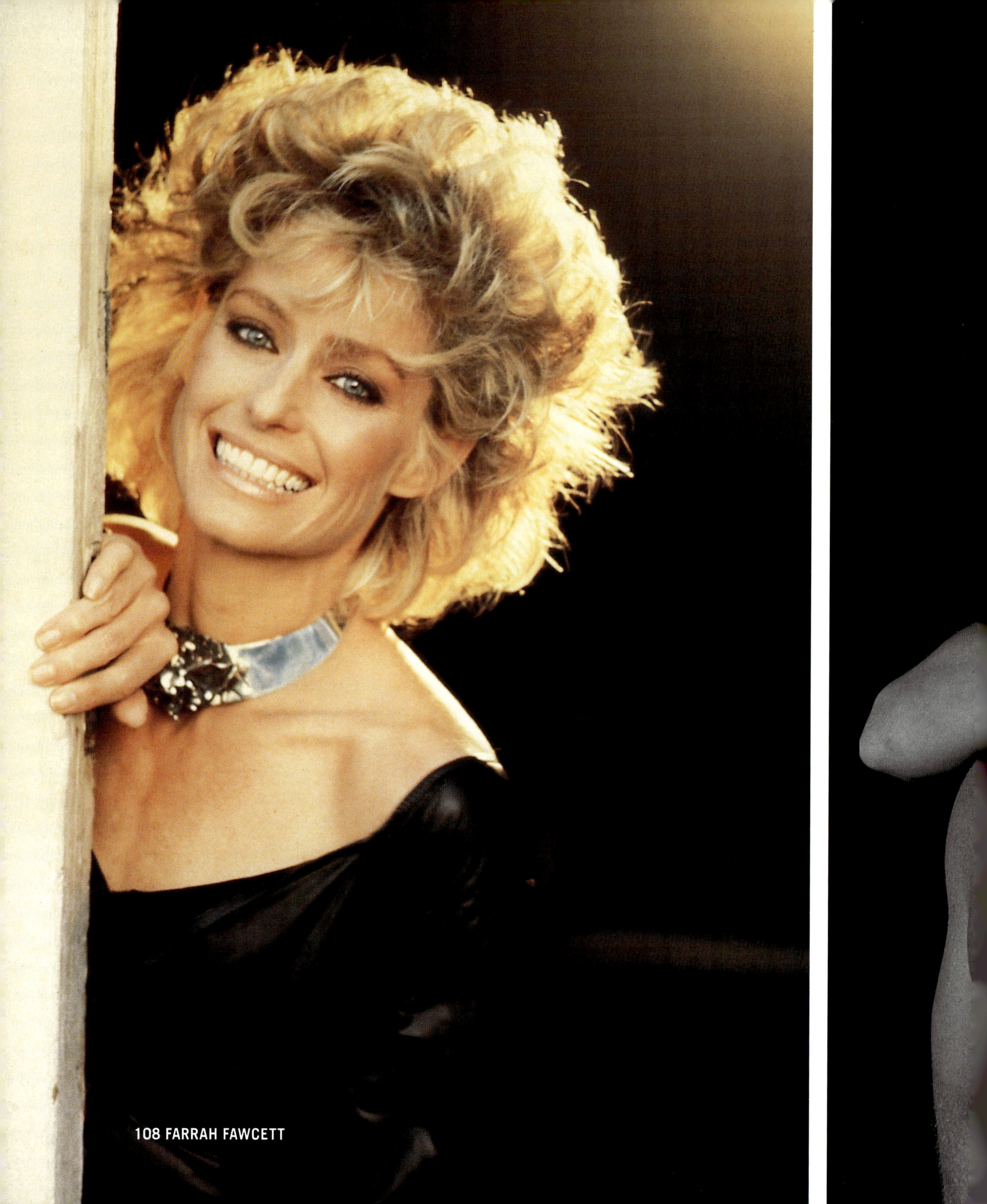

108 FARRAH FAWCETT

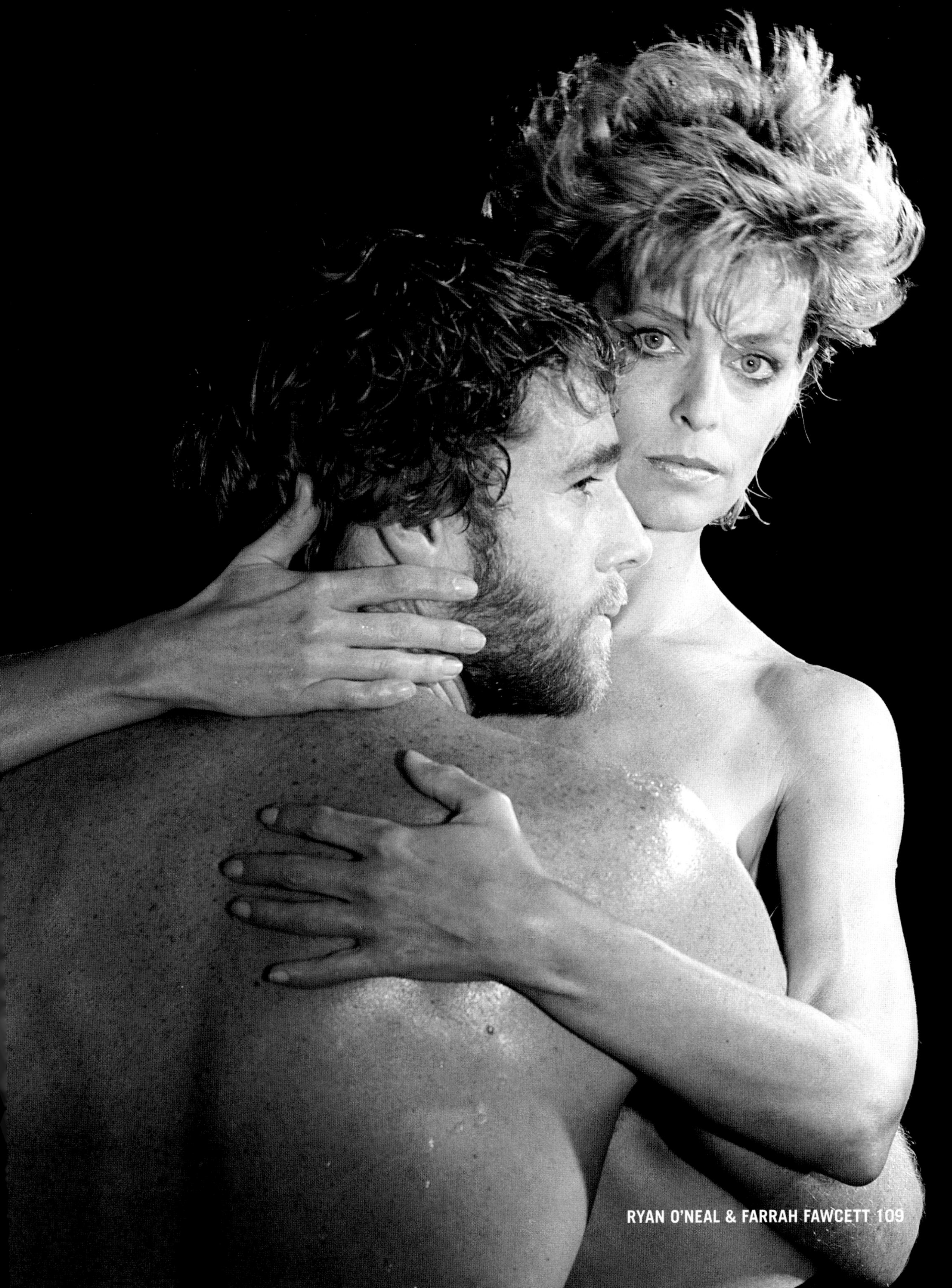
RYAN O'NEAL & FARRAH FAWCETT 109

The photographer who influenced me most, when I was starting out, was George Hurrell from the Hollywood era of the thirties and forties. In my opinion, Hurrell always lit his subjects perfectly and in the most flattering way. All the great movie stars flocked to him—men and women. I remember reading somewhere that whenever Marlene Dietrich was photographed, her key light always had to be forty-five degrees straight in front of her and above her so that there would be a shadow under her cheekbones, nose and chin. Since she had a round moon-face, this kind of light brought out her 'bones'. I tend to photograph women in that way as well. It is the key to making any woman look gorgeous in photographs. When I photographed Daryl this particular time, outside her house in Santa Monica, I made sure that the sun was shining on her already beautiful face at a forty-five degree angle. I had photographed her several times before. The photograph was used as a cover image for a British magazine.

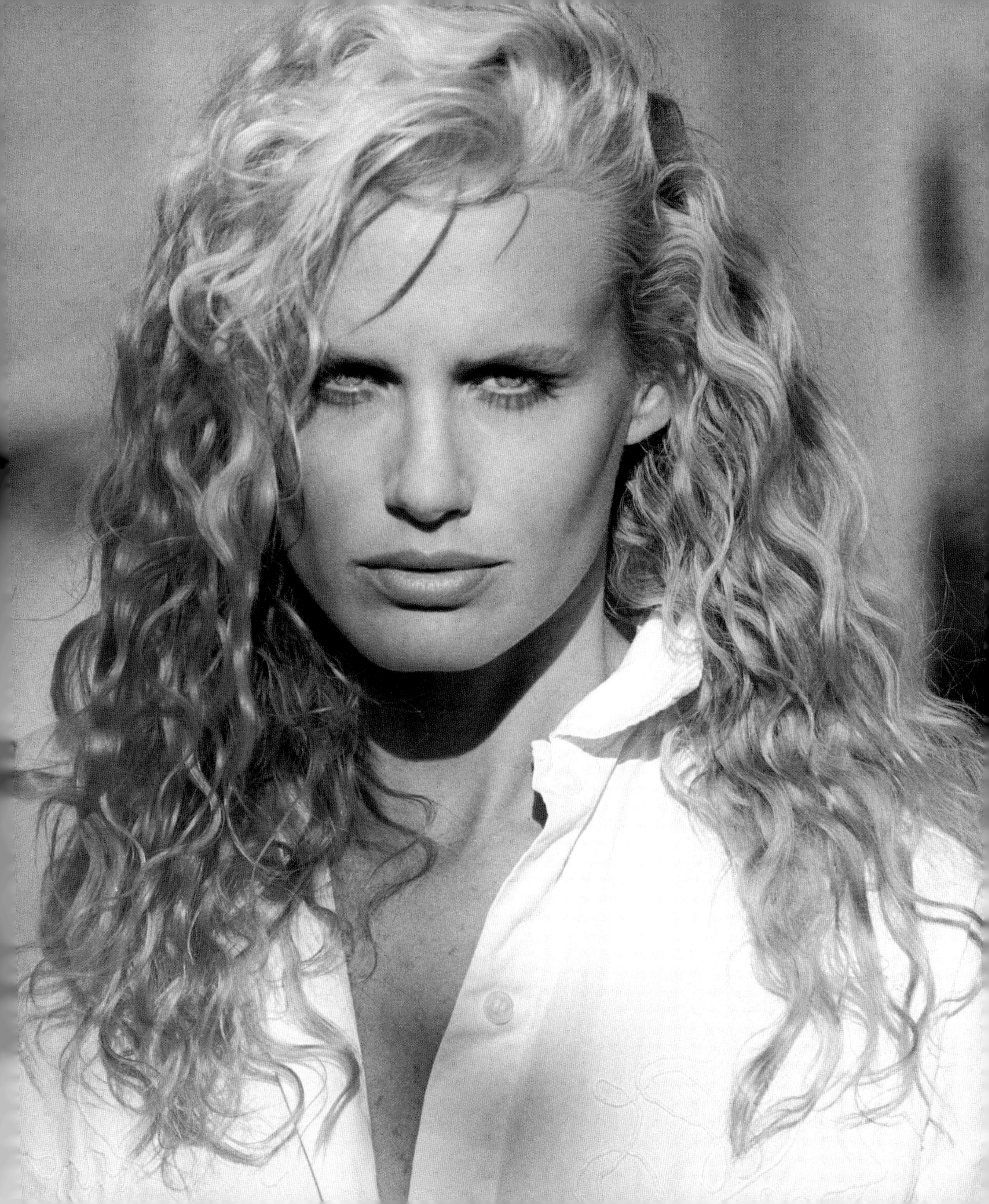

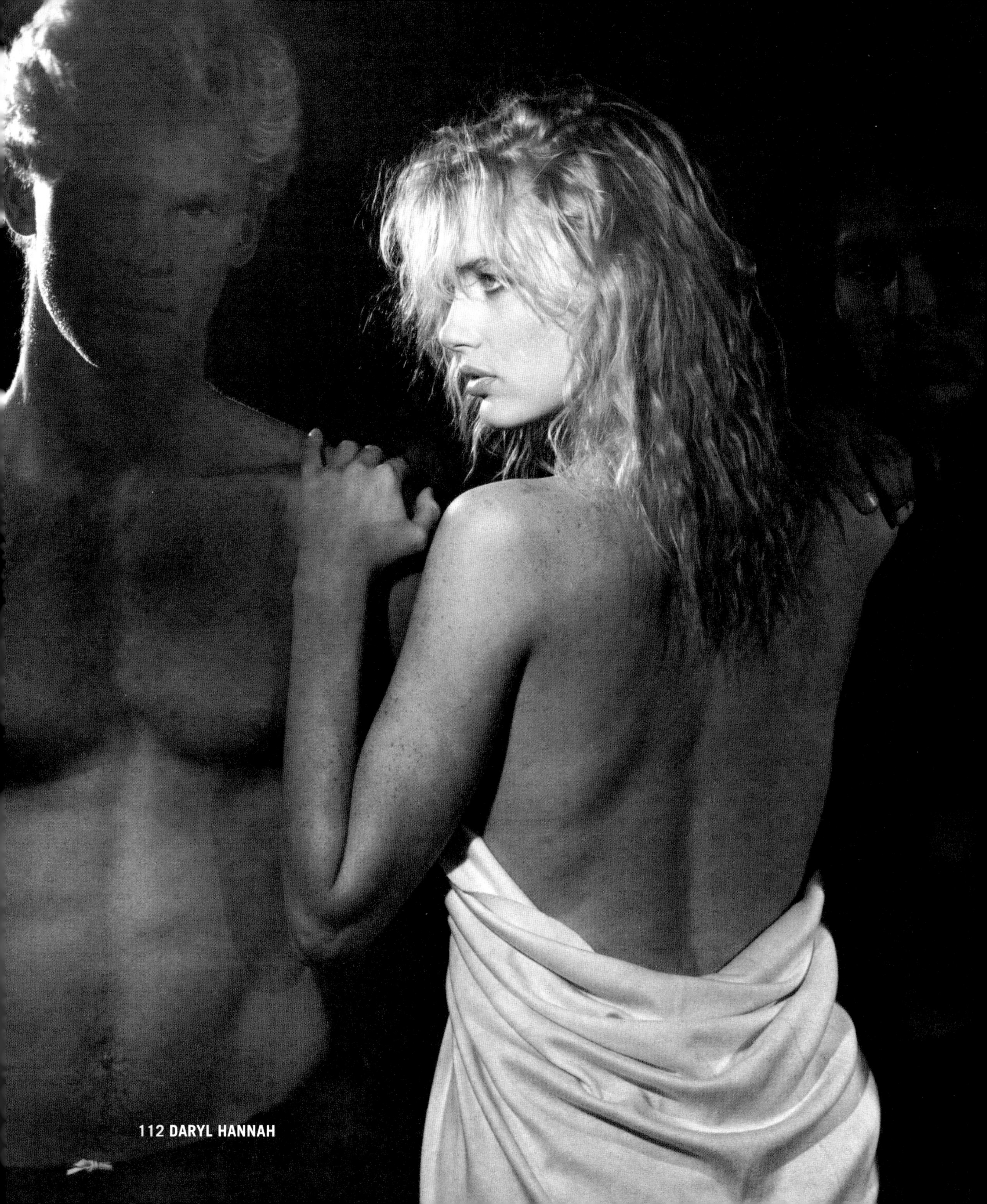
112 DARYL HANNAH

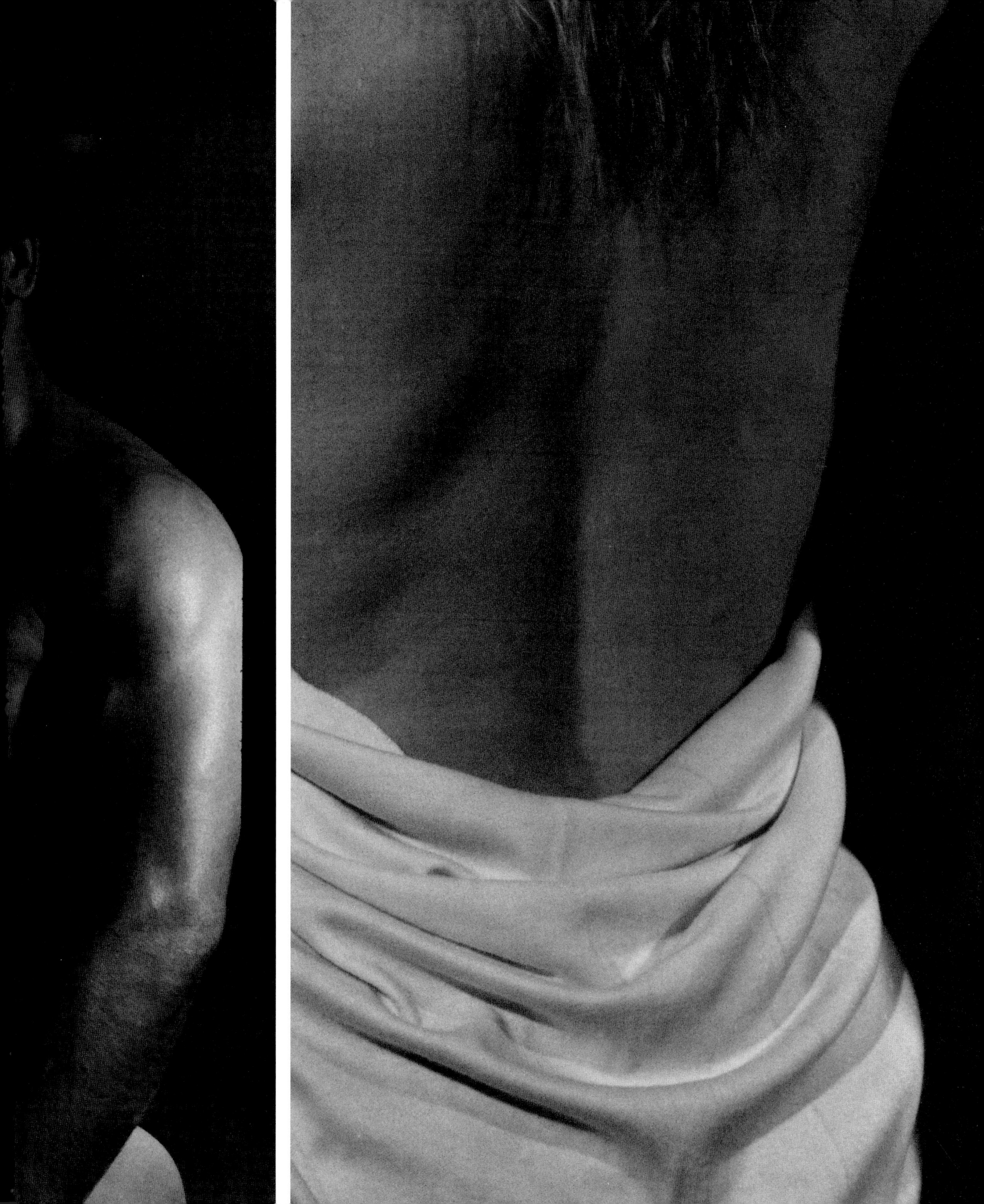

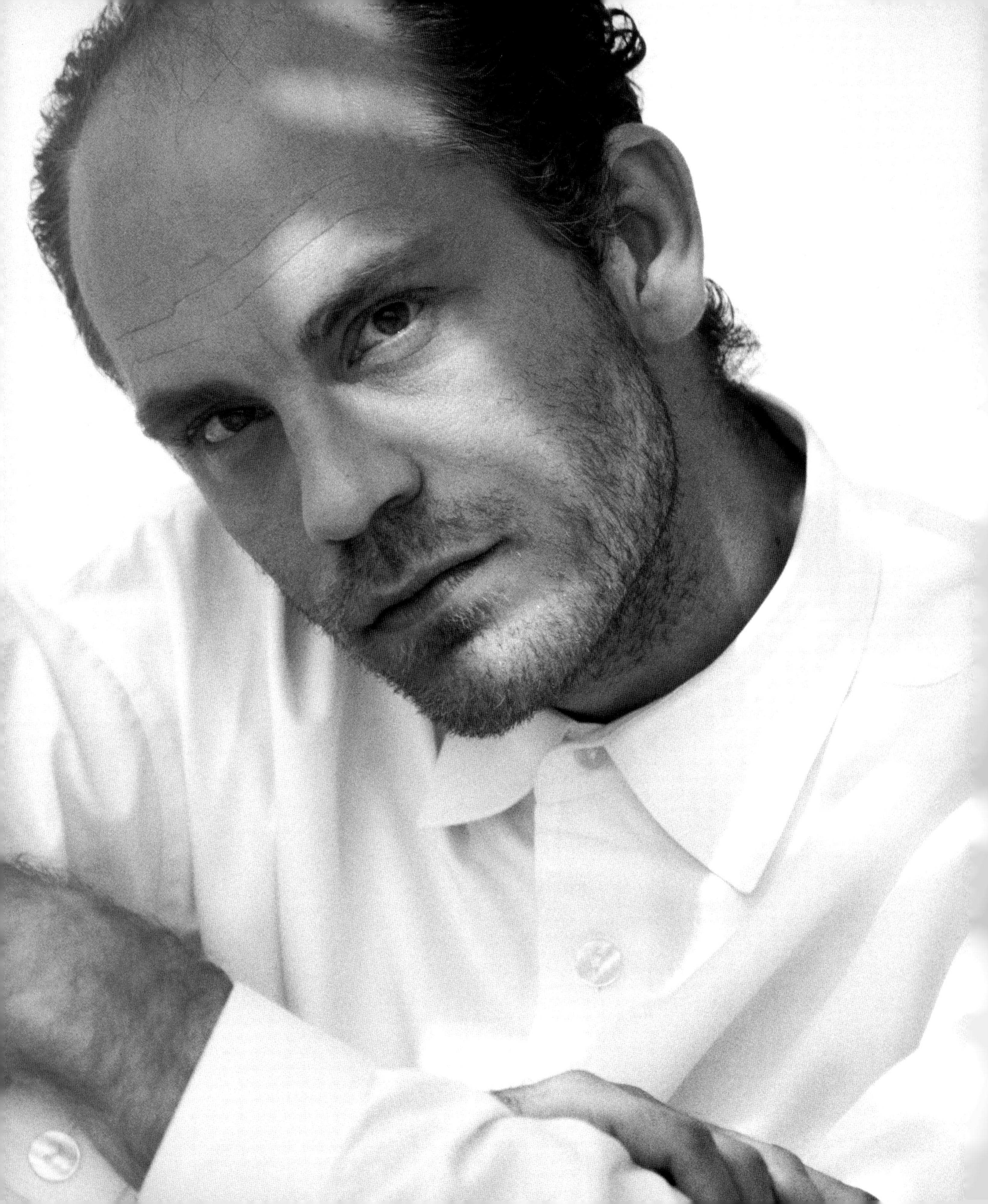

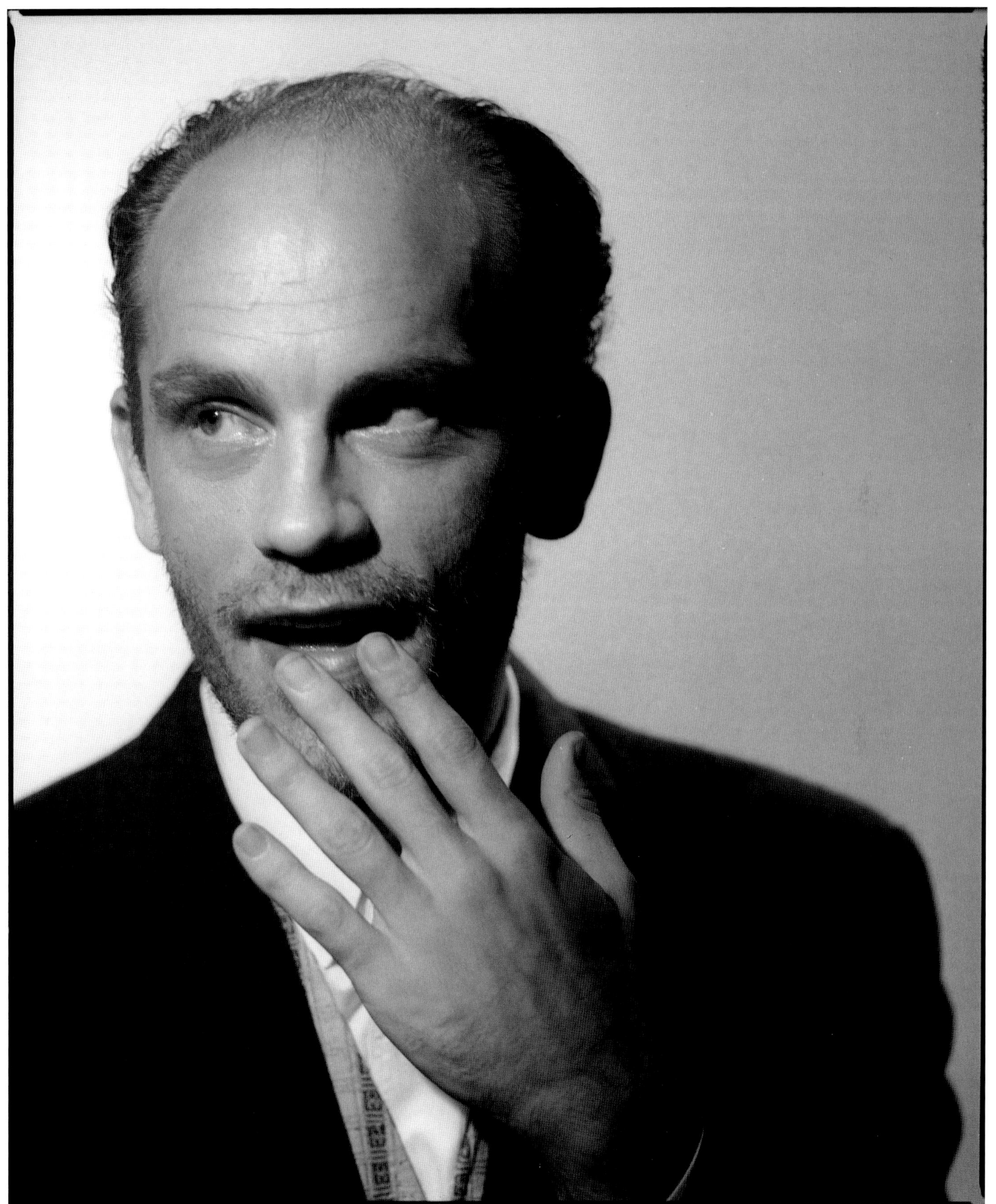

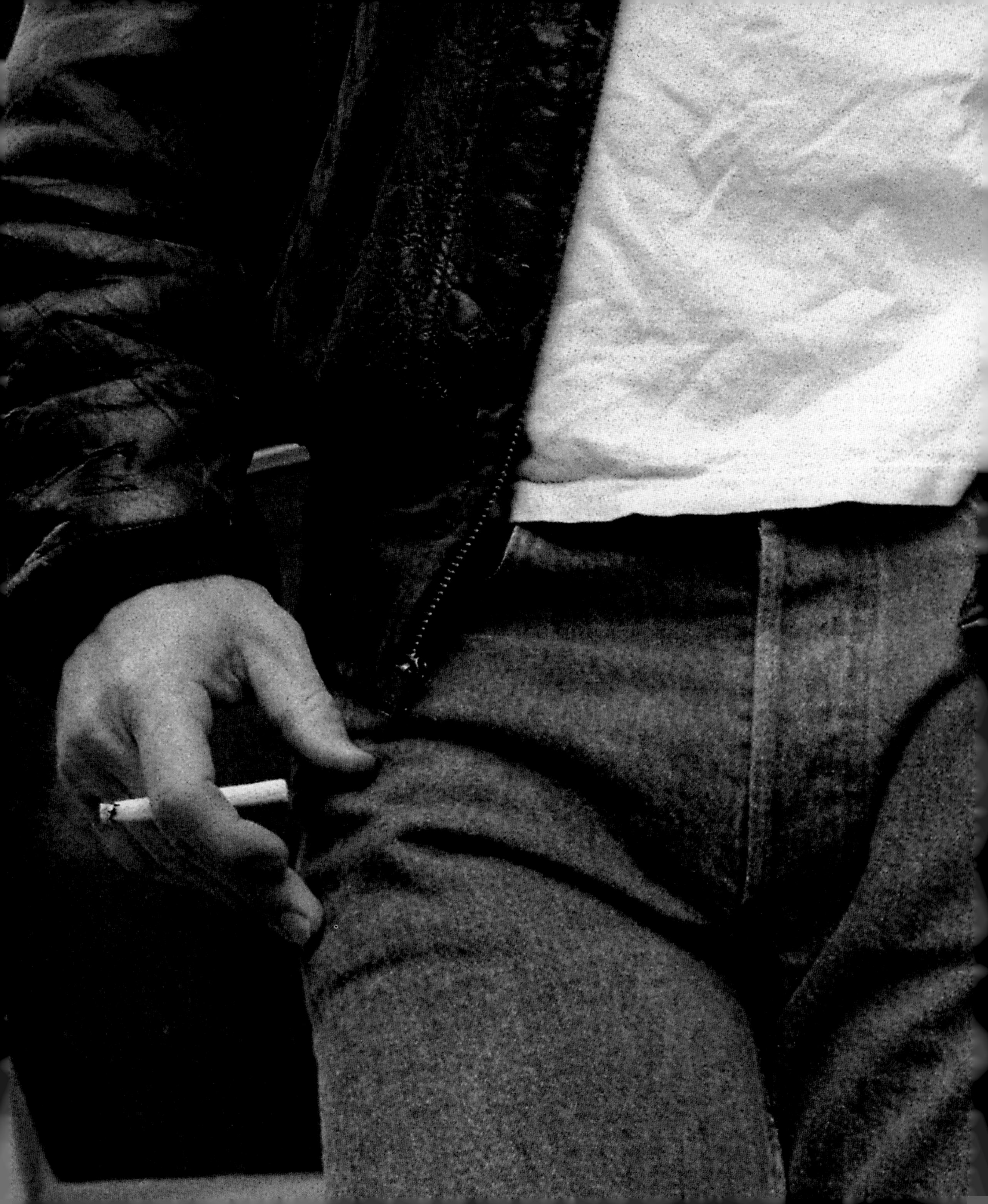

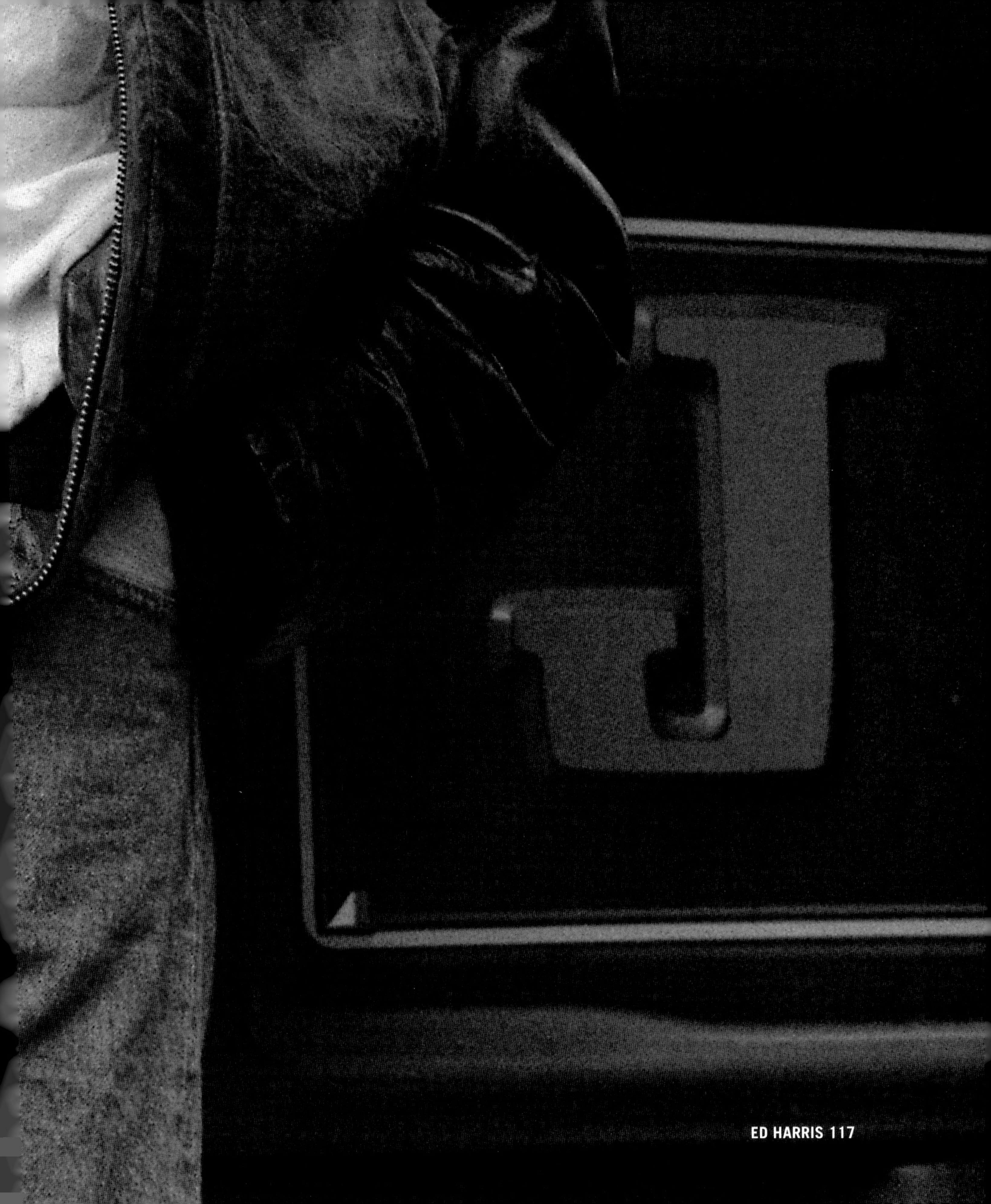

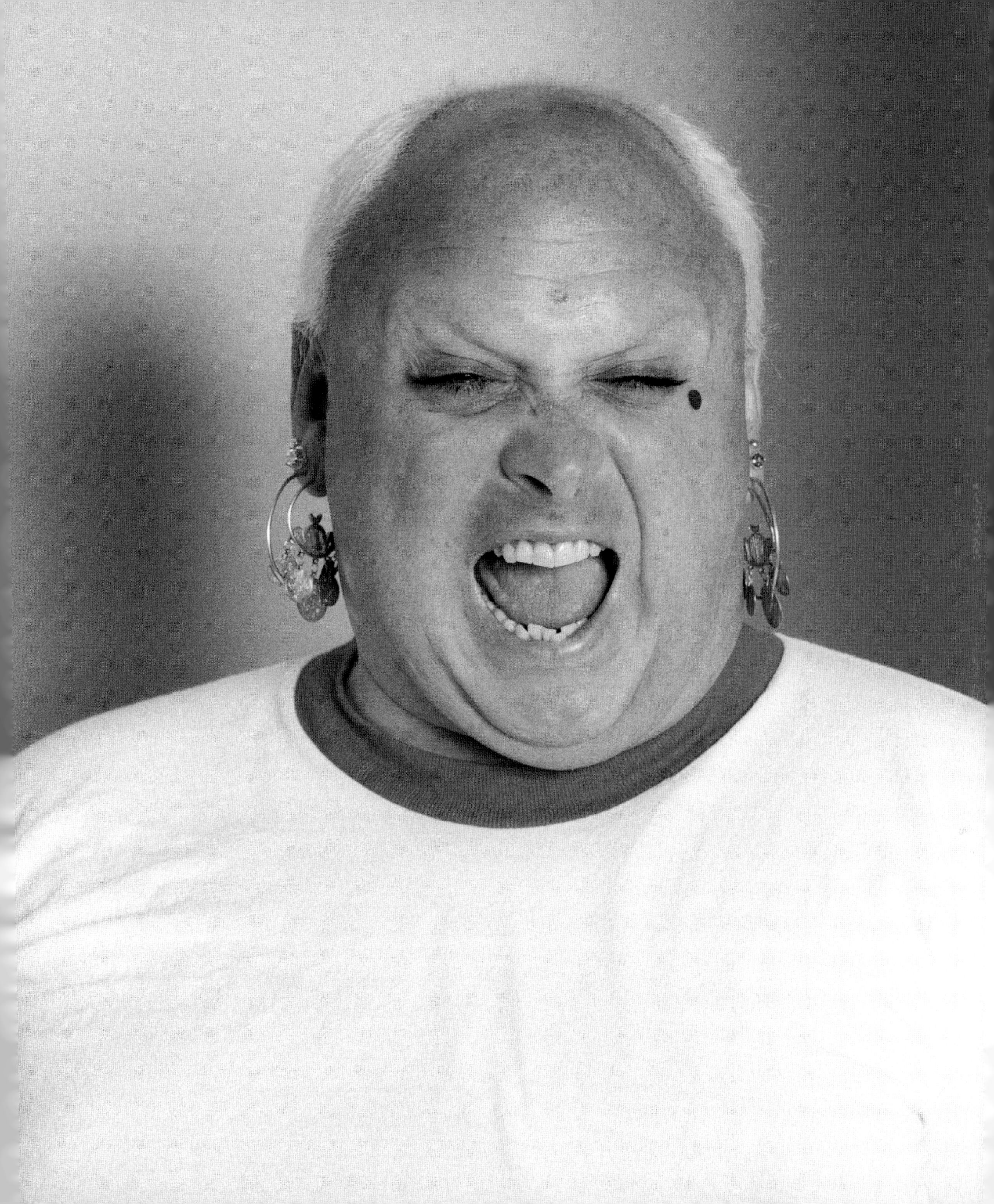

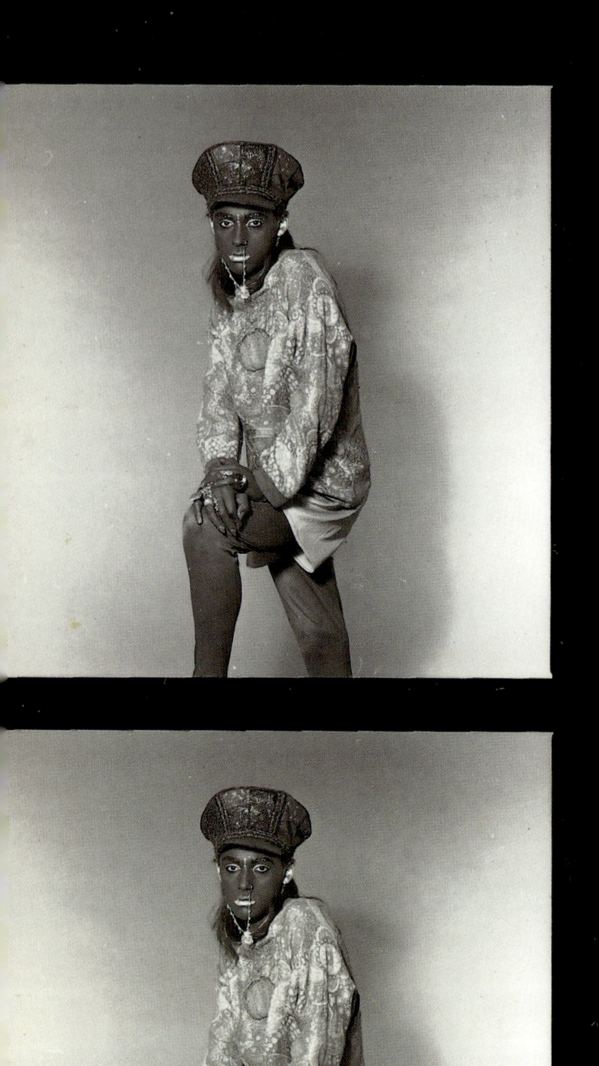

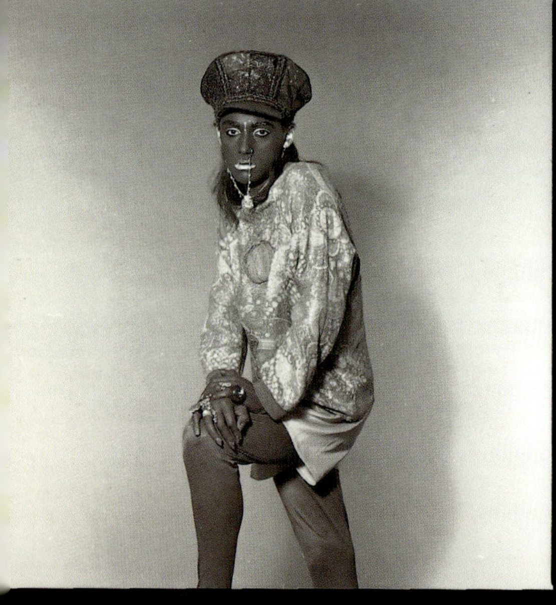

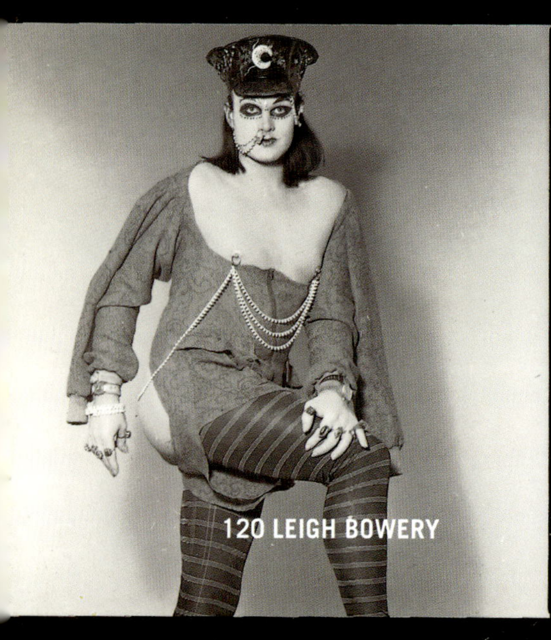
120 LEIGH BOWERY

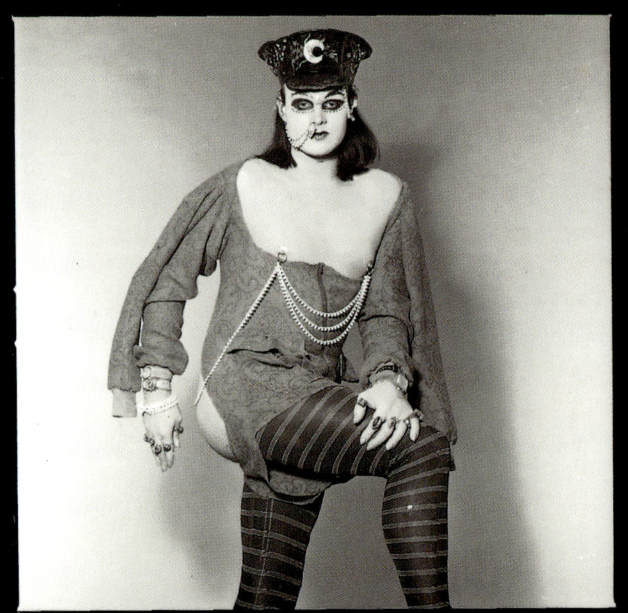

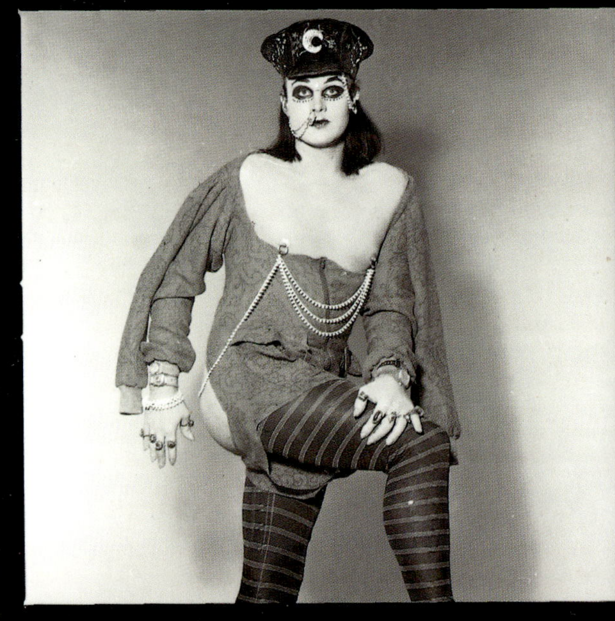

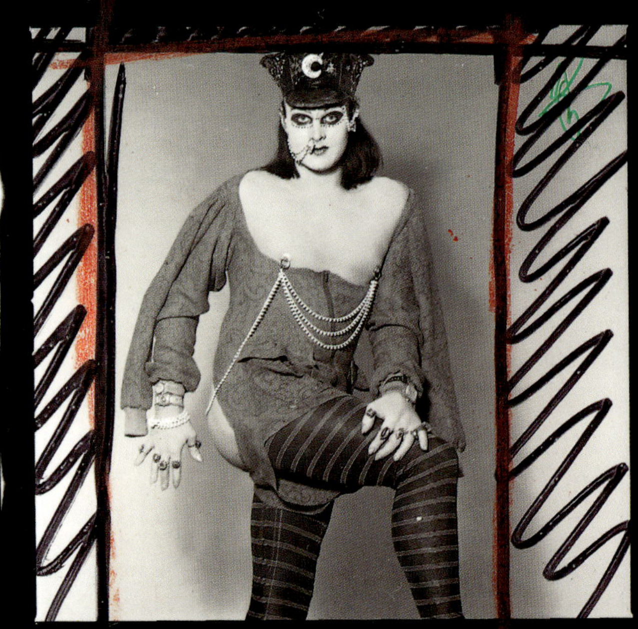

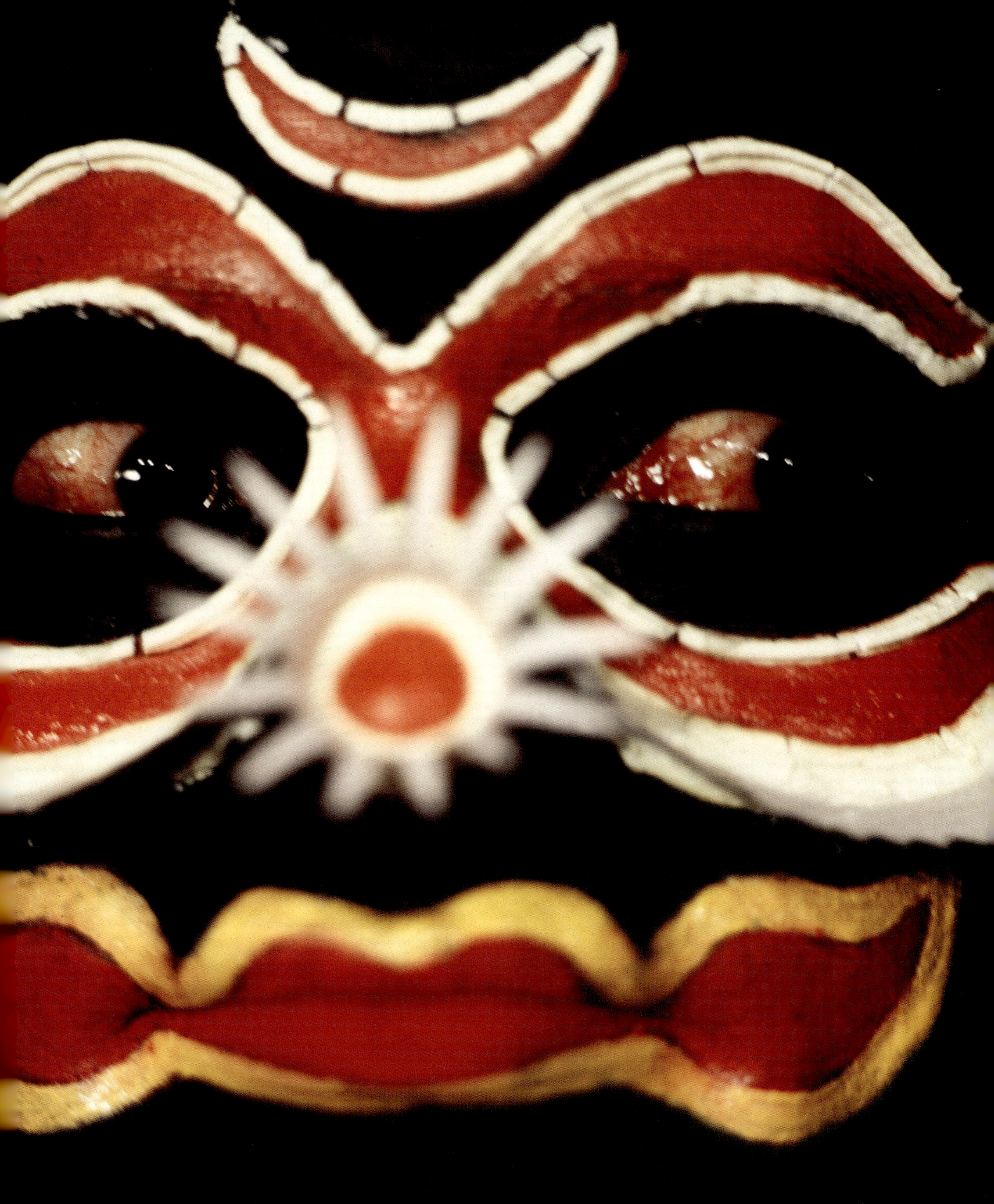

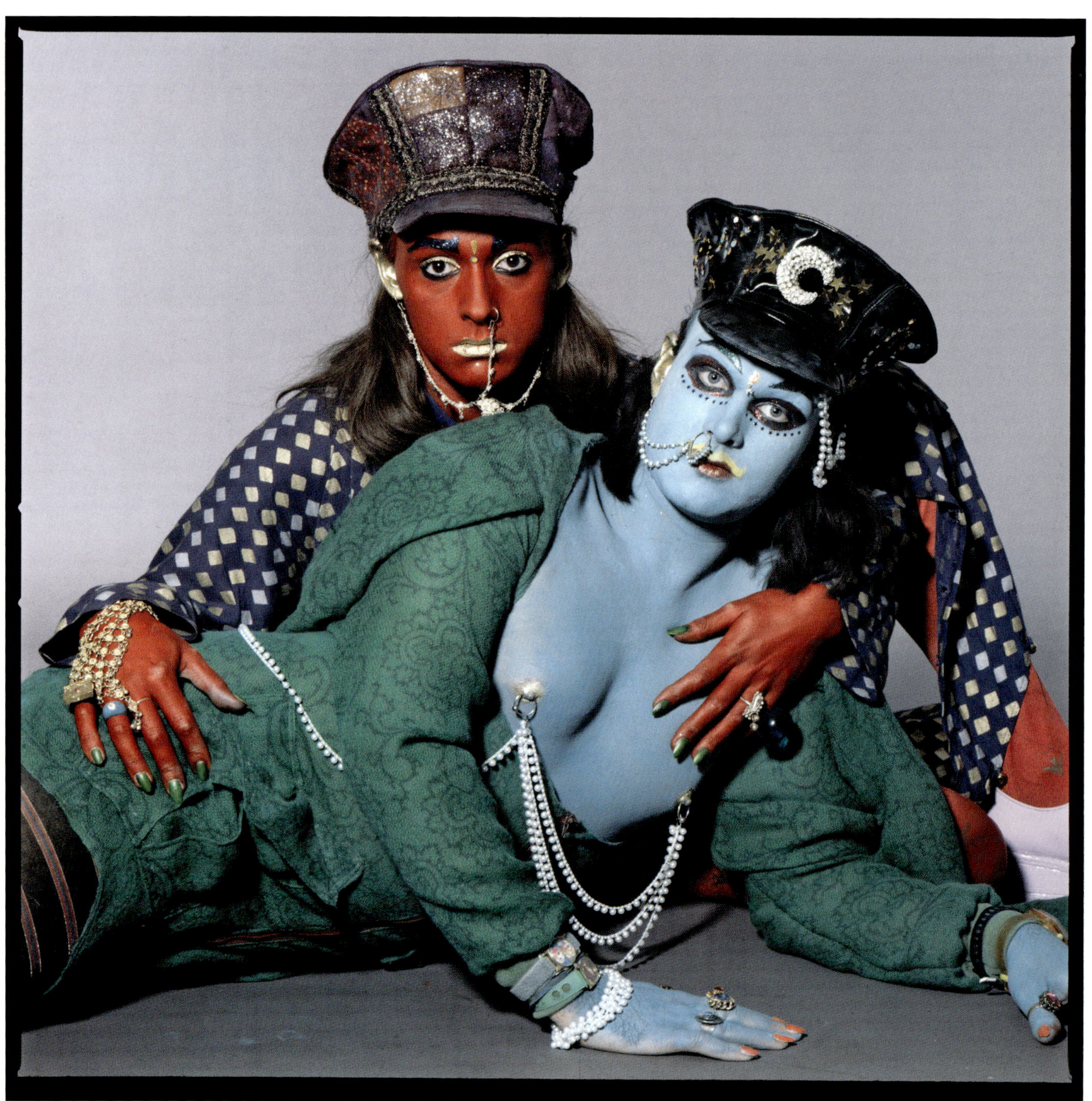

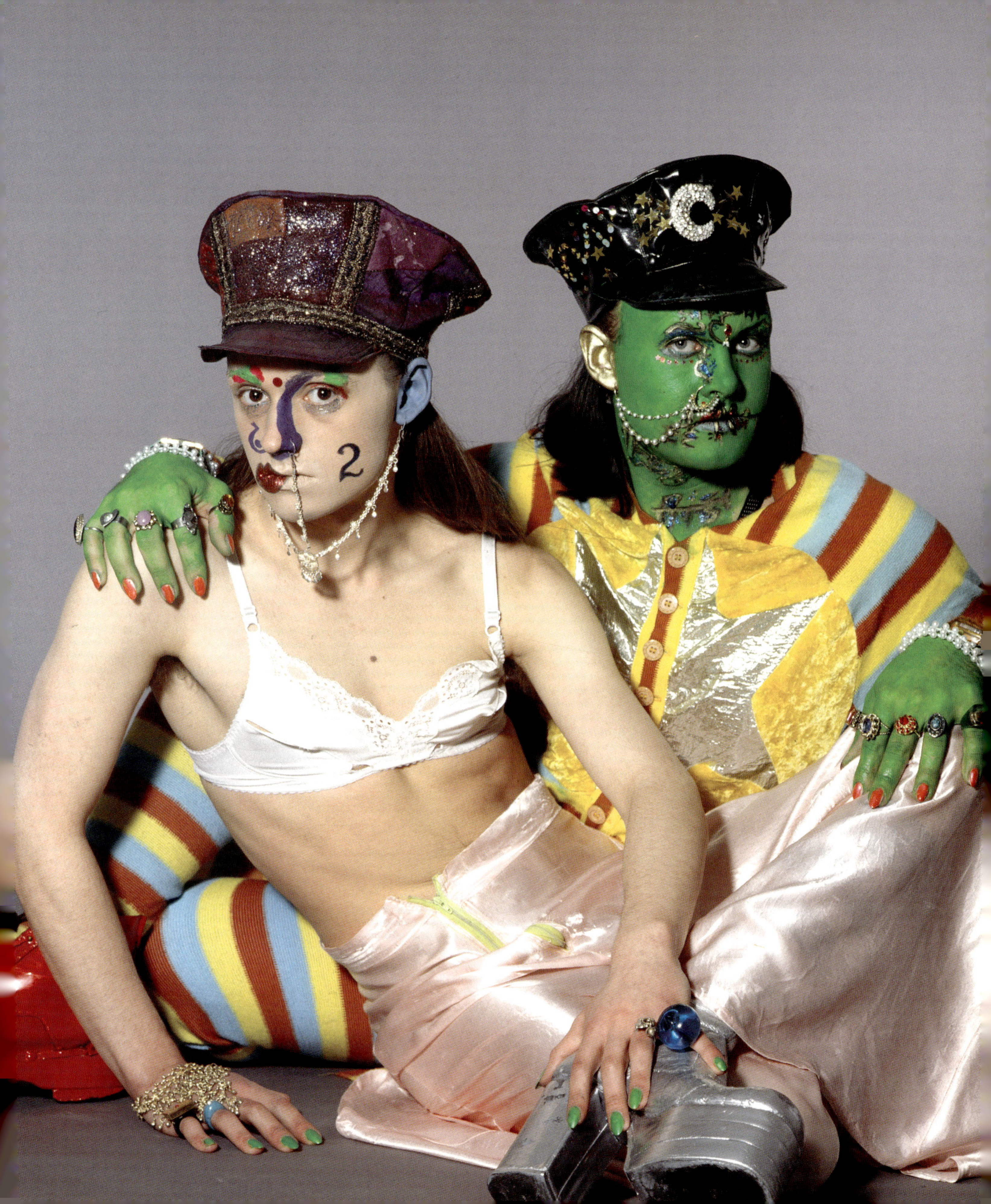

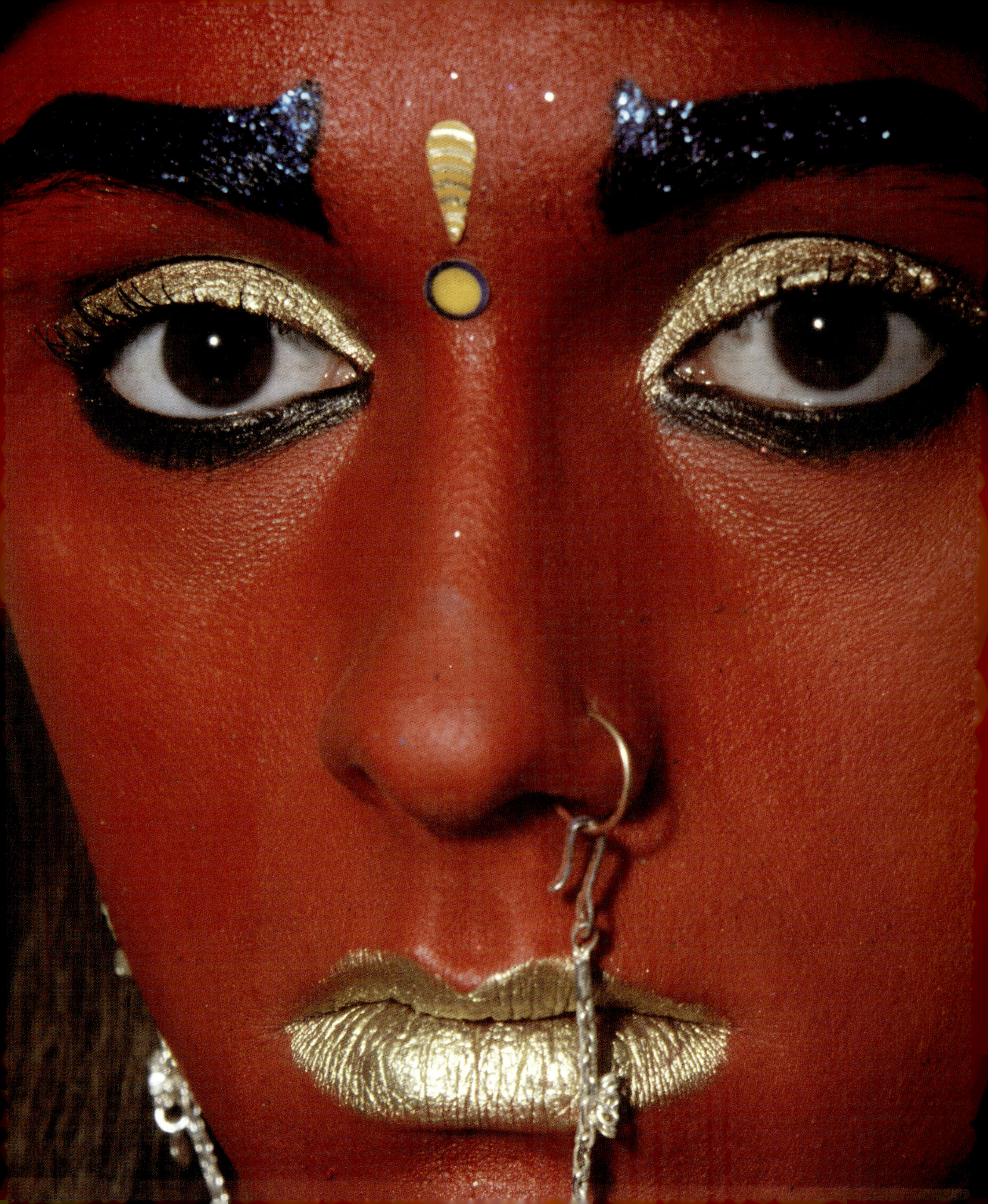

I met Leigh and Trojan in a club in SoHo in the early eighties and I was immediately wowed by the way they looked. They reminded me of the Kathakali dancers from Kerala that I had photographed a decade earlier. When I shot them in their famous "Pakis From Outer Space" look, they came all the way from the East End to my Fulham Studio in full make up on the London tube!

I met Leigh and Trojan
in a club in SoHo in the
early eighties and I was
immediately wowed by the
way they looked. They re-
minded me of the Kathakali
dancers from Kerala that
I had photographed a de-
cade earlier. When I shot
them in their famous "Pakis From Outer Space" look,
they came all the way from
the East End to my Fulham
Studio in full make up on
the London tube!

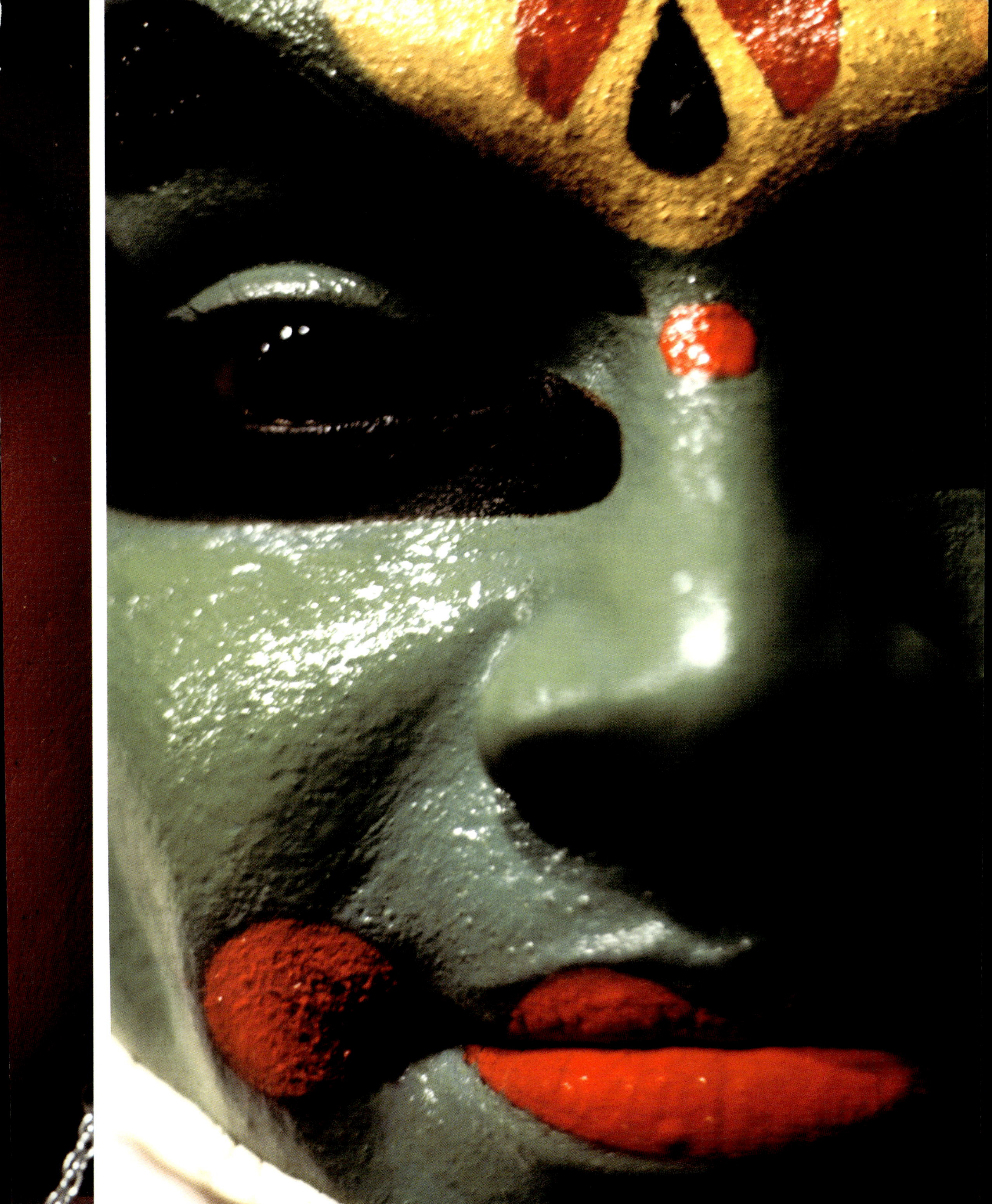

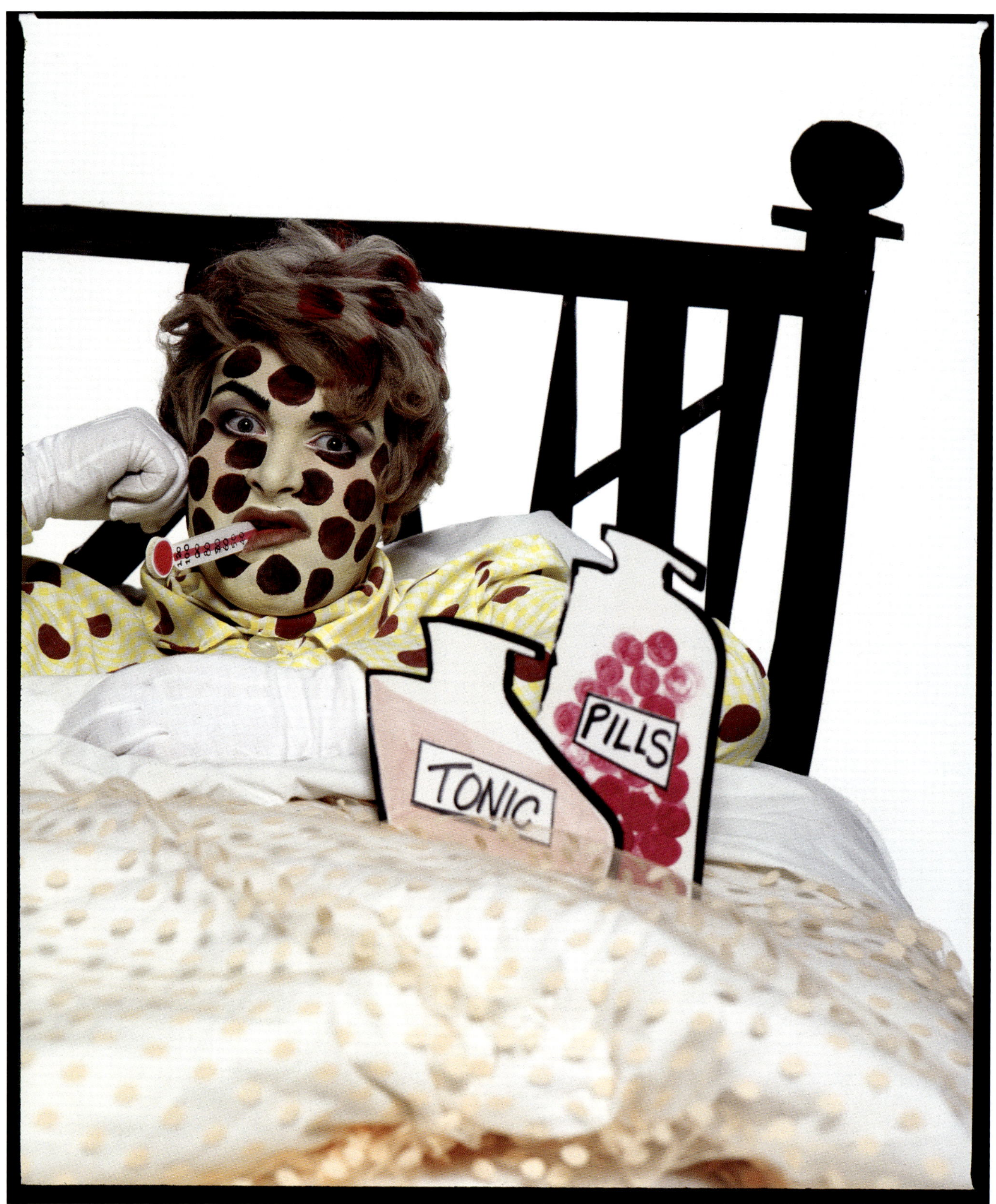

TONIC
PILLS

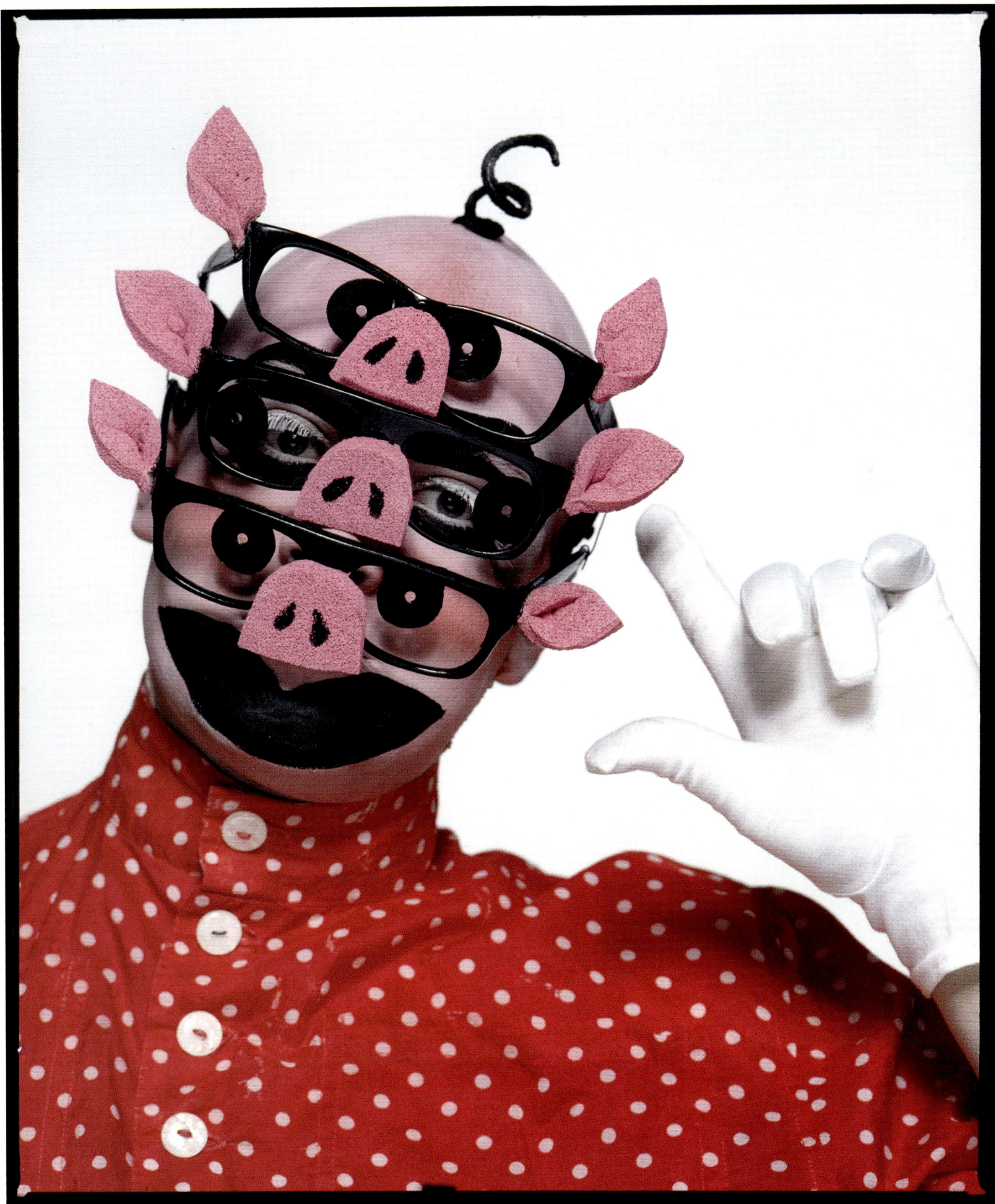

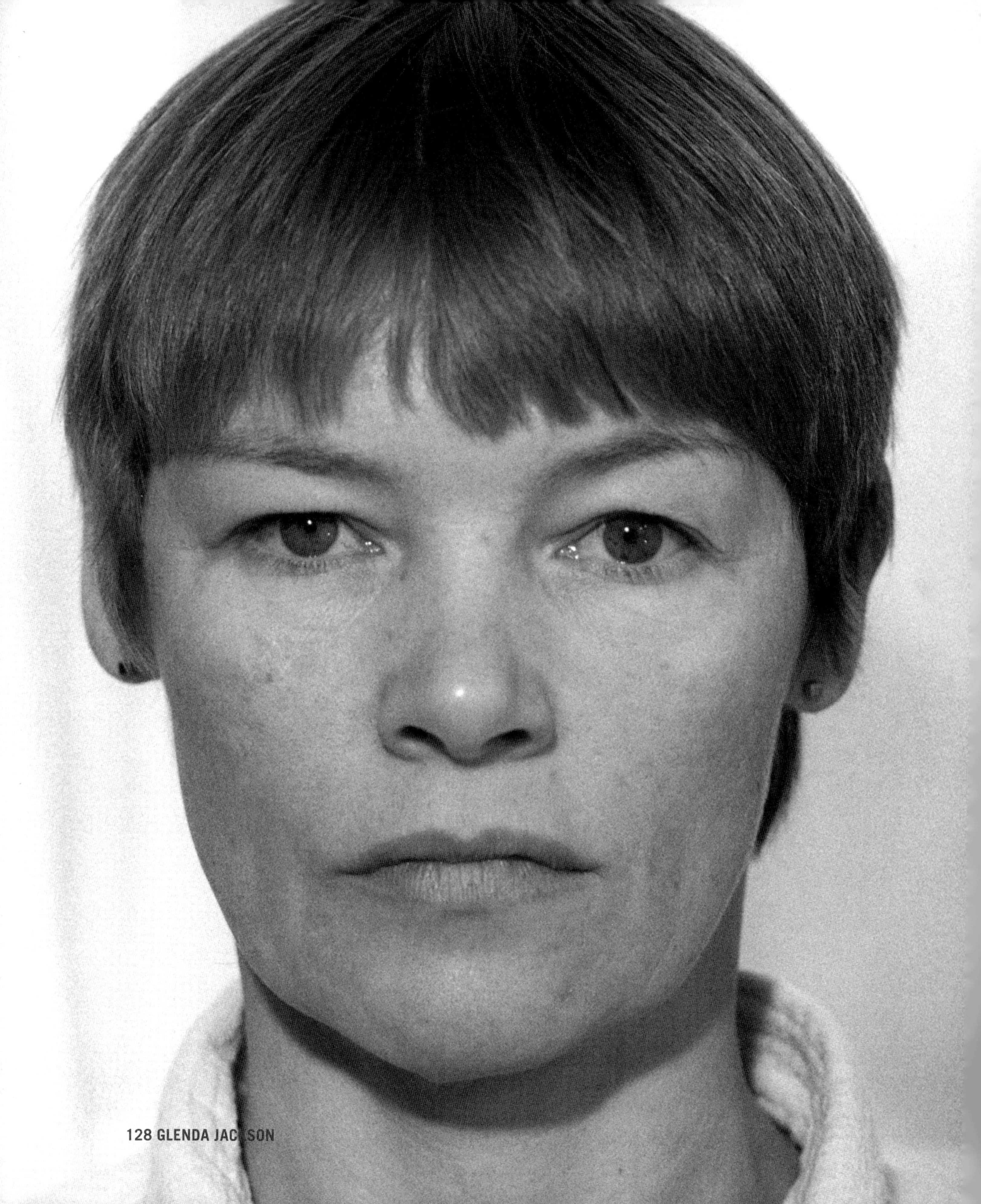
128 GLENDA JACKSON

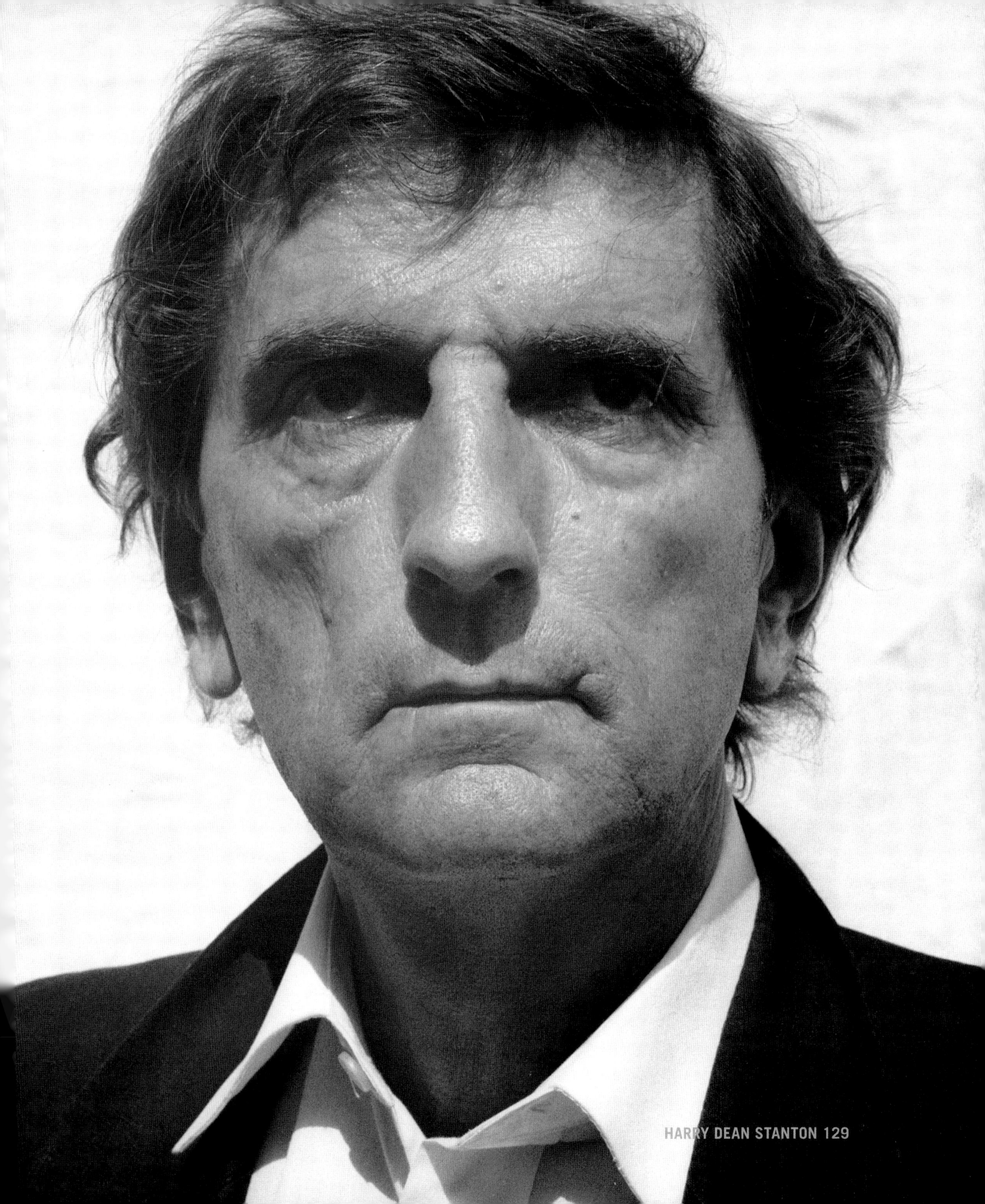
HARRY DEAN STANTON 129

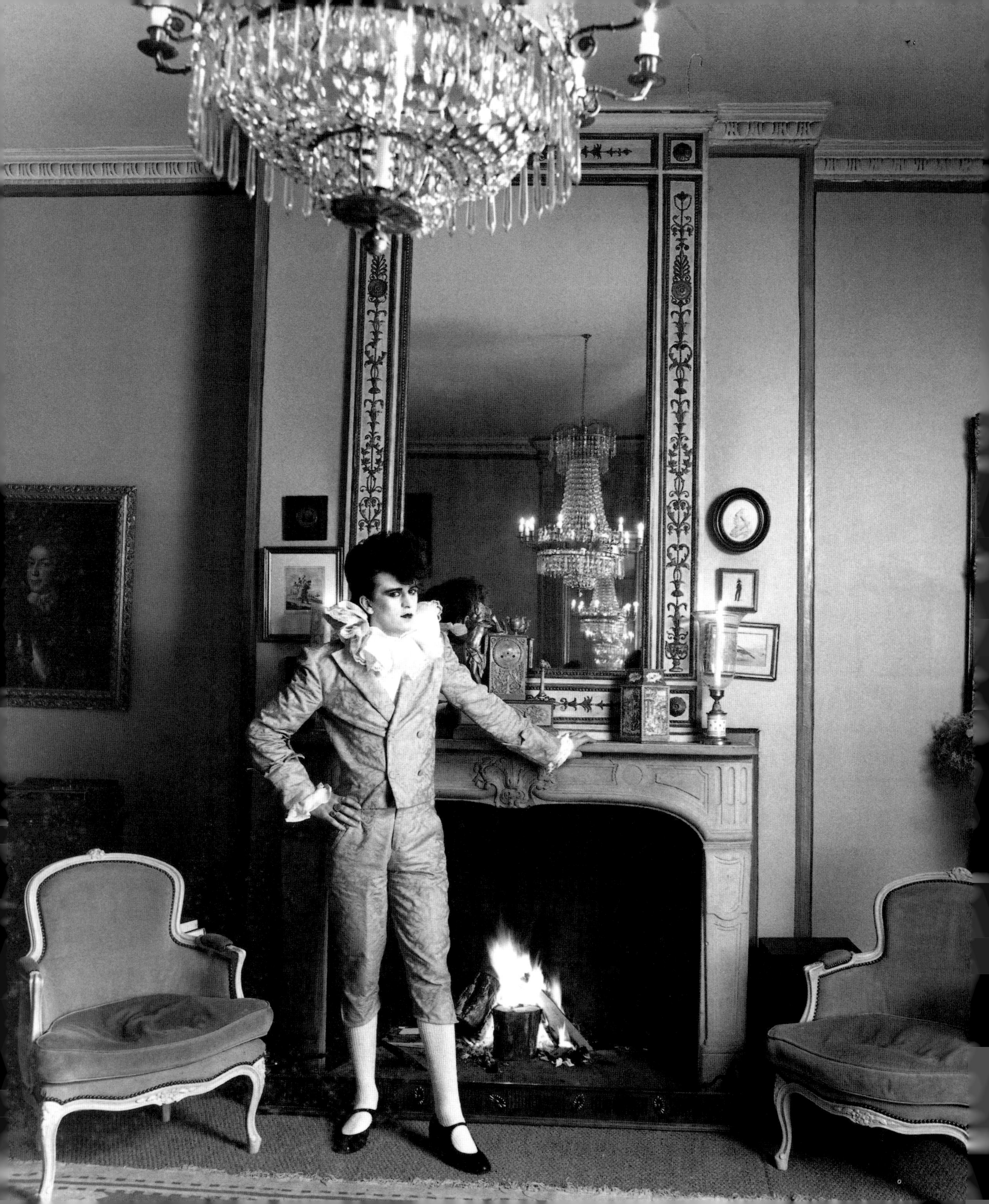

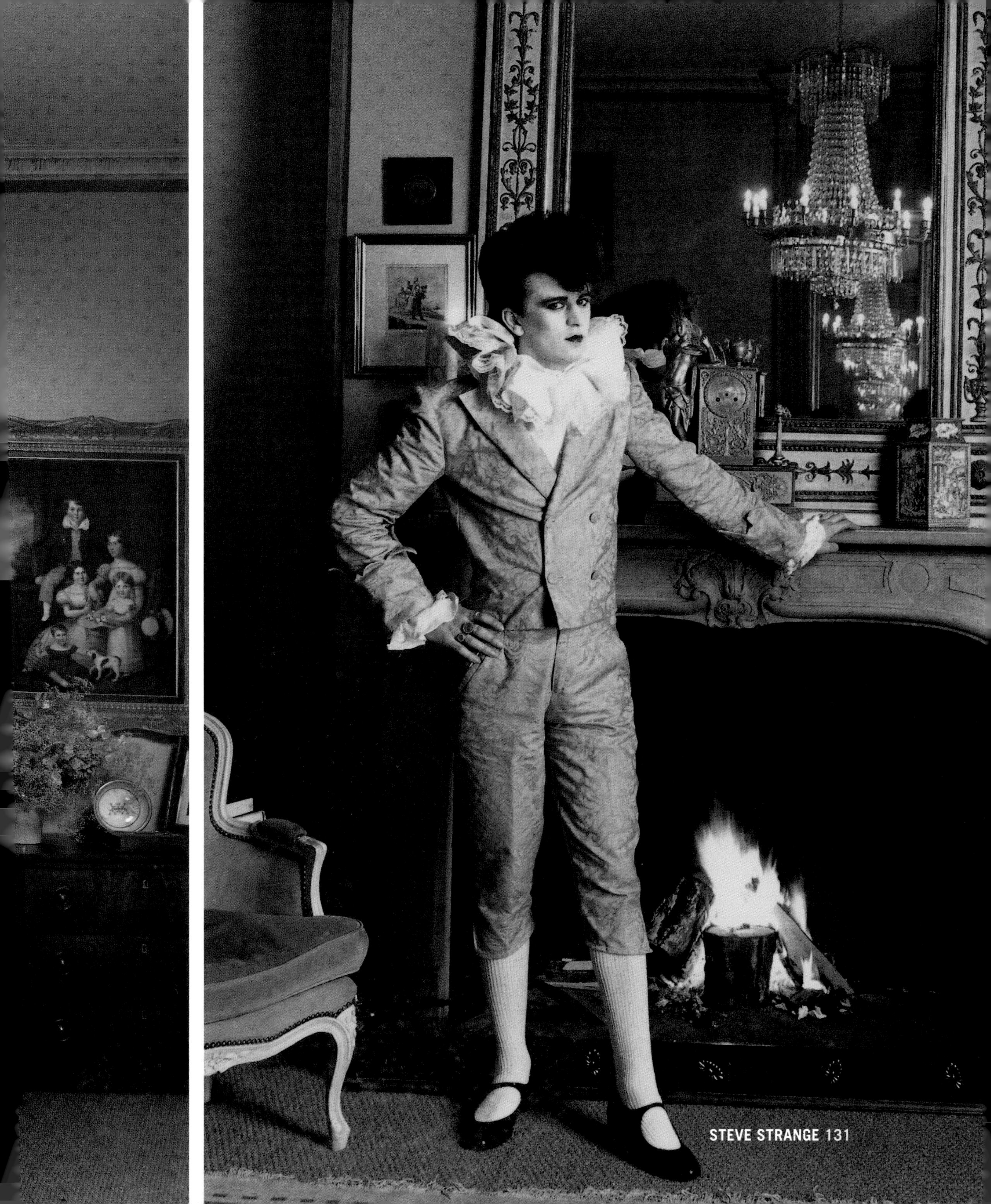
STEVE STRANGE 131

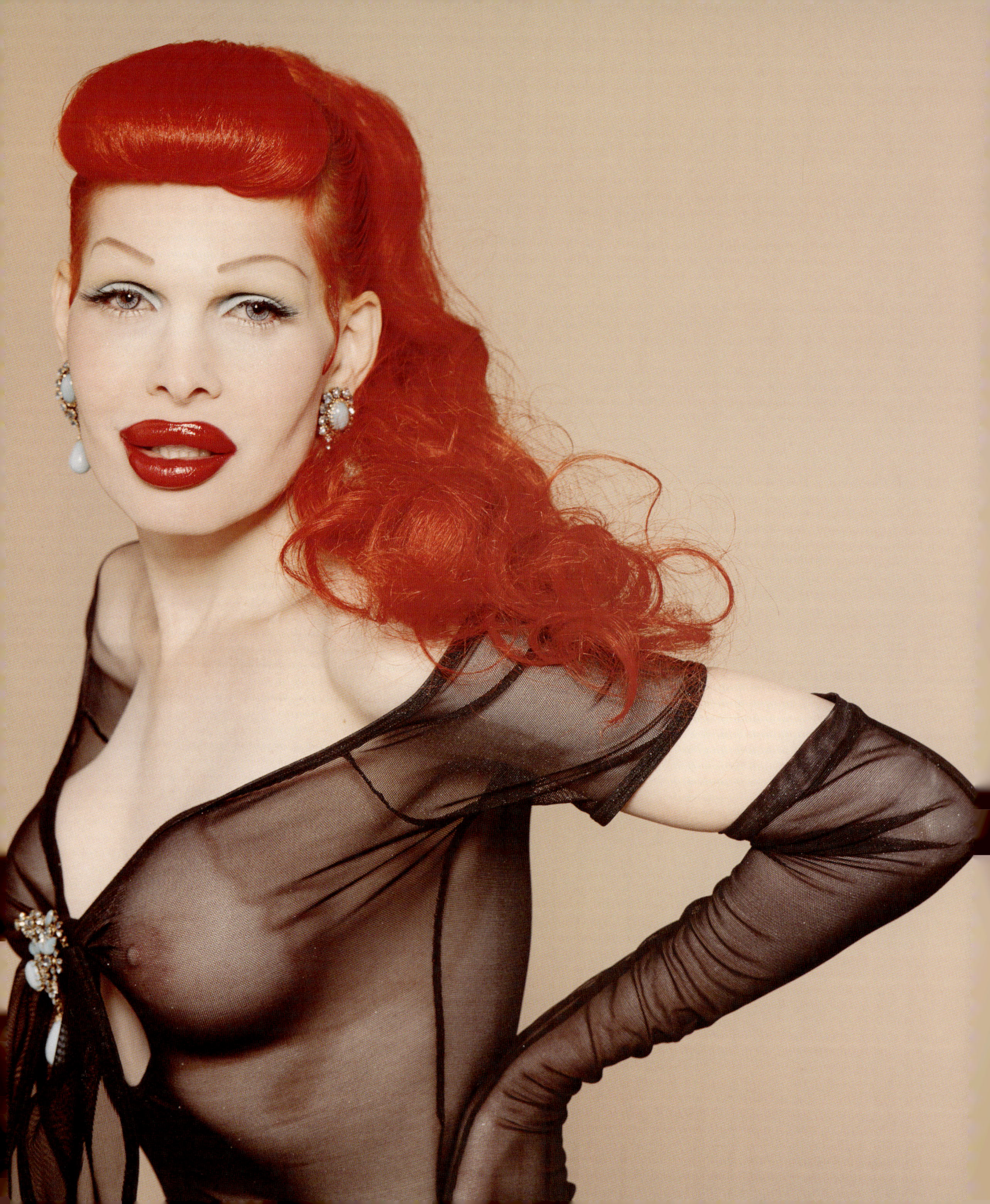

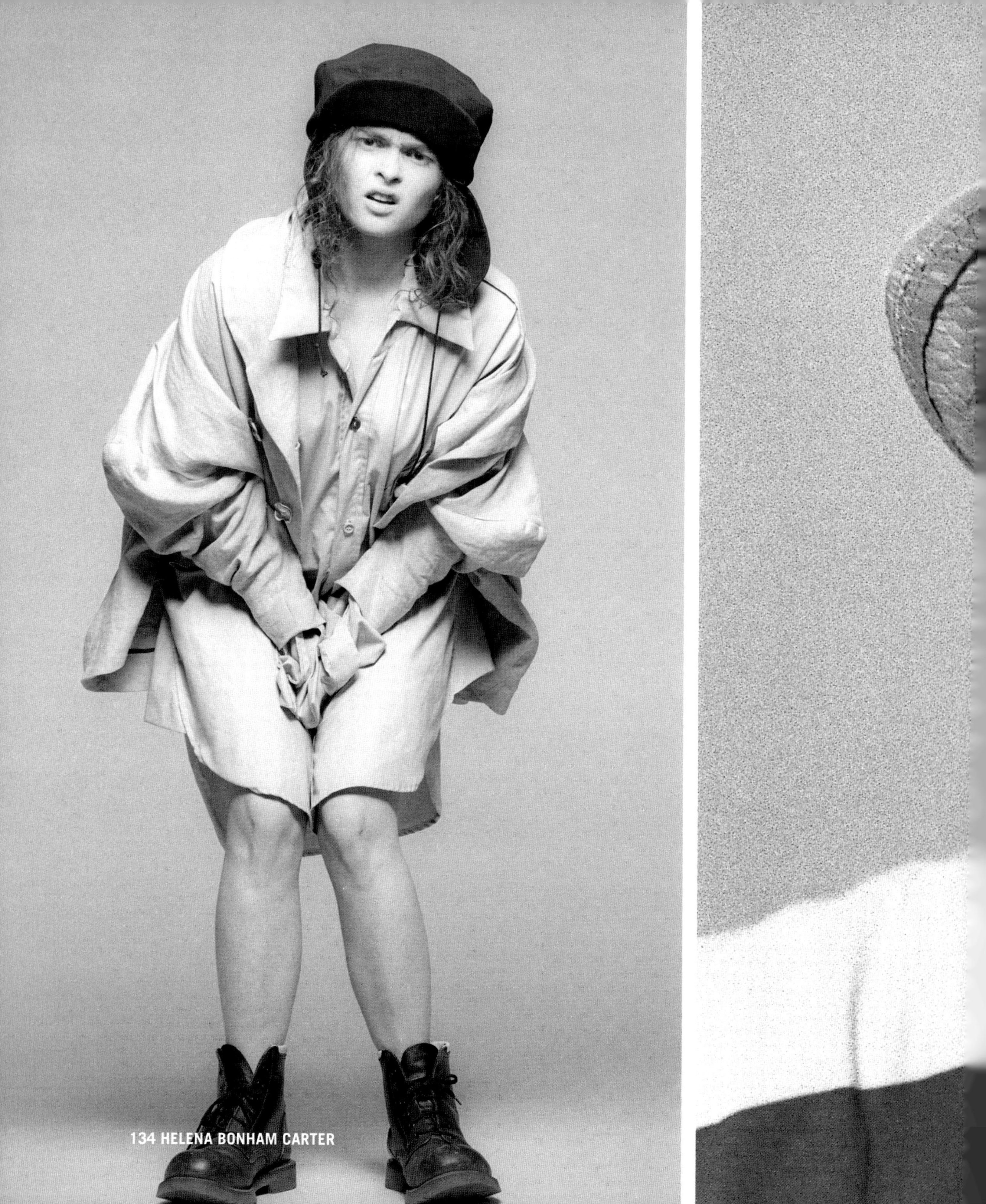
134 HELENA BONHAM CARTER

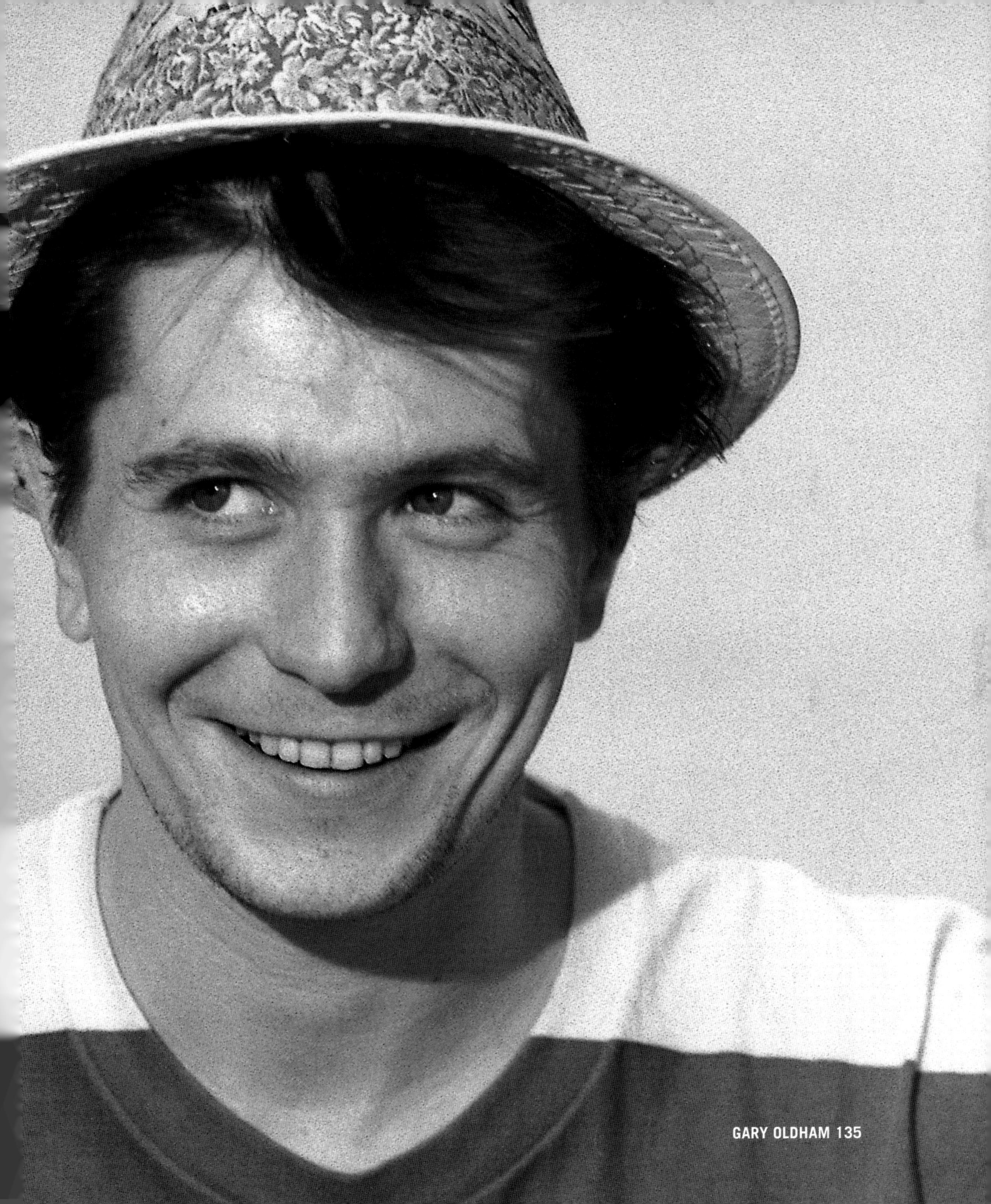
GARY OLDHAM 135

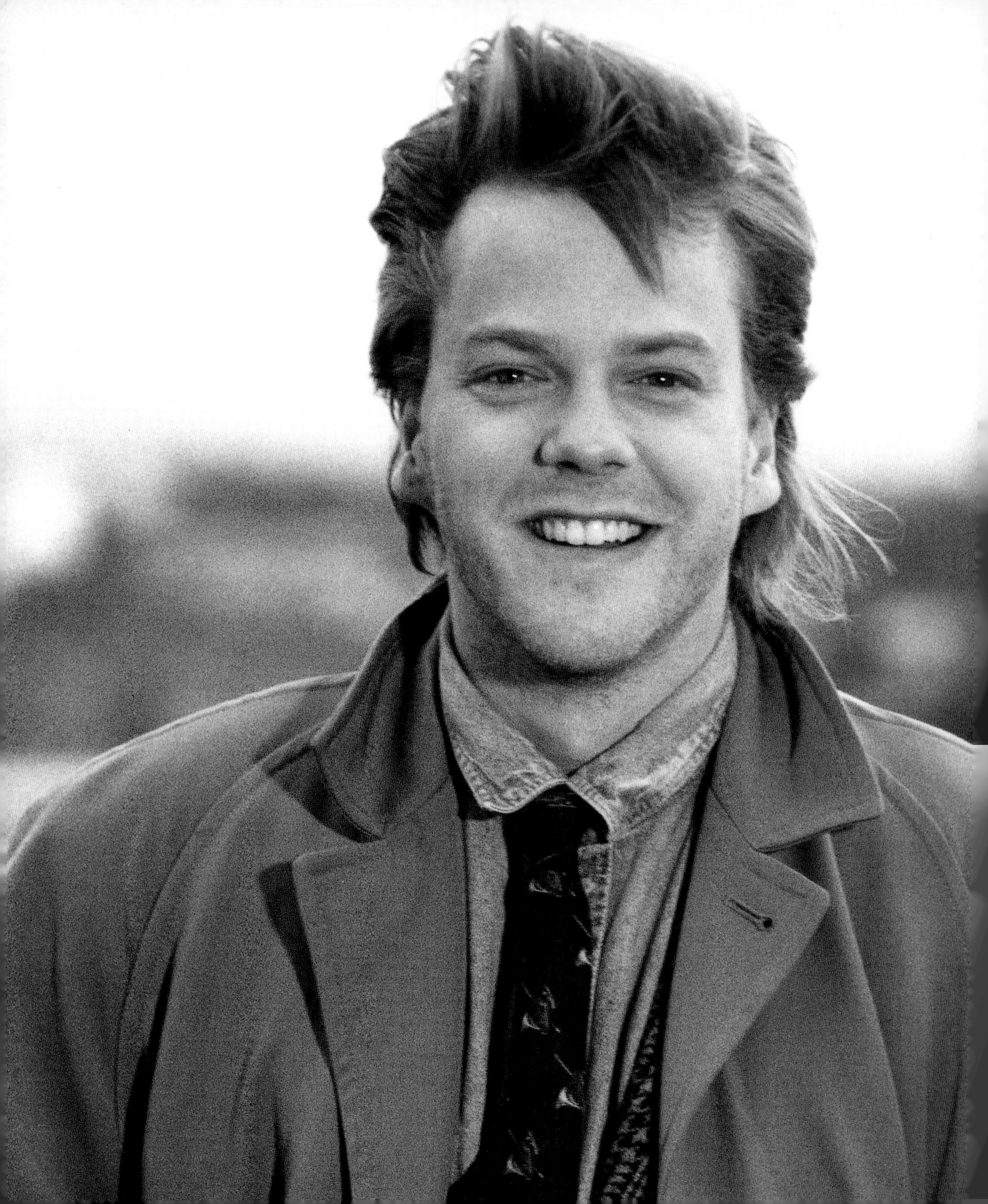

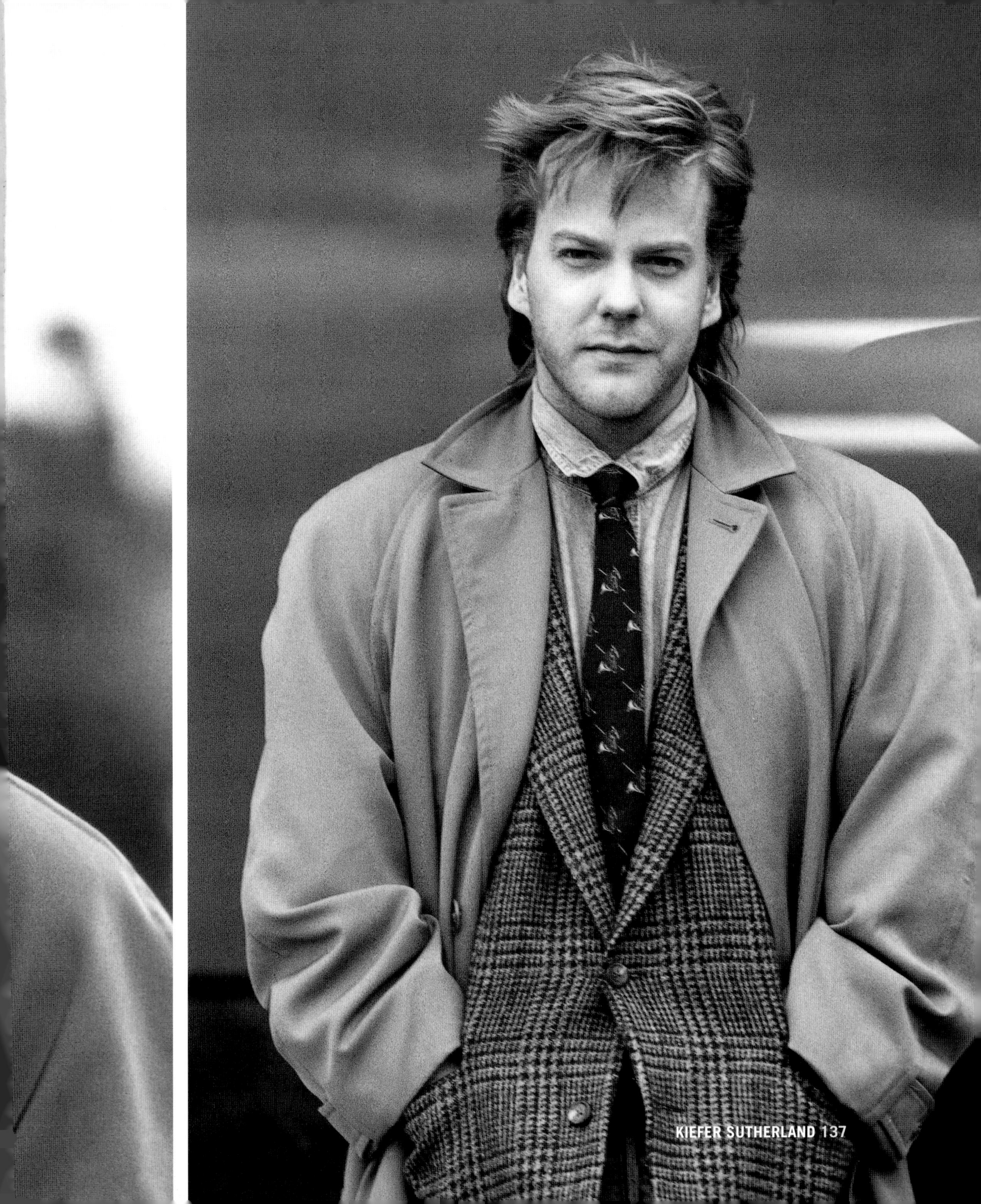

KIEFER SUTHERLAND 137

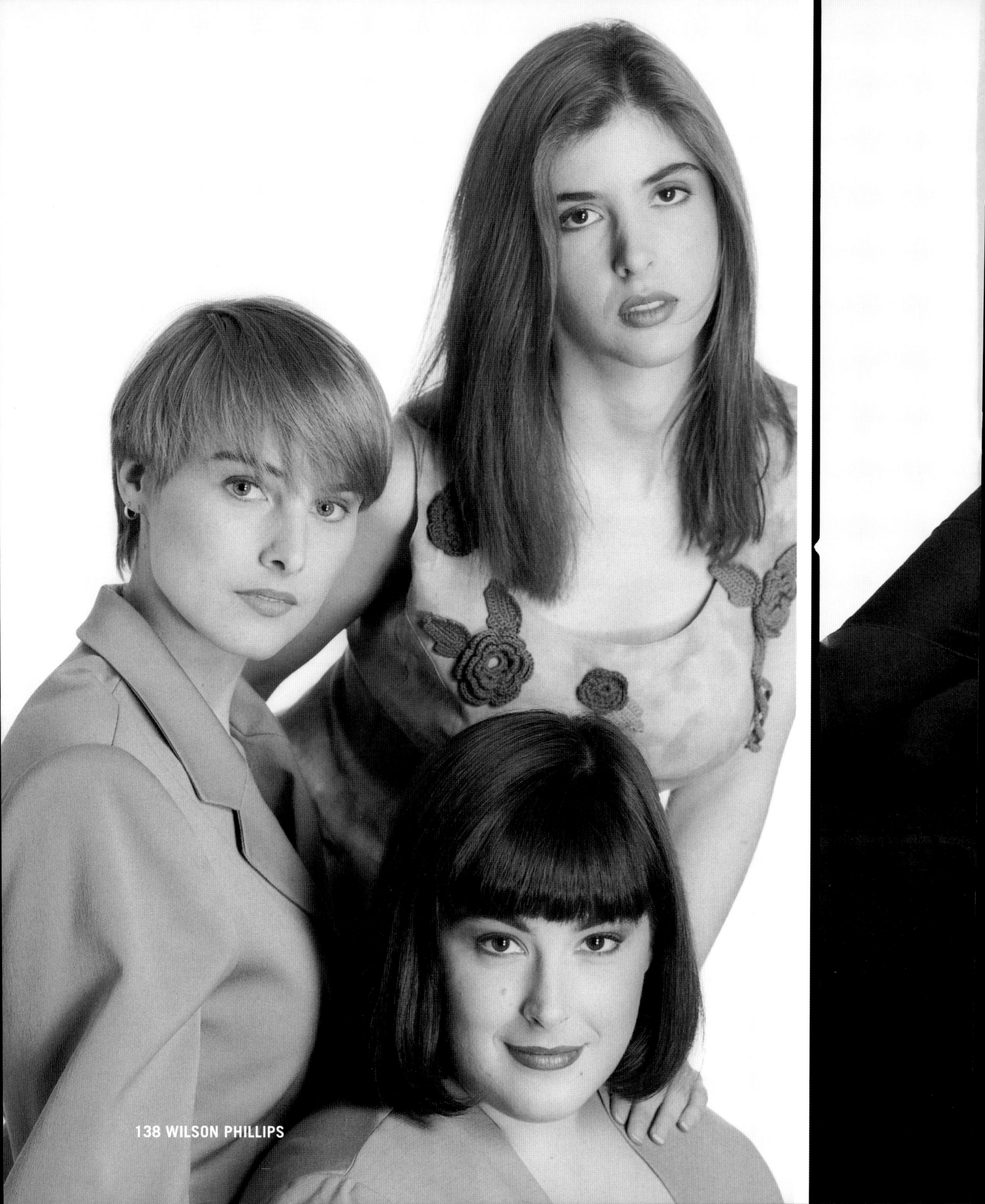
138 WILSON PHILLIPS

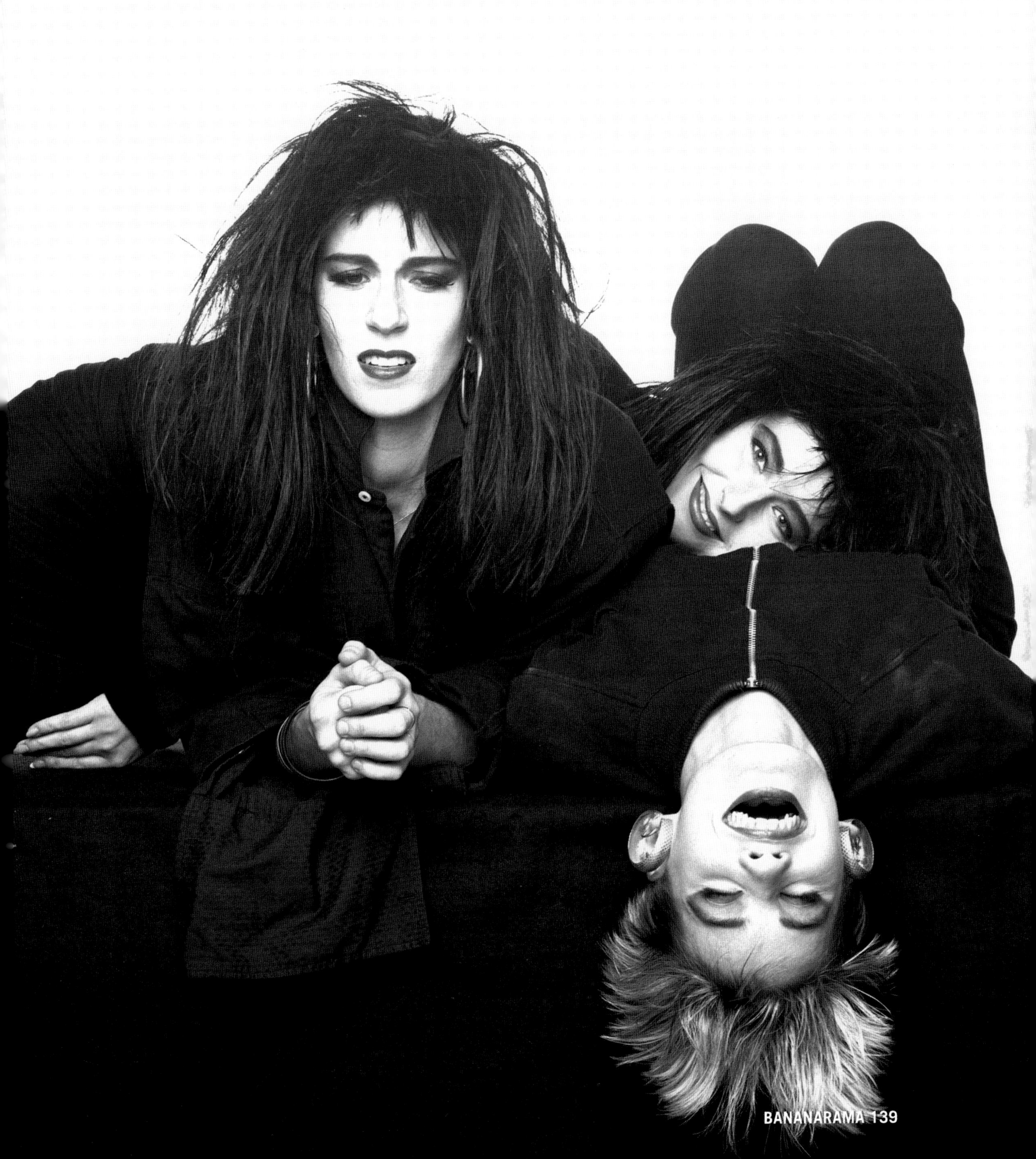
BANANARAMA 139

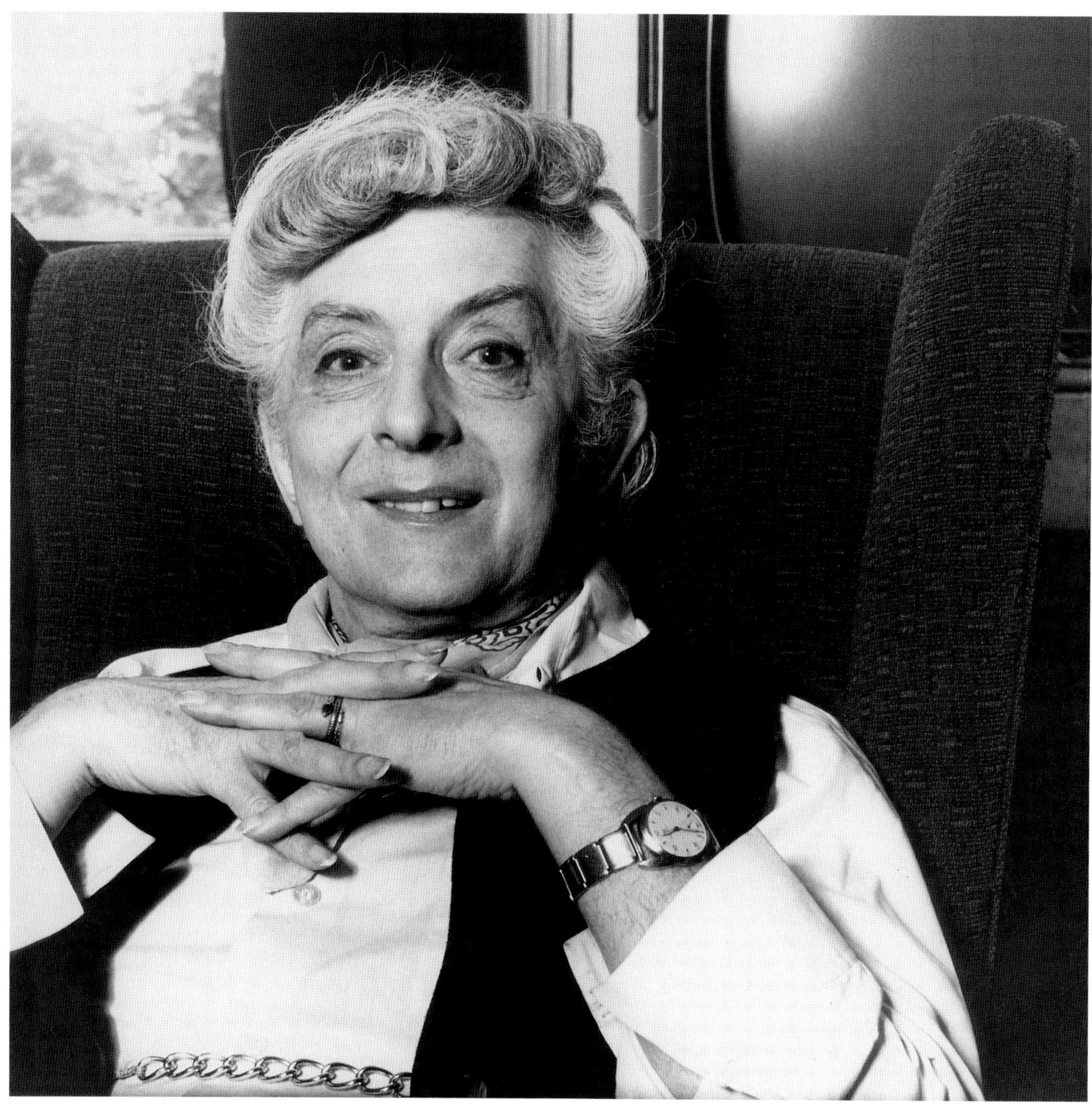

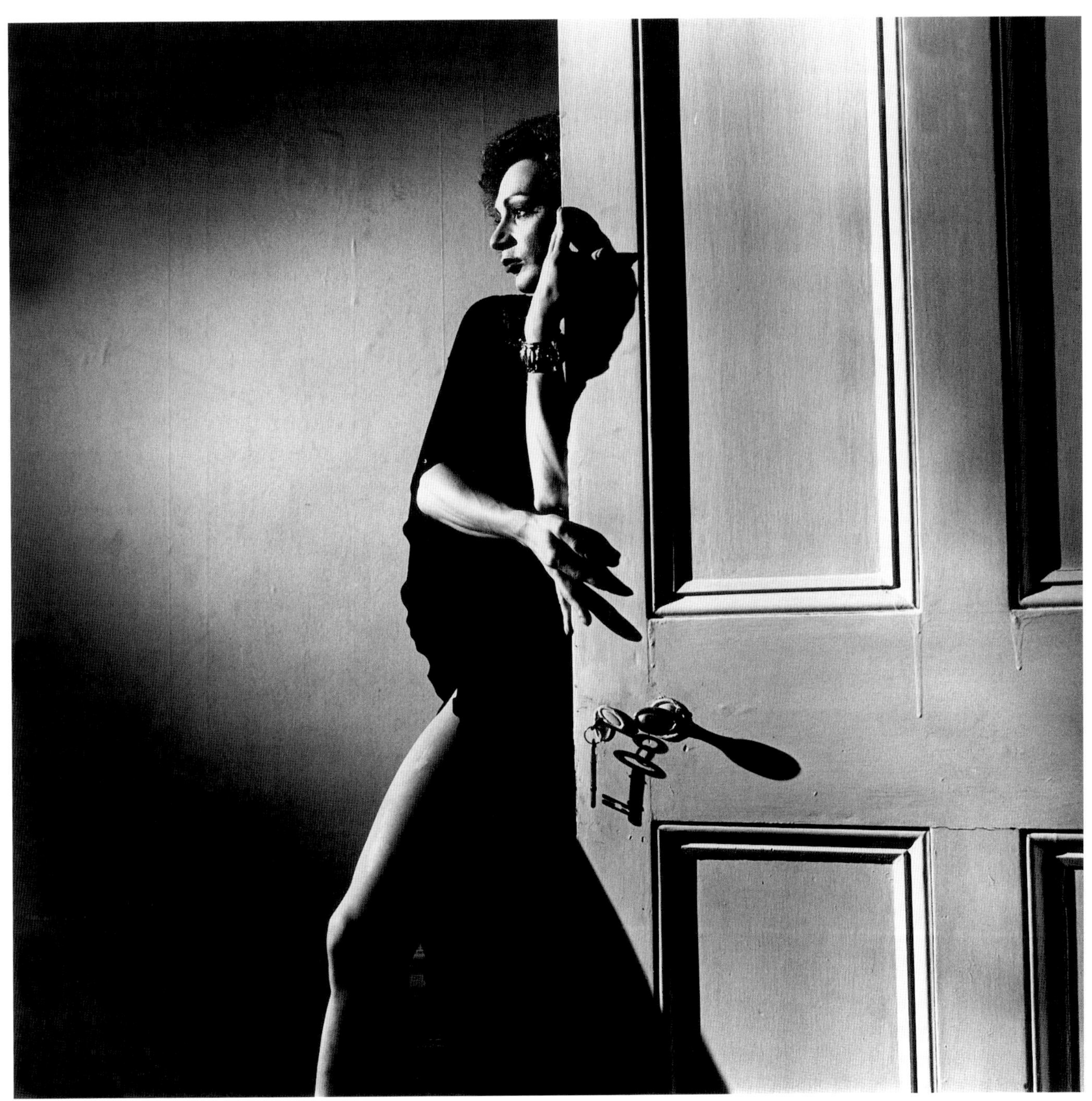

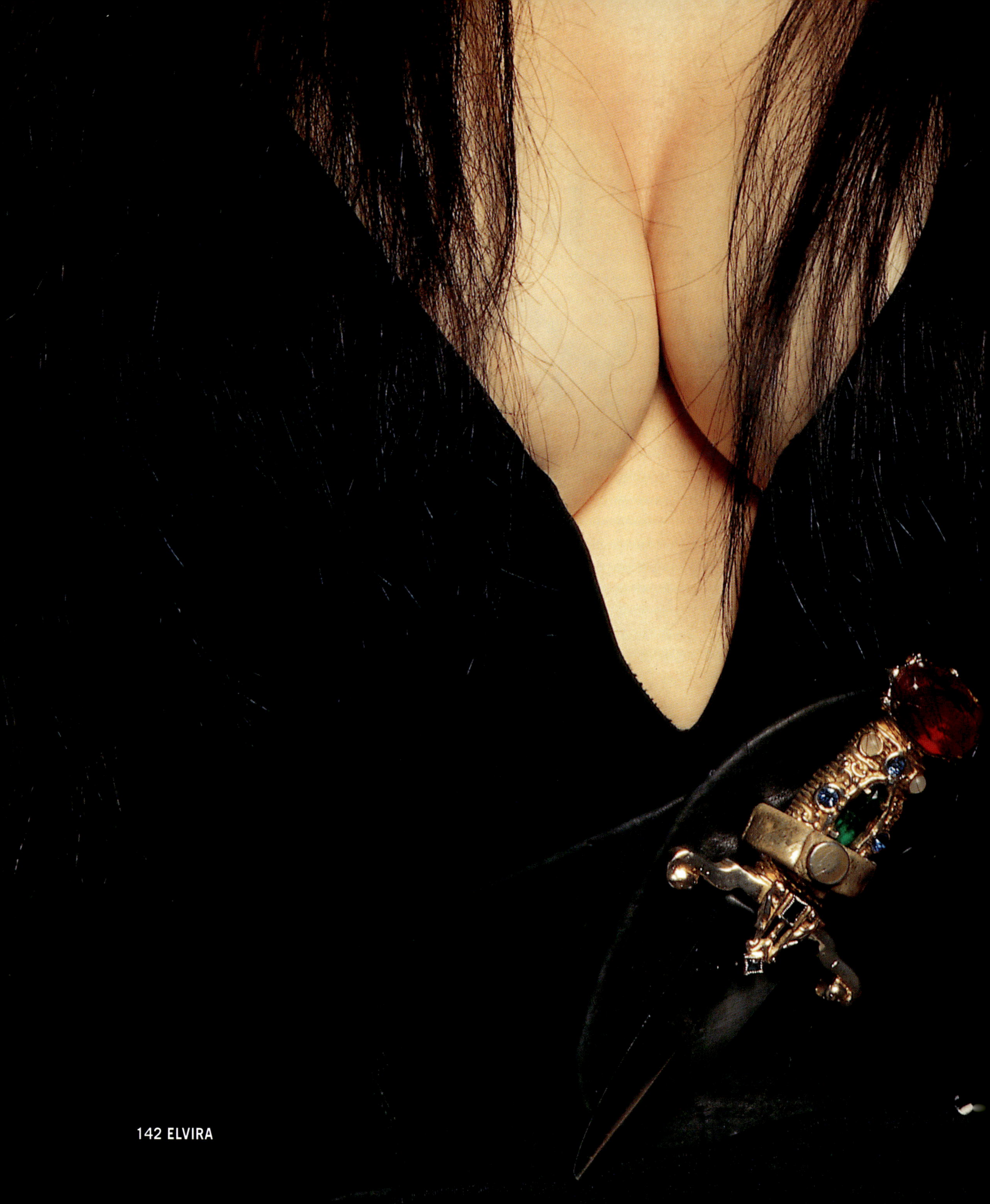
142 ELVIRA

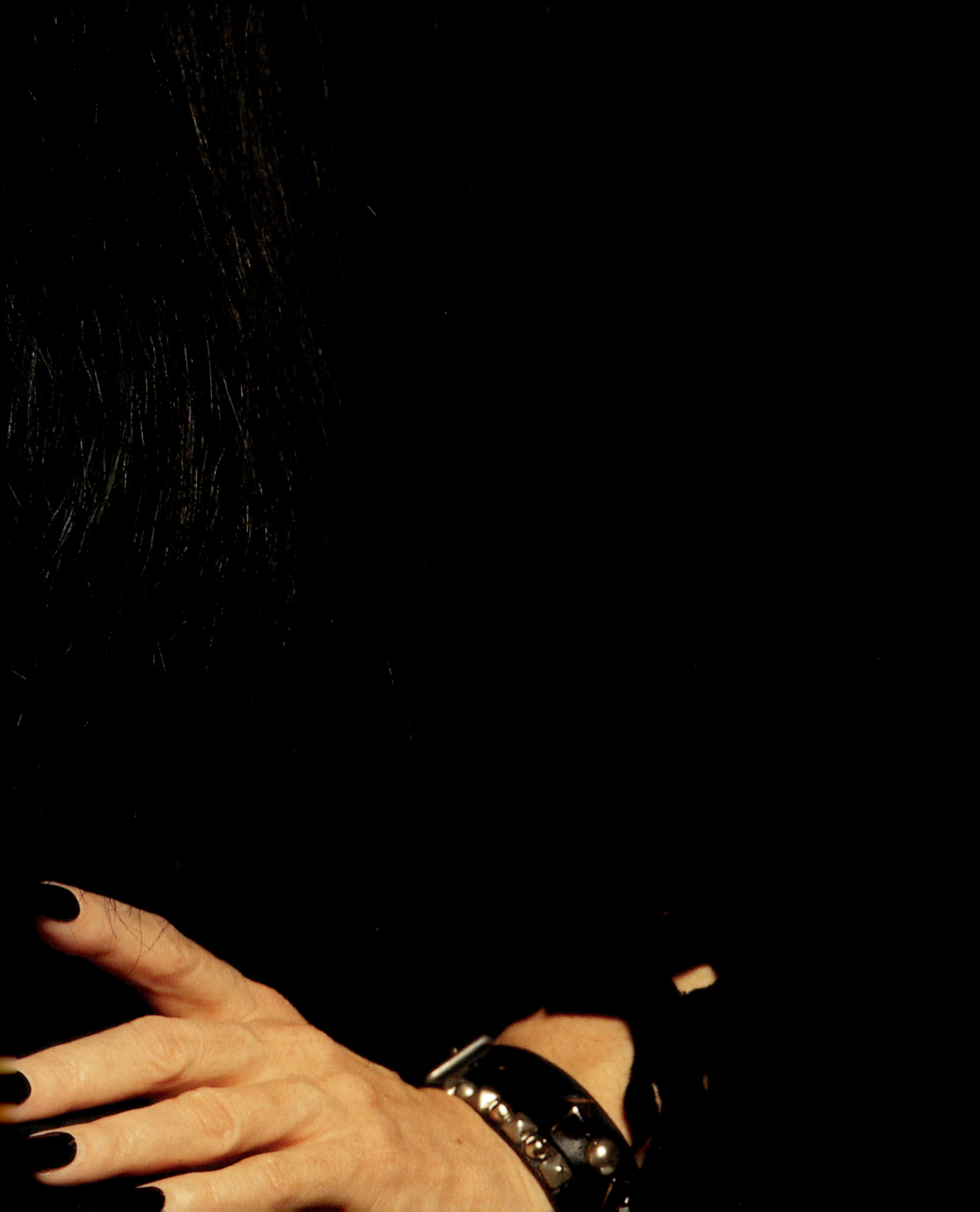

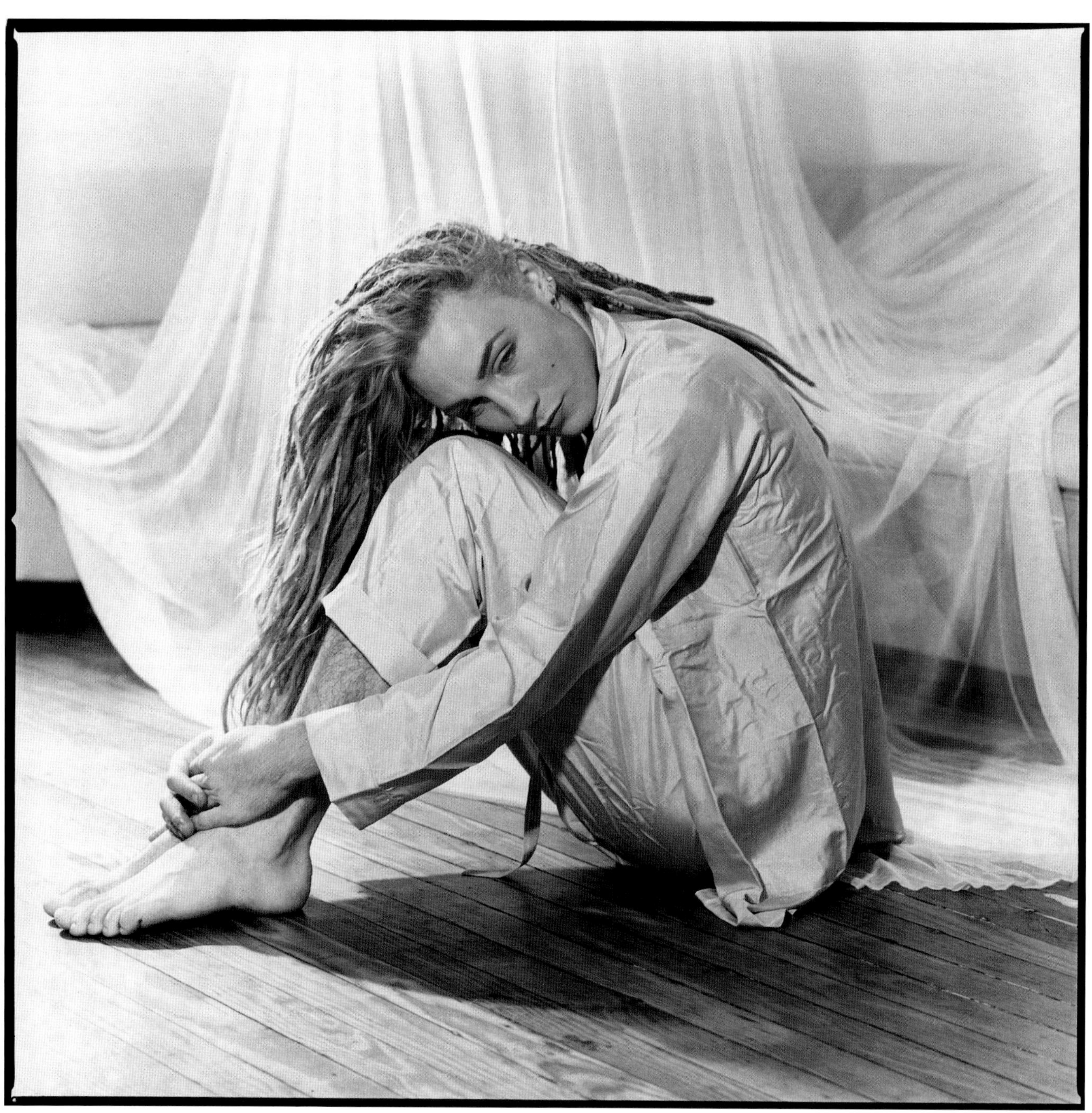

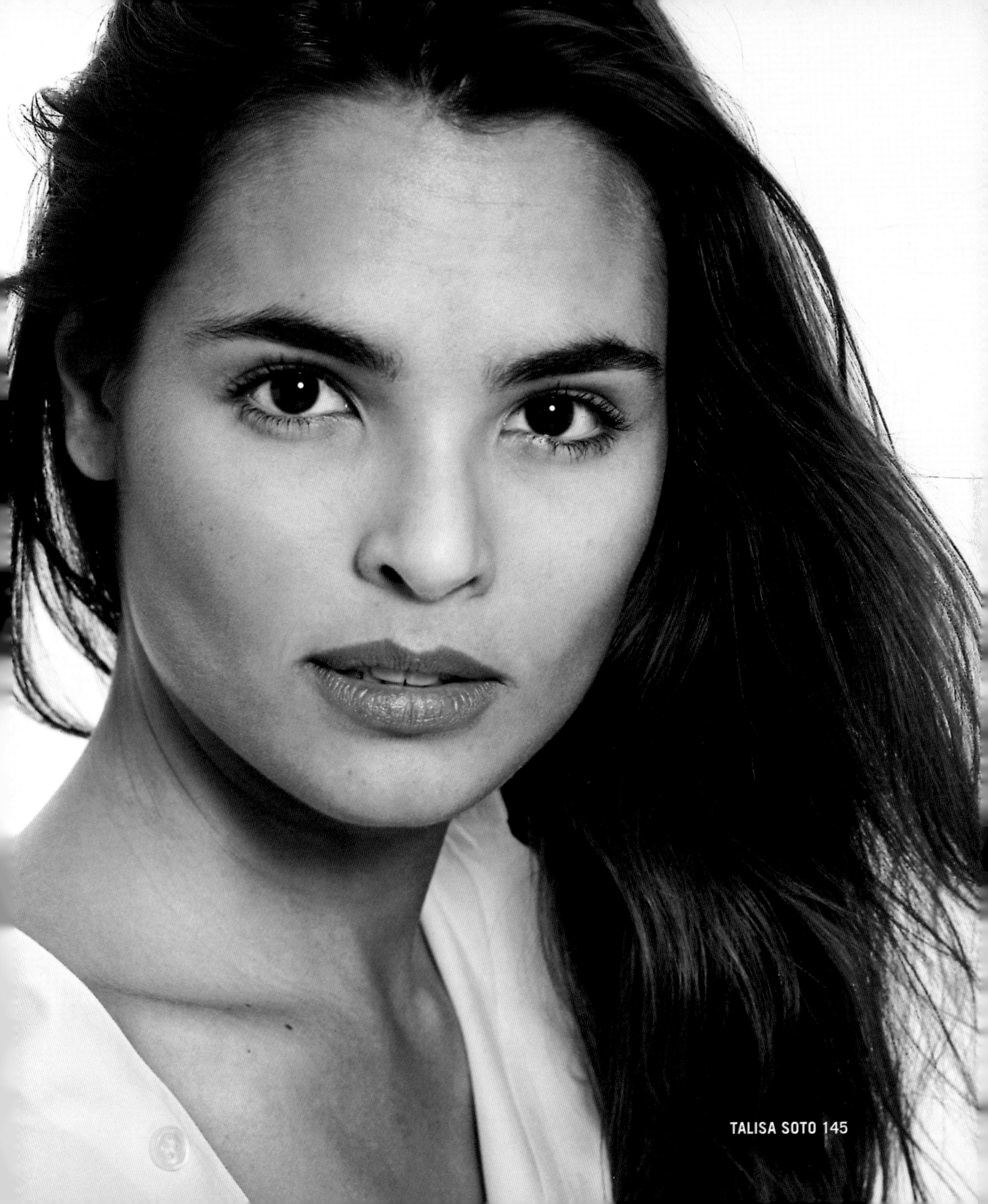
TALISA SOTO 145

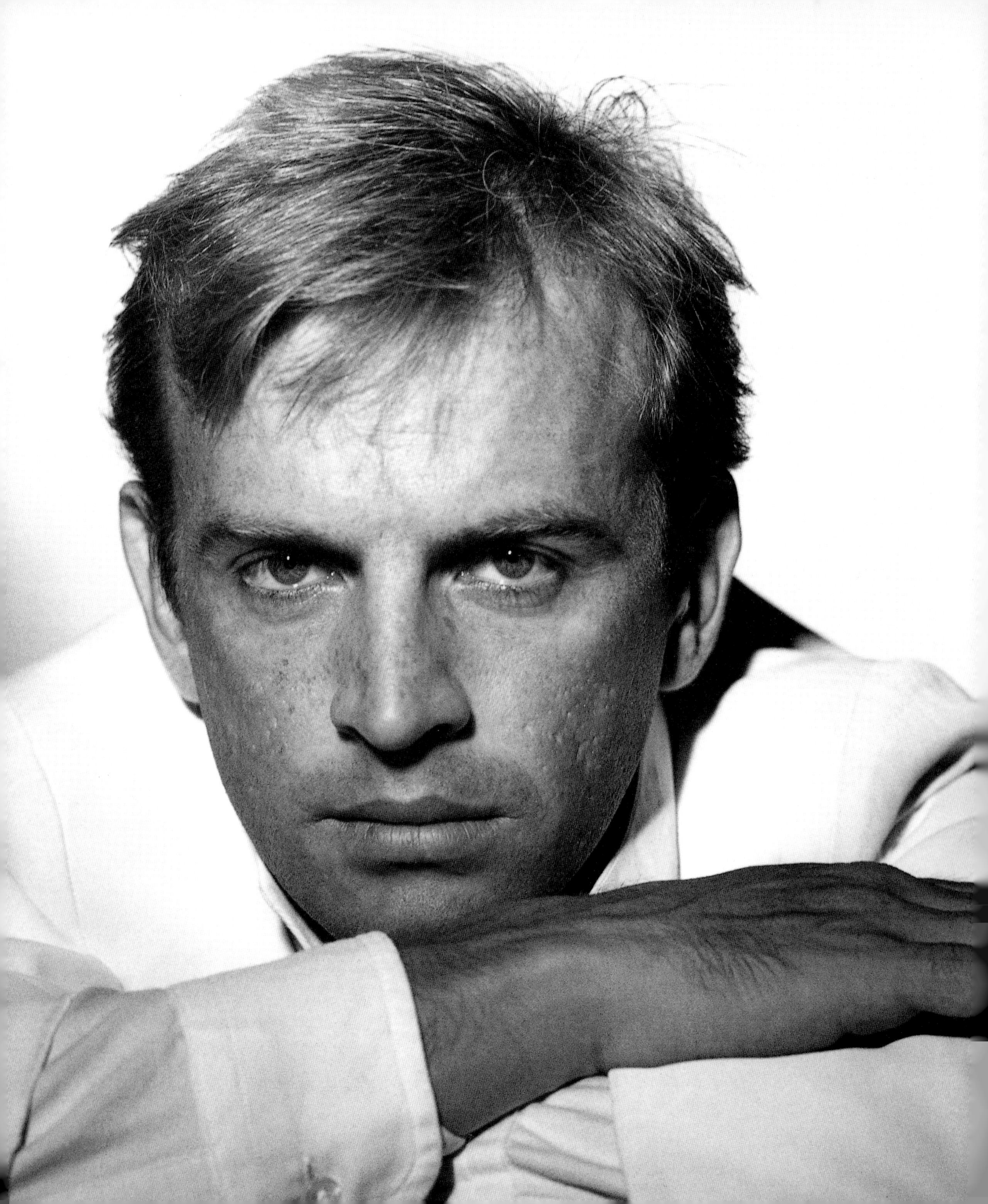

Ian was my best friend and I think the best actor of his generation. I loved his mind, his laugh, his Wildean wit and will never get over losing him at the peak of his promising career to the dreaded virus.

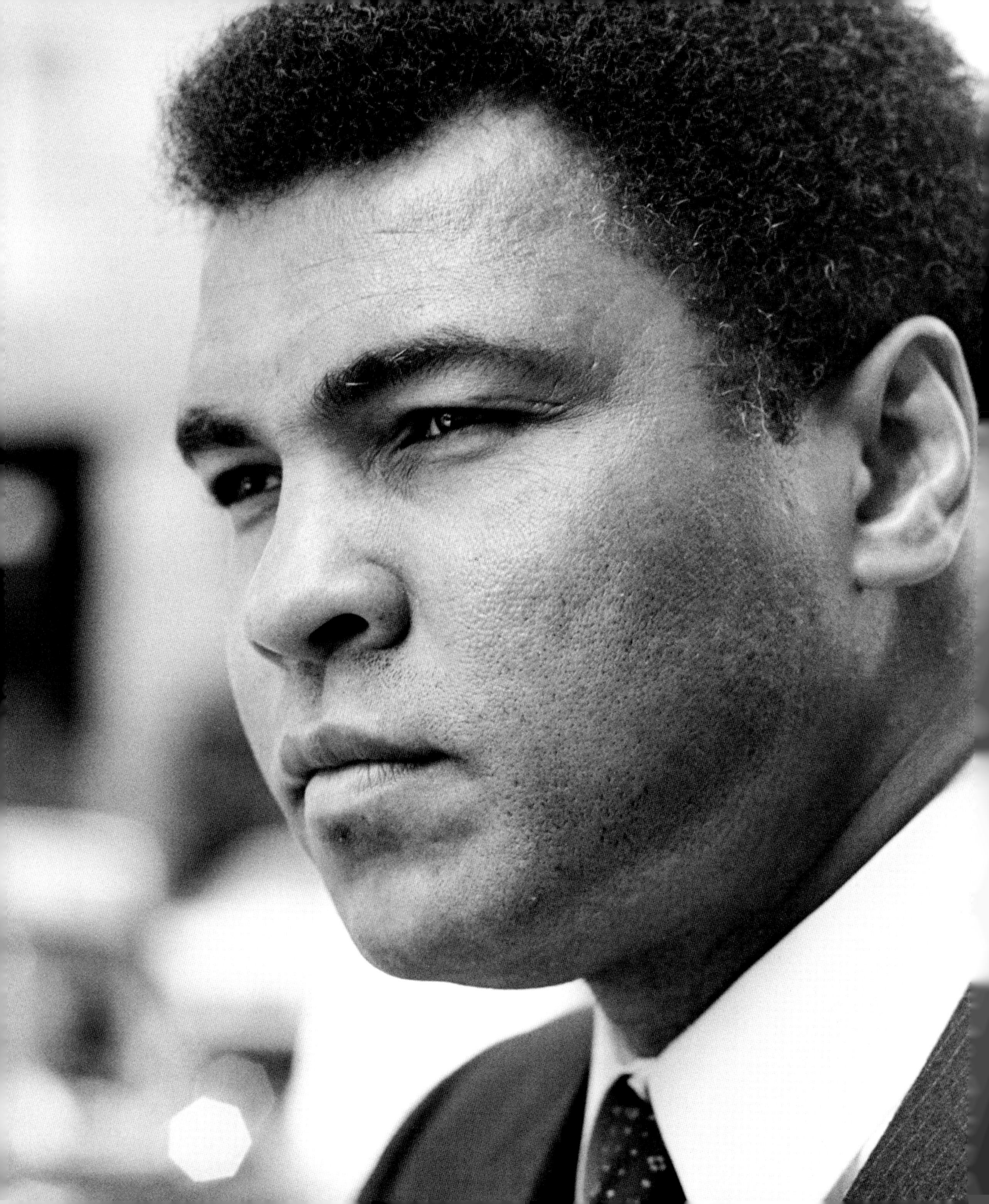

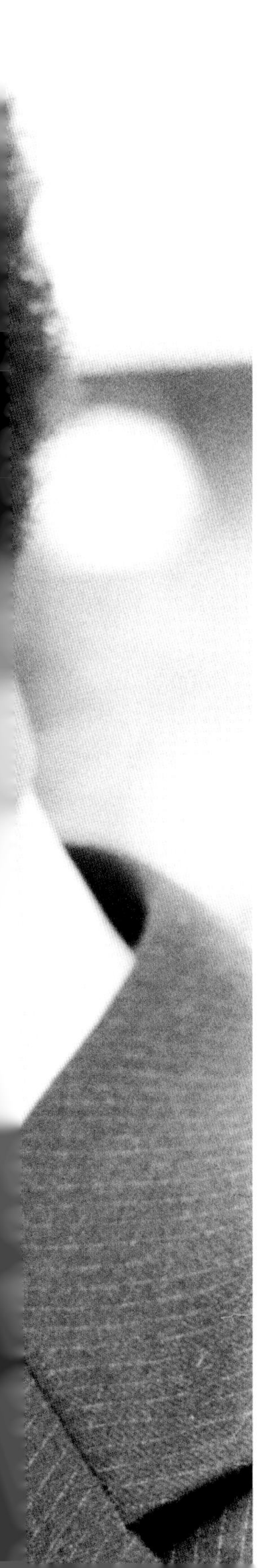

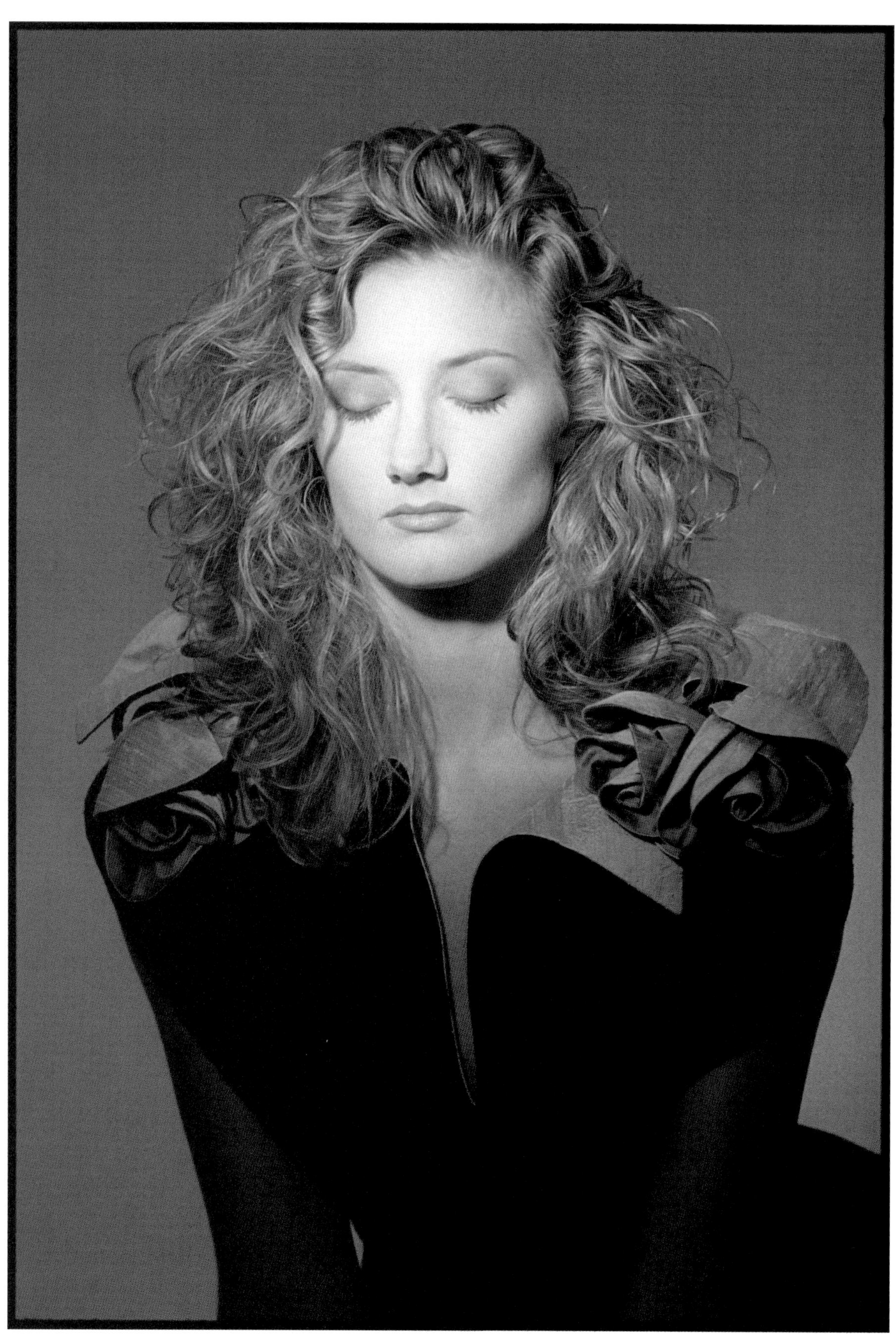

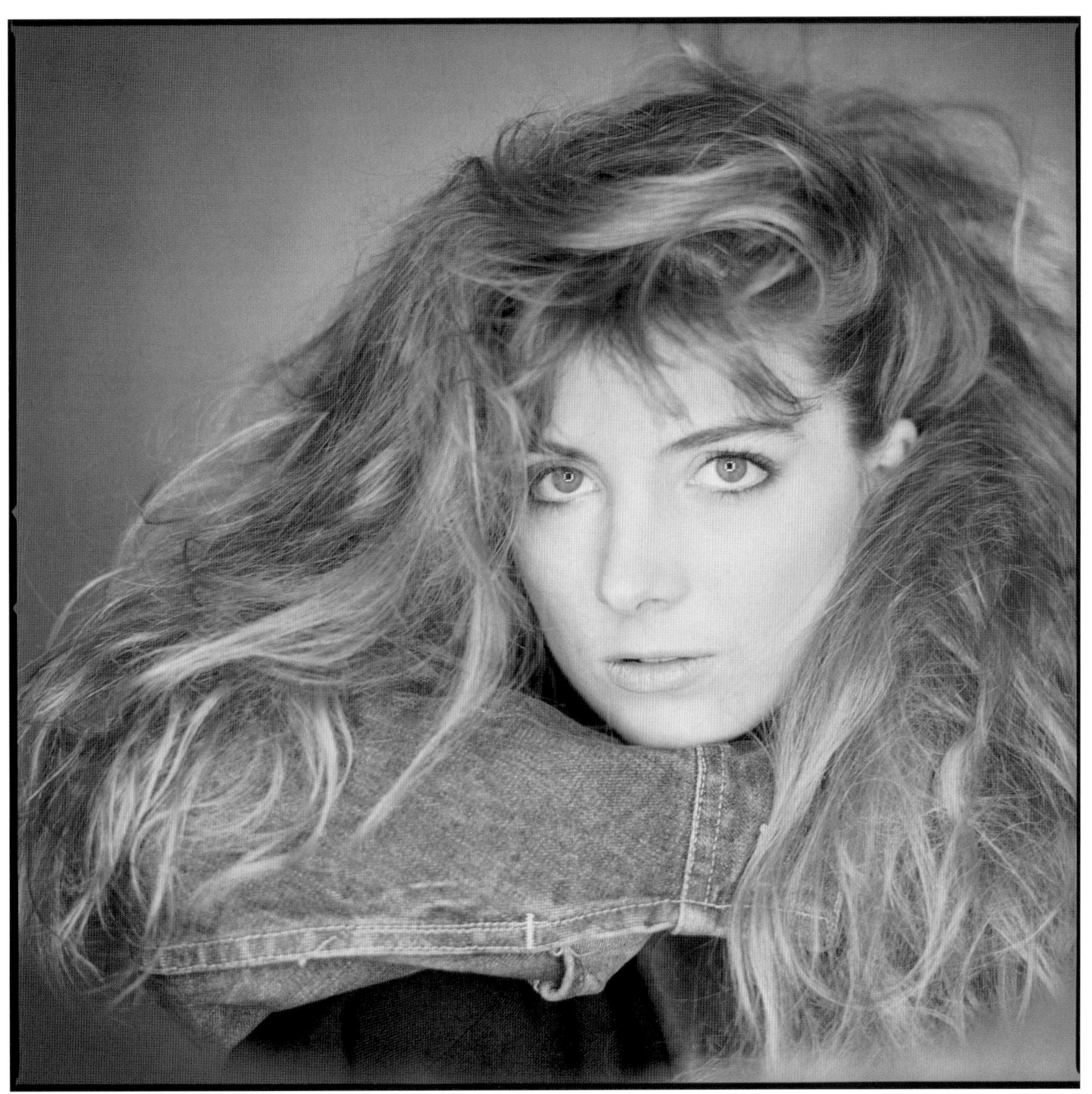

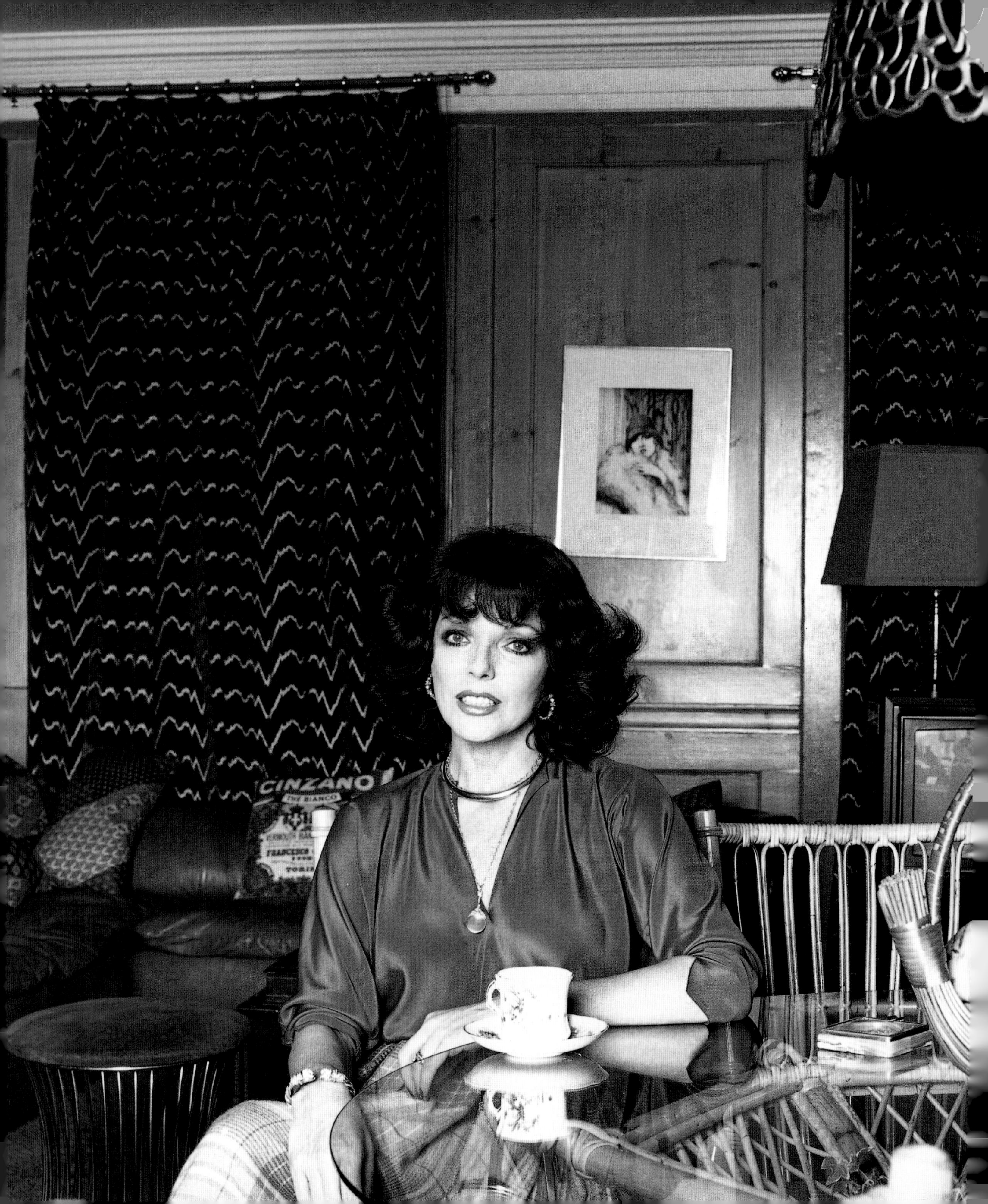
CINZANO

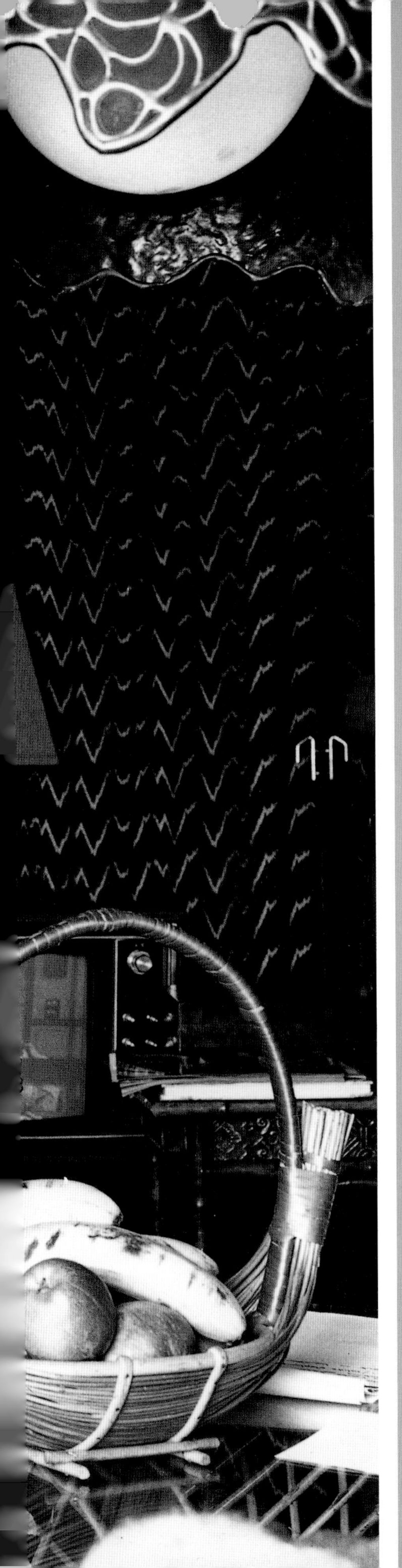

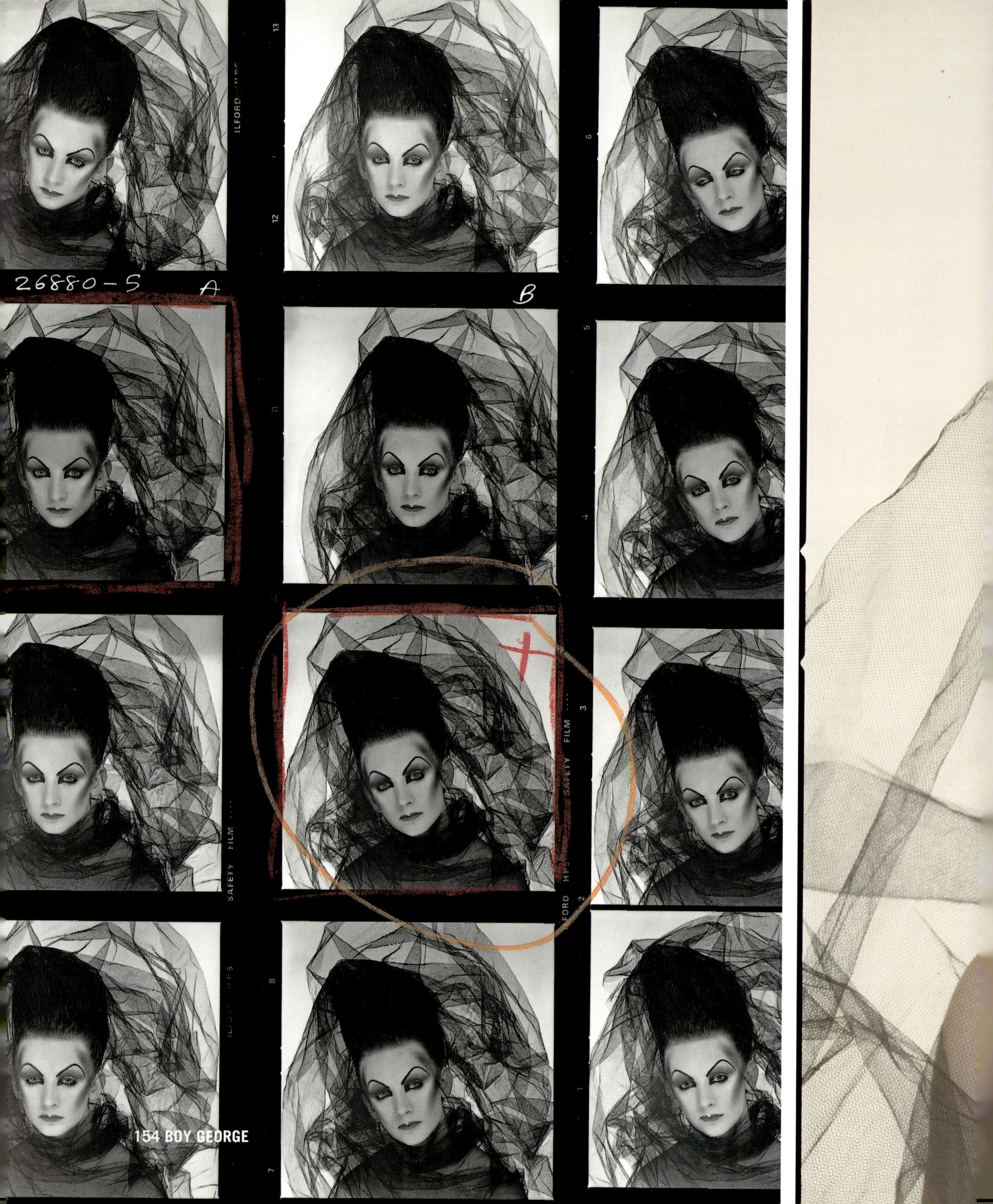
26880-5
A
B
154 BOY GEORGE

I first met Boy George in 1978 when he was living in a squat near the Post Office Tower. He came over to sit on my bed, already punked-out and painted so I decided to add to the look by wrap-ping him in black net. Later, after the *New Ro-mantics* era, I did many more sessions with him.

I first met Boy George in
1978 when he was living
in a squat near the Post
Office Tower. He came
over to sit on my bed,
already punked-out and
painted so I decided to
add to the look by wrap-
ping him in black net.
Later, after the New Ro-
mantics era, I did many
more sessions with him.

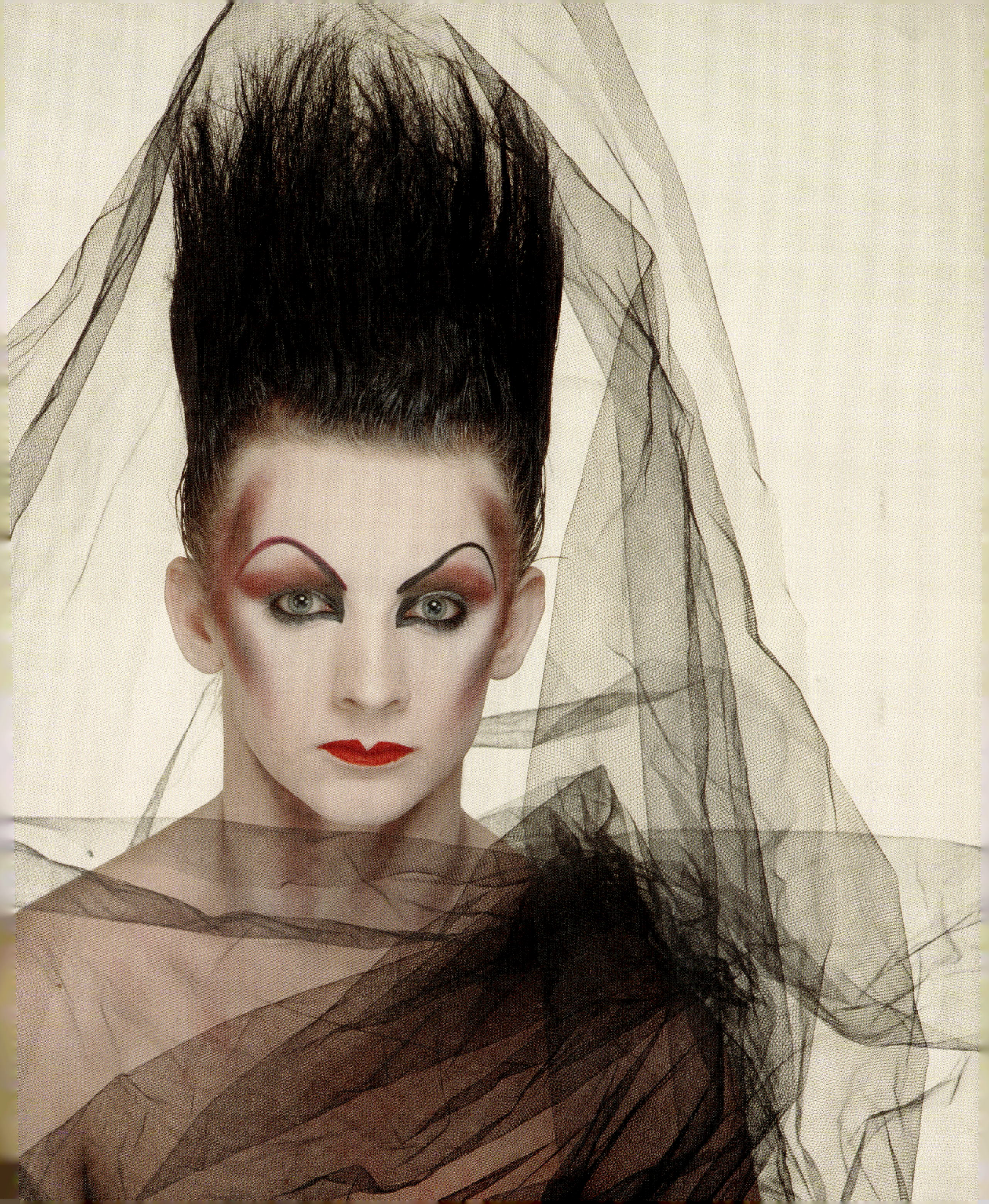

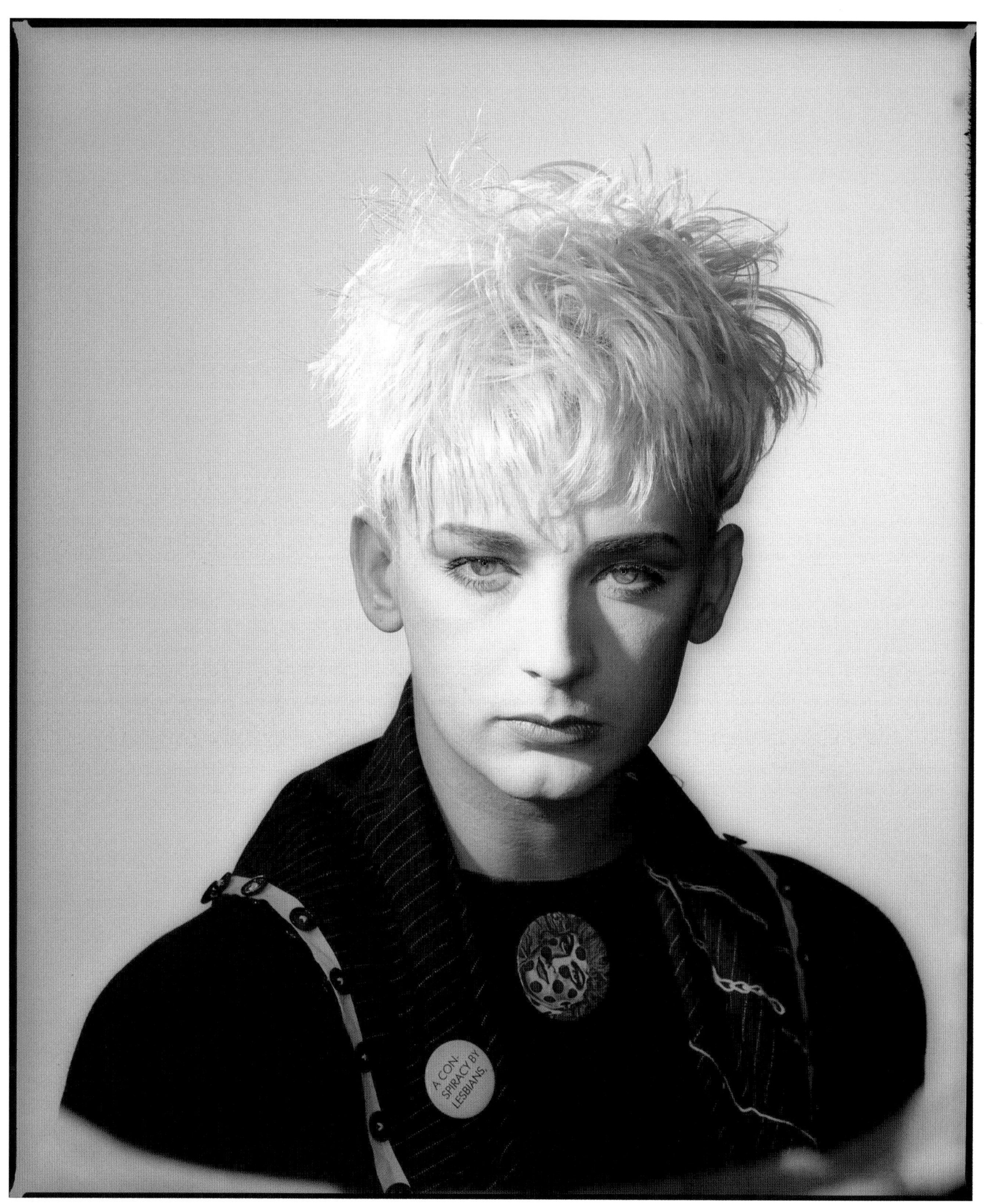

A CON-
SPIRACY BY
LESBIANS.

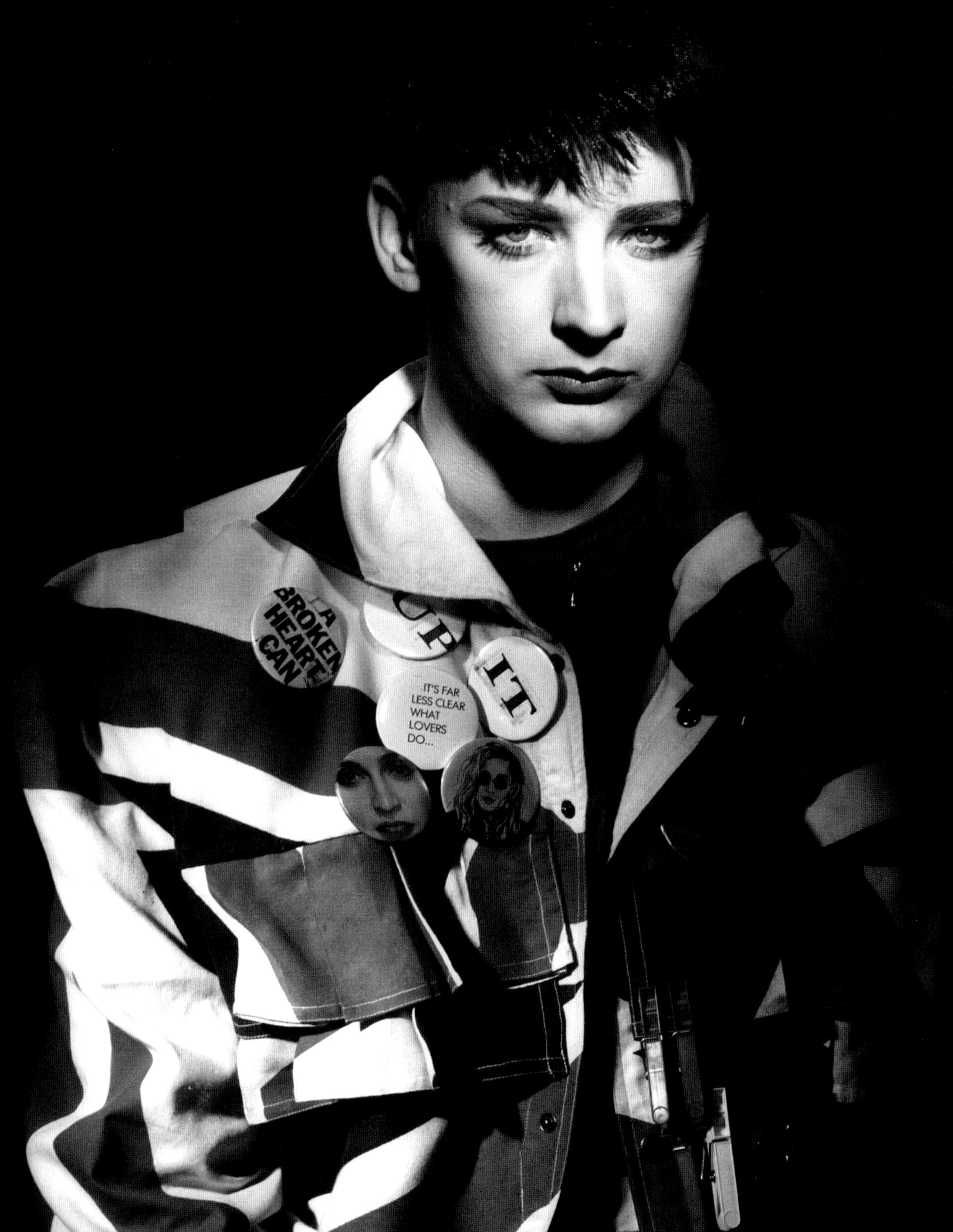

A BROKEN HEART CAN
OF
IT
IT'S FAR LESS CLEAR WHAT LOVERS DO...

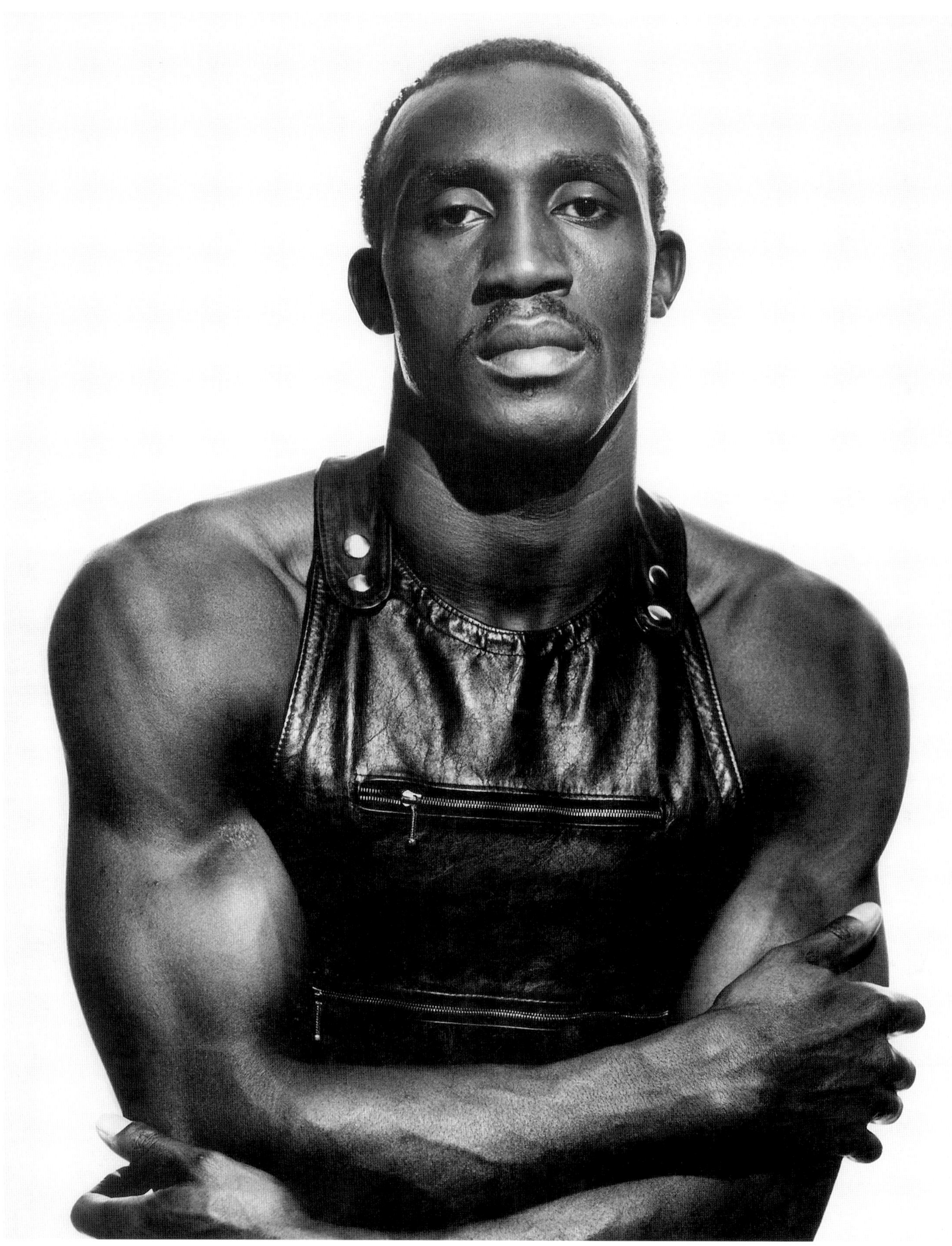

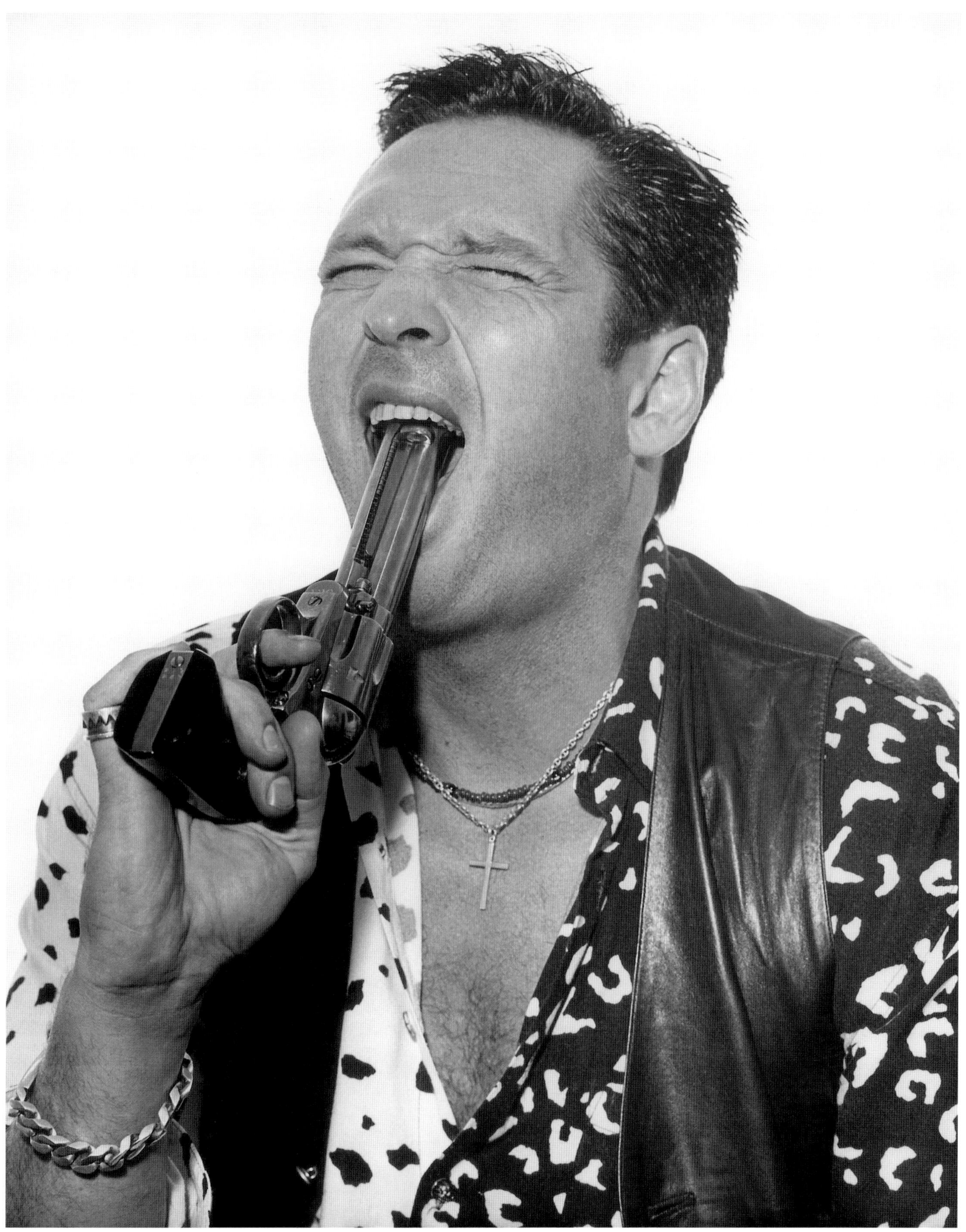

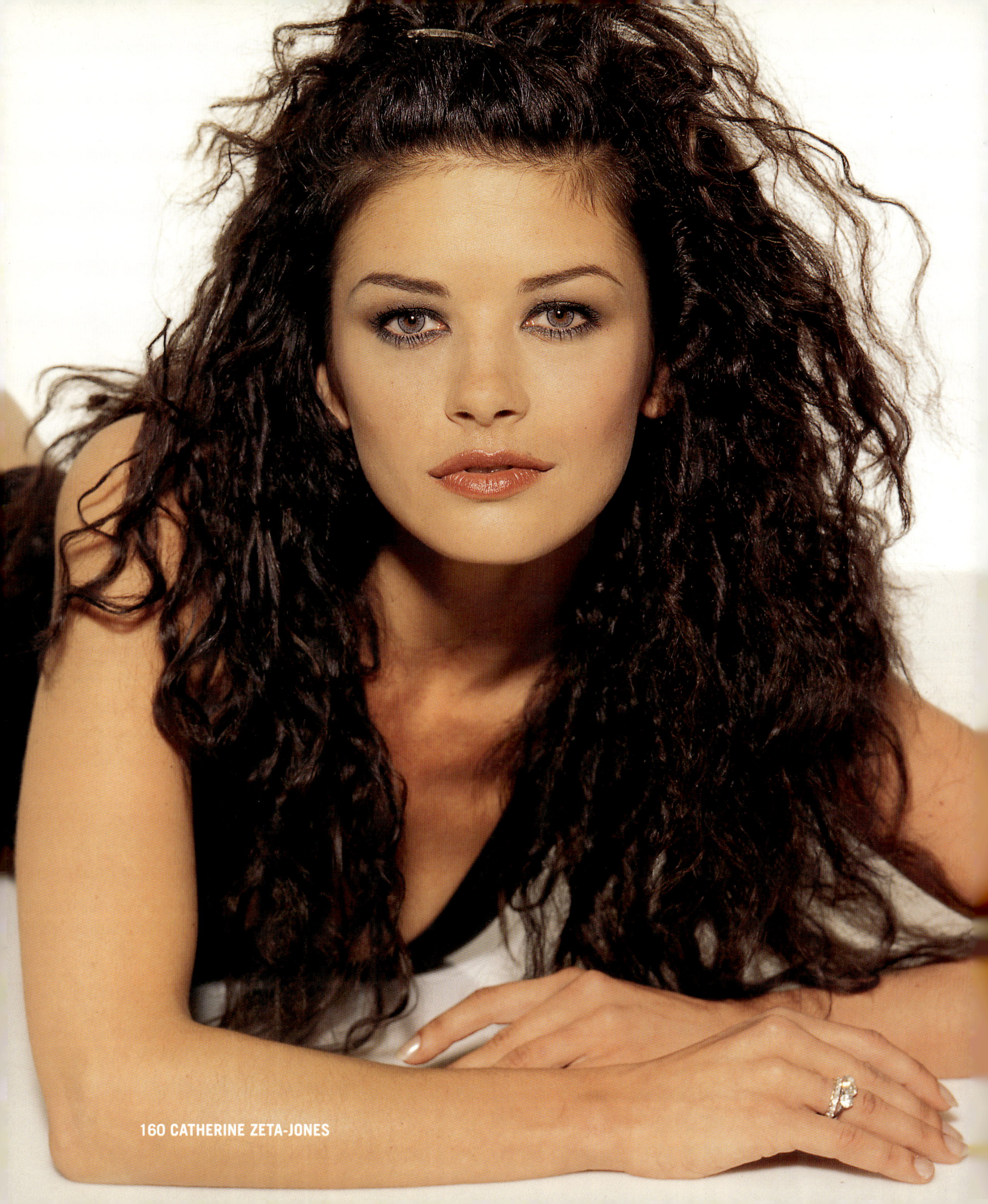
160 CATHERINE ZETA-JONES

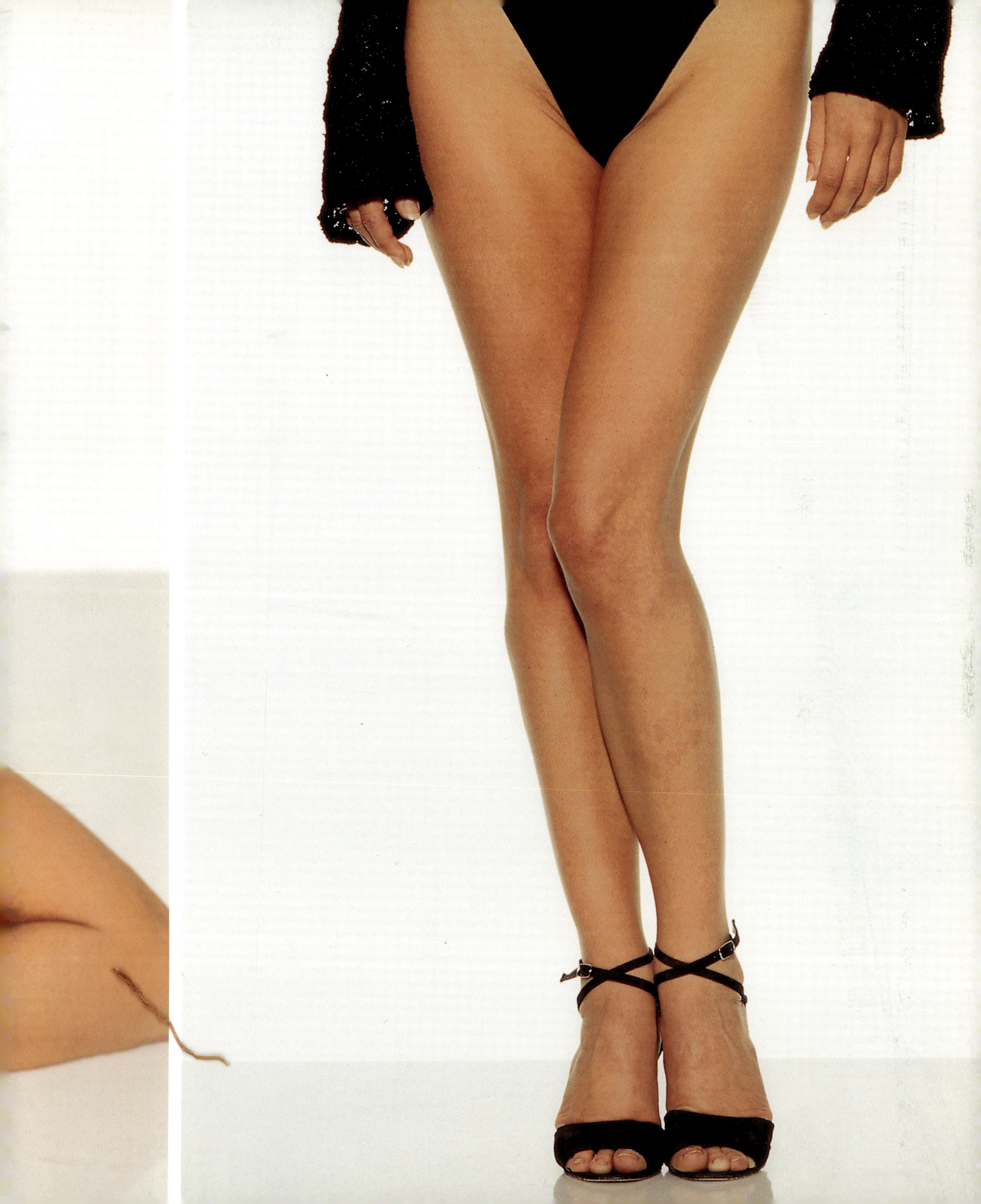

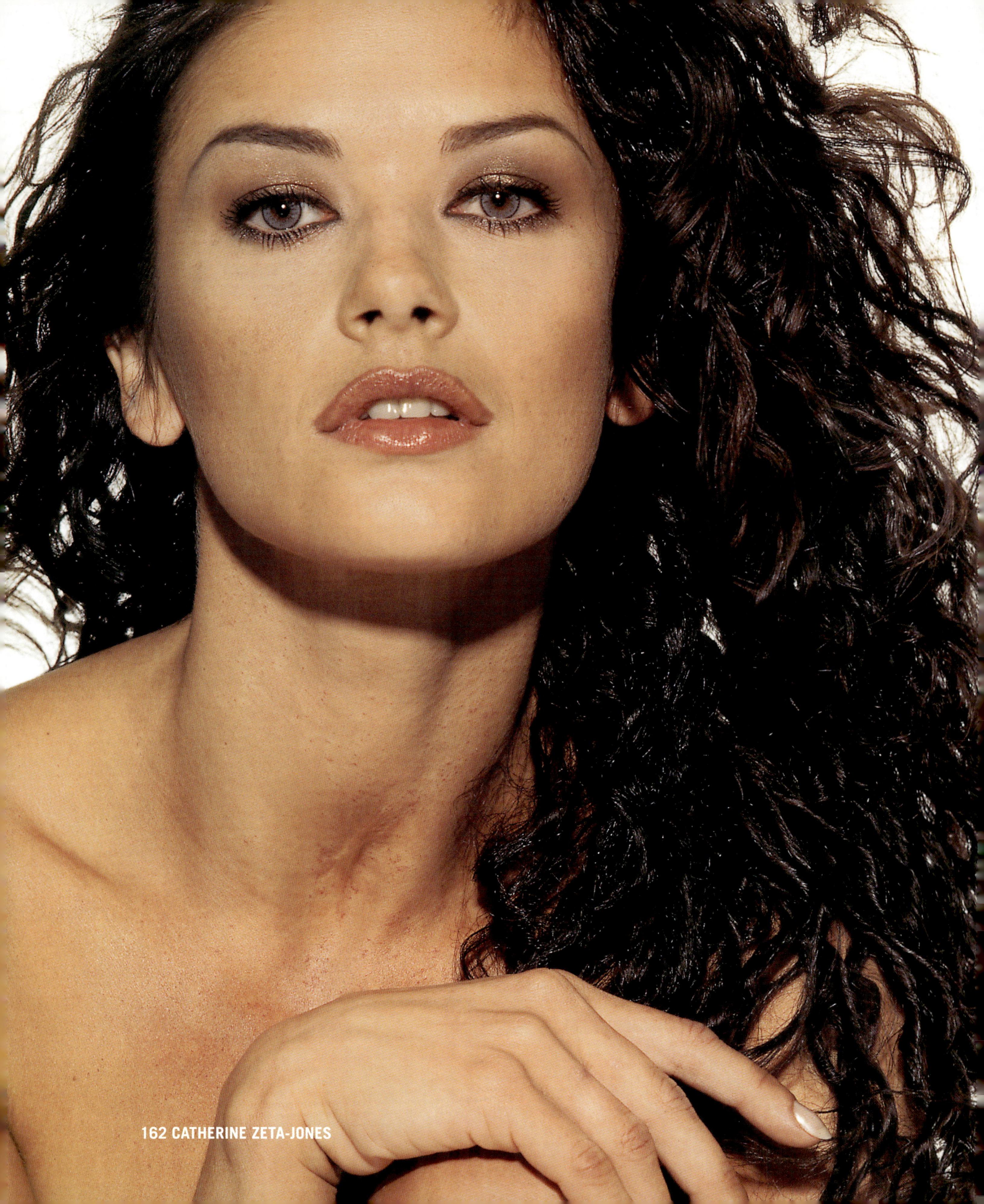
162 CATHERINE ZETA-JONES

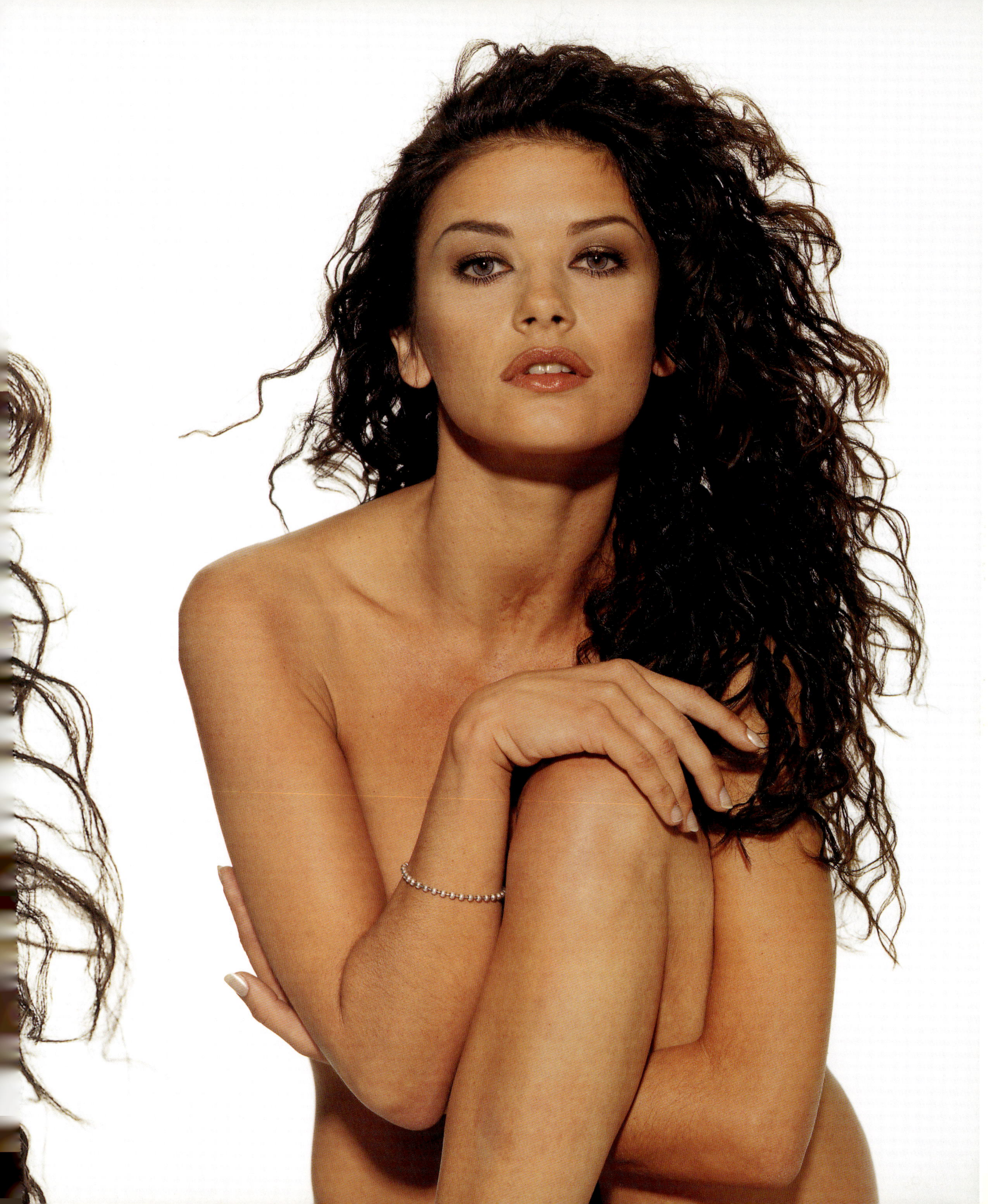

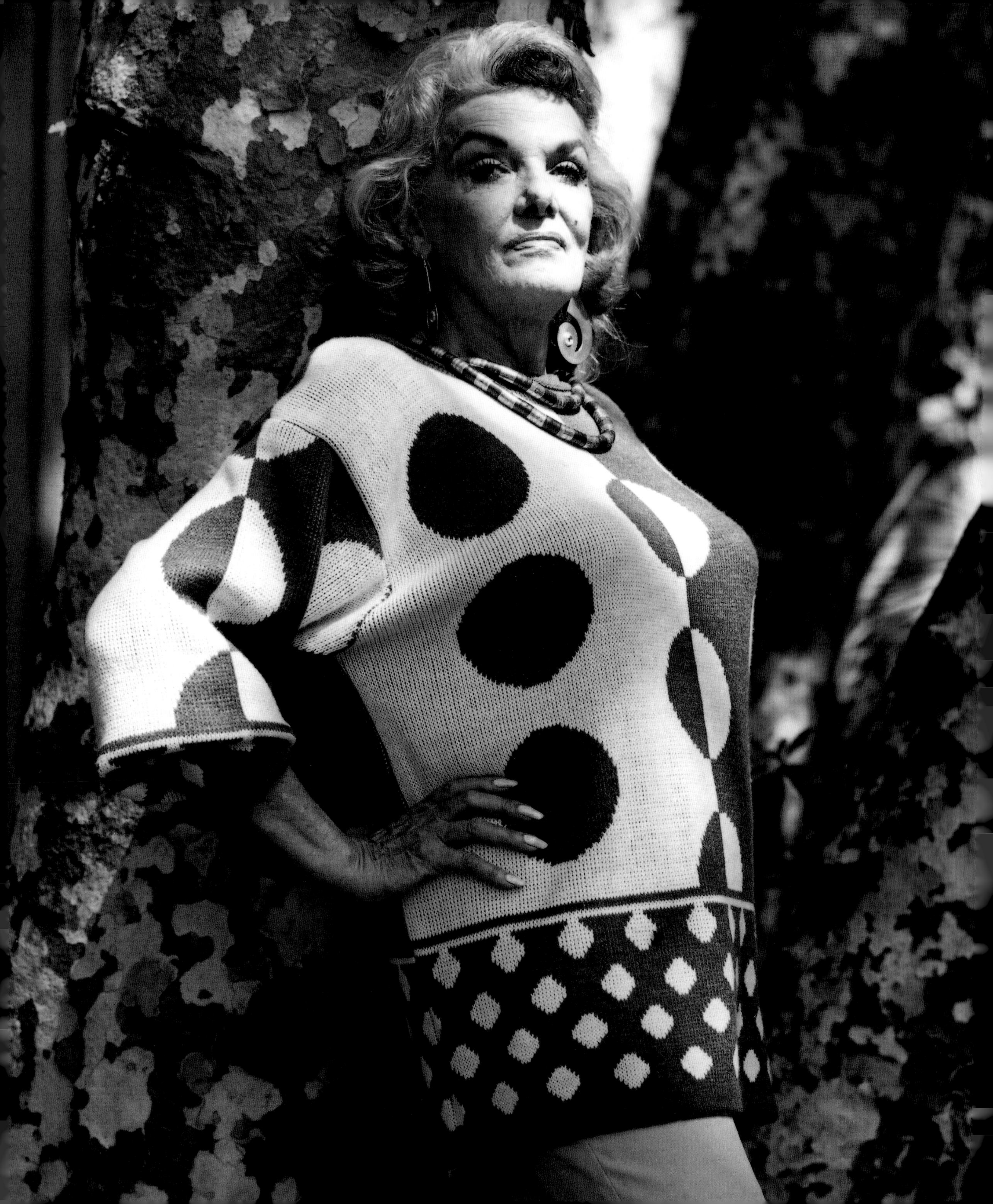

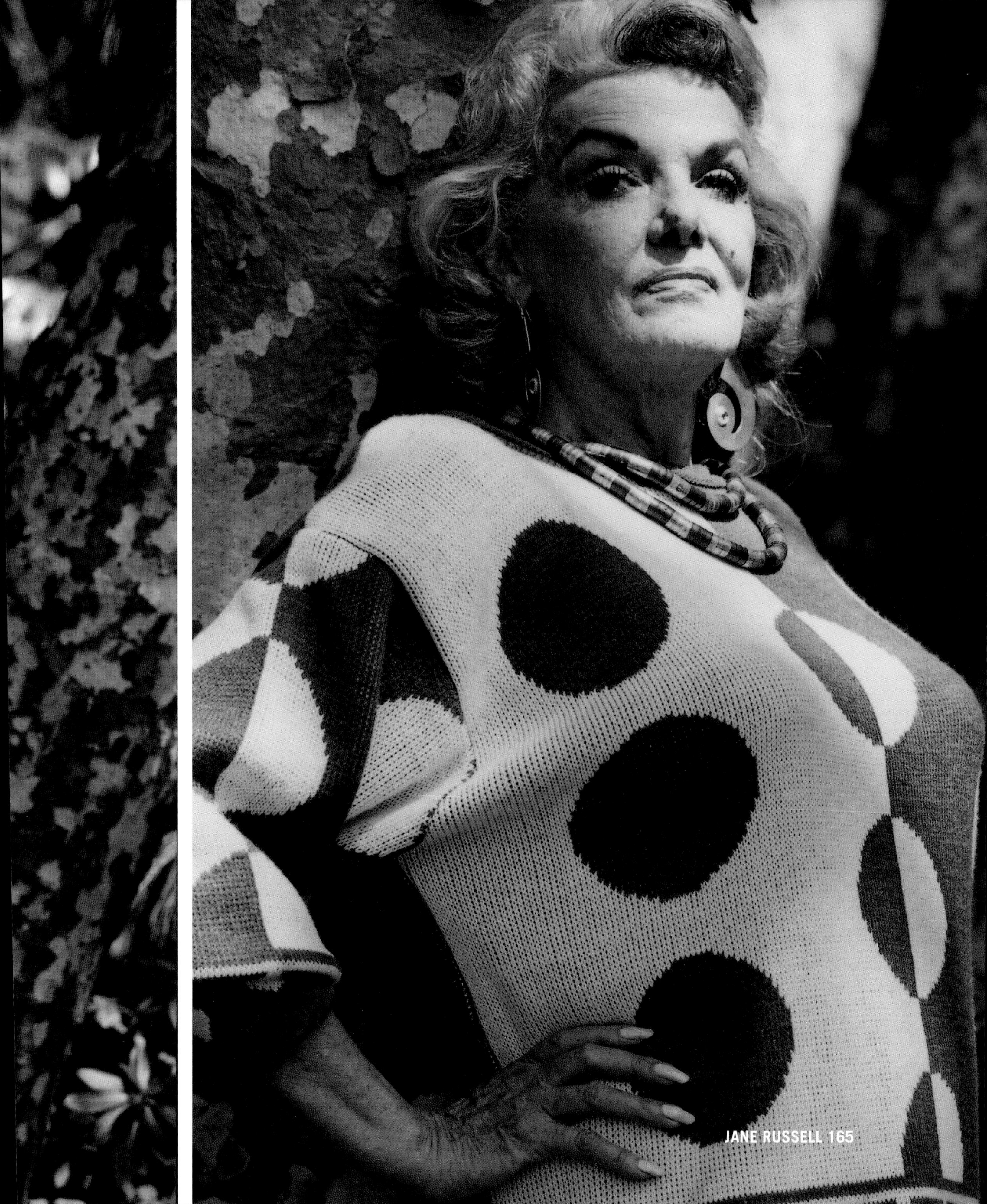
JANE RUSSELL 165

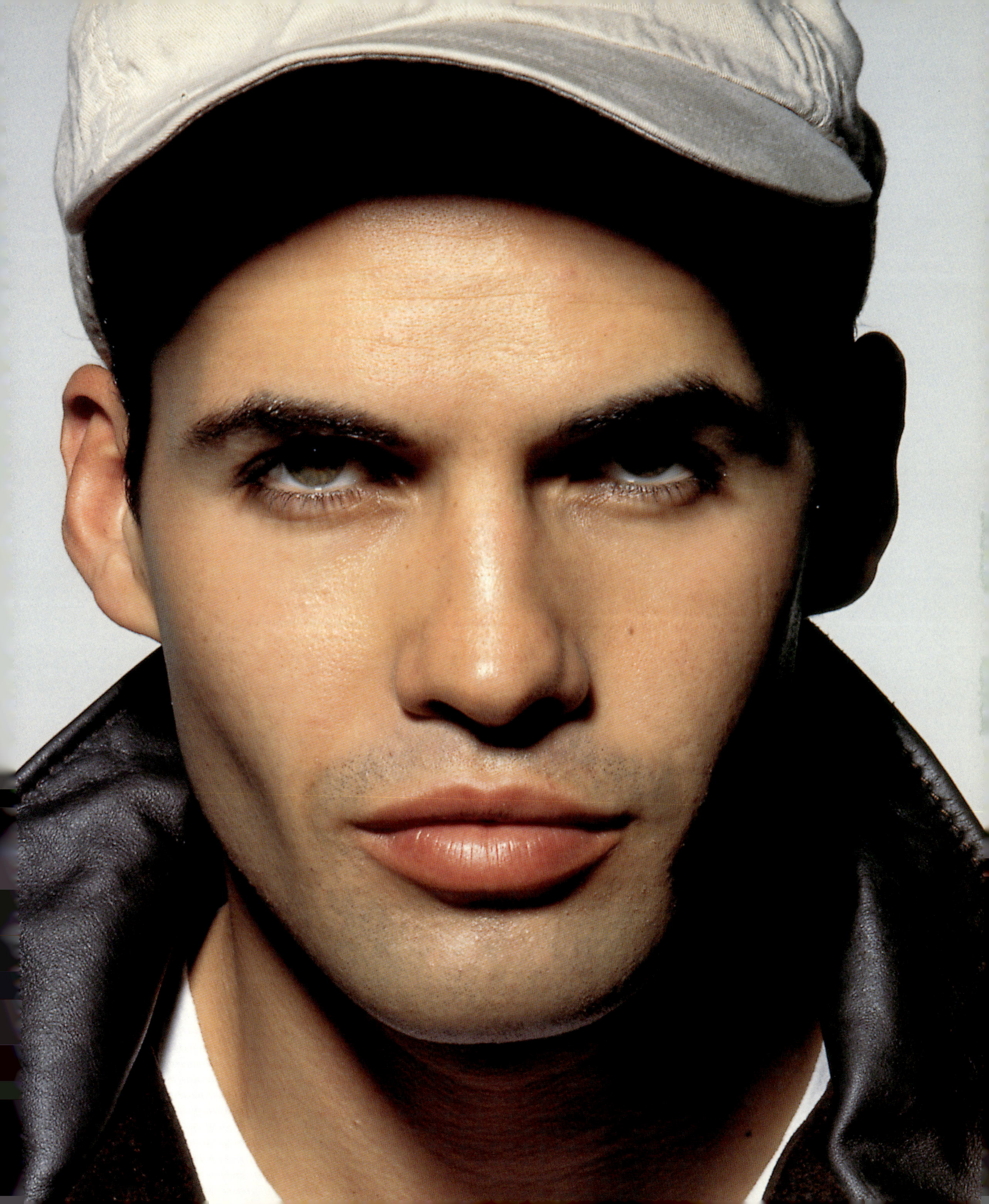

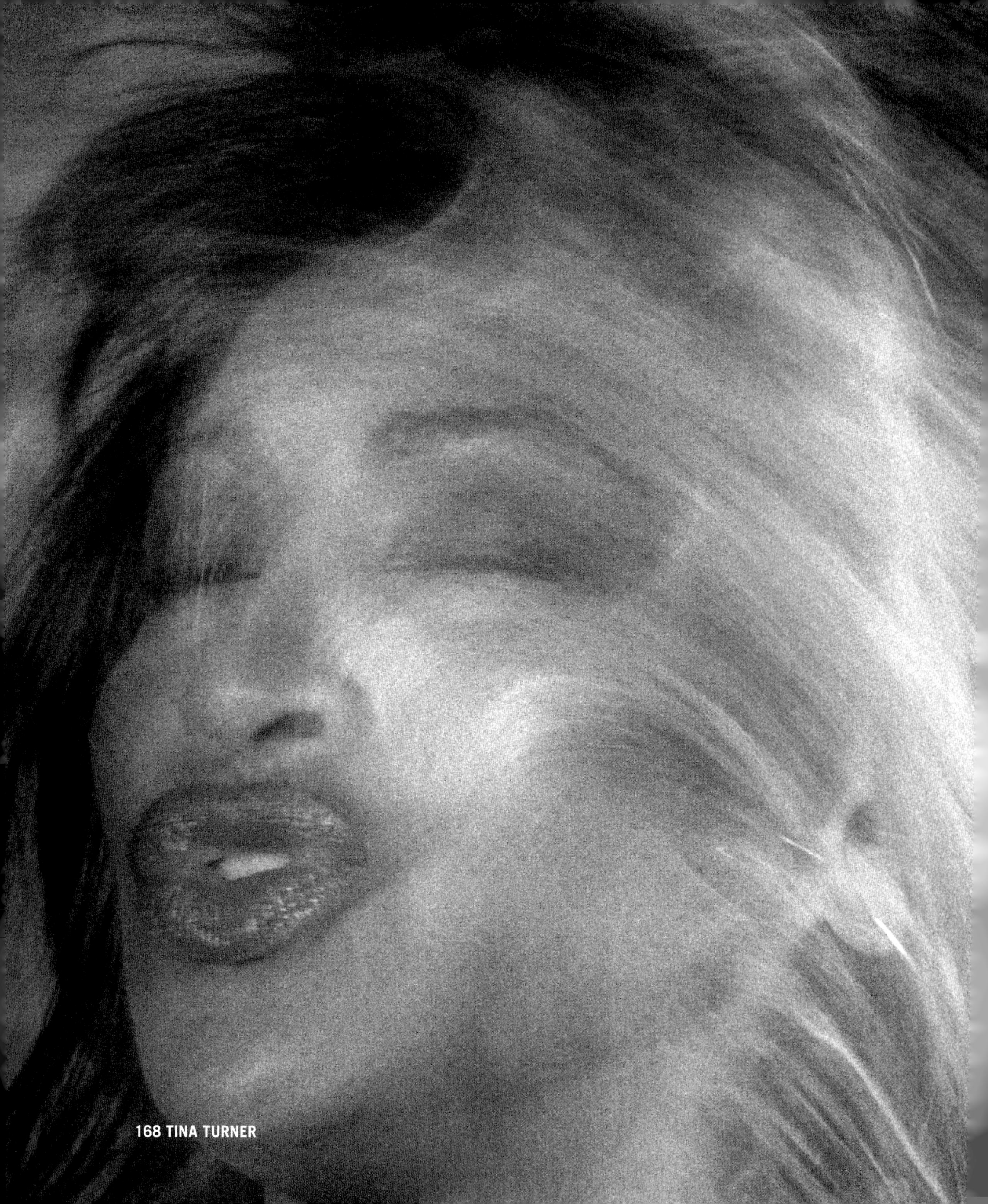
168 TINA TURNER

When I photographed her at my Beverly Boulevard studio in Silverlake, California, I couldn't wait to meet the woman I had seen perform onstage in London, years earlier, in the "Ike and Tina Turner Revue." I had been wowed by her energy and fabulosity! Our photo session was in 1982 (just after she had left Ike and before she became a solo megastar). Little did I know that she was going to change my life personally. When I went over to her house a few days after our time together to show her the contacts and obtain her approval, I noticed a little room with an ornate altar in it as I was leaving. I asked her about it. Tina Turner knelt down in front of it and I meekly copied her as she started to chant "nam-myoho-renge-kyo." Here I was, next to my heroine, kneeling beside someone who held the key to everything I wanted, compassion, energy, success, fun and courage. This was my first introduction to Buddhism and now I have been a Nichiren Buddhist for over twenty-five years.

When I photographed her at my Beverly Boulevard studio in Silverlake, California, I couldn't wait to meet the woman I had seen perform onstage in London, years earlier, in the "Ike and Tina Turner Revue." I had been wowed by her energy and fabulosity! Our photo session was in 1982 (just after she had left Ike and before she became a solo megastar). Little did I know that she was going to change my life personally. When I went over to her house a few days after our time together to show her the contacts and obtain her approval, I noticed a little room with an ornate altar in it as I was leaving. I asked her about it. Tina Turner knelt down in front of it and I meekly copied her as she started to chant "nam-myoho-renge-kyo." Here I was, next to my heroine, kneeling beside someone who held the key to everything I wanted, compassion, energy, success, fun and courage. This was my first introduction to Buddhism and now I have been a Nichiren Buddhist for over twenty-five years.

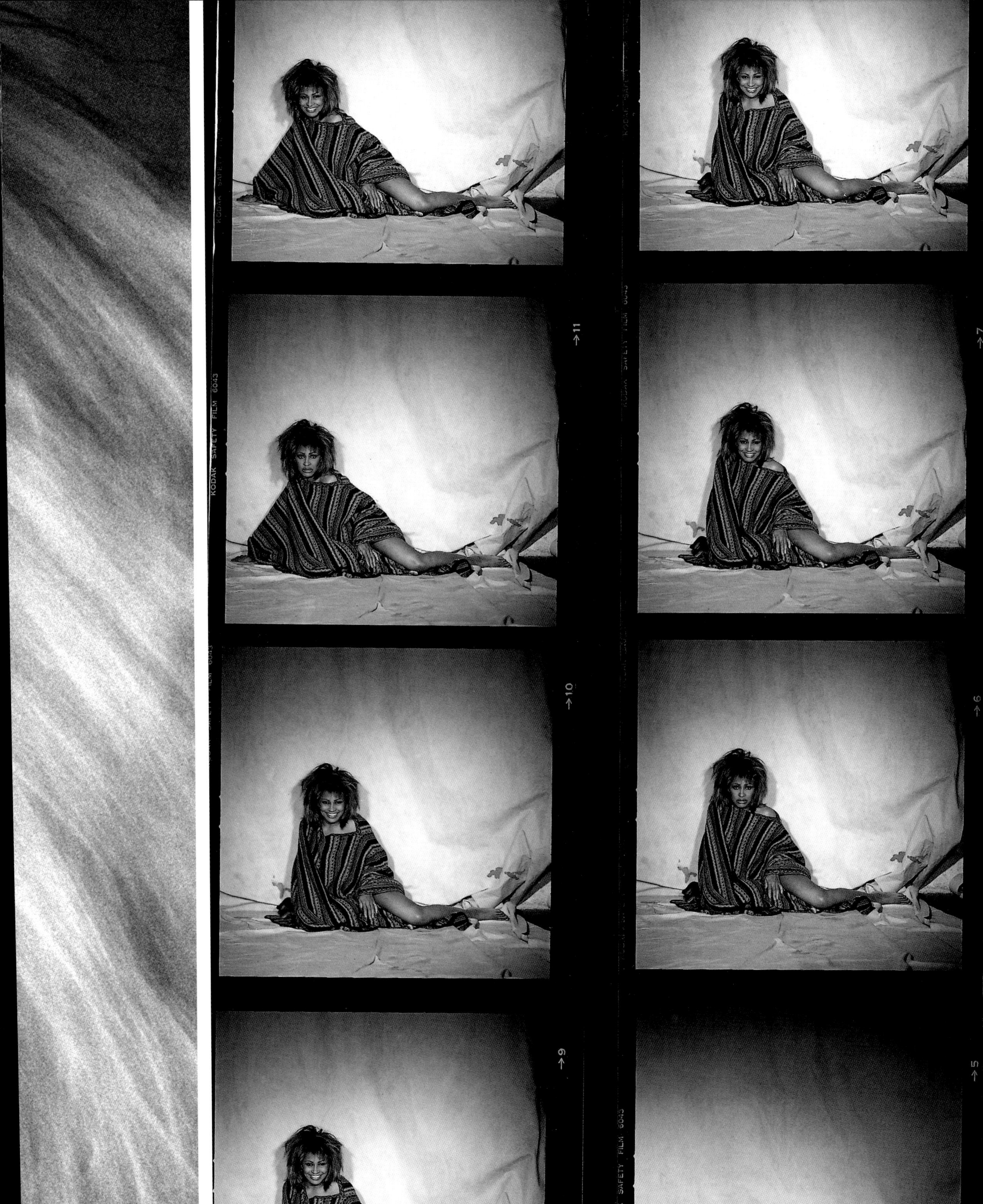

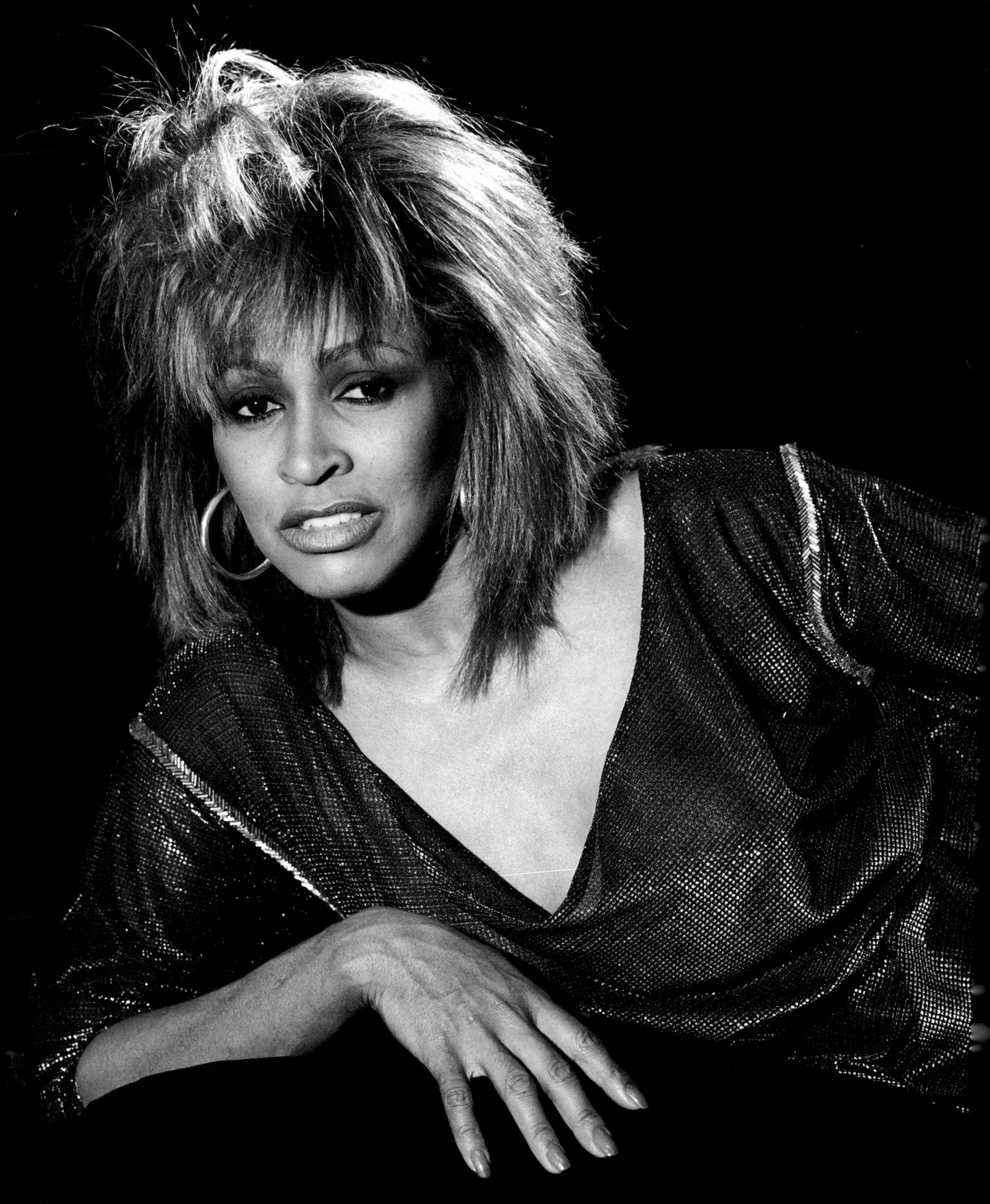

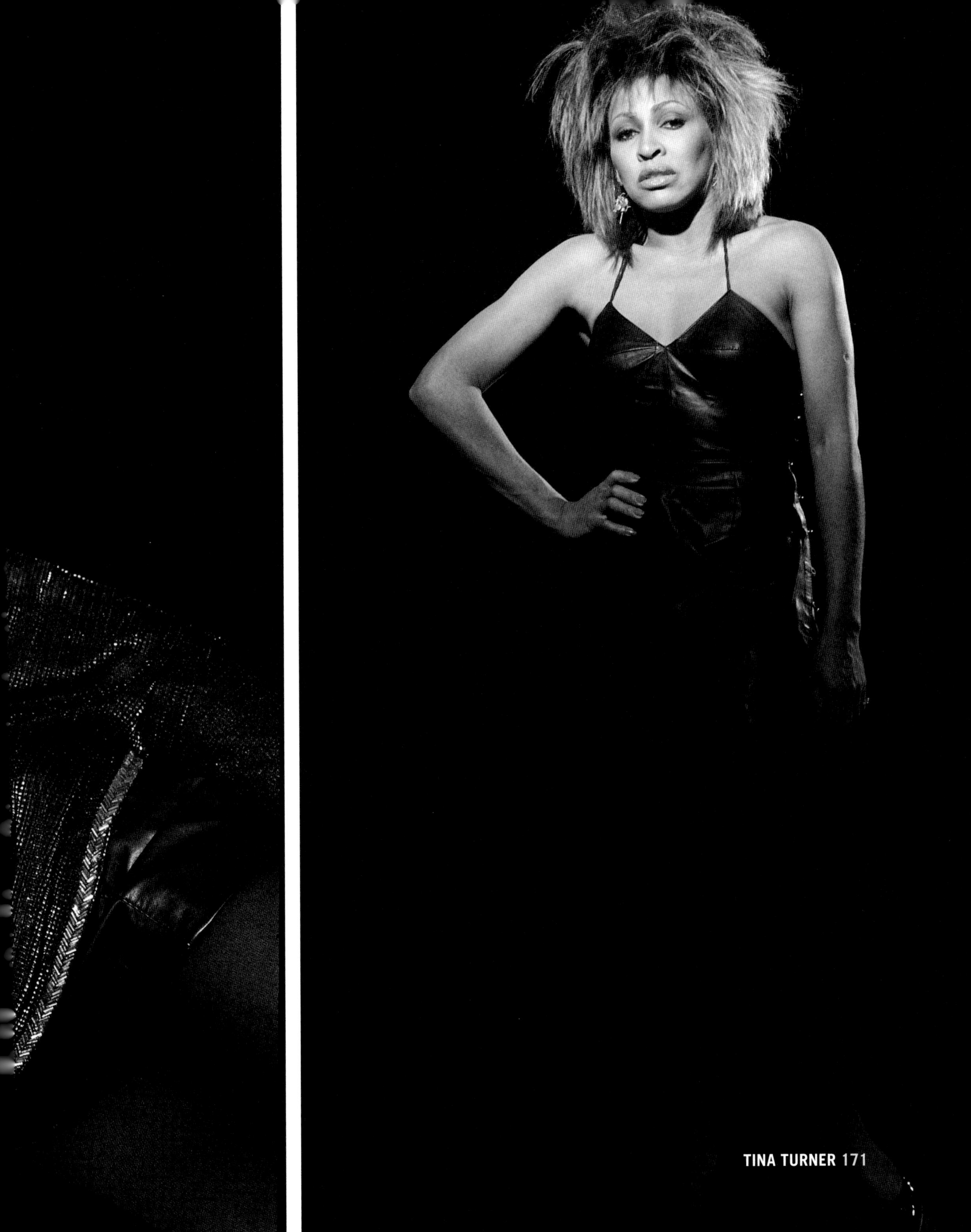
TINA TURNER 171

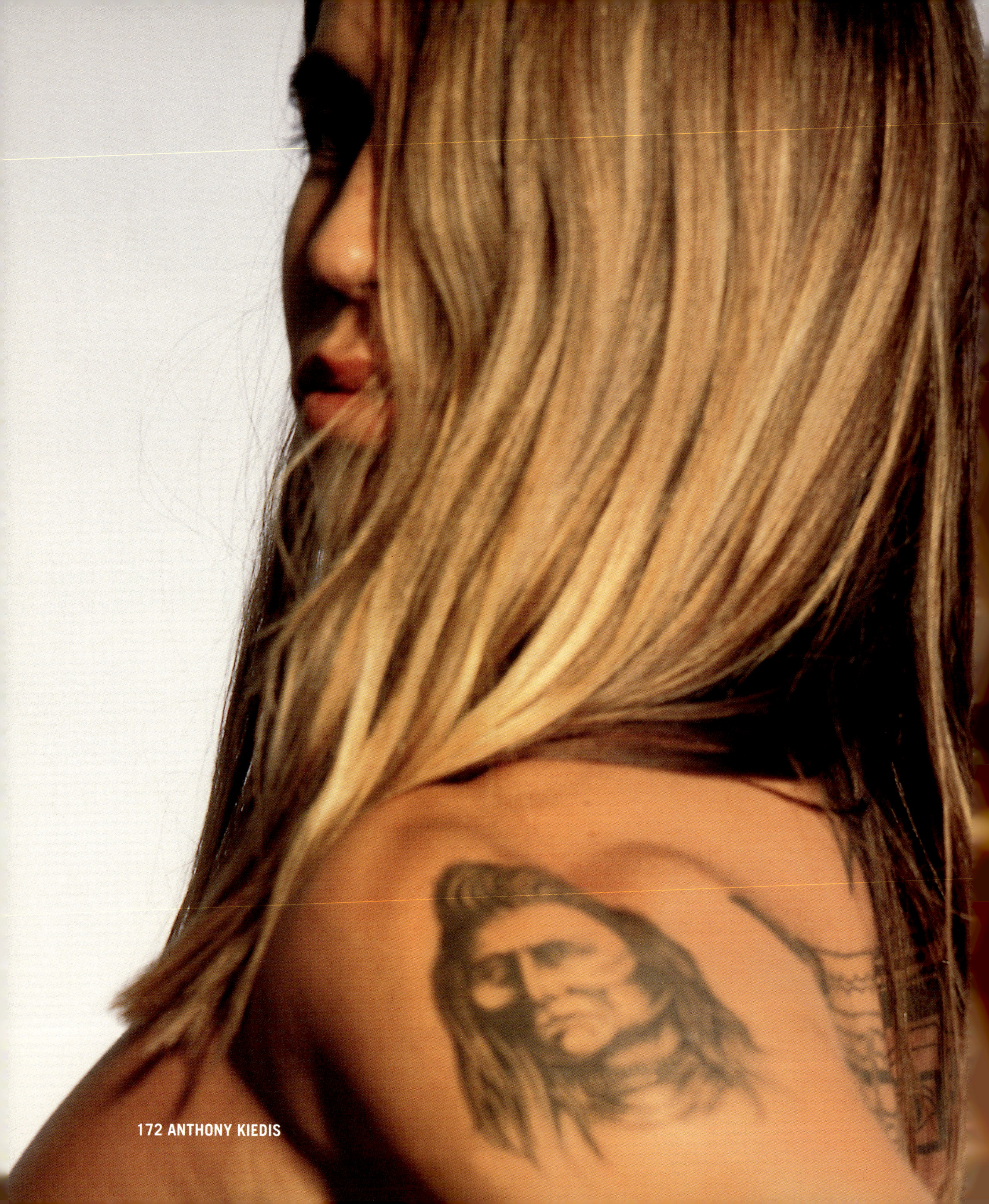

172 ANTHONY KIEDIS

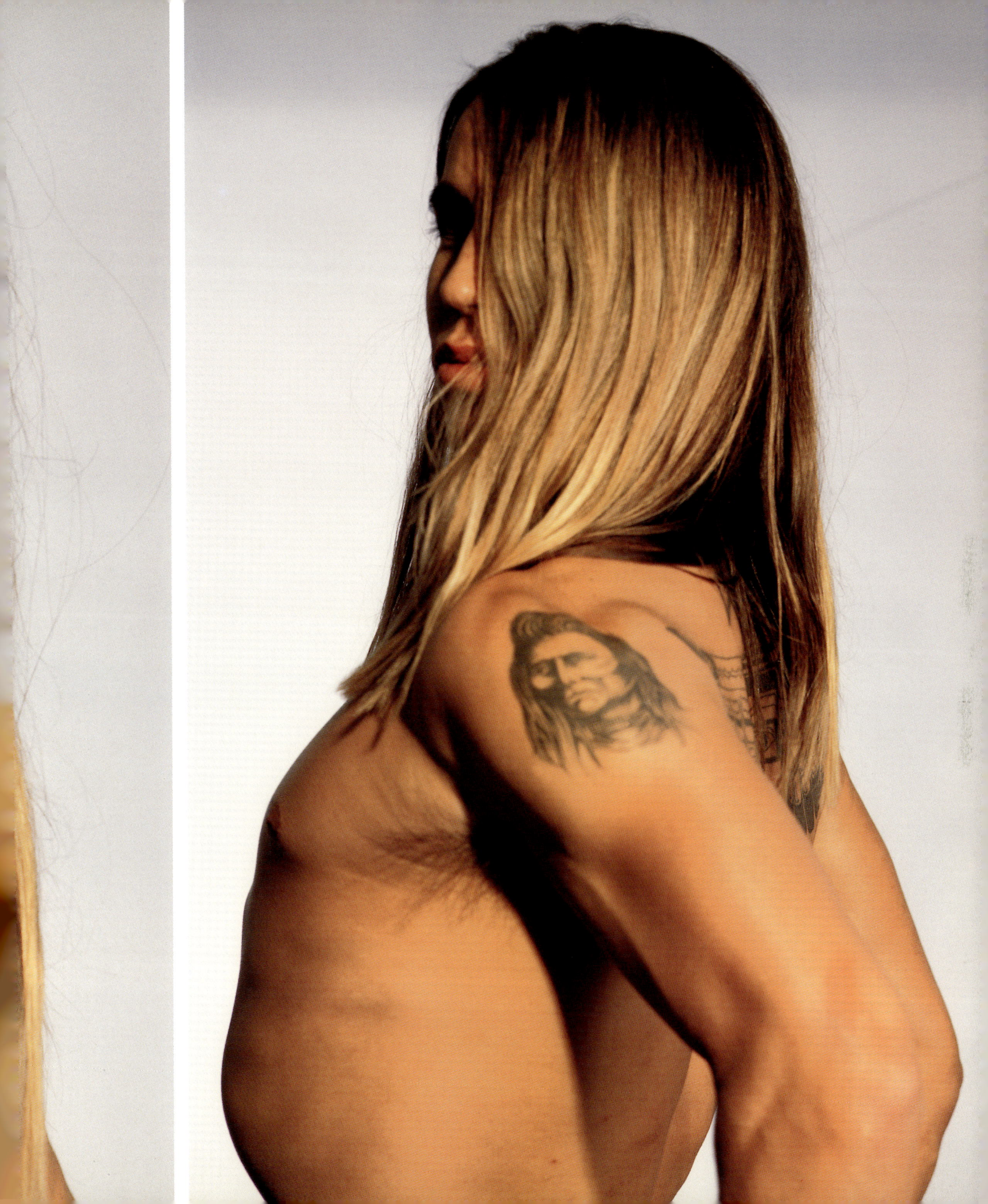

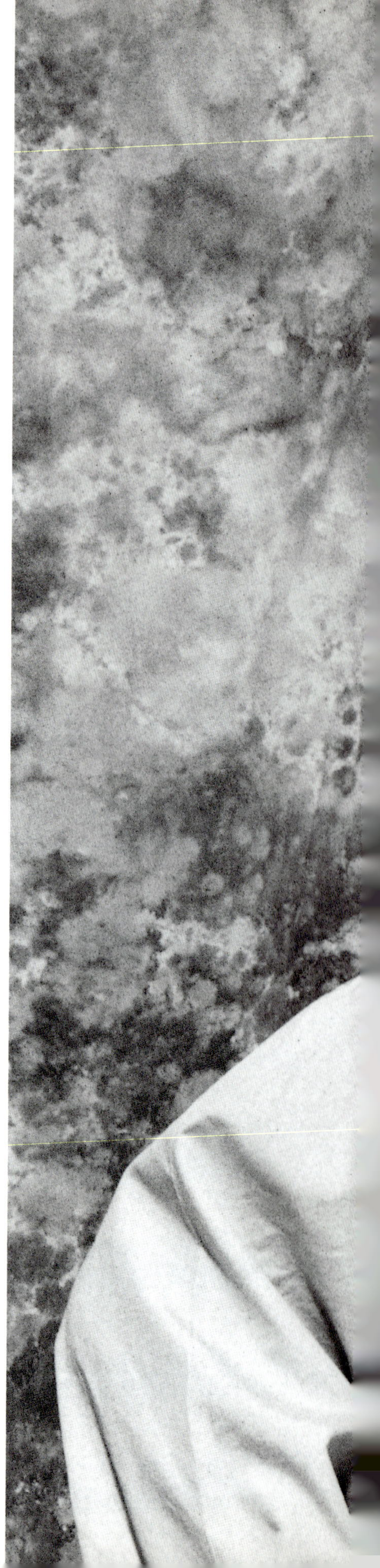

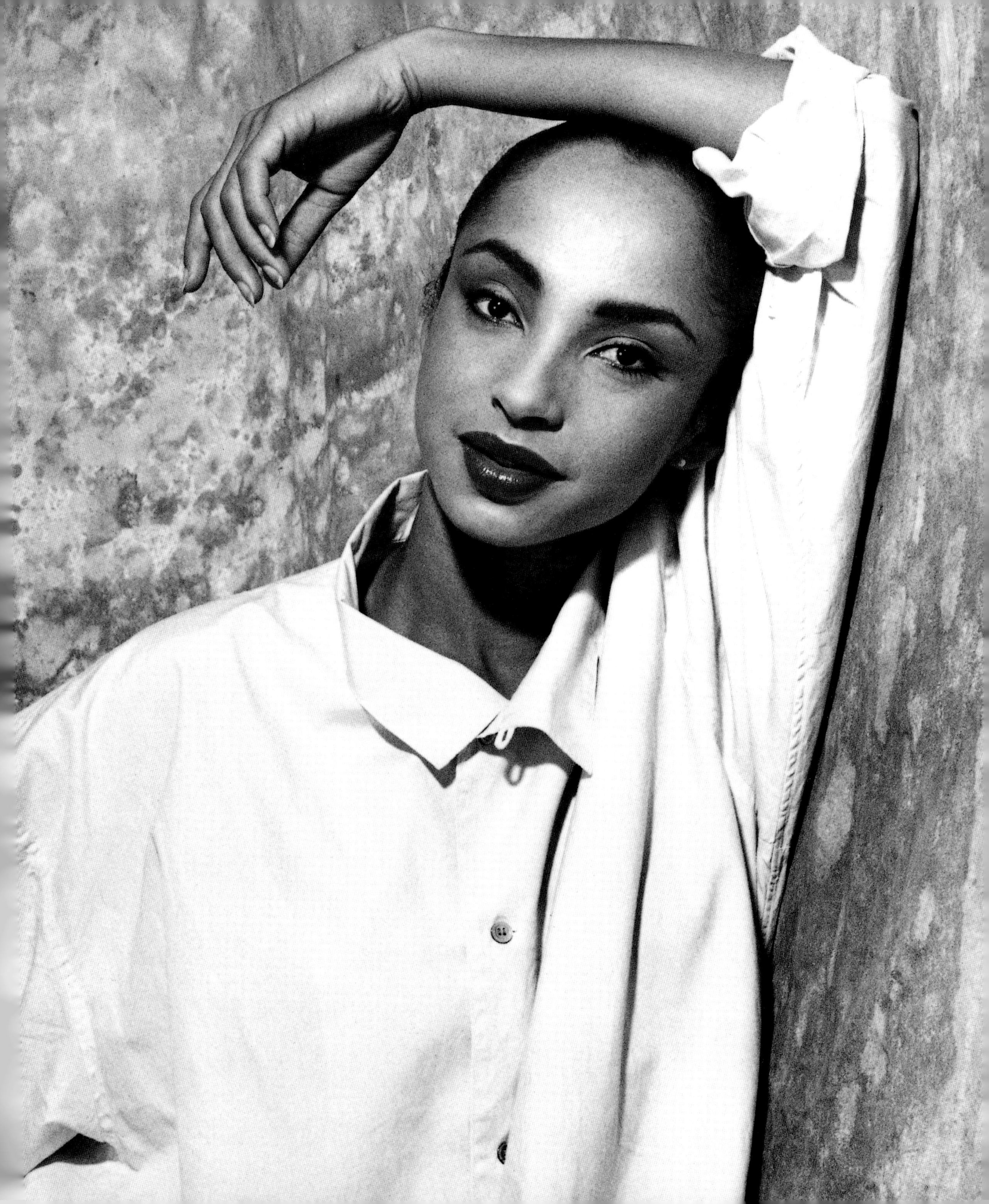

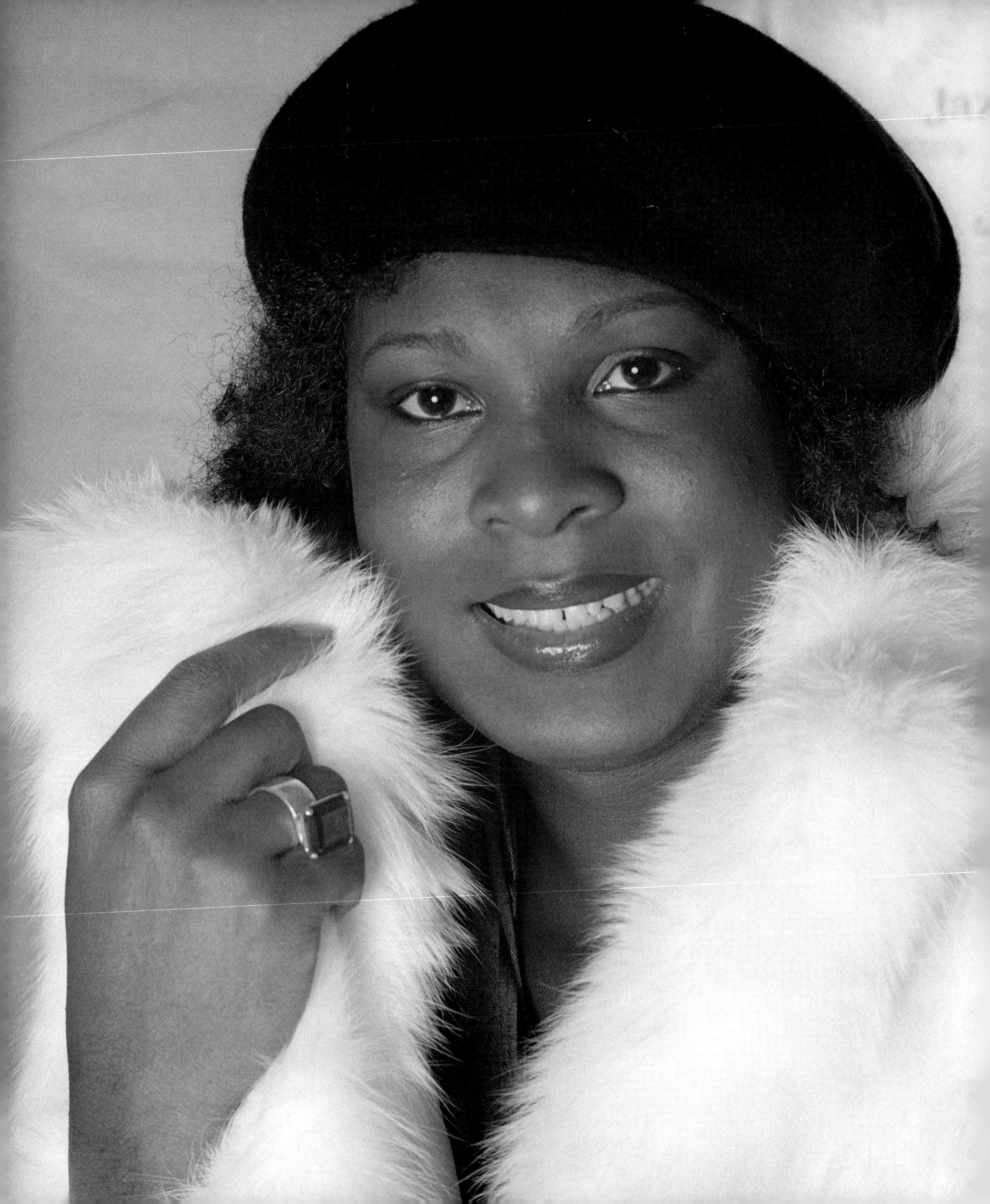

"You make me feel mighty real" was his logo, but I met Sylvester back in his "Cockette" days in San Fransisco. To me, seeing him back before his disco days, dressed in drag, with a black dress, magnolia flowers in his hair and glossed lips, crooning Billie Holiday torch songs in a small cabaret room, is where he triumphed as a star.

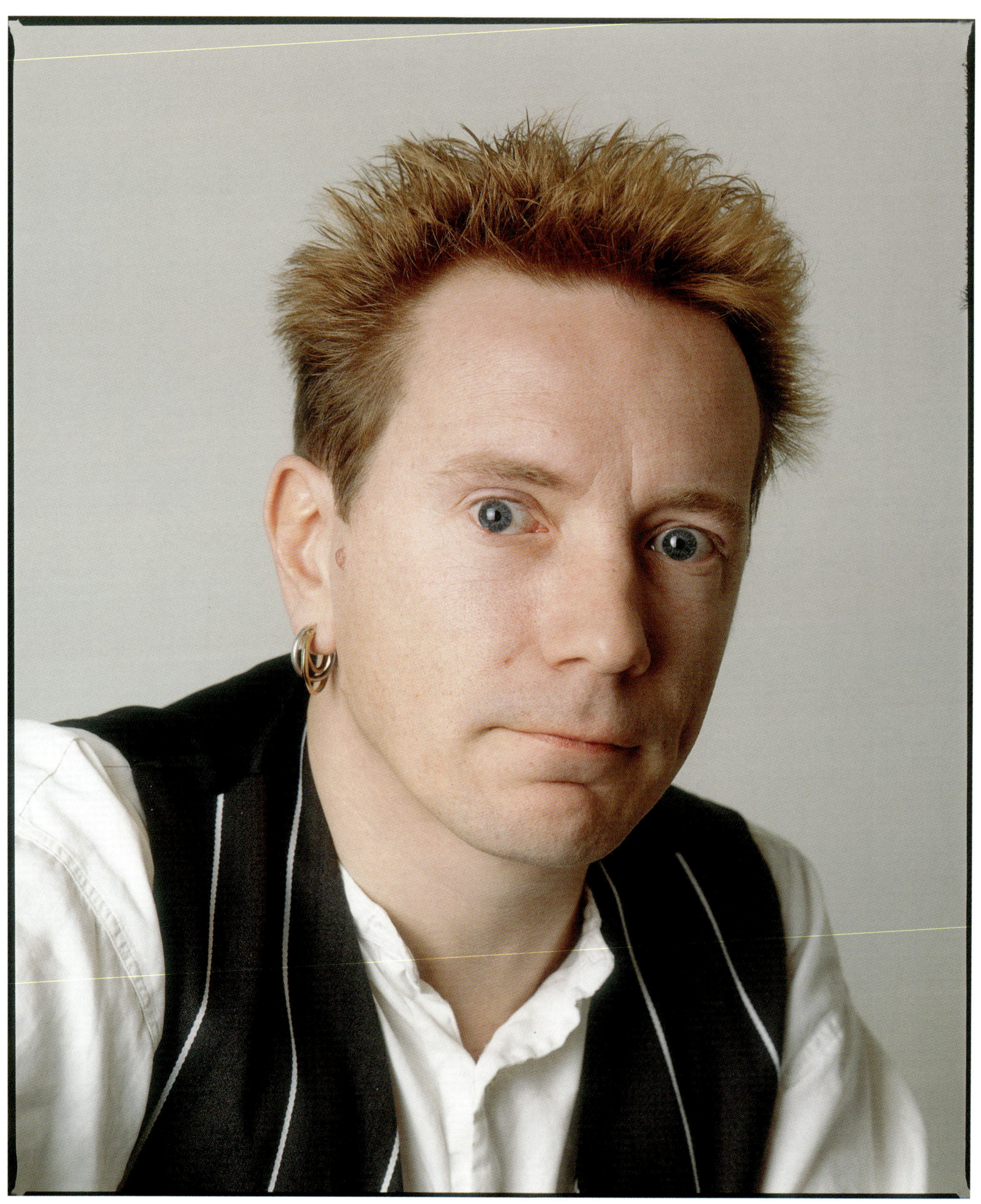

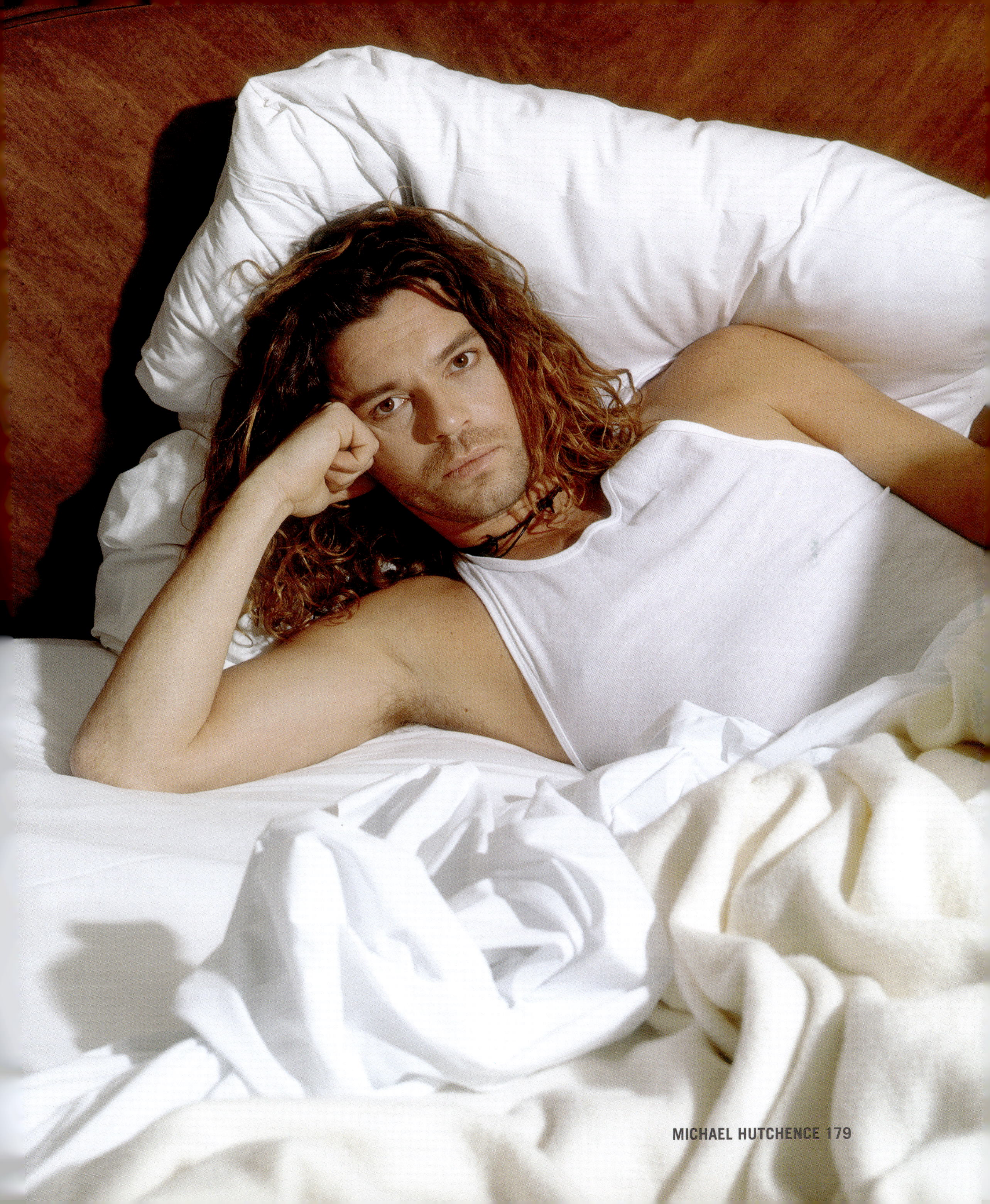MICHAEL HUTCHENCE 179

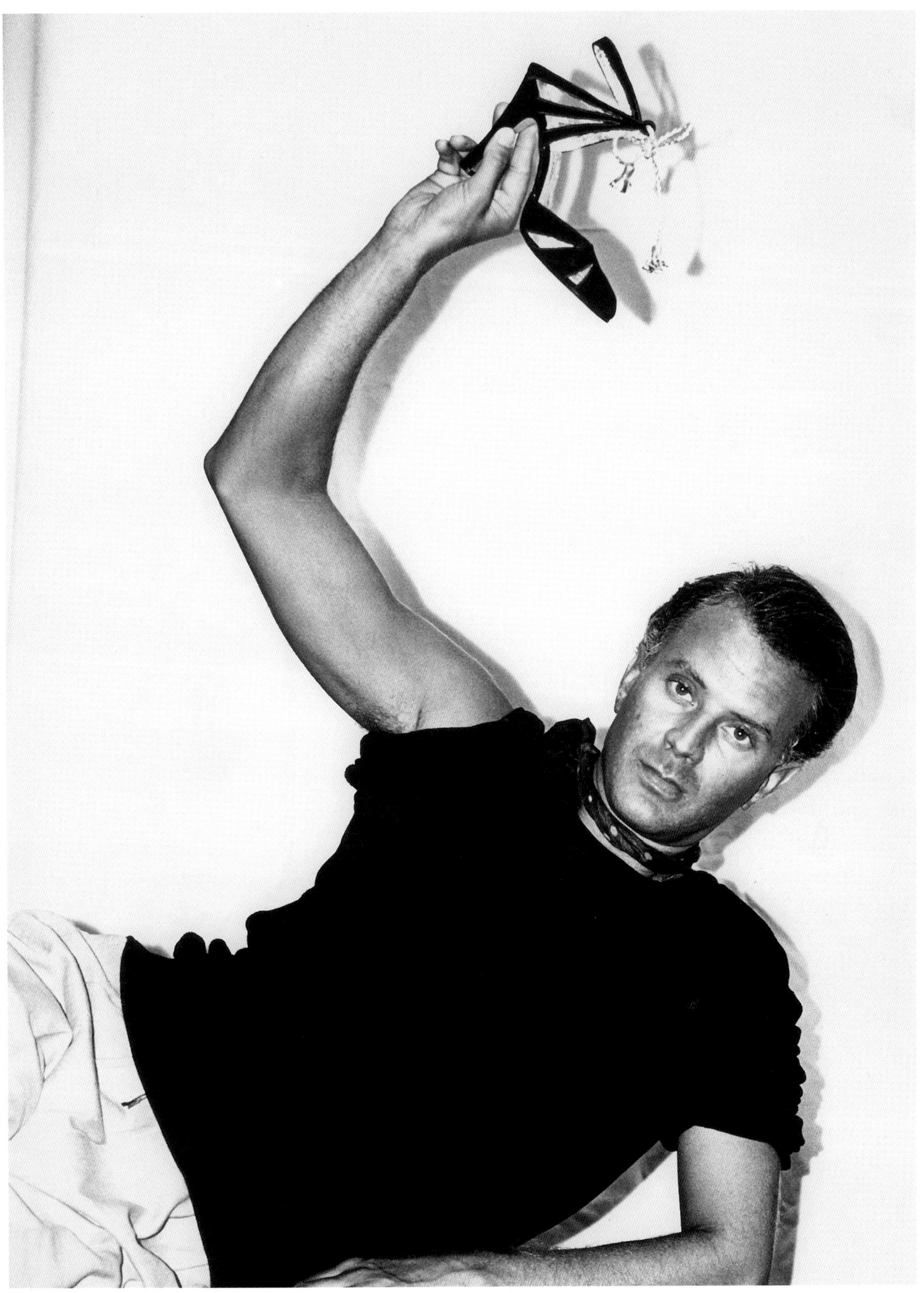

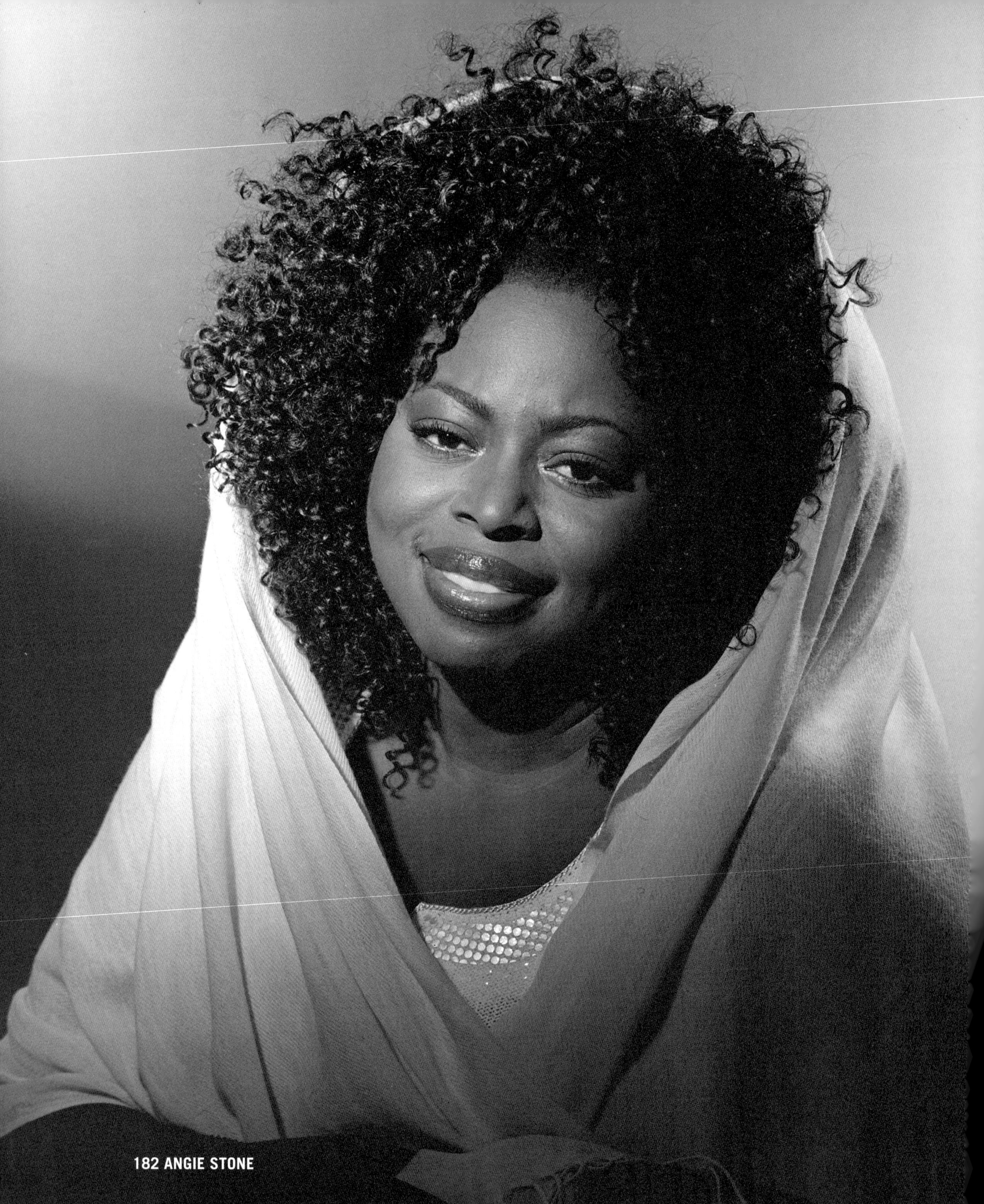

182 ANGIE STONE

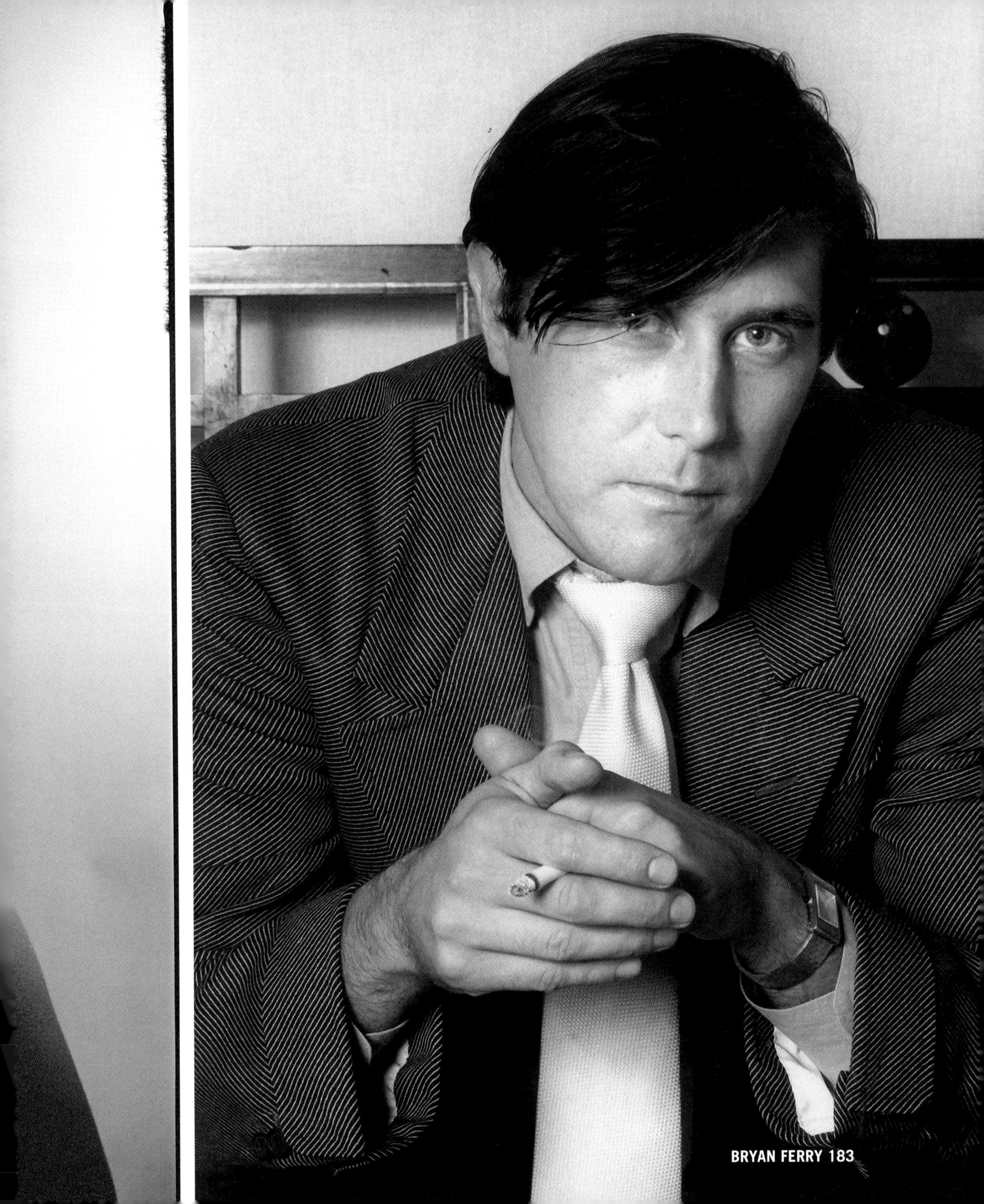

BRYAN FERRY 183

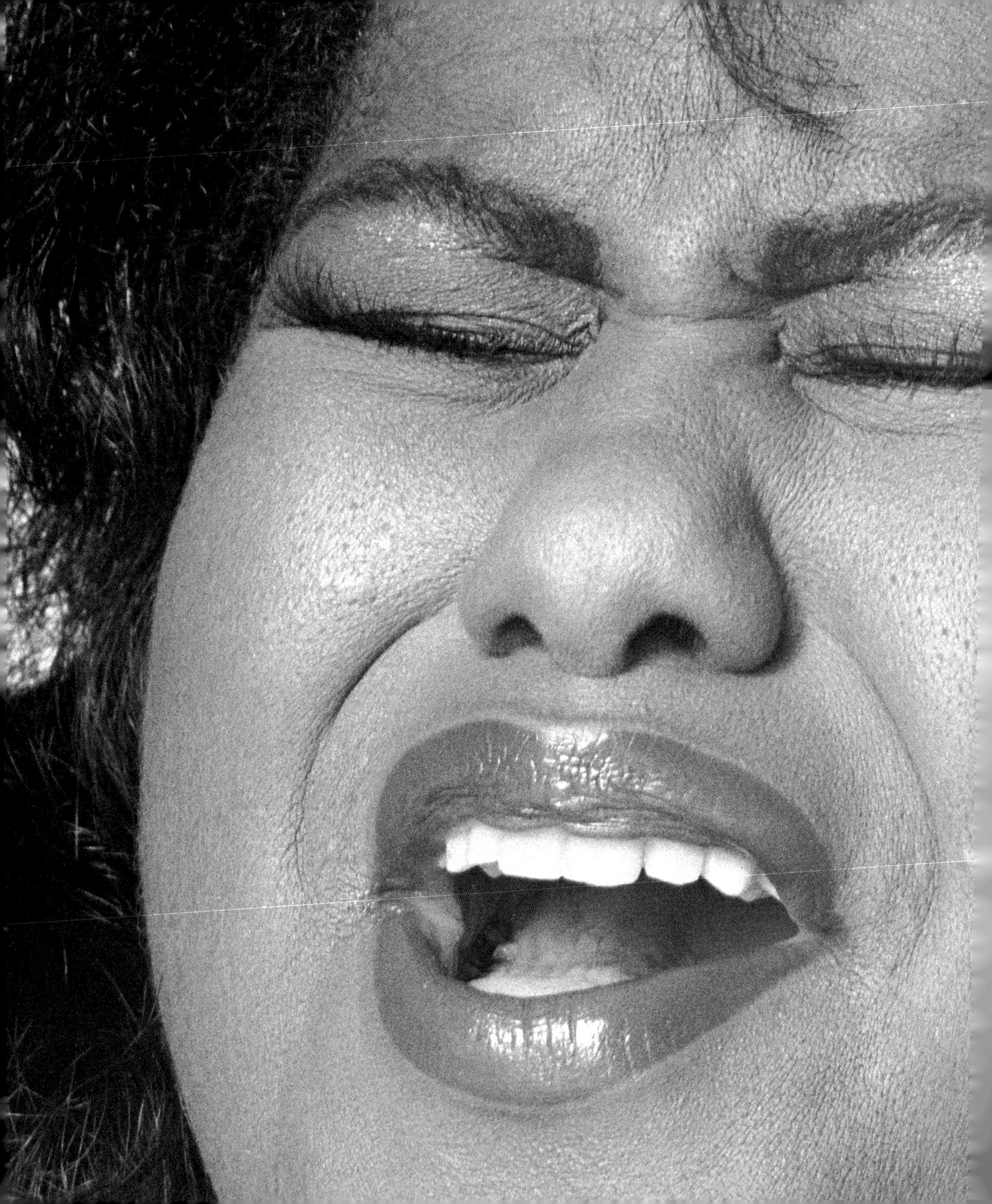

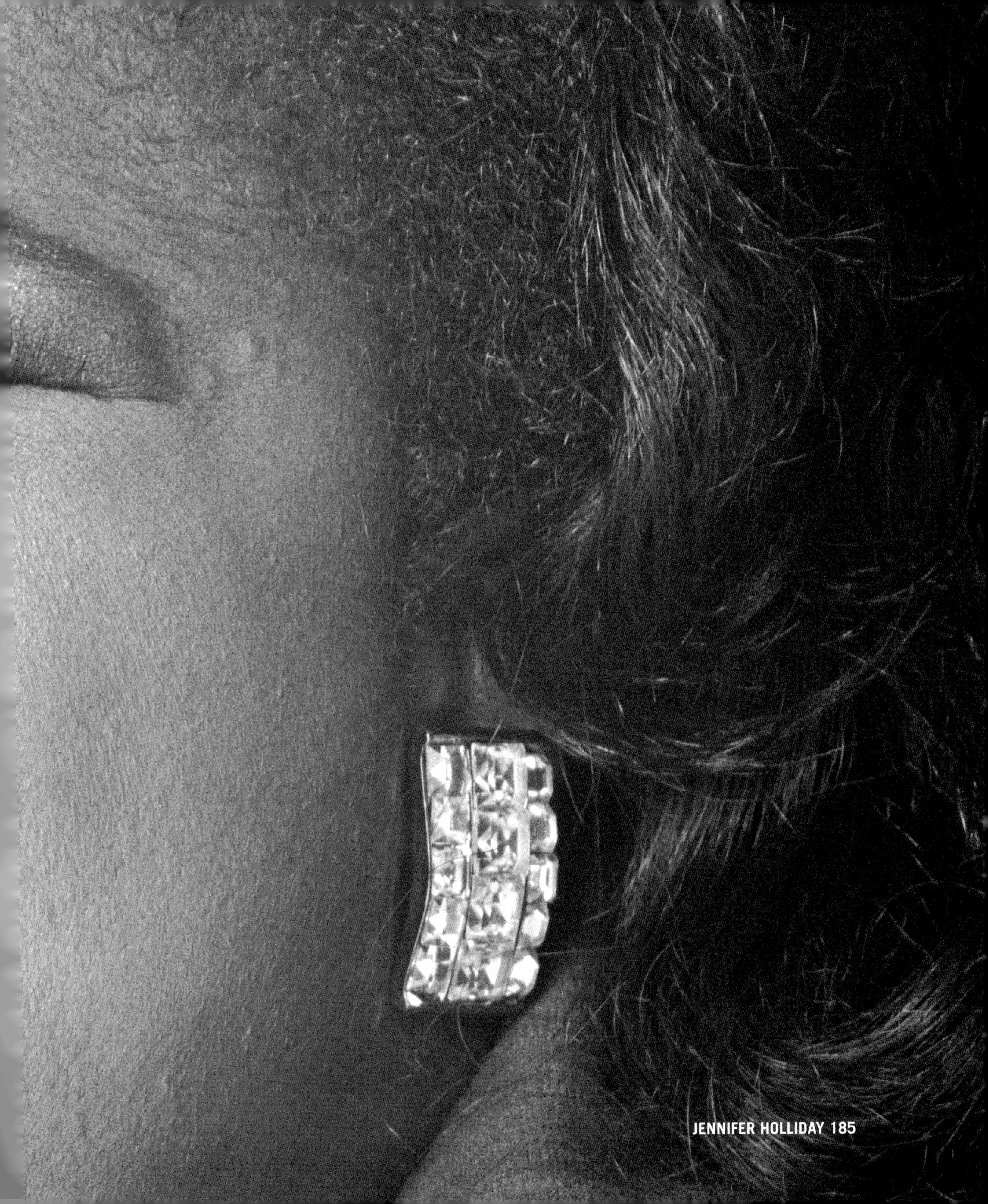
JENNIFER HOLLIDAY 185

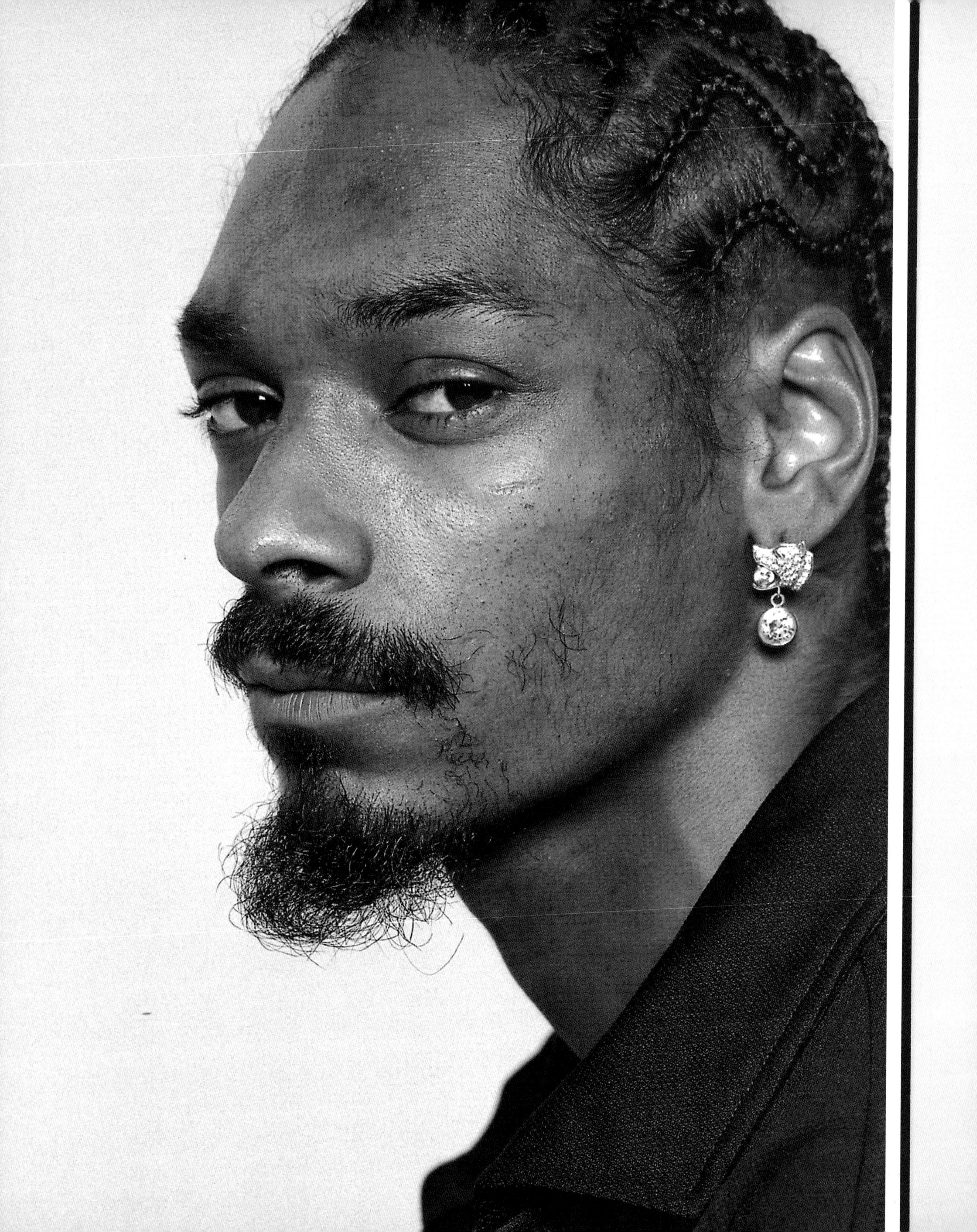

He appeared in
a cloud of smoke,
larger than life.
I remember a true
gentleman, a white
background, my
camera and his
intimidatingly
genuine eyes.

He appeared in
a cloud of smoke,
larger than life.
I remember a true
gentleman, a white
background, my
camera and his
intimidatingly
genuine eyes.

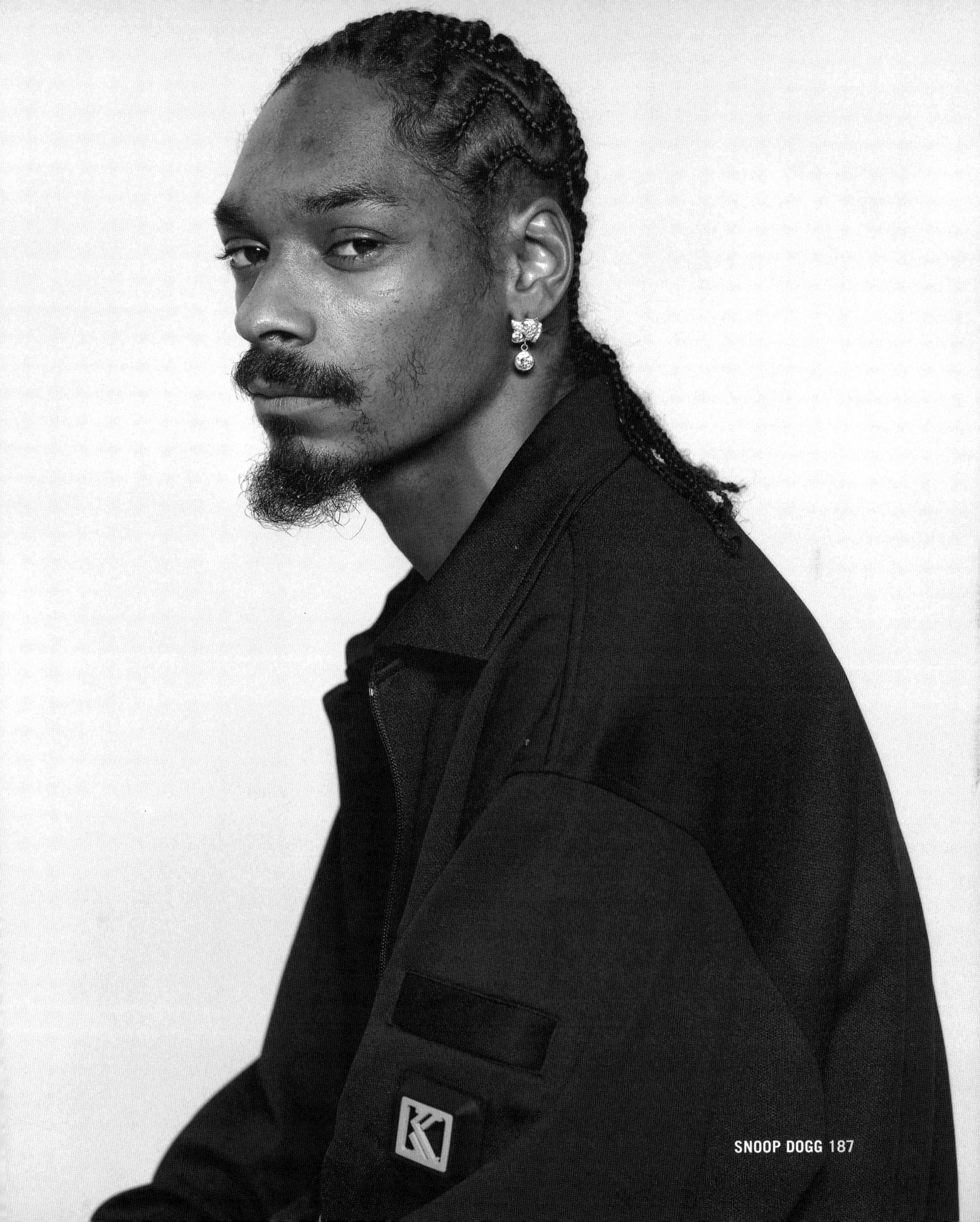
SNOOP DOGG 187

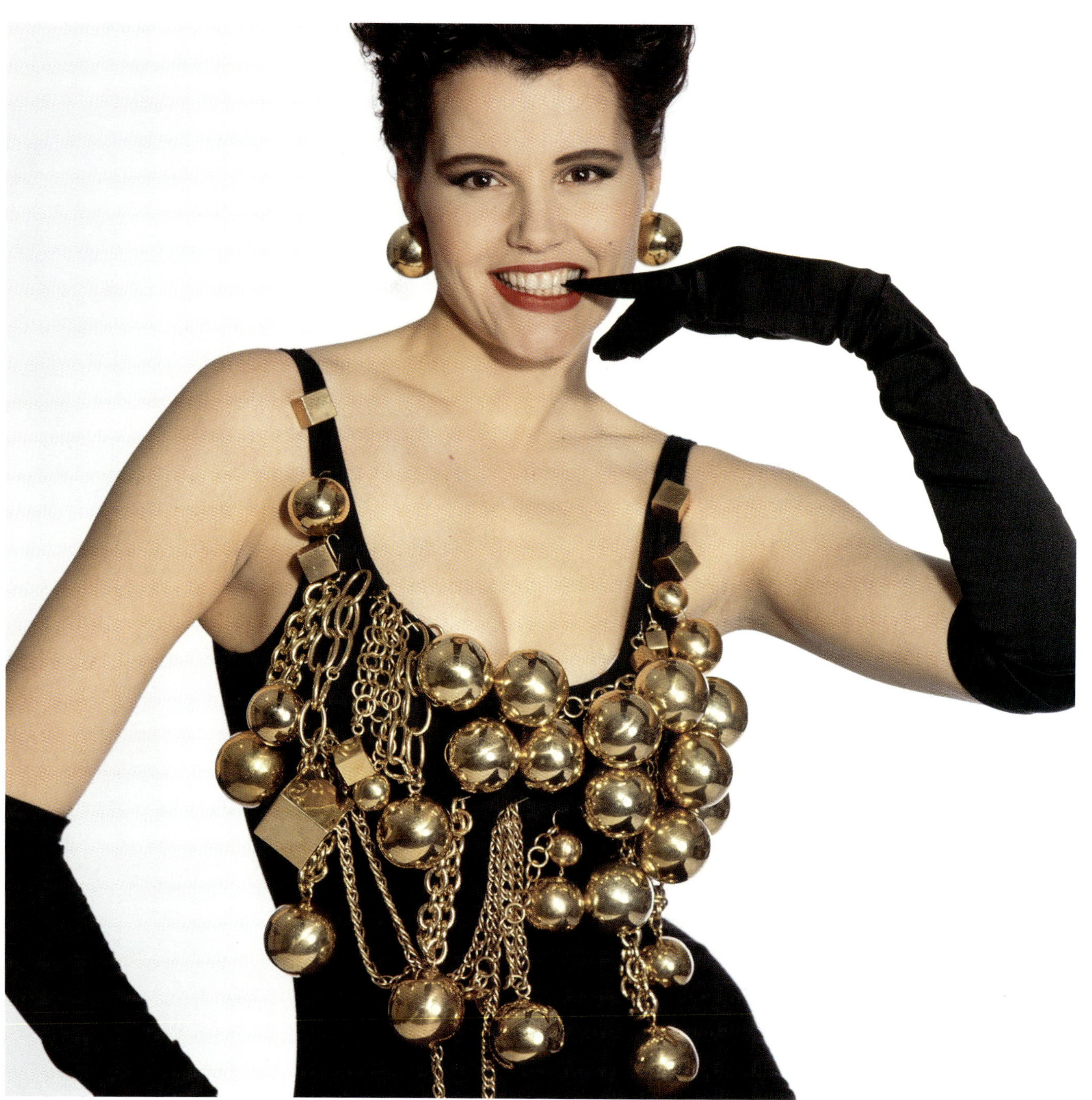

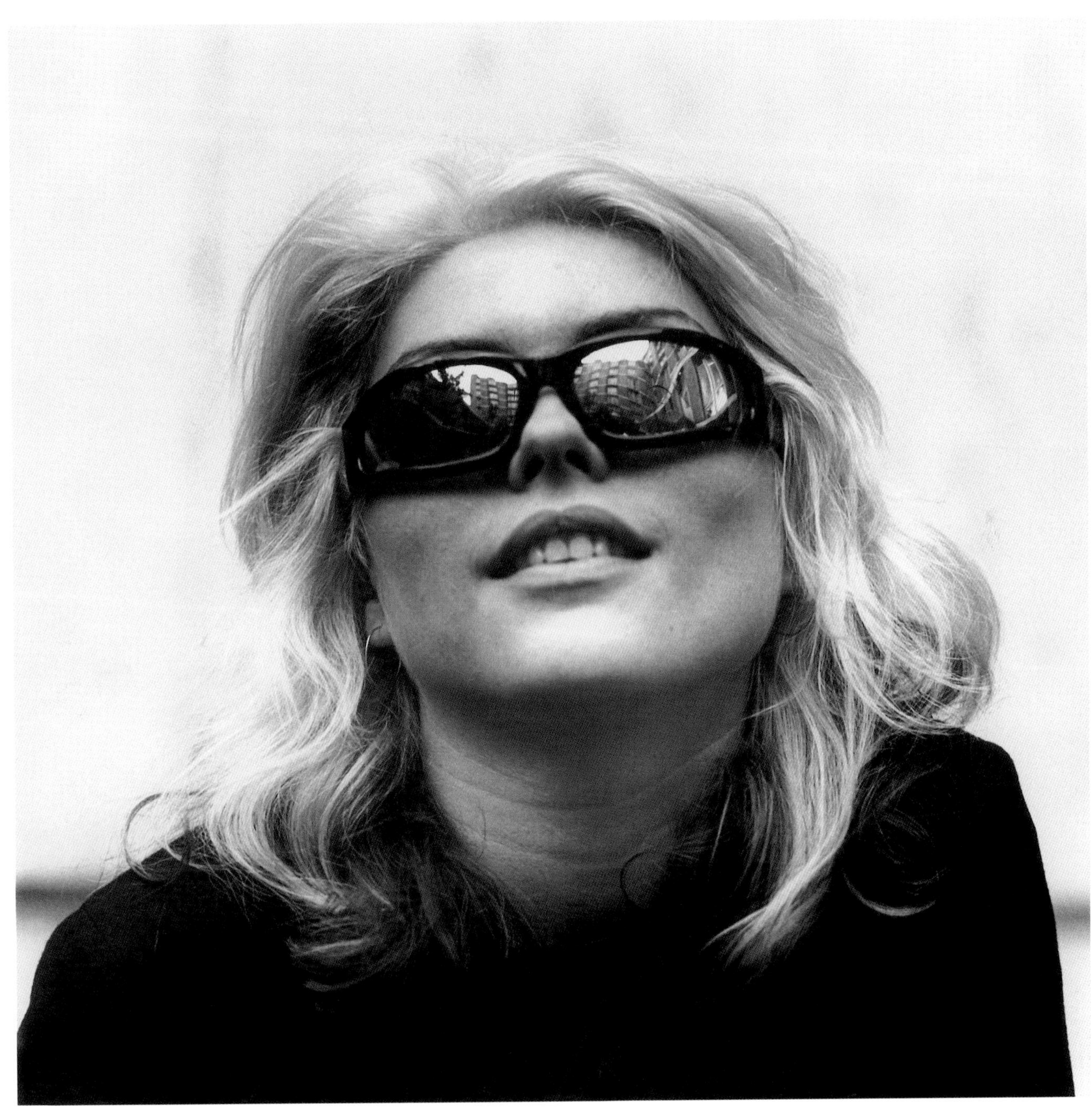

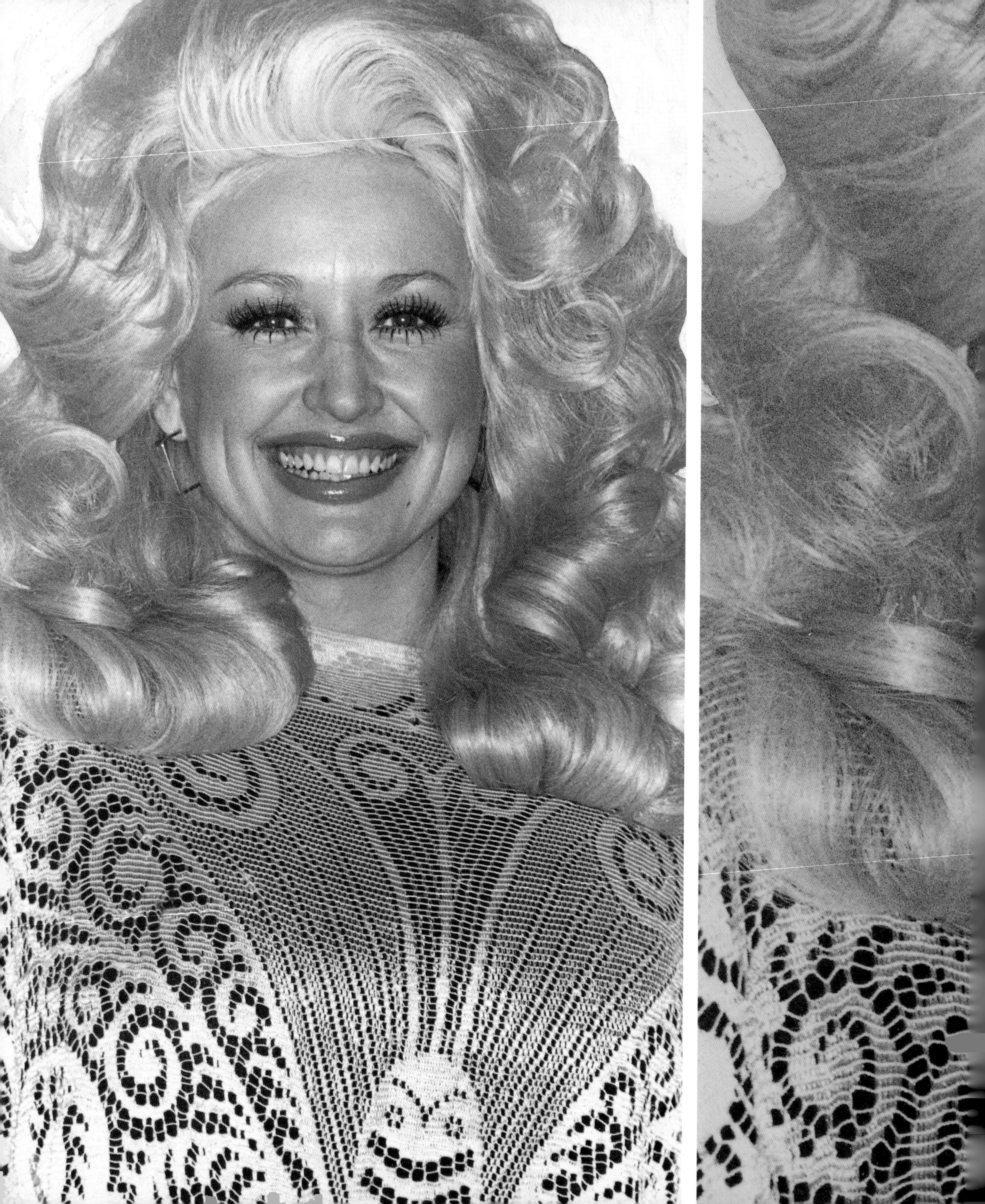

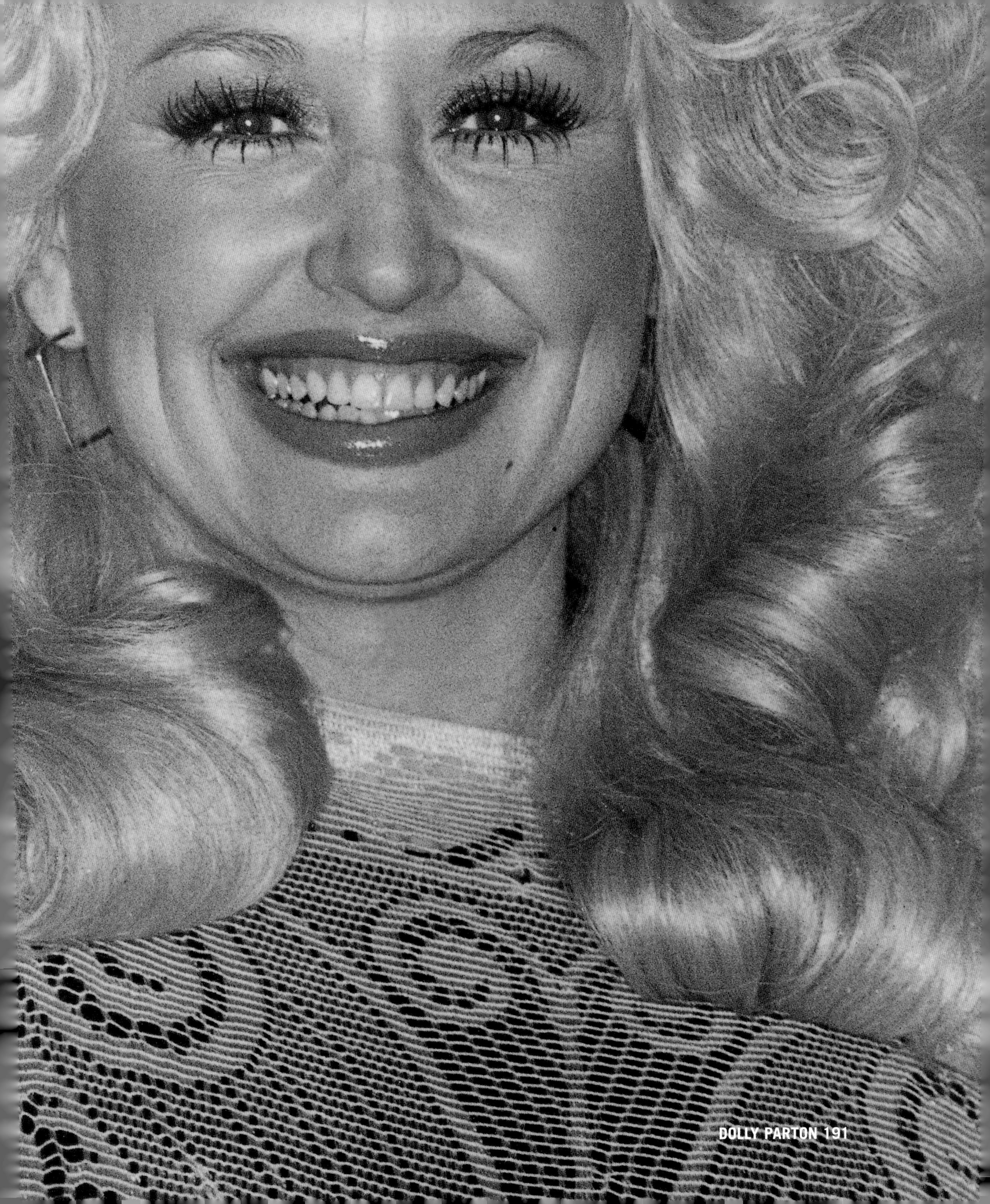
DOLLY PARTON 191

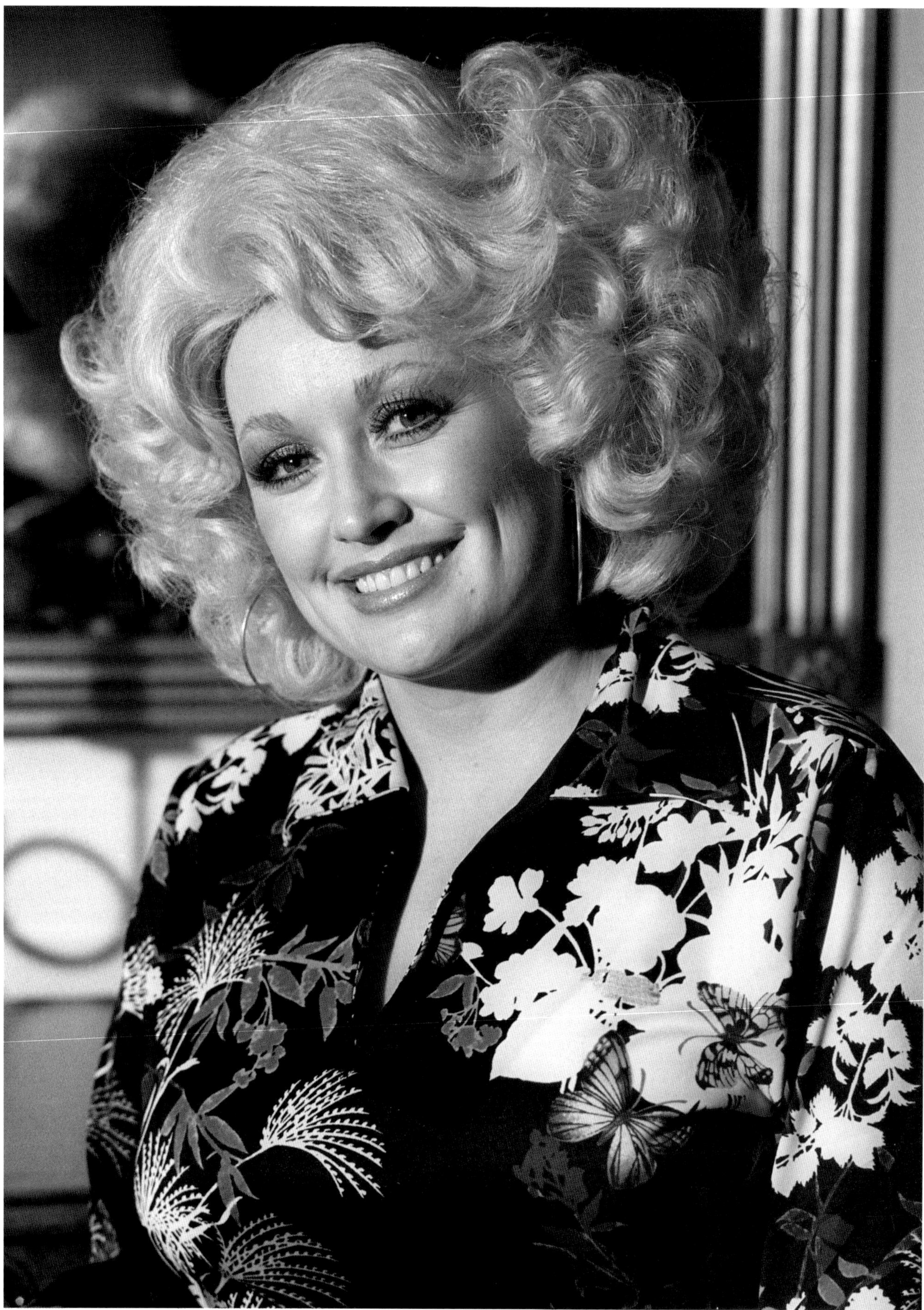

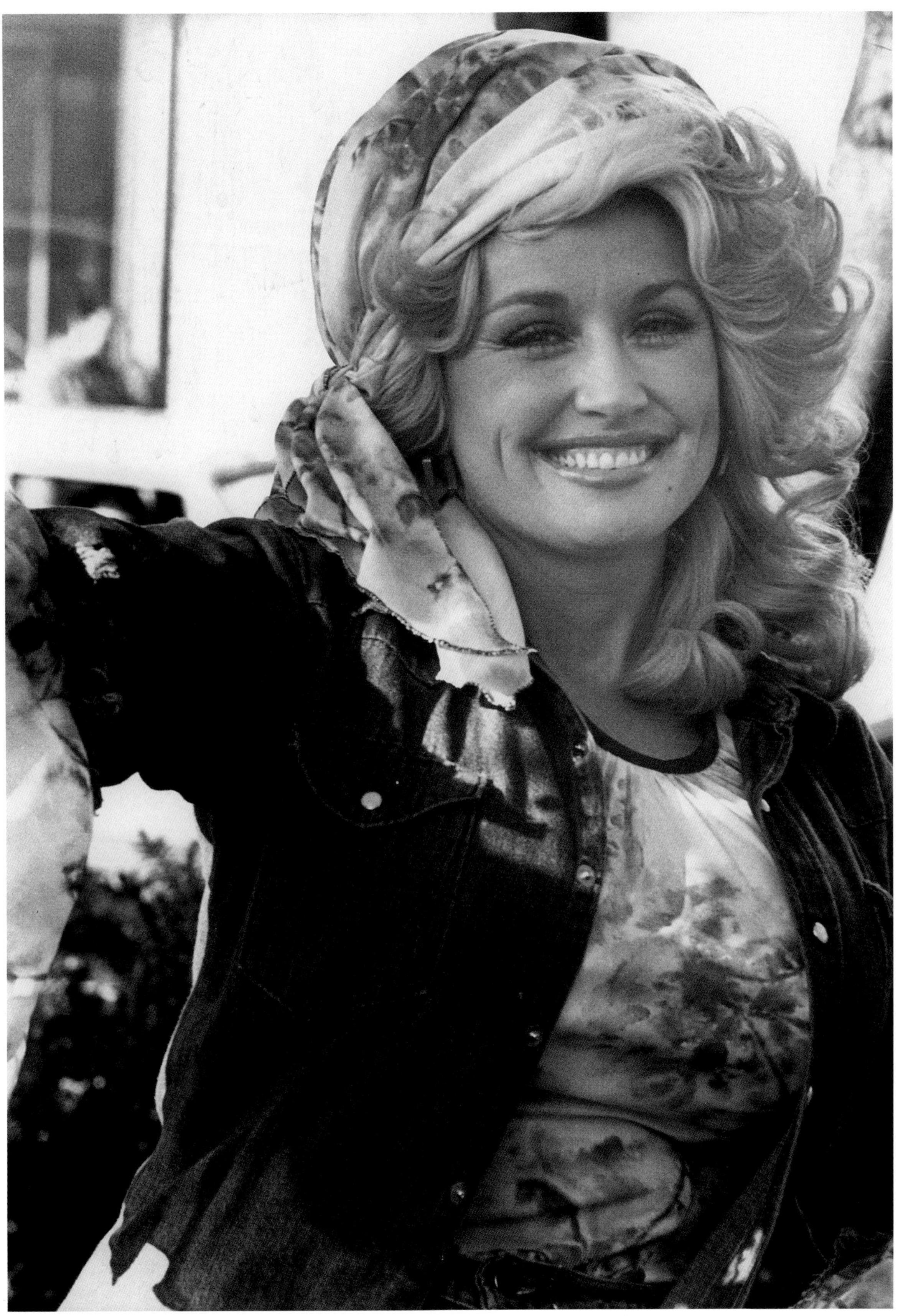

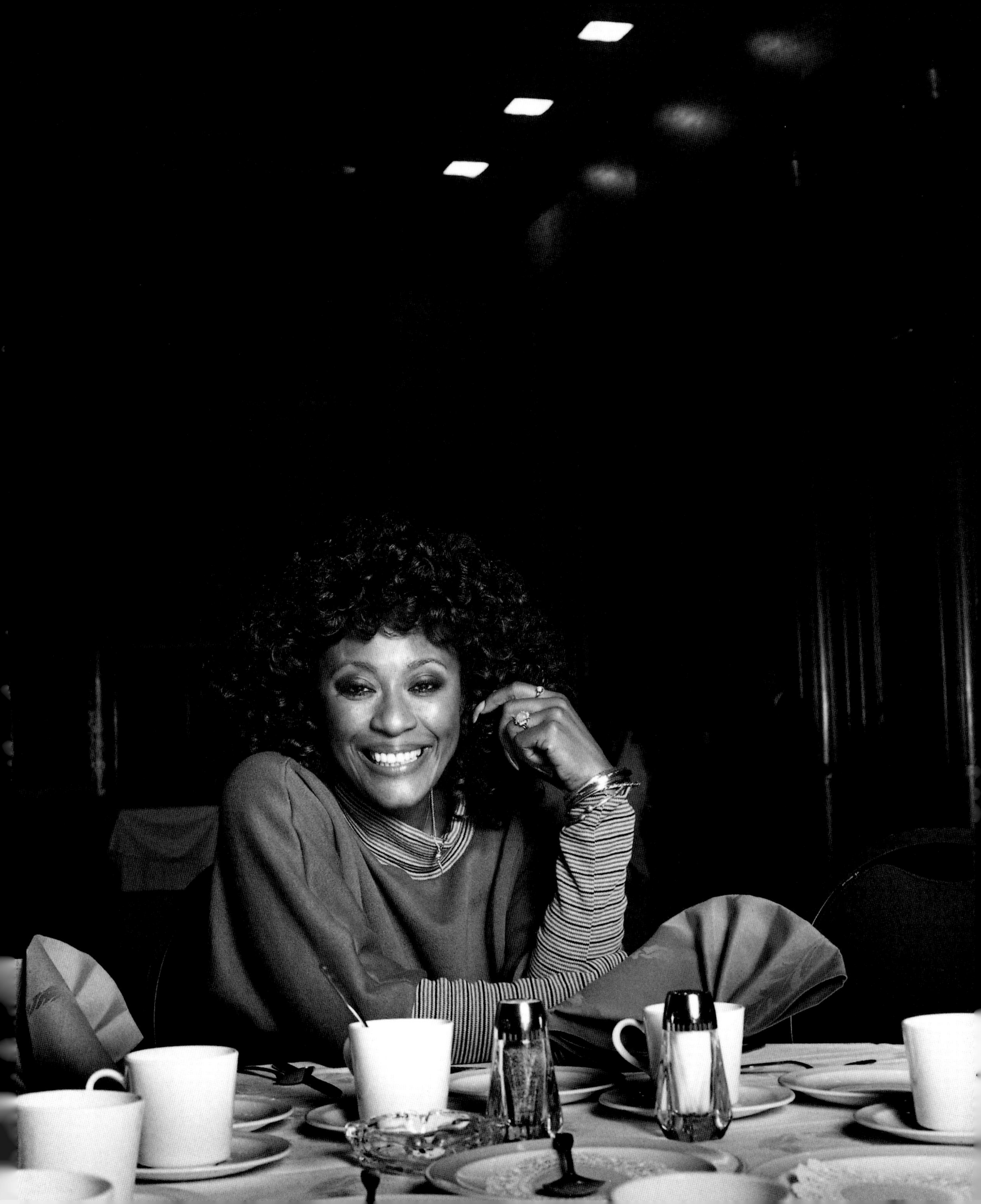

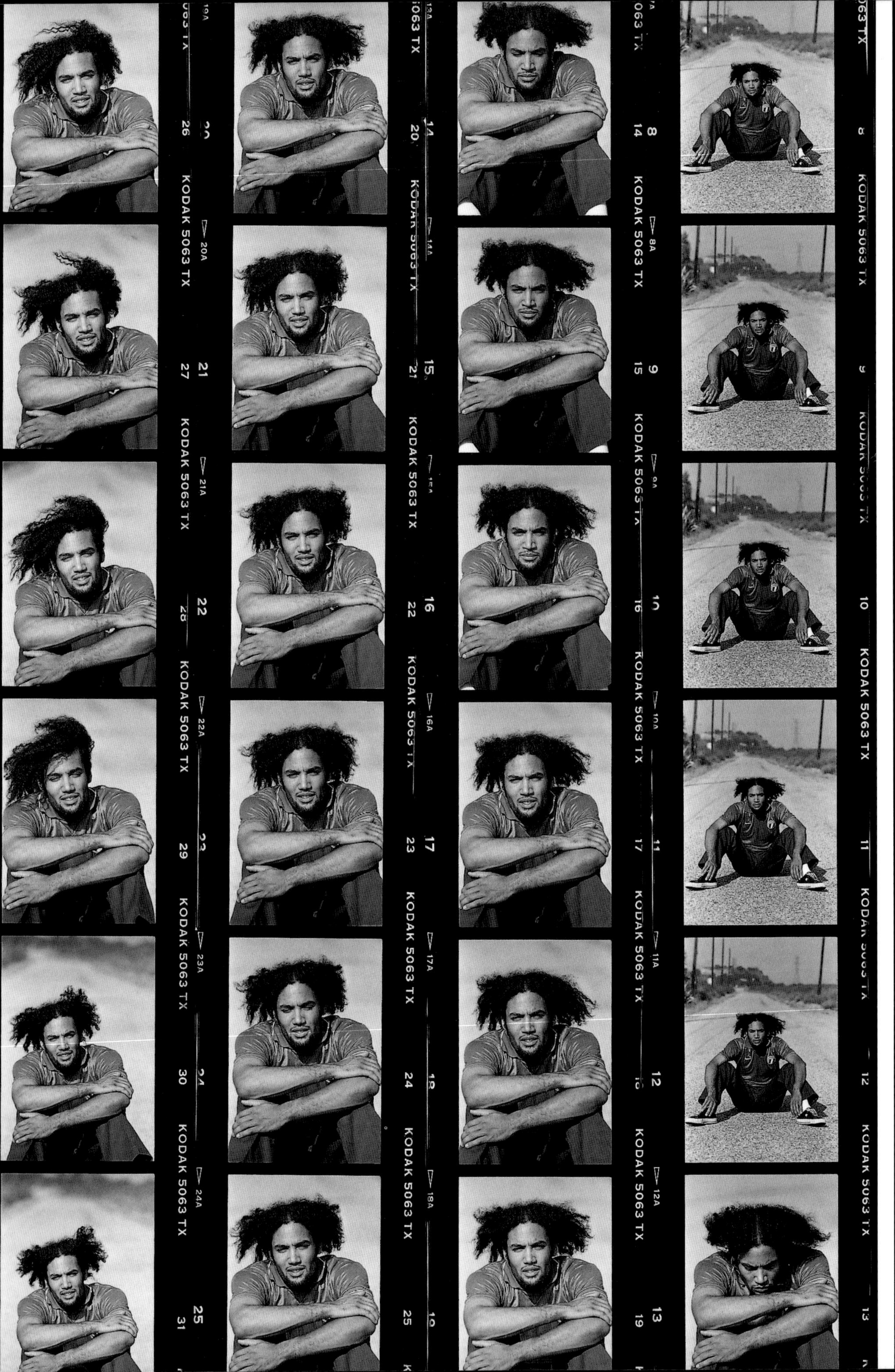

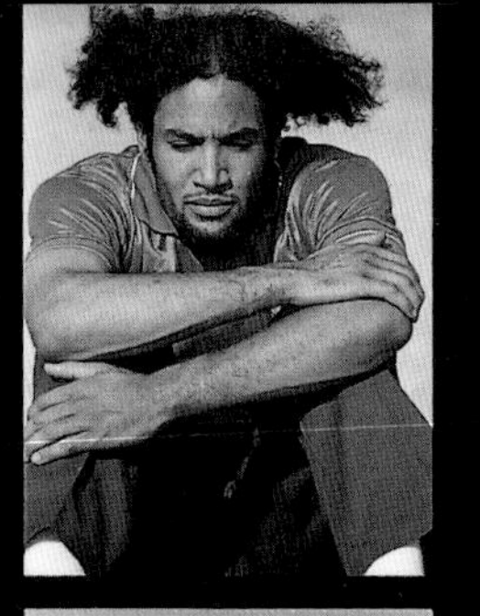
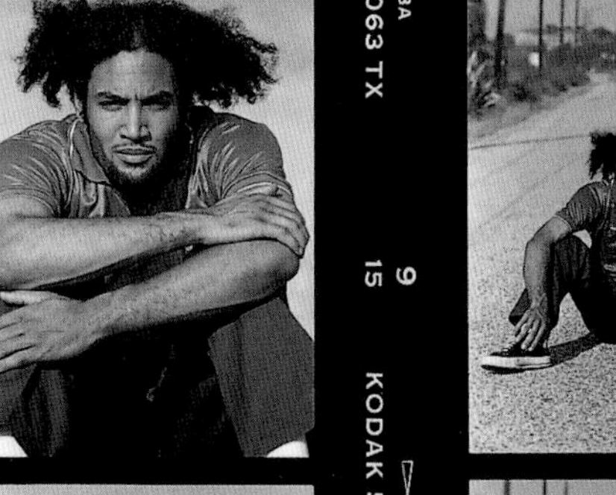
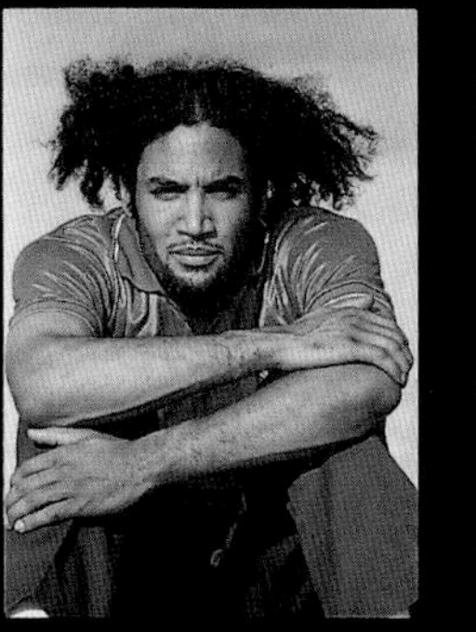
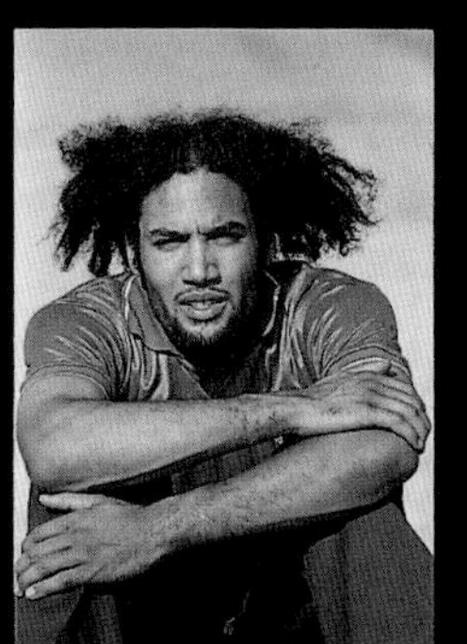
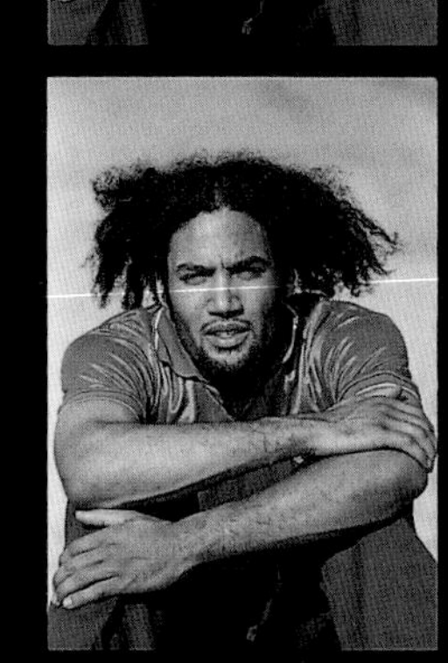
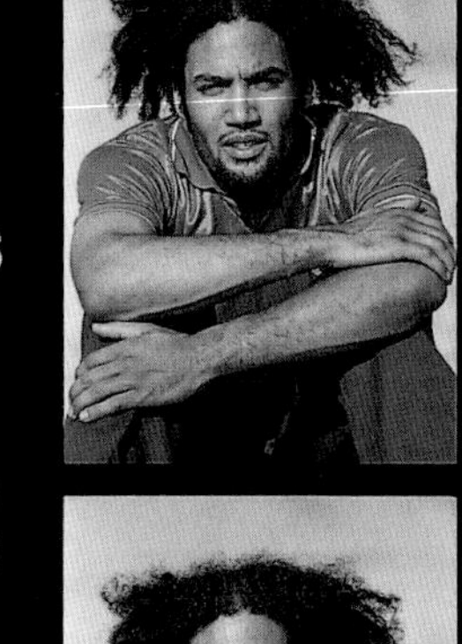
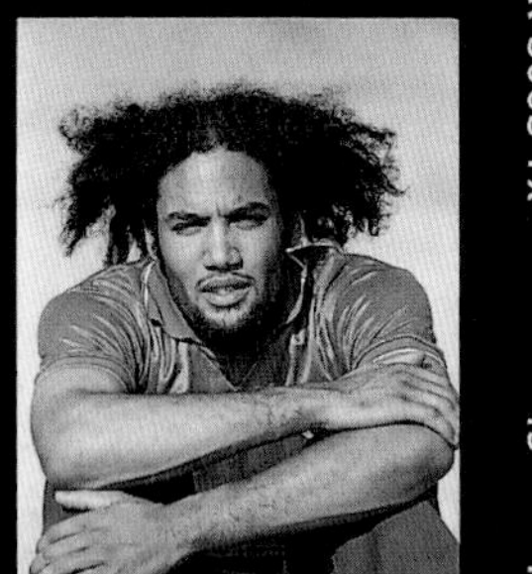
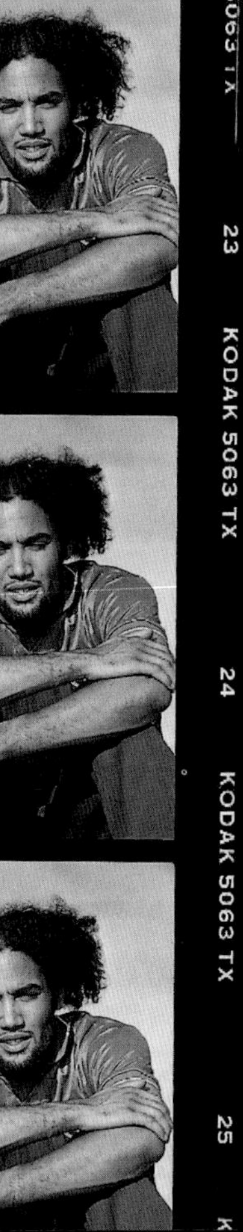
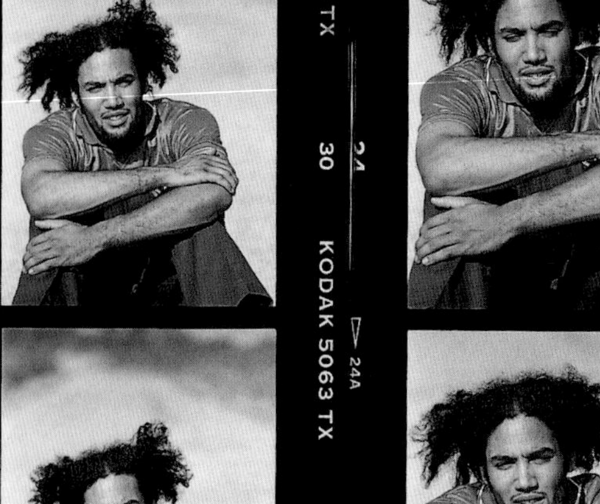
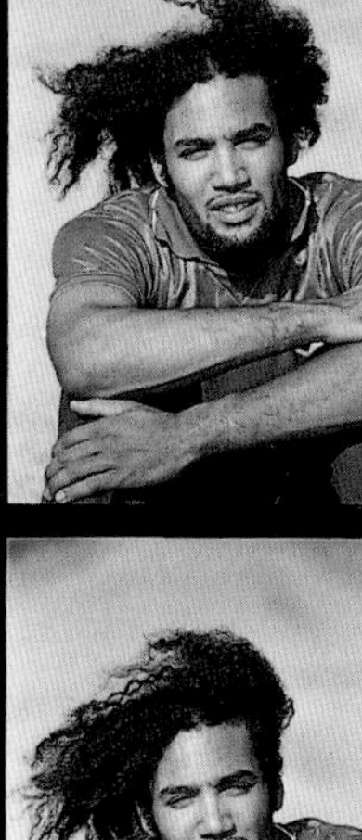
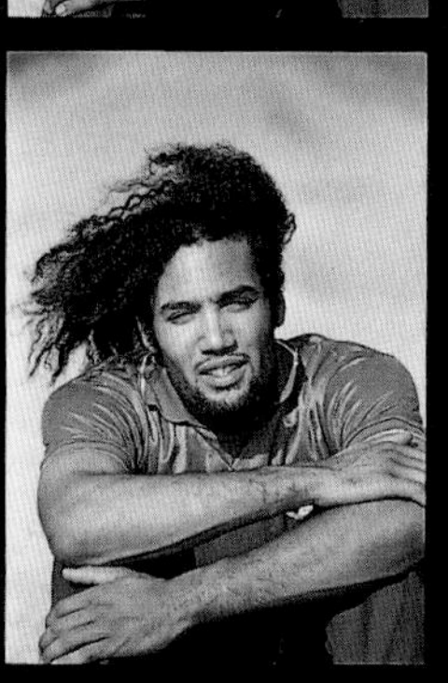
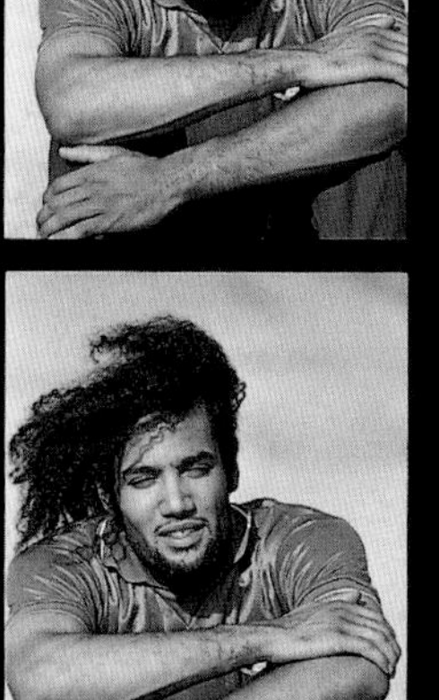
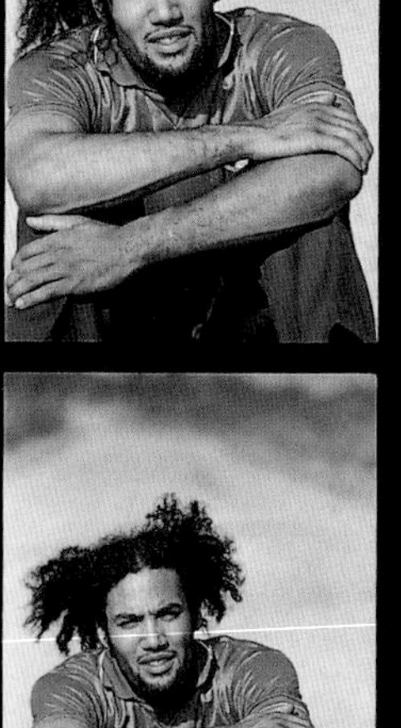
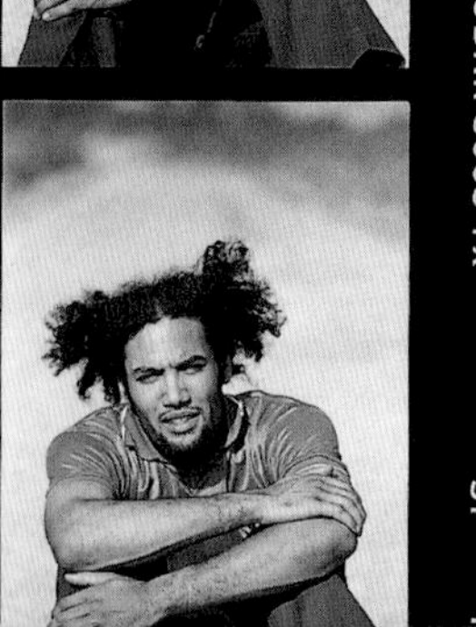

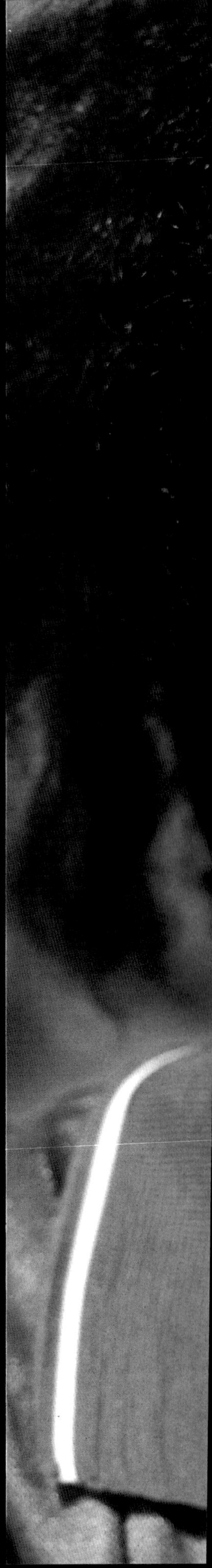

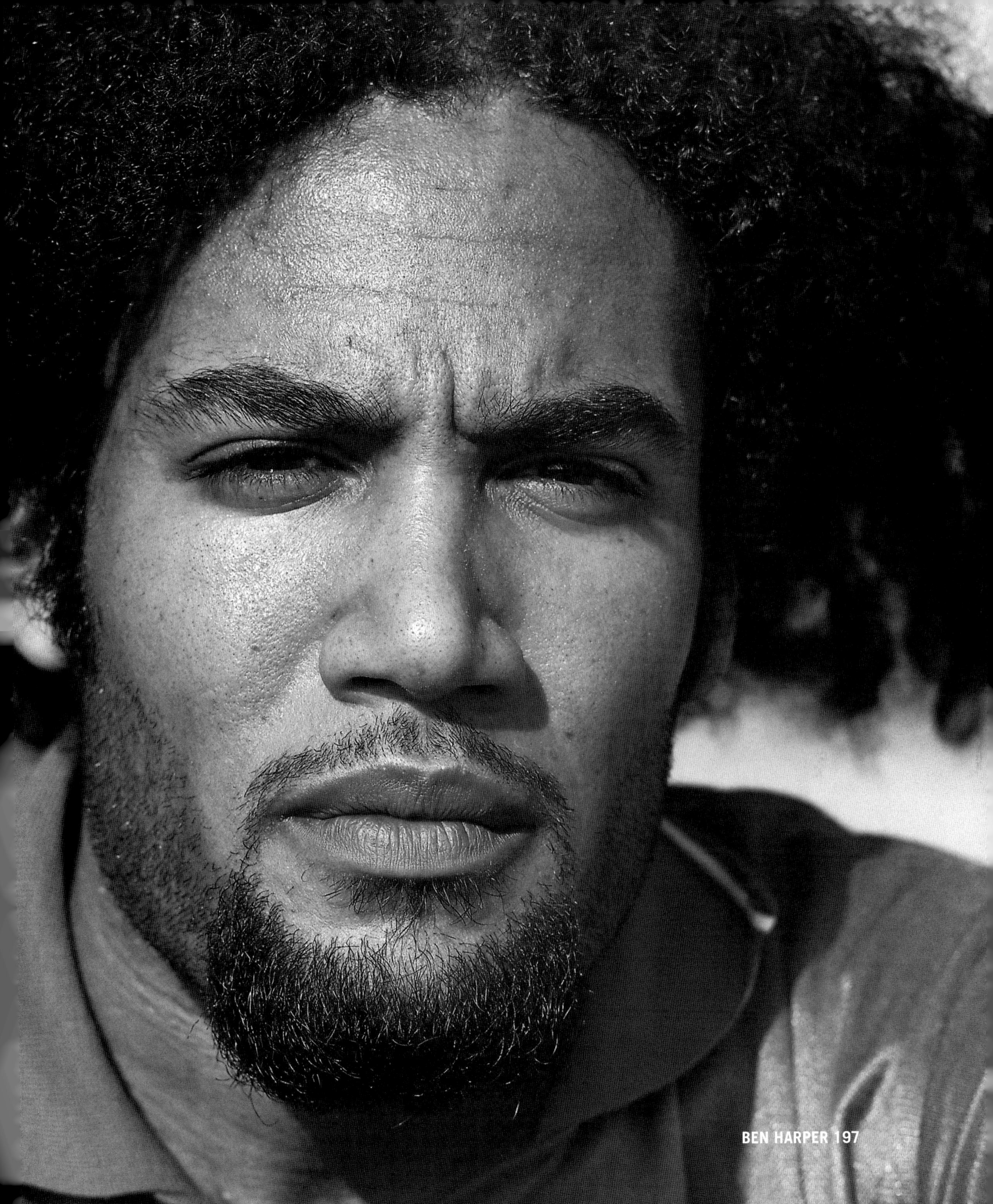
BEN HARPER 197

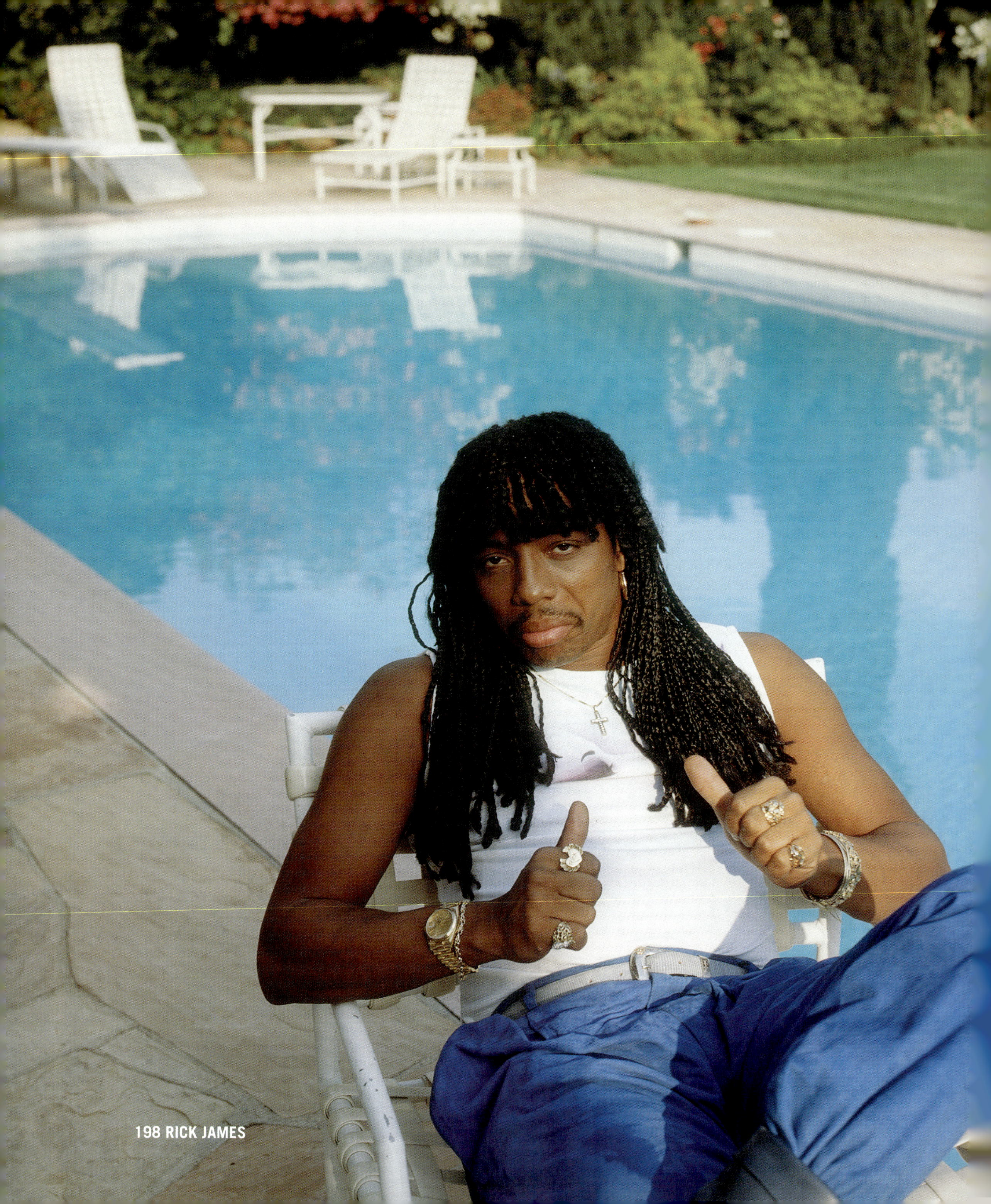
198 RICK JAMES

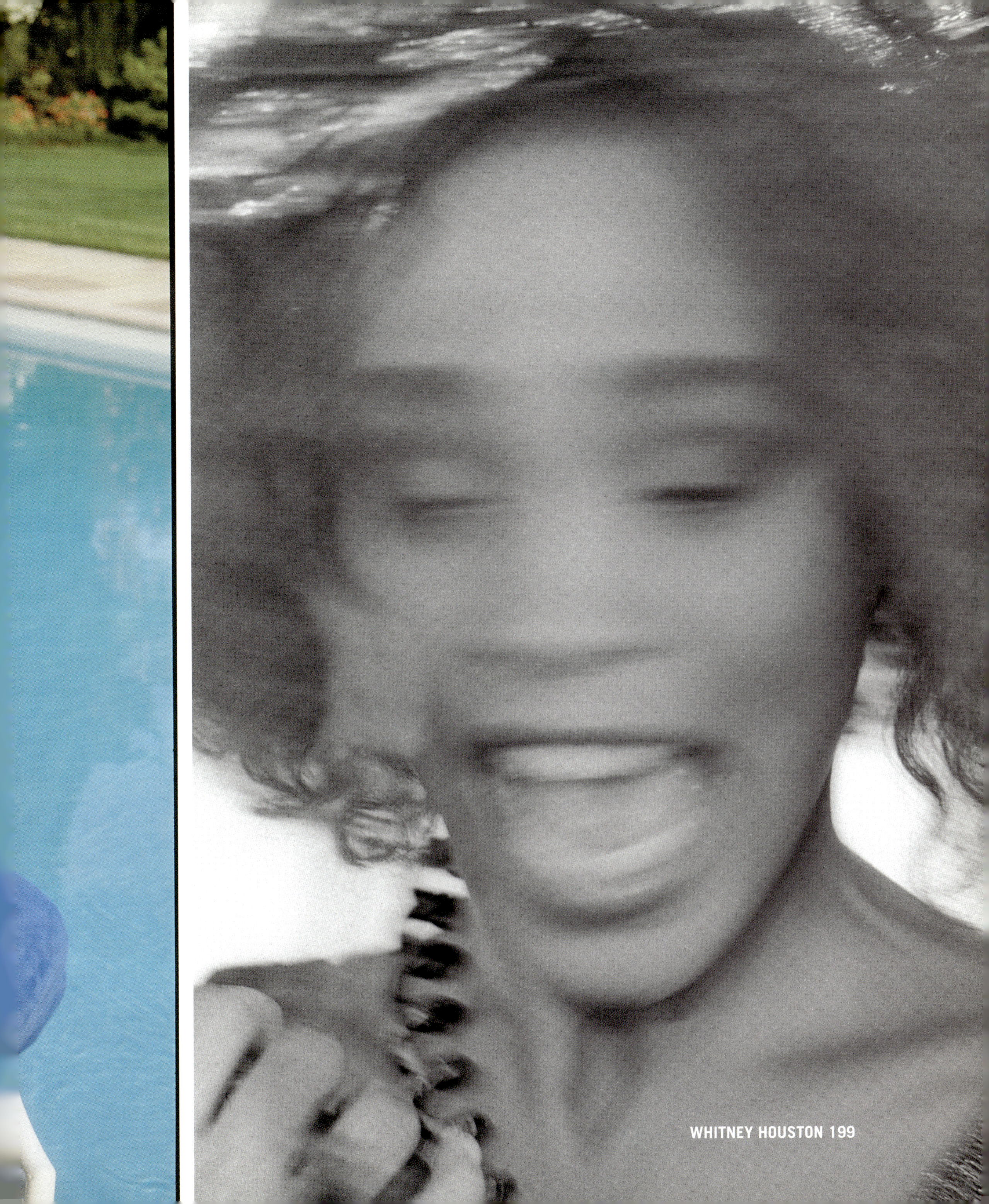
WHITNEY HOUSTON 199

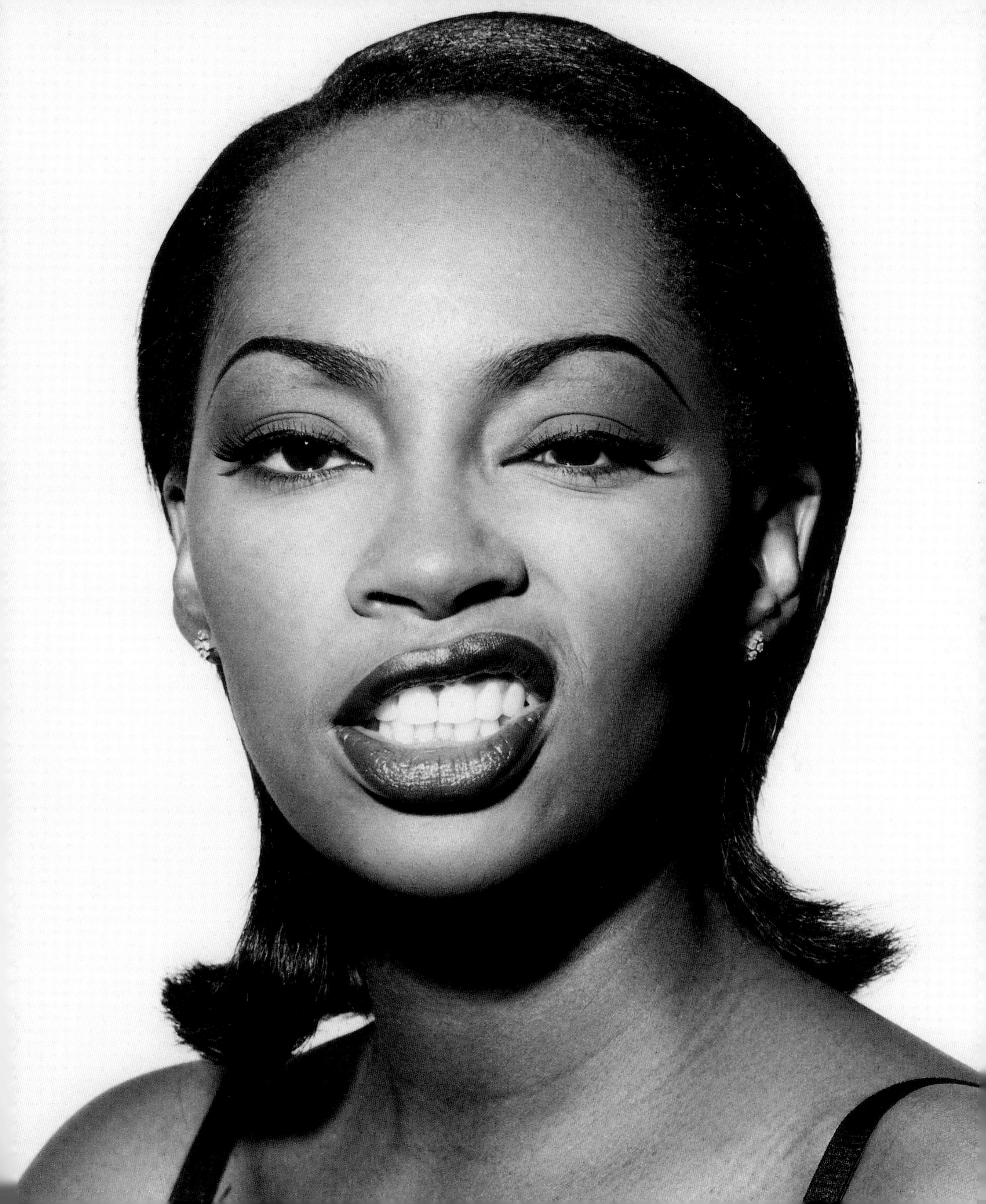

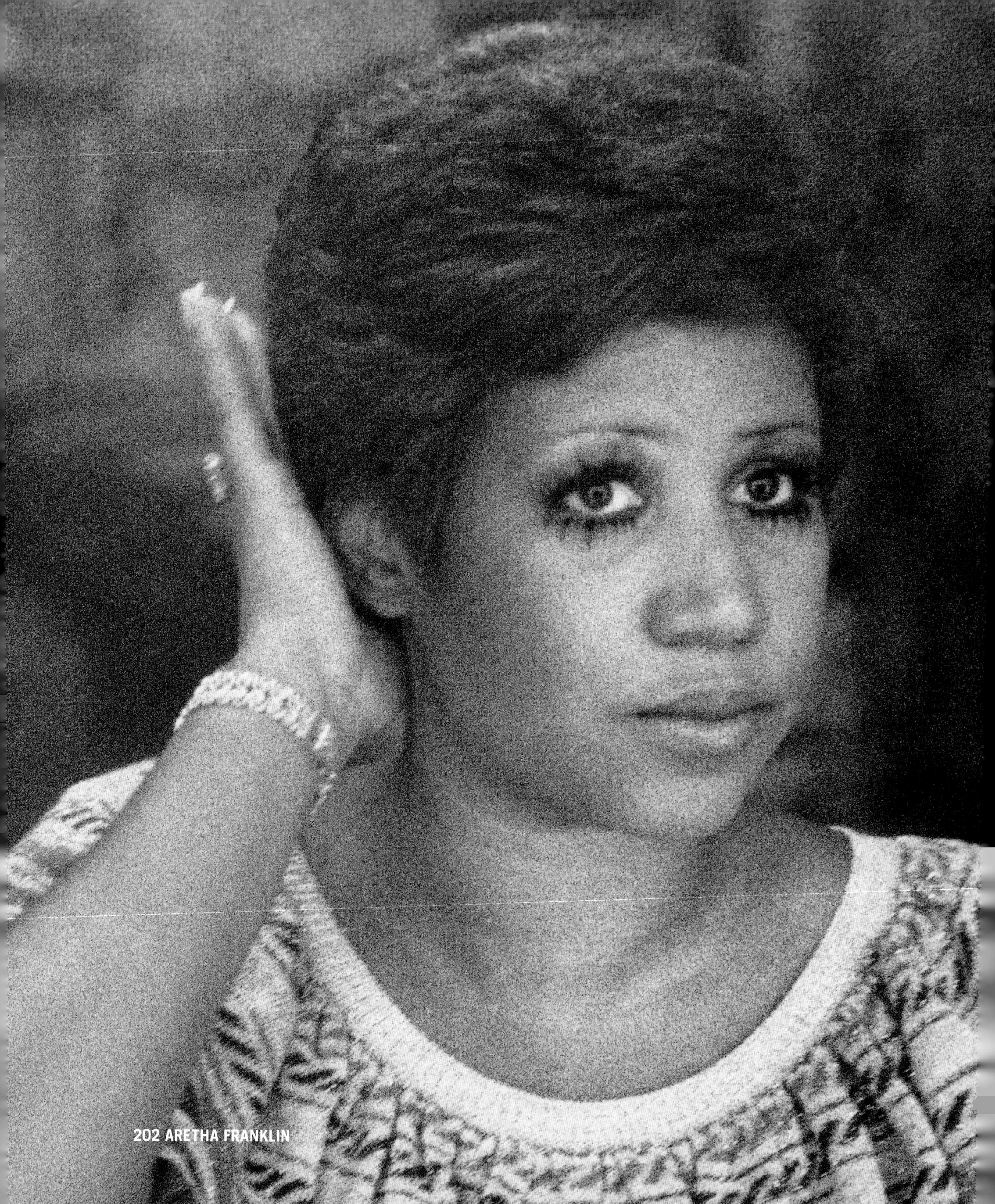
202 ARETHA FRANKLIN

I managed to shoot her in her dressing room. Casually, I said, "Aretha could you please look into my camera?" She snapped back: "Call me Miss Franklin."

I managed to
shoot her in her
dressing room.
Casually, I said,
"Aretha could you
please look into
my camera?" She
snapped back:
"Call me Miss
Franklin."

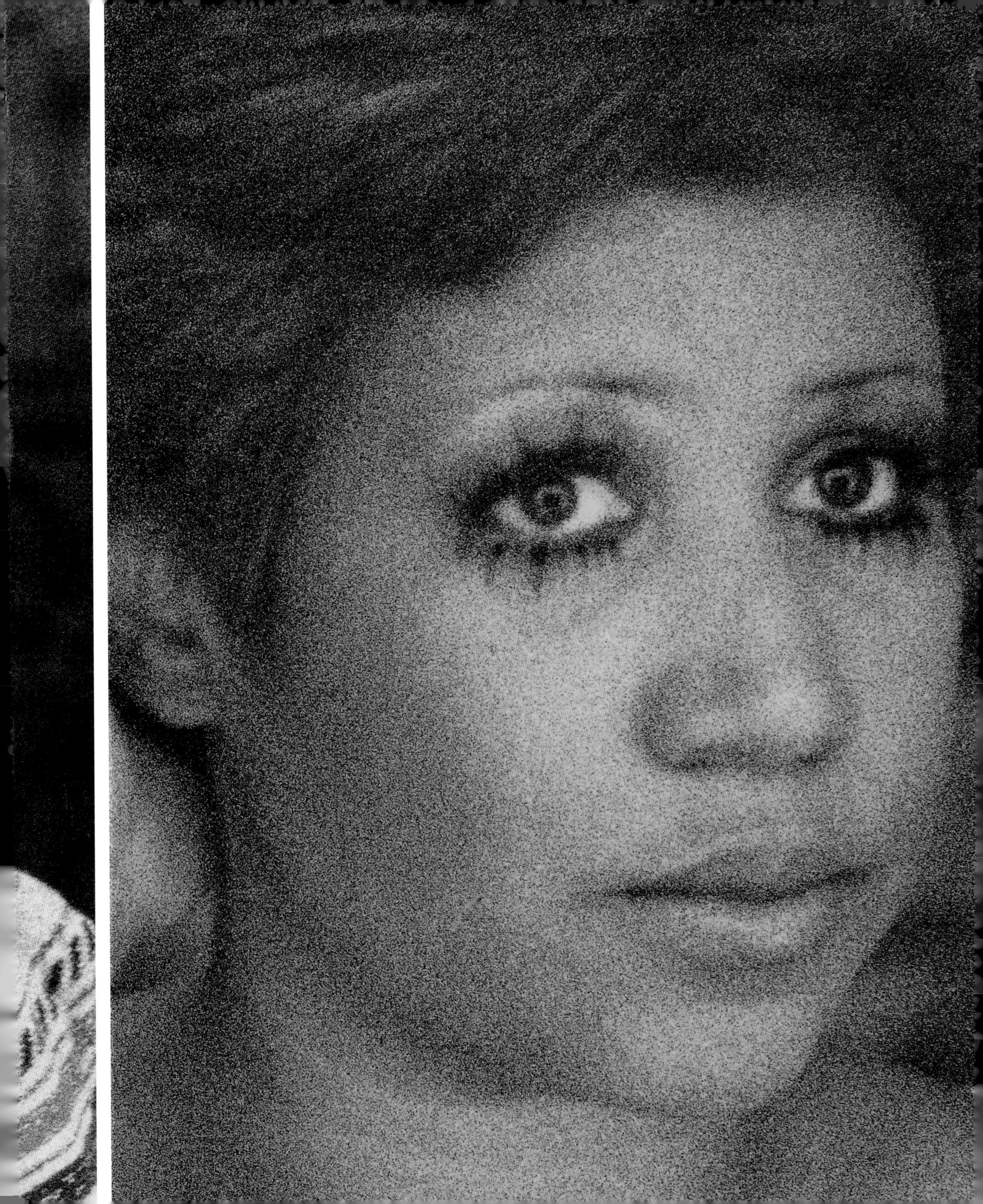

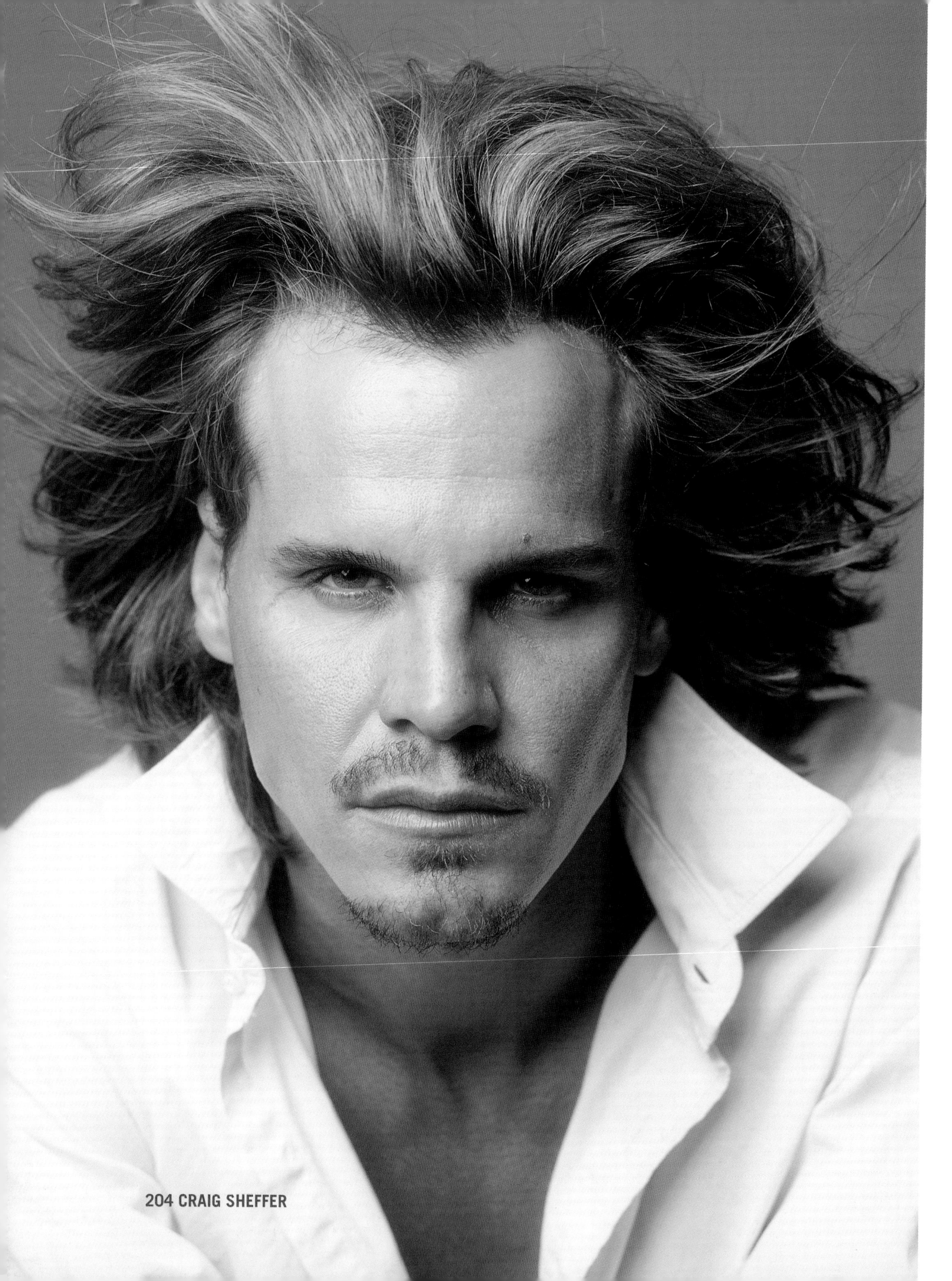
204 CRAIG SHEFFER

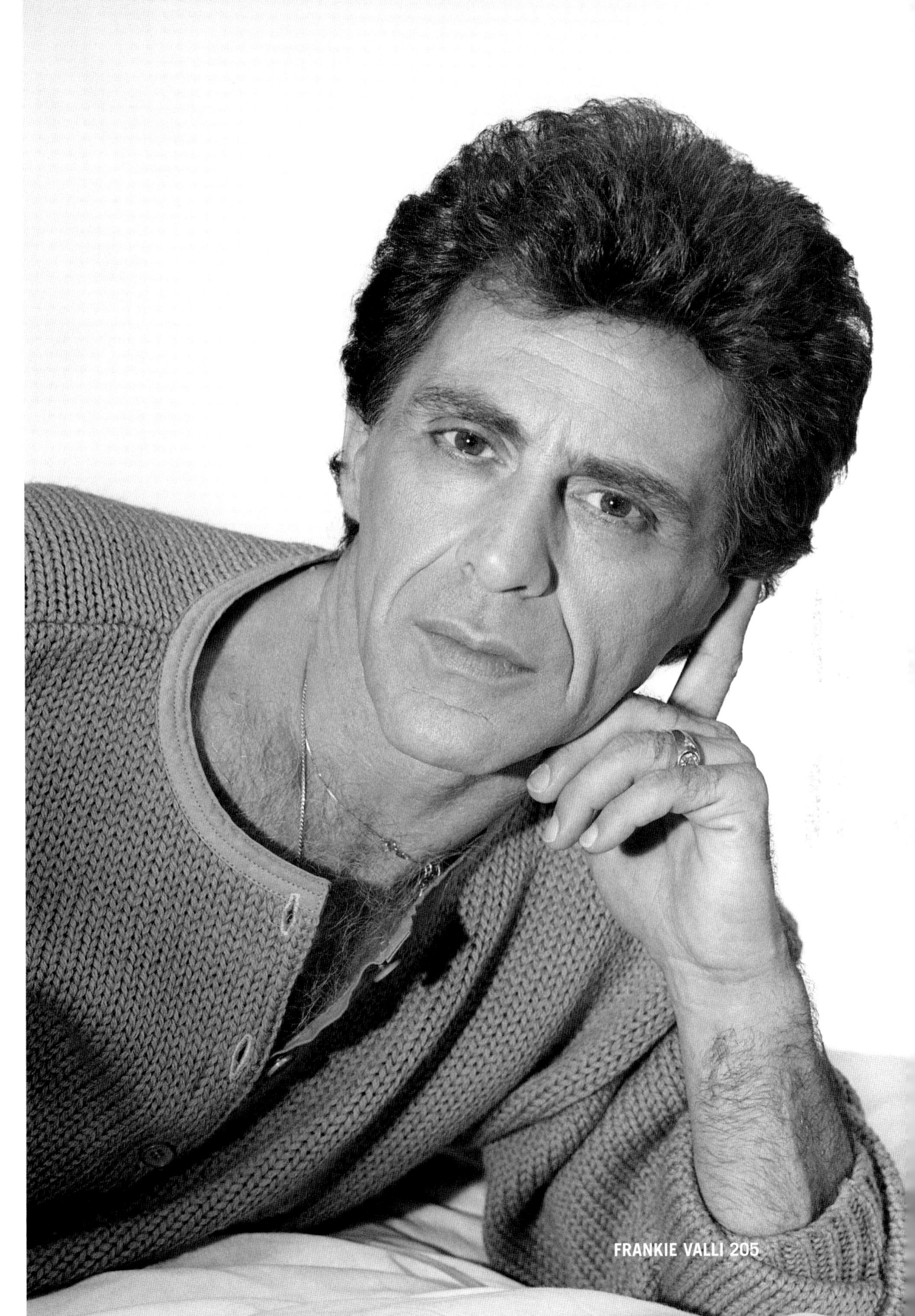
FRANKIE VALLI 205

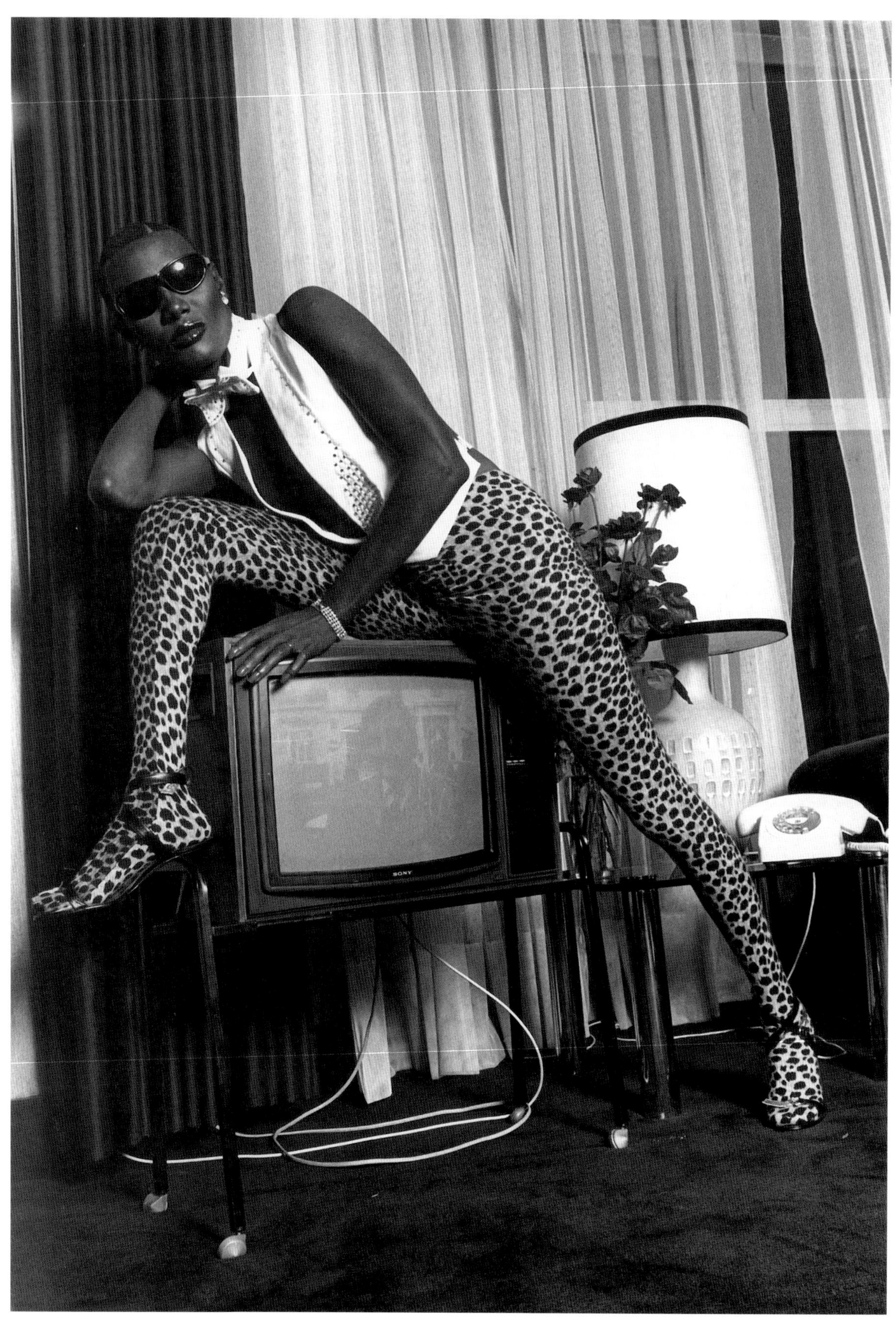

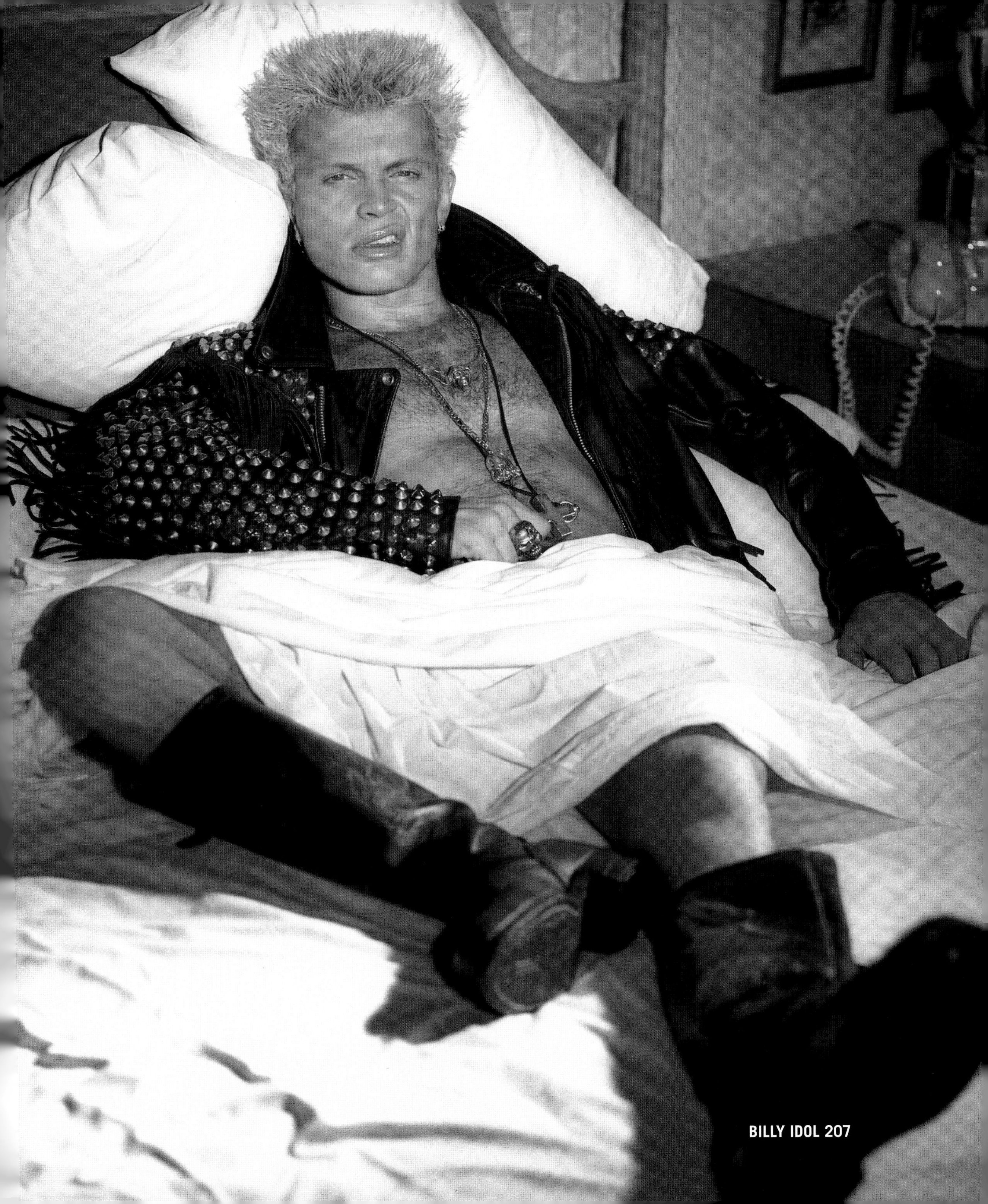
BILLY IDOL 207

In Memory of Stevie Hughes, Philip Sayer, Ian Charleson, Richard Causton, John DelNavo, My beloved Granny Selma, Lazaro Marilu, Leigh Bowery, Peter Lester, Richard Sharah, Derek Jarman, Luciana de la Martinez, Henry Tennant, Paula Owen, Benny Gannon, Roger Roberts, Paul Starr, Ray Allington, Tina Chow, Ossie Clark, Ray Petri, my father Imre and my best bull terriers Ruby and Belle.

Also Sincere Thanks to Rifat Ozbek, Lyndall Hobbs, Darrel Wright, Freddie Leibe, Gaye Sandler and Roger Miller, Ed Harris, Jose Fonseca and Dick Kreiss, Lorraine Ashton, Patti Harrison-Clapton, Kasuo Fuji, Jenny Dmitiri, Manolo Blahnik, Paul Vater, John Cigorini, Colin Gold, Simon Doonan and Johnathan Adler, Marta Hallett, Elizabeth Sullivan, John Campbell, Nick Kamen, Bryan Rabin, Connie Filipelo, David Litchfield at Ritz, The guys at Blitz, Michael Roberts, Hamish Bowles, Meriel McCooey, Robert Forrest, Deanna Madsen and Cody, Howard Napper, Denise Linn, Tatiana Patits, Dr Emanuel Lim, Lynne Franks, Prince Peter, Fay Greene, Saleem Ahmed, Paul Fortune, Gary Murie, Vivienne Westwood, Fumio and Kris Kawashima, Darren Mohamed, Melanie Sainsbury, Panos Pitsillides, Breean Brasile, Derric Lowe at L.M.G., George Lawrence, Lala Guimaraes, Baillie Walsh, Drs. Christpher Coad, Eviatar and Steven Dillon, Stephen Brown, Anwar and all he gang in Tangier, John Galliano, Siobhan Barron, Aaron and Nathan Kamstra, my 2 best assistants Nico and Colin, Jamie Morgan, Sharman Forman, Enid Graddis, Ione Skye and Donovan Leitch, Daisy Garnett, Mirella Ricciardi, Jimmy Dobson, Michael Patterson, Jackie de la Thibeeaudiere, Fiona Fox, Crispian Belfrage, Bunny Storrar, Barney Wan, Oscar Mann, Mohammed Lamki, Katherine Hamnett, Lorraine Kirke, Gaby Dellal, Marsha Hunt, Chandrika Casali, Nell Campbell, Pam Proctor, Denise and Alex Golding, Gael Boglione, Ulla Larson, John Maybury, Gregg Wolf, Joe Gaffney, Janet Street-Porter, Andrew Logan and Michael Davis, Terence Pepper, Christopher Brooks, Pamela Hansen, Heather Traber-Fitzpatrick, Kevin Landwehr, Liz Lange, Gil Doron, Jose Kendall, Julie Felix and my god-daughter Tanit, Mahendra and Tamaki Patel, Ollie Picton-Jone, Mark Arena and Jason Arbuckle, Lendon Flanagan, Lina Marquez, Chase Winton and Mark Campbell, Xiang and Juan at Luster NY, and all at Metro, London, and Robin Bell.